When Paper Collar Bandbox Soldiers Fight

A History of the 4th Regiment
West Virginia Volunteer Infantry

Philip Hatfield PhD
and
Terry Lowry

35th Star Publishing
Charleston, West Virginia
www.35thstar.com

ISBN-13, Paperback edition: 979-8-9889020-2-7
ISBN-13, Hardcover edition: 979-8-9889020-3-4
Library of Congress Control Number: 2024930915

35th Star Publishing
Charleston, West Virginia
www.35thstar.com

Cover design by Studio 6 Sense
Interior design by 35th Star Publishing

On the cover:
Painting of Siege of Vicksburg by Thure de Thulstrup, Library of Congress.
Image of Col. Joseph A.J. Lightburn courtesy of Richard A. Wolfe
Image of Col. James H. Dayton, Terry Lowry Collection
Numeral 4 gold-plated chest decoration worn by officers of the 4th West Virginia
    Infantry, courtesy of James M. Cole.
4th West Virginia Infantry Recruiting Broadside, courtesy of Gallia County
    Historical Society.

Dedication

*This work is dedicated to the loyal Mountaineer soldiers
and citizens who courageously stood for the Union,
leaving an enduring legacy of valor, devotion to duty
and the cause of liberty for all.*

Table of Contents

Preface xiii
Acknowledgments xvii

1 - 1861 - Piece by Piece: The Birth of a Regiment 1
2 - 1862 - On the Edge of Darkness 77
3 - 1863 - From Vicksburg to Missionary Ridge 145
4 - 1864-1865 - Into the Shenandoah Valley 221
5 - Anecdotes, Oddities, and Curiosities 259
6 - 4th West Virginia Infantry Monument at Vicksburg 267

Appendix A: Company Rosters 271
Appendix B: Images Gallery 359
Notes 381
Bibliography 417
Index 429
About the Authors 437

Photos/Maps/Illustrations

Map, 4th West Virginia Infantry 1861 Camps and Battles xxiv
Brigadier General Jacob D. Cox 2
Francis H. Pierpont 4
Frederick Ford 6
Captain Albert F. McCown 10
Lt. Col. John Luther Vance 12
Lt. Barney J. Rollins 14
Jesse Vincent Stevens 14
Captain William R. Brown 20
Ephraim C. Carson 22
Thomas H. Barton 24
James F. Stone 26
Cpl. Clarkson Fogg 28
Maj. Henry Grayum 30
Joseph A.J. Lightburn 36
Lt. Col. James R. Hall and Maj. John T. Hall 40
Dr. John R. Philson 43
Martin Van Buren Lightburn 44
Boone Court House Map 48
Roan County Court House 50
Post-war sketch of the skirmish at Reedy, WV 54
Wiliam M. Hovey 54
Calvin A. Sheppard 60
James W. Dale 62
Sketch, Camp Lightburn, seen from the rear – Ceredo House 72
4th West Virginia Infantry National Flag 82
Philemon B. Stanbury 94
Milton Stewart 102
Maj. John T. Hall 106
William L. McMaster 108
Lt. Charles Holstein 114
Daniel A. Russell 118

James H. Ralston 122
Wartime sketch of the Battle of Charleston 126
Image, Fording the Ohio River – September 13th, 1862 130
Map, Lightburn's Retreat 134
New Map of Vicksburg 144
Sketch of Grant's Canal by William V. Brown 146
Head of Grant's Canal 150
Chaplain George Woodhull 156
Capt. William S. Hall 157
James H. Dayton 158
Hand drawn map, 4th West Va. assault path on Stockade Redan 168
Brigadier General Hugh Ewing 168
Map, Vicksburg Assault 170
Major Arza Goodspeed 172
Major Arza Goodspeed 172
Robert Henry Sampson, Jr. 177
Lt. Finley D. Ong 180
Post-war image of John Douglas 182
4th West Virginia Infantry Regimental Flag 184
Vicksburg NPS Marker, movement of Ewing's Brigade 184
Image, monument to Col. J.A.J. Lightburn, Vicksburg NPS 185
West Virginia monument at Vicksburg National Park featuring
     bust of Major Arza Goodspeed 186
Vicksburg NPS monument commemorating 4th West Virginia
     casualties 187
Map, Vicksburg Assault 188
Post-war image, William Barringer 192
William Bumgarner 192
Post-war image, James C. Summers 192
Vicksburg, 1863 196
Assault on Stockade Redan 196
Sketch of Bastion in Front of Brig. Gen. Ewing 198
Assistant Surgeon Homer C. Waterman 203
Alpheus Beall 205

Captain William Grayum 207
Map of Missionary Ridge 212
Post-war image, John Perry Wolfe 214
Major General William T. Sherman 226
Map of Hunter's Lynchburg Campaign 230
Map, Sherman's Atlanta Campaign showing Rebel Defenses 234
Map, Cool Spring 238
Captain Benjamin D. Boswell 245
Lt. Col. Jacob Weddle 252
Maj. Gen. George C. Crook 254
Brig. Gen. Benjamin F. Kelley 254
Recruiting Broadside 258
4th West Virginia Sutler Token 264
Obverse, 4th West Virginia Sutler Token 264
Image, West Virginia State Museum display featuring Civil War
    cartridge box of Lt. Col. James R. Hall 265
Image, metal numeral '4' uniform attachment 266
Image, dedication of Arza Goodspeed monument 269

Preface

Numerous published and unpublished histories of the 4th West Virginia Volunteer Infantry in the American Civil War have been written, with the most prominent being the *Autobiography of Dr. Thomas H. Barton including a History of the 4th Regt. West Va. Vol. In'fy* (Infantry), published in Charleston, West Virginia, in 1890. This volume has often been considered the definitive history of the regiment because Barton served as hospital steward for the regiment during a large portion of the war, and he often provided first person accounts of people and events. But following the fall of Vicksburg, Mississippi, in 1863, his time with the regiment was minimal at best, with his accounts less personal and seemingly based on information he gathered from comrades and friends.

Barton was not alone in his fondness for the 4th West Virginia Volunteer Infantry. Major Benjamin D. Boswell submitted two hand-written histories of the regiment to the West Virginia Adjutant General, which were partially used in Theodore F. Lang's book *Loyal West Virginia 1861 – 1865* in 1895. James F. Stone also published a small history of one of the regimental companies called *Company F: 4th West Virginia Volunteer Infantry* in 1914 at Ravenswood, West Virginia.

Modern day historians, including Francis Lightburn Cressman, a direct descendant of General Joseph A.J. Lightburn, have also studied the 4th West Virginia Infantry, through sources either published, unpublished, or in digital format online. The most important source for studying the 4th West Virginia Volunteer Infantry remains the letters, diaries and journals of the soldiers who served, such as William V. Brown, Clarkson Fogg, William Grayum, Adolphus De Bussey, William Safreed, and other veterans who left detailed accounts of their personal experiences in the regiment; such are heavily cited in this work without apology. While we both recognize the importance of critical studies-published secondary sources and are keenly aware that first person accounts can often be biased, we firmly believe that no one is better qualified to narrate the soldiers' experience than those who themselves carried the arduous burdens of battle and campaign. Our goal is therefore to articulate the individual soldiers' narratives of the regiment's experiences from day to day across the war, and less on analysis of larger campaign strategies and battle tactics. More simply put: to allow the veterans to tell the stories in their own words.

Hopefully, the reader will find that this study has resulted in a thorough history of the 4th West Virginia Volunteer Infantry, bringing to life the character and personalities of the soldiers composing the regiment, from their early organization in western Virginia and Ohio to Vicksburg and their final struggles in the Shenandoah Valley. The 4th West Virginia has a proud and fierce history of Union soldiers representing West Virginia, which became the thirty-fifth state during the Civil War.

Lowry's interest in the regiment developed when his grandmother informed him his great grandfather served with the 4th West Virginia. He later discovered two great-uncles were also in the regiment. Dr. Hatfield was first drawn to the story of this regiment in 2005 while on leave from the military; he toured the Vicksburg battlefield and was captivated by stories of their role in that bloody and decisive affair, and he began accumulating soldier letters and other records documenting their gallant service. Our mutual interest and research have culminated in this present work, which we humbly present for your consideration.

Terry Lowry
Philip Hatfield, Ph.D.

Acknowledgments

There are many organizations and individuals who kindly assisted us in the creation of this work, without whom it would not have been possible to provide the depth and breadth of this regiment's Civil War service as we hoped to present, including Joe Geiger and the excellent staff at the West Virginia State Archives for assisting in locating manuscripts, photos, maps and other original sources included in this work; John Cuthbert and the entire staff of the West Virginia University Regional History Collection, Morgantown, West Virginia; the staff at the Ohio University Library, Athens, Ohio, for assistance with the William V. Brown Collection; the Gallia County Historical Society, Gallipolis, Ohio; Meigs County Historical Society, Pomeroy, Ohio; author-historian Tim McKinney, Fayetteville, West Virginia, for sharing a wealth of information and his expertise on the 4th West Virginia Infantry; Richard Wolfe, Bridgeport, West Virginia, for sharing his expertise and extensive West Virginia Civil War Collection; and Eugene Smith, The Plains, Ohio, for information on D.A. Russell and for sharing his extensive collection of 4th West Virginia Infantry materials.

In addition, Brian Abbott, Parkersburg, West Virginia, for sharing photographs of soldiers in the 4th West Virginia (cited individually herein); Keith Ashby, of the Sons of Union Veterans Camp Number Seven, Pomeroy, Ohio; Carol R. Austin, Garden Grove, California; and Vena (Grayum) Petit Jean of Portland, Oregon, for information on the Grayum brothers. Lieutenant Eric M. Beal, United States Navy, Kaneohe, Hawaii, shared source material related to Adjutant Alpheus Beal, and thanks to Anthony Collins, Washington, West Virginia, for information on Morris Dennis and James M. Cole, Elkview, West Virginia, for allowing us to include his photo of James C. Summers and the brass numeral 4 (shown on the cover of this book), which belonged to Summers.

We also recognize the valuable contributions of Claudia Wilson Cooper, Cross Lanes, West Virginia, for data related to Richard Carte of this regiment; James C. Cline, Beverly, Ohio, for information on John P. Wolfe; and Heidi Eads for sharing information related to Captain E.C. Carson and Daniel Burrows, in addition to Norma M. Frank, Bridgeport, Ohio, for contributing information on Joseph Nicholson. Much thanks also to Charles L. Hayley, Petersburg, Virginia, for allowing use of William Barringer's photograph and other information related to his service in this regiment; to Dallas Hill for data related to Winfield/Swinfield Hill; William K. Holbrook, King George, Virginia, and Danny Roush for information and photo of Gilbert Roush; and further, Glenna Ivy and Isabell McKee, Buchanan Dam, Texas, for photos and information on William Henry Nessmith; and Brian Kesterson, Vienna, West Virginia, provided information and a photograph of James F. Stone. Lewis Leigh, Jr., Leesburg, Virginia and Wayne Farley, Bridgeport, West Virginia contributed important information related to Arthur Watts Pomeroy.

We further recognize and thank Frances Lightburn, Jane Lew, West Virginia, for kindly sharing information on General Joseph A. Lightburn. Thanks also to James and May Persinger, Nitro, West Virginia, for material on Arthur Forbes and Mark Philson, Mercer, Pennsylvania for information and photo of John Rush Philson. William Schneck provided information about the 1864 train wreck, and Richard

Shepherd, Boerne, Texas, shared information on Finley Ong. John and Mary Lou Snodgrass, Pfafftown, North Carolina, shared information related to William Burdette and his service in the regiment; David Waterman, Lebanon, Missouri, shared information on "Saunders;" and, Edelene Wood, Parkersburg, West Virginia, contributed information on William H. Wood.

Authors' Caveat

West Virginia became the thirty-fifth state on June 20, 1863. Prior to that date, Union regiments from western Virginia during the Civil War were known as Virginia regiments. However, for convenience and to avoid confusion, all such regiments including the 4th are referred to herein as West Virginia regiments.

Jane Lew, Lewis County. W. Va.
Nov. 14th 1868

Daniel A Russell Esqr.
My Dear Sir

Your very polite note was received today extending me an invitation to attend a Reunion of the 4th Va Vol Infy in reply to which I am sorry to say that my family and business arrangements are such that I cannot attend. Please say to those brave officers and men that I am truly sorry that I cannot be with them and although I have not had the pleasure of meeting with them since the termination of the war, yet I hold them in remembrance for their bravery. I never shall forget their intrepid charge at Vicksburg, their gallantry at Missionary Ridge, and in fact wherever it was their lot to be placed. They have a record which they may be proud of, a record that will be handed down to Generations. A name that will live long in the history of this country. Please give them one and all my best wishes. Please accept my thanks for your very kind invitation to share your hospitality.

And believe me
Truly Yours
J.A.J. Lightburn

[Source: Daniel A. Russell Collection]

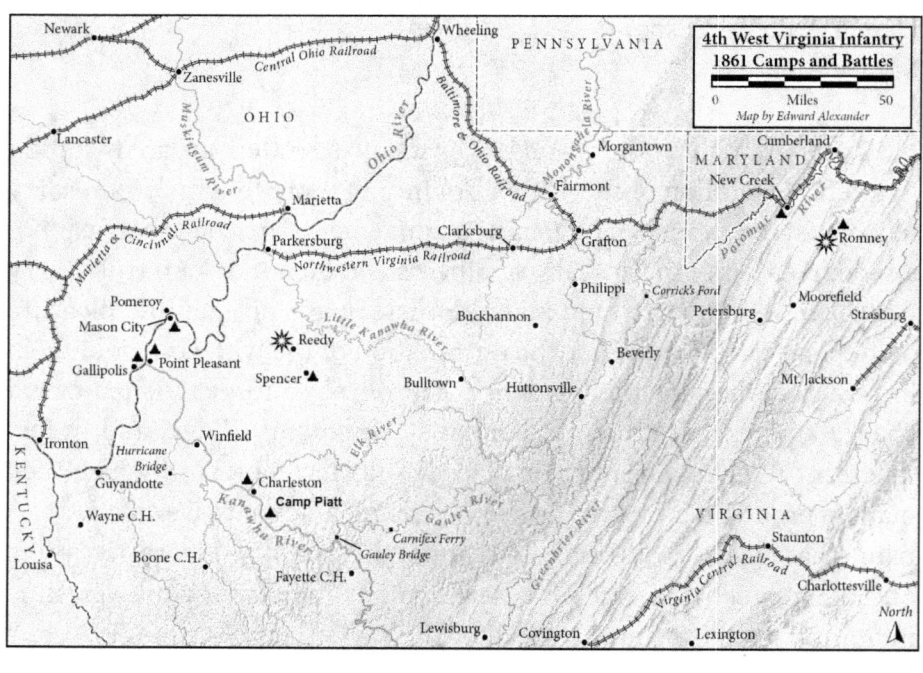

Newark

Wheeling   PENNSYLVANIA

Central Ohio Railroad

Zanesville

OHIO

Lancaster

Muskingum River

Ohio River

Baltimore & Ohio Railroad

Monongahela River

Morgantown

Cumberland

MARYLAND

New Creek

Marietta

Fairmont

Potomac River

Marietta & Cincinnati Railroad

Parkersburg   Clarksburg   Grafton

Northwestern Virginia Railroad

Romney

Philippi   Corrick's Ford

Moorefield

Petersburg

Strasburg

Pomeroy

Little Kanawha River

Buckhannon

Mason City

Reedy

Beverly

Gallipolis   Point Pleasant

Spencer

Bulltown   Huttonsville

Mt. Jackson

Winfield

Elk River

KENTUCKY

Ironton

Hurricane
Bridge

Guyandotte

Charleston

Camp Piatt

Kanawha River

Gauley River

Greenbrier River

VIRGINIA

Wayne C.H.

Carnifex Ferry

Gauley Bridge

Staunton

Louisa

Boone C.H.

Fayette C.H.

Virginia Central Railroad

Charlottesville

Lewisburg   Covington   Lexington

North

1

1861
Piece by Piece: The Birth of a Regiment

The 4th (West) Virginia Volunteer Infantry, or 4th Loyal Virginia Infantry, was organized between June 17 and August 22, 1861, although Major Benjamin D. Boswell claimed that the first company was mustered into Federal service on June 5. The regiment was composed primarily of men from the Ohio counties of Athens, Gallia, Lawrence and Meigs, and the (West) Virginia counties of Jackson, Lewis, Mason and Wayne. Additionally, the bulk of Company H came from the Elk River area of Kanawha County, and Company K from the northeastern section of (West) Virginia in Hampshire County. Geographically isolated from the other companies of the regiment in 1861, Company K was mustered in at Grafton in Taylor County, (West) Virginia.

The first year of the war the 4th West Virginia Volunteer Infantry spent organizing, drilling, scouting, skirmishing with bushwhackers, and participating in a few small expeditions, all within the boundaries of present-day West Virginia, except a brief jaunt into eastern Kentucky by a few companies late in the year. The regiment served unattached the District of the Kanawha, until March of 1862 and primarily protected the supply line and rear of Generals Jacob D. Cox

1

Brigadier General Jacob D. Cox.
Oberlin College, Oberlin, Ohio.

and William S. Rosecrans in the Kanawha Valley of (West) Virginia and the surrounding vicinity.

The second year brought more of the same until the 1862 Kanawha Valley Campaign and the battle of Charleston. During this period the 4th West Virginia was with the 4th Brigade, Kanawha Division, under General Jacob D. Cox until August, when they were placed in the District of the Kanawha, commanded by Colonel Joseph A.J. Lightburn. Upon Cox's return to the Kanawha Valley in October, the regiment served with the Department of the Ohio until January of 1863.

As the year 1863 opened, the regiment was placed with the 3rd Brigade, 2nd Division, 15th Army Corps, Army of the Tennessee. This change would move the boys south to participate in General Ulysses S. Grant's Vicksburg Campaign and hard fighting at Vicksburg as well as at Jackson, Mississippi, and Chattanooga, Tennessee, all under General William T. Sherman. In October they were placed with the 2nd Brigade, 2nd Division, 15th Army Corps, Army of the Tennessee, until May of 1864.

Following a brief veterans furlough, the regiment was assigned to the 2nd Brigade, 1st Infantry Division, Army of West Virginia. They moved to the Shenandoah Valley of Virginia in 1864 and participated in most of the battles there, including Lynchburg, Snicker's Ferry, Winchester, and Cedar Creek. At the same time, the non-veterans of the 4th West Virginia were kept in the South and consolidated with the 8th Missouri Infantry, fighting in General Sherman's Atlanta Campaign at Resaca, Dallas, and Kennesaw Mountain. By late 1864 the regiment's ranks were so depleted from combat, disease, and miscellaneous contributing factors that they had to consolidate with the 1st West Virginia Infantry to form the 2nd Veteran West Virginia Infantry.

When the war ended in 1865, the 4th West Virginia could boast of six Medal of Honor recipients and their colonel, Joseph A.J. Lightburn, rising to the rank of brigadier general. In addition, it was the only West Virginia regiment to fight in both the Western and the Eastern Theaters and the most traveled West Virginia regiment. On a darker note, the 4th West Virginia had the highest casualties among the

Francis H. Pierpont.
Library of Virginia, Richmond, Virginia.

Federal regiments engaged in the May 19, 1863 assault on Stockade Redan at Vicksburg, Mississippi.

Militia

The first Union regiment in western Virginia organized in May 1861. President Abraham Lincoln soon authorized Francis H. Pierpont, governor of the Restored Government of Virginia, which would lay the foundation for the new state of West Virginia, to begin recruiting for new state regiments in June 1861, intending to protect Union citizens. At that time, the state militia system was in shambles from years of peacetime neglect. Despite the Federal Militia Act of 1792, which required men ages 18 to 45 to be liable for militia duty, they rarely attended muster more than the minimum: once every three years. Those events were usually no more than a social gathering in lieu of a strict military discipline and training regimen.[1]

A militia officer in Hampshire County recalled, "on muster days the boys composing our battalion assembled at some stated place, generally a central location, and after drilling usually indulged in horse-trading, or 'swapping;' talk of, and appoint log-rolling's, rail-mauling's, house raisings, apple cuttings, corn-huskings, and many other kinds of 'frolics' as they were entitled by those sturdy farmers, and each of them would invariably terminate in the evening in a jovial old time, 'hoe-down' dance ..." When the Virginia Assembly later passed the Militia Act of 1860 requiring state militia units to hold regular drill as talk of war darkened the horizon, the majority of regiments in western Virginia existed only on paper. By April 1861, many of the newly formed volunteer companies tended to operate as loosely organized independent companies, ostensibly under the state adjutant general's authority, but in reality, most did little more than serve as local patrol groups protecting Union citizens. Beyond that, they were of minimal effect in the first few months of the war.[2]

Frederick Ford.
National Tribune, public domain.

A Regiment is Born

The legacy of the 4th West Virginia Volunteer Infantry began in June 1861, as numerous militia and home guard units began forming along the Ohio River bordering western Virginia. Frederick Ford, a native of Point Pleasant, (West) Virginia, and pilot of a steamboat on the Ohio River, recalled this early period when he later wrote in *The National Tribune*: "I began at my own expense, to recruit a company, though not commissioned to do so. Appearances in that part of the country indicated that its services would soon be needed. I had succeeded in nearly filling the company with men who were loyal and true, when I received a dispatch from the Secretary of War, asking me to act as Pilot on one of the boats which the Government was fitting out for active service on the rivers. I consented, willing to serve my country in whatever capacity I could be most useful. I turned over to the government the recruits I had secured, and they became part of the 4th West Virginia. I was not, however, reimbursed for the expense I had incurred, nor have I been to this day." [June 3, 1886].[3]

Mason City

In early June 1861 a military encampment was established at Mason City in Mason County, (West) Virginia, across the Ohio River from Pomeroy, Ohio. The camp was situated on the Lewis Anderson farm on the western boundary of the town. Structures such as the Welch Methodist Church on Third Street, the Wallace House on Horton, and several others were commandeered for barracks.[4]

The Three Faces of Company A

The genesis of Company A of the 4th West Virginia is somewhat conflicting and should be viewed in context of how the different incarnations of that unit eventually became Company A. Major Benjamin D. Boswell claimed the first company of the 4th regiment was organized on June 5; however, the earliest known version may have been organized in Lewis County, (West) Virginia, by Joseph Andrew Jackson Lightburn, who was commissioned as colonel of the 4th West Virginia on August 22. In a July 20 letter to General James S. Wheat, Lightburn indicated he had formed a company at Jane Lew known as "Co. number 4 of the line" prior to June 1861. He also mentioned that there had been two companies at Jane Lew, "one in the town and one outside the town – one Union and one secessionist." Lightburn further indicated his group had "formed themselves into a company, designated as such before I received my commission.... [they were] almost unanimously Union....it would be well enough to state that 80 stands of arms were received some of which are in very bad condition...." Lightburn's company was eventually re-designated as Company A at Point Pleasant in November 1861.[5]

Lightburn was appointed adjutant of the 192nd Regiment Virginia Militia from Lewis County with the rank of captain on July 11 and enlisted in the Federal Army as a corporal on July 13. The confusing dual role prompted Lightburn to write Joseph Blackwell Jackson from Jane Lew on July 13 to inquire about various rules and regulations of the Militia Act, posing questions regarding drilling the militia, providing music, and to ask if he was to work with both the Jane Lew company and the company from Harrison County.[6]

The 192nd Regiment was known as the "Virginia Foot Volunteers" and was assigned to the 20th Virginia Brigade, commanded by Brigadier General C. B. Conrad during 1860-1861. This brigade was comprised of the 129th along with the 125th Virginia Regiment (Lewis County) and the 133rd Virginia Regiment (Upshur County). Lightburn's company was briefly designated as 1st Company, 4th Regiment, in late July 1861, although Lightburn also signed documents as adjutant of the 192nd Militia as late as July 27.[7]

There were two other early incarnations of Company A, Captain James Dayton's Company and Captain Welton's Company, both of which were scheduled to be mustered in on the same day. Captain Dayton's Company was from the upper Potomac region of western Virginia located at New Creek Station in Hampshire County. This unit was organized by James Hart Dayton, who was also later served as colonel of the 4th regiment. Twenty-four-year-old Dayton owned a lucrative mercantile business at New Creek Station when the war began. A post-war pension application indicates Dayton had started recruiting for a company shortly after the war began, and he enlisted in the Union Army on June 17 at Piedmont. This company is identified in early records as "Captain Dayton's Co. Western Virginia Volunteers," as well as Company A in July 1861, but was later redesignated as Company K in December 1861. Dayton's original company was comprised of men from Allegheny County, Maryland, Hampshire County, (West) Virginia, and the area now known as Mineral County, West Virginia.[8]

On June 17, Dayton had approximately 101 men gathered at New Creek, Hampshire County, (West) Virginia, but, due to communications being cut off, the mustering officer could not reach the area and a force of secessionists attacked the unarmed company, dispersed part of it and took the other portion prisoner. As a result, the company would not be mustered in until July 20, and it would be designated Company K near the end of 1861, much to the chagrin of Dayton and his men, who thought they deserved to be Company A.[9]

While Dayton's men waited to be mustered in, Major James Oakes, 2nd Regiment U.S. Cavalry, performed a muster-in on June 17 at Mason City of foot soldiers under Henry Samuel Welton, as Captain Welton's Company Virginia Foot Volunteers. With Dayton's Company yet to be mustered, Welton's Company officially became Company A of the 4th West Virginia Infantry. Lightburn had also reportedly promised Welton's company they would be Company A.[10]

Captain Welton, who was born in Connecticut in 1827, moved to (West) Virginia prior to the war. He organized his company of foot soldiers at New Haven in Mason County, but his time with the regiment was short as he resigned on September 1, 1861, and was replaced by Tilton B. Rockhill. Welton recruited a new company the following year, and on May 25, 1862, with men he had recruited at Gallipolis after he had left the 4th West Virginia, he departed the city, arriving at Indianapolis on May 28, where "Morrison" died of typhoid

Captain Albert F. McCown.
Courtesy St. Albans Historical Society.

fever. The men were designated as Company H, 1st Battalion, 19th U.S. Infantry, with Welton as captain, and departed Indianapolis for Washington City on the same day. They would go on to serve in many engagements, including Chickamauga.[11]

Captain Welton's replacement in the 4th West Virginia, Tilton B. Rockhill, was a shoemaker who was born in 1825 in either Massachusetts or New Jersey. In 1860 he was living in a hotel at Salisbury near Pomeroy, Meigs County, Ohio.[12]

Albert F. McCown of Mason City was elected 1st lieutenant of Company A, but he resigned soon afterward, becoming a captain in the 106th Militia of Mason County in 1862 and later a major in the 13th West Virginia Infantry. Apparently, his time with the 4th West Virginia was so brief he does not appear on any official regimental records. McCown was replaced by Dioclesian "Dan" A. Smith, who also resigned on either August 31 or September 1. Smith was born circa 1827 in Virginia and eventually moved to Meigs County, Ohio. In 1862 he would become a major in the 92nd Ohio Infantry.[13] John W. Davis was elected 2nd lieutenant of Company A on July 17, 1861. He was born circa 1838.[14]

A member of the newly organized Company A said that of the 164 men comprising the company, "... 125 were enrolled in fifteen minutes." Private Lewis Love of the company said at Mason City they were "armed and drew some underclothing." Love also recalled: "Company A was composed mostly of Virginians, who knew more about the geography of the country, the roads and cow paths through the mountains than those companies from Ohio. So we were on the scout for bushwhackers for more of the time."[15]

Company B

On July 5, Company B, also known as John Luther Vance's Company Virginia Foot Soldiers, of the 4th West Virginia Infantry, was organized and mustered in at Mason City by Major James Oakes, 2nd U. S. Cavalry, with Vance as captain and William C. Bailey and Barlow W. Curtiss as 1st and 2nd lieutenants, respectively.

Lt. Col. John Luther Vance.
Terry Lowry Collection.

John Luther Vance was born July 19, 1839, at Gallipolis, Gallia County, Ohio. He received his early education at Gallipolis in his father's county printing office at age 11 and at the Gallia Academy. At the age of 17 he was a teacher in schools adjoining Gallipolis, and at age 18 was deputy clerk of the Courts of Gallia County. During the fall of 1860, Vance entered the Cincinnati Law School and was also appointed to the staff of Chief Constable of the Ohio Militia. In April of 1861, a day after graduation from law school, he was ordered to Gallipolis for military duty, where he recruited and organized the first military companies in the county. He began recruiting the first three-years company on June 3, and on July 5, Vance was mustered in as captain of Company B, 4th West Virginia Infantry. He would go on to serve as major and lieutenant colonel of the regiment.[16]

Postwar articles and information from former members of his company, some possibly politically motivated, portrayed Vance as a strict disciplinarian, an alcoholic, and very self-centered. Private Louis Everett, Company K, from Hampshire County, said: "His cruelty toward his men were past all bearing. Especially when intoxicated, and on one occasion, when he was president of a court martial, he sentenced two of his men, for a trivial offence, to wear the ball and chain for eleven months, or until his term of office expired." Private Everett added: "When the news of the Emancipation Proclamation reached us [at Point Pleasant September 22, 1862], and was hailed with shouts of applause, he on the contrary, made a vigorous speech in opposition, and denounced President Lincoln in bitter terms. He even went so far as to tell his men they were fighting for a 'damned black republic'."[17]

William C. Bailey, who was born circa 1832-34, joined the company on July 5 at Mason City and was mustered in as 1st lieutenant the same day.[18] Barlow W. Curtiss was born August 10, 1833, in Ohio, and worked as a tinner in the fabricated steel industry at Gallipolis, Ohio. By 1860, he was working in the same trade but in Memphis, Tennessee; however, the outbreak of the war and a strong Southern sentiment in Memphis may have contributed to his return to Ohio.[19]

Lt. Barney J. Rollins.
Courtesy Robert J. Keathley.

Jesse Vincent Stevens.
Meigs County Historical Society.

The July 19 edition of the *Pomeroy Weekly Telegraph* noted of Vance's company, "We understand they are fully equipped and ready for service."[20]

Company C

Also mustered in on July 5 at Mason City by Major James Oakes, 2nd U. S. Cavalry, was Captain Thomas Jefferson Smith's Company of (West) Virginia Foot Volunteers, as Company C, with Smith as captain, Barney J. Rollins of Mason County as 1st lieutenant and Jesse Vinton Stevens as 2nd lieutenant.

Captain Smith was born April 28, 1825, in Wheeling, Ohio County, (West) Virginia, and in 1850 was a shoemaker at Pomeroy, Meigs County, Ohio. In 1899 Corporal George W. Gilliland, who served in Company C of the regiment, wrote: "My first captain was Thomas J. Smith, of Pomeroy, and I understand he was a shoemaker by trade. He was a jolly, good officer and a man whom I held in high esteem. He called our company the 'tadygomillions.' The boys would sometimes go out foraging. It was not stealing, only foraging. When the boys would return, they sometimes had chickens, roasting ears, sweet potatoes or something else good to eat. Our captain would say 'boys don't forget your superior officer,' and we would always divide. That sounded much better to us than to hear him say. 'I will put you fellows in the guard house for ten or fifteen days.'"[21]

Lieutenant Barney J. Rollins was born December 7, 1820, in either Braxton County or Lewis County, (West) Virginia, depending on the source. Rollins was a farmer in District 38, Mason County, (West) Virginia, in the 1850 census. He joined the company on July 5 at Mason City and was mustered in as 1st lieutenant the same day.[22]

Jesse Vinton Stevens (Stephens) was born August 28, 1827, in (West) Virginia or Ohio. On November 18, 1852, he was appointed postmaster at Downington, Meigs County, Ohio, and the 1860 census lists him as a miller at Pomeroy, Meigs County, Ohio. Stevens enrolled as a 2nd lieutenant in Company C, 4th West Virginia Infantry, on July 5 at Mason City, (West) Virginia. He was appointed 1st lieutenant on

September 1 and regimental quarter master on October 18, although his service record states this also transpired on September 1.[23]

Corporal George W. Gilliland, Company C, recalled: "I have often thought about the first suit of Uncle Sam's clothes. The blouse was just five times bigger than I was. I rolled up my new pants three times and they were too long and I looked more like a 'paddy' than I did a seventeen-year-old soldier boy."[24]

Company D

July 8 saw the muster-in at Mason City of Captain Arza Mathias Goodspeed's Company, (West) Virginia Foot Volunteers, as Company D. Corporal James B.C. Vale said he enlisted at the school lot in Columbia Township, Meigs County, Ohio, on June 27 and was mustered into Company D as a private on July 8 at Mason City. Arza Goodspeed served as captain of the company, with John Mallernee as 1st lieutenant and Adam Bratton as 2nd lieutenant.[25]

Arza Mathias Goodspeed was born in Athens County, Ohio, September 17, 1839, and resided in Athens in 1850 and 1860. Goodspeed also attended Ohio University at Athens. He joined the 3rd Ohio Volunteer infantry (three months organization) on April 19, 1861, at the age of 21 and was appointed 2nd lieutenant May 4, 1861. Goodspeed was mustered out on July 8 to accept promotion to captain of Company D, 4th West Virginia Infantry.[26]

John Mallernee, also from Athens, served as 1st lieutenant. He was born about 1839-1840 and in 1850 resided at Moorefield in Harrison County, Ohio. In 1860 he was an artist living in Athens, Ohio. He enlisted April 19, 1861, in Company C, 3rd Ohio Volunteer Infantry (three months organization) and was appointed corporal. Mustered out June 16, he enlisted as a 1st lieutenant in Company D, 4th West Virginia Infantry.[27]

Adam Bratton Sr., of Meigs County, Ohio, performed the duties of 2nd lieutenant but the governor refused to commission him due to drunkenness. Bratton was born September 23, 1816 or 1817 (probably in West Virginia), and in 1860 was a farmer in Pomeroy, Meigs County,

Ohio. He performed the duties of 2nd lieutenant until October 25, at which time he was discharged by Colonel Joseph A.J. Lightburn.[28]

Bratton was replaced the same day by George W. Hankinson (Hankinsson), who was born January 28, 1836, in Ohio or Pennsylvania, and in 1850 resided at Circleville, Pickaway County, Ohio. According to the 1860 census he was a farmer at Walnut, Pickaway County, Ohio. Afterwards he served as a private in Company C, 3rd Ohio Volunteer Infantry (three months organization), from April 19 to June 16. Hankisson enrolled in Company D of the 4th West Virginia at Mason City as a sergeant on July 8 and was promoted to 2nd lieutenant October 25, all within the first few months of the war.[29]

William Van Brown of Company D said: "Co. D will go wherever Capt. Goodspeed says, it makes no difference where that is. Every man loves him and thinks he is the best officer in Va. I don't believe there is a man in the Co. who would not willingly risk his life to save the Captain's. We have the best Co. and the best officers in the Reg't without doubt. I heard the Col. say to the Adjutant one day when we were coming off of the Battalion drill just as we passed them, says he, 'There is the best Co. in the Reg't.'"[30]

Corporal James B.C. Vale of Company D claimed that at Mason City the company "got white wool shirts, and blue pants, and no blouses, and....armed with the old U. S. muskets, cartridges – one ball and three buckshot." This conflicts with some members who claimed they were not issued any government clothing until they were at Point Pleasant. Vale also said they drilled a little bit and he performed his first picket duty.[31]

The Move to Point Pleasant, (West) Virginia
July 18, 1861

William Van Brown, Company D, wrote his mother from Mason County on July 18, one day after General Jacob D. Cox's Federal forces suffered a defeat along the Kanawha River at Scary Creek, Putnam County, (West) Virginia. He informed her: "We are going to leave here this forenoon as soon as we can get off. We are going to Point Pleasant

16 or 20 miles below here. Our uniforms are down on the wharf boat, we will get them as soon as we can get our breakfast. We get three pair pants, three shirts, 3 pair socks, 2 pair shoes, three coats (our coats have not come yet), 1 hat, 3 pair drawers, 1 blanket. I don't know what they are sending us to Point Pleasant for, I suppose it is just to get us out of this hell hole."[32] James B.C. Vale, Company D, said they had their first dress parade at Point Pleasant.[33]

William V. Brown also spoke of a recent event in which he, Wallace Beckley, Pearley Bratton, and John W. Bradshaw, all of Company D, and two little boys as guides, went to pick blackberries and encountered about seven or eight young boys en route. One, possibly by the name of French, got into a harmless verbal exchange with Beckley, who charged bayonets on the boy, believing his gun to be unloaded. Beckley ran the gun through a fence, hitting the cock of the gun on the fence. "The gun went off, the ball striking him [the boy] two inches left of the backbone. He died in two or three hours."[34]

Joseph A.J. Lightburn was commissioned adjutant of the 192nd Militia of Lewis County, (West) Virginia, on July 11, and on July 13 he enlisted in the Federal army. He would soon thereafter be made colonel of the 4th West Virginia Volunteer Infantry. His first impression of the men who volunteered for the 4th Regiment from western Virginia was that they were "...hardy mountaineers, accustomed to the chase....", while he noted also that the Ohioans were largely farmers and tradesmen such as machinists, clerks, teachers, and river boat mechanics.[35]

By July 19, companies A, B and C of the 4th West Virginia had departed Mason City for Point Pleasant, (West) Virginia, at the mouth of the Kanawha River. Just south across the Ohio River was Gallipolis in Gallia County, Ohio.

Before companies E through I of the 4th West Virginia were mustered on July 20, an unarmed company that originally hoped to be Company A of the 4th Regiment had been attacked at New Creek in Hampshire County, (West) Virginia, on June 17. They had gradually arrived at Grafton between that time and July 20 and were assigned various military duties such as guard and picket chores. During this period of time, they were mustered in as Company K of the regiment at Grafton in Taylor County, (West) Virginia, by Captain Crane. James Hart Dayton was appointed captain of the company while James J. Mansell was appointed 1st lieutenant and Alpheus Beall was made 2nd lieutenant.[36]

James Hart Dayton was born on December 25, 1836, in Hampshire County, (West) Virginia, where his father had an extensive plantation along the Potomac River with many slaves. Dayton received his education on the plantation. He also worked as a passenger conductor on the Baltimore and Ohio Railroad, married in 1859, and was a resident of New Creek in Hampshire County in 1860. For many years prior to the Civil War, he served as captain of the Romney Greys and was commissioned captain in the 4th West Virginia Infantry on June 17, 1861.[37]

James J. Mansell was born September 24, 1830, in Liberty Township, Trumbull County, Ohio. He served in the Mexican War, enlisting June 1846 at Cumberland, Maryland, as a private in Company L, 1st Virginia Volunteers, and was discharged at Fort Monroe July 1848. Mansell became 1st lieutenant of Company K on July 22, 1861.[38]

Alpheus Beall was born circa 1841 in Missouri and in 1850 lived in District 5, Allegany County, Maryland. Beall was an engineer living at Frostburg, Allegany County, Maryland, in 1860. He joined Company K on July 12 at New Creek, Hampshire County, (West) Virginia and was mustered in as 2nd lieutenant on July 20, 1861.[39]

Also on July 20, Adjutant Joseph Andrew Jackson Lightburn of the 192nd Militia wrote General James S. Wheat from Jane Lew, Lewis County, (West) Virginia, and he enclosed a certificate for the organization of a volunteer company primarily composed of "Company no. 4 of the line," who had formed themselves into a company before Lightburn's commission. He said he assembled and organized the company and considered transferring the remnants of Company 4 to Company 3, because their district to cover was much smaller and their drill field easily accessible to everyone. Lightburn complained that he had been issued 80 arms in poor condition, which he wished replaced, and pointed out that the lower end of the county

Captain William R. Brown.
Larry Strayer Collection.

was composed of the loyal Union men of the 192nd Militia while the upper end favored secession, resulting, in essence, in two companies. Lightburn's references to Company No. 4 seem to indicate this was the beginning of the 4th West Virginia Infantry.[40]

Company E

On July 22, Captain William Robert Brown's Company, (West) Virginia Foot Volunteer Regiment, was mustered in by Major Oakes as Company E, with Brown serving as captain, Philemon B. Stanbery as 1st lieutenant, and Ephraim C. Carson as 2nd lieutenant.

William Robert Brown was born October 11, 1823, in Pennsylvania. As he grew older he visited Canada, Iowa, Kansas Territory, and New Orleans before finally settling in Pomeroy in Meigs County, Ohio. He worked as a foreman in machine shops and brass foundries. With the outbreak of the war, he reportedly took 40 men from his machine and brass foundries and enlisted them for service in his newly formed military company. He enlisted July 22, 1861, at Mason City, as captain of Company E of the 4th West Virginia; Brown would be promoted to lieutenant colonel of the 13th West Virginia Infantry September 16, 1862, and eventually be breveted a brigadier general.[41]

Philemon Beecher Stanbery was promoted to 1st lieutenant and adjutant on August 22. He was born May 5, 1832, at Lancaster, Fairfield County, Ohio. At a young age his family moved to Zanesville, where he studied law, and he was admitted to the bar at Gallipolis before returning to Lancaster to practice law. Educated in the public schools, he attended Kinsley Military Academy near West Point between the ages of 13 and 17. He matriculated from Kenyon College after two years, then entered Ohio University at Athens, Ohio. Following graduation in 1853, he worked as a surveyor on the Ohio Central Railroad and the Little Miami Railroad. In 1856 he removed to Indianola, Iowa, where he was admitted to the bar and opened a practice at Fort Des Moines. Two years later he moved to Leavenworth, Kansas, and following two years at that place, he moved to Pomeroy, Ohio, and established a law practice. At the outbreak of the war, he enlisted and was appointed a

Ephraim C. Carson.
Terry Lowry Collection.

1st lieutenant in Captain William R. Brown's Company, Virginia Foot Volunteers, later Company E, 4th West Virginia, on July 22. He was also commissioned adjutant of the 4th West Virginia on August 22, 1861, according to records.[42]

Ephraim C. Carson was born April 25, 1833, in Pennsylvania. In 1850 he was in the farming industry at Sutton in Meigs County, Ohio, and in 1860 was a clerk at Salisbury, near Pomeroy, in Meigs County. He was appointed 1st lieutenant of Company E on July 22, 1861.[43]

Captain Brown and Stanbery had run recruiting ads in the *Pomeroy Weekly Telegraph* as early as July 12. Most of the men of Company E were from Racine, Pomeroy and Syracuse of Ohio, and Mason County of (West) Virginia. Dr. Thomas H. Barton of Syracuse, Ohio, who later served as a hospital steward with the regiment, recalled that about the first of June an independent company of militia was formed at Syracuse, which would soon provide many members of Company E of the 4th West Virginia. This was confirmed by the July 12 edition of the *Pomeroy Weekly Telegraph* newspaper, which states: "Persons wishing to volunteer in the defense of their country, can now have the opportunity at almost any place in our county. W. R. Brown and P. B. Stanbery, of Pomeroy, are now raising one company." The newspaper followed up on July 19, reporting: "Those who have volunteered in Capt. Wm. Brown's Company, are requested to report themselves to Pomeroy on Monday next. Still a few more men are wanted – only a few, however – and those wishing to enlist had better make haste, or the Company will be full. No better Company has been raised than this one." A subsequent column in the paper added: "they have about 80 on the roll, leaving room for some twenty more....A finer set of fellows than those already enrolled, cannot be found. It will be a splendid Company when full, and one in which it will be an honor to serve." On August 9, the *Pomeroy Weekly Telegraph* referred to them as a "crack company" and claimed that about 70 of the men were members of the Temperance Association.[44]

The company moved to Mason City, elected officers, drilled extensively, and went on dress parade. Thomas Barton remembered that, "When on parade, my little daughter, then in her fifth year, would sometimes march by my side with a regular step, and as much of a soldier bearing as anyone in the company." Britton Cook and Dr. Barton, both of Syracuse, had assisted in raising the company. Barton recalled: "In taking this step, I was actuated by motives of patriotism. I shouldered my musket in defense of the Union; but I had no idea of abandoning my profession, and intended, if spared, to resume the practice of medicine at the expiration of my term of service. My wife was patriotic, and readily gave her consent to my enlistment. But it was hard to part with the loved ones, not knowing whether or not I would ever return; and when I was about to bid

Thomas H. Barton.
From *Autobiography of Thomas H. Barton...*

farewell to those who were near and dear to me, my little daughter said, 'Doc, you must not go to war, for you will get shot.'"[45]

Private John G. Farrar, Company E, recalled he enlisted on July 9 and: "Britton Cook came up on Thomas Fork getting signers. I and Melvin Murray put our names down....we elected our officers by ballot," and the officers appointed the non-commissioned officers.[46]

Company F

As early as July 15, a large number of Murraysville, Jackson County, (West) Virginia men had enlisted in Company F. Among them was Private James F. Stone, who claimed "At Long Bottom, Ohio," they picked up some additional recruits: "We were a motley squad of men and boys. We marched through Bashan and Chester, Ohio, to Pomeroy, crossed the river and went into quarters in an old building....when we had been in camp a few days Capt. Welton of Co. A, and Capt. Thomas Smith, of Co. C, came up to where Co. F boys were quartered to look us over, and report on what our boys needed to make real soldiers of them. Capt. Smith told Capt. Welton in his report that we needed 'New

Noses, New Toeses and New Clotheses.'" Stone went on to relate, "And this was literally true for Wm. Massingham had no nose and I forget who needed toes, but nearly all of us needed new clothes."[47]

The "Pork and Beans" Battle

In 1914 James F. Stone, a veteran of Company F, remembered first being a member of a home guard unit from Murraysville and said they were called out when Confederate General Henry A. Wise was at Ripley in Jackson County and threatening Ravenswood, Murraysville, and other points in the county. Referring to the home guard he said: "...people from Long Bottom came over armed with squirrel rifles, shot guns, corn cutters, etc. Capt. [Richard Channing Moore] Lovell, with a company of home guards, came up from Mason City with men and boys he had gathered up in the Pomeroy Bend. Our battle line was formed on the hill just back of Murraysville between the old graveyard and the Pond Creek road near the old log schoolhouse; but after a day or two of excitement the 'army' went to their respective homes with no loss of life. The headquarters of that little, inexperienced body of men and boys was at A. C. Tidd's home in Murraysville, and it was christened the 'Pork and Beans battle.'" Upon arriving at Ravenswood, Stone saw his first mustered soldiers: "Capt. Stinchcomb's company [probably James Stinchcomb of the 17th Ohio Volunteer Infantry], and possibly other volunteers. I think they were three months men. We stayed only one night in Ravenswood. Some of us slept on the upper porch of the Ravenswood House and then returned to our homes the next day."[48]

Private Lewis Love, Captain Welton's Company (Company A), discussed another such event by the tense new recruits at Mason City when he wrote: "...a report came in that a force of rebels, some 400 or 500 strong, were in the Roush Settlement and marching on Mason City....Capt. Welton ordered his men to take position on the bluff south of town. This movement so excited the citizens that they gathered such belongings as they could carry on their backs, or get other transportation for, and there was a regular exodus to Pomeroy,

James F. Stone.
Terry Lowry Collection.

just across the Ohio River, all available watercraft being brought into service....The people were terribly excited, running in all directions with their bundles of household goods." Love believed Captain Welton only had the men participate in this event as camp life had become monotonous. Following the reaction of the citizens, Welton never attempted such an affair again.[49]

The Department of the Ohio issued Order No. 1 at Grafton, (West) Virginia, on July 24, announcing that General George B. McClellan was relieved of command of the department and replaced by General William S. Rosecrans, who would henceforth command both the Department of the Ohio and Army of Occupation in Western Virginia. The army would consist of four brigades composed mostly of Ohio, Indiana and Kentucky soldiers, and the 4th brigade would be called the Brigade of the Kanawha. The 4th West Virginia Infantry was not mentioned as it was still in the process of organization.[50]

On July 25, Clarkson Fogg of Company E wrote from the barracks in Mason County: "We were sworn into the service of the U.S. on Monday last and are now on drill. We expect to get our arms by the first of next week....this is undoubtedly the best company yet mustered into service in this section – officers and men all in good spirits, very seldom one who drinks liquor....our Co. is the Honor Co. It will carry the colors and the music. There are 3 other companies here each about half full....officers drill 5 hours each day – the privates 3 hours." Dr. Barton of the company also indicated that while at Mason City, they received: "...their arms and accoutrement's and donned the blue uniforms. The muskets were of the old pattern, used by the armies of Generals Scott and Taylor in the Mexican War.[51]

Captain William Henry Harrison Russell's Company of (West) Virginia Foot Volunteers was mustered in as Company F on July 30 at Mason City, with Russell as captain, William S. Hall as 1st lieutenant, and Finley Davis Ong as 2nd lieutenant.

Russell was born November 25, 1840, at Amity, Allegany County, New York, and in the 1850 census he resided with his parents at Wirt, Allegany County, New York. In the 1850 New York state census he was again listed with his parents in the state. Sometime after that his

Cpl. Clarkson Fogg.
Private Collection.

family moved to Ravenswood, Jackson County, (West) Virginia, where they were living in 1860. He enlisted at Mason City on July 30 as captain of Captain Russell's Company, Virginia Foot Volunteers, and as captain of Company F, 4th West Virginia, on August 22.[52]

William H. H. Russell was apparently a favorite among his men, as noted by Corporal Adolphus De Bussey of Company F when he wrote: "We had a big time about our Captain. He is the best like[d] man at this post and the best like[d] man in the regiment. The other officers are jealous of him as he is putting us ahead of their men. He has a call for Lieutenant Colonel, and they want us to give him up but the boys will not hear to it."[53]

Nevertheless, Russell's time as captain was short because he was commissioned lieutenant colonel of the regiment on August 27. This opened the captaincy of the company to George W. Storey on September 1, 1861. Born circa 1829-1830 in New Hampshire, Storey was a clerk at Troy, Athens County, Ohio, in 1850 and had the same occupation in Pomeroy, Meigs County, Ohio, in 1860.[54]

William S. Hall was born circa 1831 in [West] Virginia. In his pension he claimed he had been a resident of Murraysville, Jackson County, at least ten years prior to his enlistment. His pension also indicates that at the time of his enlistment he was living at Long Bottom, Meigs County, Ohio, and entered the service as a private on July 20. According to Hall, he was commissioned as 1st lieutenant in Company F of the 4th West Virginia "fourteen days later," although his official record states he was commissioned July 30.[55]

Finley Davis Ong was born April 23, 1822, in Ohio, and in 1850 he was a mill wright working in Madison, Iowa. In 1860 Ong was a boat builder residing in Murraysville, Jackson County, (West) Virginia. He was designated as a 2nd lieutenant July 30, 1861, at Mason City.[56]

This was the sixth company mustered in for the regiment. Major Richard Channing Moore Lovell of Pierpont's staff, brevet colonel of cavalry, state troops (militia), reported he had mustered in 83 men for the company so far, without Major Oakes present, as Lovell was fearful that possible bad news from Kanawha County might instill fear in the new company. Lovell also wrote on August 1 that the lieutenant

Maj. Henry Grayum.
Terry Lowry Collection.

governor and he would be meeting the following day to appoint officers for the regiment.[57]

According to Lovell, there were two other companies in barracks awaiting muster, including a cavalry company and a company of Kanawha County sharpshooters under a John B. Booram, who had served with General Cox as a scout and fought at Scary Creek. Booram, who would be appointed 1st lieutenant in Company H of the 4th West Virginia, requested his men be armed with the army rifles with minie balls.[58]

A description of Company F's first weapons was provided by James F. Stone, who wrote:

> After we were fully equipped for active service, our arms were of an ancient type, the old musket with cartridge ball, and three buckshot wound in paper at the end of the ounce ball. I remember the first time the 4th Va. Regt. Was given a test of firing by volley. When we came back to quarters many of the boys had black and blue shoulders for those muskets kicked with a vengeance.[59]

Company G

Company G of the 4th West Virginia Infantry was mustered in at Mason City by Major Richard Channing Moore Lovell on August 11. Henry Grayum, born November 14, 1818, in Gallipolis, Gallia County, Ohio, was commissioned captain effective July 1, and later promoted to Major on May 19, 1863.[60]

The company's 1st lieutenant was John DeLille. Born circa 1829 in Ohio, in 1850 DeLille lived in Pomeroy, Meigs County, Ohio, and worked as a lab worker, possibly in the photography business, since he was a photo artist in the 1870 census. He joined the company July 18, 1861, and was mustered in August 11 at Mason City, with his commission as 1st lieutenant effective from July 18.[61]

The position of 2nd lieutenant went to Cincinnatus Benjamin "Nat" Blake. Born January 8, 1830, at Blake's Landing, near Swan Creek,

Gallia County, Ohio, in 1850 he was working as a farmer in Gallia County. Blake joined Company G on July 28, 1861, at Mason City, and was appointed 2nd lieutenant August 11.[62]

Lieutenant Blake noted Captain Henry Grayum developed a reputation for getting "mad as Boston" whenever his men would get excited at the mere mention that Confederates may be lurking nearby. In order to calm that fear, Blake would assemble the men and relate a good story. As an example, he said he would address them with, "I call out attention, Co. G, our Captain discovered a cat in the commissary department and whilst you get in readiness he will surround and rout the cat," which was a joke that calmed the men.[63]

According to a postwar interview, William Foreman (Forman) joined the 4th West Virginia sometime prior to September 16, although he does not appear on any official records of the regiment. He claimed he was a resident of Lawrence County, Ohio, when he enlisted. Foreman recalled a sad incident during this time:

> When loading a government wagon on a boat at Point Pleasant the ropes broke and let the wagon down on him killing him almost instantly. I thought that it was a very bad way to begin ....We went into camp at Mason City where we remained a month or perhaps six weeks before we were mustered into the service, and when we went home our clothes had become so worn that some of us had to peel pawpaw bars and use it to tie our clothes on. All the warfare we saw while in camp was a number of fights between some of the boys. Not being satisfied with that kind of 'warfare' I enlisted in the 5th [West] Virginia [Infantry]" on September 16, 1861. He would later be shot in the back at Cedar Mountain, Virginia, in August of 1862, which caused the loss of the use of his right arm and led to a medical discharge.[64]

A good example of the fighting amongst each other was told by Corporal George W. Gilliland, Company C, who wrote:

I was very much amused one day while in camp at two members of my company, [Private] Samuel Crawford and a fat fellow by the name of [Private] Caleb Williams got into a scrap. Caleb started for a rock and Sam picked up a piece of brick, blazed away and hit Caleb. But the funny part was to hear Caleb grunt when his rear part and the piece of brick came in contact with each other. It was several days before Caleb could sit down with any degree of comfort and converse with his comrades.[65]

Point Pleasant
August 1, 1861

Private John G. Farrar noted that on August 1, Company E was ordered to Point Pleasant at the mouth of the Kanawha River. The company took a transport down the Ohio River, where they studied military tactics. Farrar indicated they drilled about eight hours a day. Private Lewis Love, Company A, recalled that the full complement of clothing was assigned, and they went through "military maneuvers, manual of arms, and target practice" on a daily basis. Love also commented on slavery, writing that while at Point Pleasant "the colonel received orders to guard the Kanawha River and intercept all slaves who were trying to escape. The soldiers were ordered to search every boat or skiff for runaways, and if any were caught to have them returned to their master. This order was obeyed but no slaves were caught. The boys were determined not to herd negroes for rebels. It was an order that could well not be enforced." Love followed with a typical remark expressed by many whites at the time: "We knew a slave could build breastworks and drive an army team as well as a white man. We thought the masters could look after them better than those who had no experience in the business, and he better lay down his arms, come home and behave himself."[66]

According to James B.C. Vale of Company D, he and Milton Conner went home on leave on August 2 and when they returned the following day they found companies B and D had been ordered to Charleston. As a result, Vale and Sergeant Conner, who was very sick with measles, went up the Kanawha River to join them.[67]

William Van Brown, Company D, recalled that on August 7 his company was at Point Pleasant quartered in the courthouse (They would move their camp about a mile outside of town the following day). He added, "We are all well here except six or seven who have got the measles." There had also been a recent near insurrection in the company because the men had not yet received their uniforms and blankets. In addition, Brown noted that the company of Captain John L. Vance had arrived in camp.[68]

The week before, Private Brown had been part of a detachment to guard a supply train of 75 wagons to General Jacob D. Cox at Gauley Bridge. Ten men from each of the companies of the regiment were selected, with initial advance camping at such places as Buffalo, Poca, and the property of secessionist "Capt. Earley." Along the route Brown witnessed much of the damage in the aftermath of General Henry A. Wise's recent occupation of the Kanawha Valley, including the Scary Creek battlefield and, later, the wire suspension bridge over the Elk River at Charleston.[69]

Upon arrival at Charleston the detachment refused to proceed to Gauley Bridge unless they were furnished horses. The request was met, and they advanced to Simm's Creek, (Simmons Creek) "one mile above Malone and 11 miles above Charleston," Smithers Creek, and Cannelton.   When they arrived at Gauley Bridge they found that General Cox had been arrested on a trumped up charge of treason, initiated mostly by jealous officers, which was quickly dropped. Colonel John W. Lowe, the Union field commander in the late Scary Creek fight, was also met with such claims against him that likewise were dismissed. Colonel Lowe and two companies of his 12th Ohio accompanied the detachment back to Charleston, where Lowe's men were to guard the town. In Lowe's opinion the 4th West Virginia boys had done the best marching he had ever seen.[70]

Corporal Adolphus De Bussey, a regimental musician in Company F, wrote his mother describing the camp at Point Pleasant: "There was 1500 soldiers here when we came. 1200 left for Charleston on

[August] the 3rd and two hundred left this morning for Guyandotte and Barboursville....There is 1400 soldiers here now. We got our guns the 5th of August. I do not know when we will get our uniforms and blankets. Some of the boys have been in the service two months and have not got their blankets yet. The boys are in good health and full of mischief."[71]

During this period, Captain James H. Dayton, Company K, was robbed. He owned a a dry goods store at New Creek, which secessionist guerrillas had robbed, taking $10,000 worth of goods, and "...fed their cavalry horses in his store drawers, shot a man who was lying asleep at the door, and perpetrated all sorts of outrages."[72]

Possibly associated with this destruction was Zachquill "Zack" Cochran, born in Monongalia County in 1814 and sheriff of Taylor County from 1859 to 1861. Cochran developed an early hatred for the Union army "...for ordering him to confiscate farm animals of the region." Consequently, he resigned as sheriff and joined the Confederate cause, assisting the movement of Southern soldiers, hiding them by day and moving them to safety under the cover of darkness.[73]

Whether or not Cochran was directly involved is unknown, but Captain Dayton had a score to settle with area guerrillas and found an opportunity when General Benjamin F. Kelley received information that a large body of them were lodged west of Grafton, within a few miles of Webster. Dayton and about 50 men of Company K (yet recognized by themselves as Company A), 4th West Virginia Infantry, were dispatched from Webster to disarm the rebels. After scouting for about 24 hours, Dayton and his men came upon the guerrillas at about noon, August 13, near Grafton, Taylor County, (West) Virginia, on the Jonathan Curry farm along the Fairmont and Webster Road. The rebel force numbered about 200, including the noted 'vile secessionist' Curry and former Taylor County Sheriff Zack Cochran. A severe hour-long fight ensued in which, reportedly, 21 guerillas were killed, including two members of the Curry family, and the remainder put to flight, with no loss to Dayton's command.[74]

Another account of this event places it on August 15-16, indicating it involved 75 members of the 25th Ohio Volunteer Infantry and notes

Joseph A.J. Lightburn.
Terry Lowry Collection.

that the two-day expedition covered two miles by rail and 36 by foot. Dayton's Company of the 4th West Virginia would not join the remainder of the regiment until December 29.[75]

Joseph Andrew Jackson Lightburn
"Corporal Joe"

The assorted companies of the newly forming 4th West Virginia Infantry received a commander on August 14 at Wheeling, (West) Virginia, when Joseph Andrew Jackson Lightburn, adjutant of the 192nd Militia (Lewis County), was appointed colonel. According to *The Findlay Jeffersonian* (Ohio) newspaper of August 16, Governor Francis Pierpont first offered command of the 4th West Virginia Infantry to Colonel James Neibling of the 21st Ohio Infantry, based upon his gallant performance in the early Kanawha Valley campaign, but he refused the offer, preferring to remain with his regiment.[76]

Joseph Andrew Jackson Lightburn was born September 21, 1824, at Webster, Westmoreland County, Pennsylvania, and then moved with his family to Broad Run, Lewis County, (West) Virginia, in the spring of 1838, when he was only 14 years old. One of his neighbors and best friends was Thomas Jonathan "Stonewall" Jackson, with whom he often went fishing. Lightburn and Jackson were among four district boys considered for an appointment to West Point, but neither received the post. Instead, Gibson Jackson Butcher got the assignment, but he soon found he was not suited for West Point life and dropped out, creating an opening for "Stonewall" Jackson. Lightburn found himself "out of the race," but during the Mexican War he enlisted in the U.S. Army on December 4, 1846, at Newport Barracks, Kentucky. During his service he was primarily involved in recruiting in such places as Cincinnati, Ohio; Fort Wayne, Indiana; Chicago, Illinois; Detroit, Michigan; Memphis, Tennessee; and New Orleans, Louisiana. He never left the United States, and as such, never saw combat. He was honorably discharged December 5, 1851, with the rank of sergeant.[77]

Lightburn returned to work the family farm and mill and in 1855 married his stepsister. The new couple built a home in the area, and on April 16, 1859, Lightburn was licensed to preach by the local Broad Run Church. Following the seizure of Harpers Ferry in 1859, Lightburn became involved in politics as a strong Union supporter, making speeches and serving as a delegate to the Second Wheeling Convention after the war erupted. He enlisted as adjutant of the 192nd Regiment Virginia Militia (Lewis County) on July 11 and enlisted in the U.S. service July 13, although he continued to sign documents as adjutant of the 192nd Militia as late as July 27. Throughout his Civil War career he would carry the nickname "Corporal Joe," bestowed upon him by his soldiers in reference to the rank with which he began his military career and a nickname he much appreciated.[78]

Company H

Company H of the 4th West Virginia was mustered in at Point Pleasant on August 18, with Patrick H. Brunker as captain, his commission dating from August 1; John B. Booram as 1st Lieutenant; and Henderson F. Donnally as 2nd Lieutenant. Brunker was born in 1833 (or 1835). Sources differ on where he was born, including Ireland, Pennsylvania, and New York, but according to the 1850 census, he was then a resident of Brady's Bend, Armstrong County, Pennsylvania. By the 1860 census, his family resided in Meigs County, Ohio, although he is listed as a resident at a hotel in town under the name E. Brunker. He was appointed a corporal of Company F, 18th Ohio Volunteer Infantry, on April 20, and mustered out with the company August 28. Brunker was appointed captain of Company H of the 4th West Virginia on August 18 or 22.[79]

John B. Booram was born September 10, 1810, in Mason County, (West) Virginia. In 1860 Booram was a boatman at Charleston, Kanawha County, (West) Virginia. Prior to joining the 4th West Virginia, he served on Pierpont's staff as chief of cavalry (militia), and he was a scout with General Cox and fought at Scary Creek. He joined Company H on August 1 at Point Pleasant and was mustered in August 22 as 1st lieutenant.[80]

Born February 23, 1840, in Meigs County, Ohio, Henderson F. Donnally lived with his family at Salisbury in Mason County in 1850. Donnally joined Company H of the 4th West Virginia on August 18 as a 2nd lieutenant and was mustered in at Point Pleasant on August 22.[81]

The companies at Point Pleasant began to develop and be equipped, as noted by Corporal Adolphus De Bussey, Company F, who wrote in August: "We got our blankets today. We got one pair of pants, two pairs of drawers, two pairs of socks, two undershirts, one pair shoes and hat, one overshirt. We get one more overshirt and overcoat a piece." He also noted there had been a false alarm the previous day of secessionist soldiers coming in their direction.[82]

Events began to develop quickly for the regiment when, on August 21, General William Starke Rosecrans, at Clarksburg, sent a telegram to Governor Francis H. Pierpont at Wheeling, stating, "Col Lightburn has been ordered to Point Pleasant to take command of the last & the 7 companies of his regiment on the Kanawha 3 more companies will be required to fill the regiment one 1 of which I suppose is Dayton's." Rosecrans requested that Pierpont "Indicate the companies you have selected and the names & dates of the Lieut Colonel & major & adjutant & quartermaster commission so that I may have the entire regimental organization." Looking beyond the 4th West Virginia, Rosecrans continued: "For the organization of the next Regt there seems to be nearly companies enough already reported about to ask for a mustering officer. I beg your excellency to hurry up those organizations. Genl Kelley has been directed as soon as notice is given to detail an officer to muster them in. Q-Master Ransom will be directed to furnish camp equipage & your Excellency has the clothing & equipment. Arms to be supplied on requisition by Lieut Crispin who will have orders to that effect."[83]

Colonel Lightburn arrived at Point Pleasant on the 20th, and on the 22nd of the month he wrote to General Jacob D. Cox, commanding the Army of the Kanawha, that he had arrived at Point Pleasant. Lightburn also reported that tensions in his area were growing, and that he was beginning to form the larger body of volunteer companies there into the 4th West Virginia regiment. He wrote to General James S. Wheat

Lieut. Col. JAMES R. HALL, U. S. A   Maj. JOHN T. HALL. U. S. A.

SON OF JOHN AND OLIVIA HALL   SON OF JOHN AND OLIVIA HALL

KILLED IN THE BATTLE OF CEDAR CREEK VA   KILLED IN THE BATTLE OF KENNEDY'S HILL VA
October 19th, 1864.   August 6th, 1862.

(Young, patriotic brave, and generous, they gallantly fell in defence of their Country, with their faces to the foe.)

Lt. Col. James R. Hall and Maj. John T. Hall.
St. Albans Historical Society.

on August 20 of their status: "...6 companies are now in Point Pleasant, 2 in Charleston...I want help in drilling...I should like to have two rifle companies or rather rifles for two companies to be used as scouts or flanking companies..." Lightburn also requested copies of Hardee's 1855 drill manuals for Rifle and Light Infantry for his officers to study and train their new recruits. On August 24, Lightburn issued "Order No. 1," stating he had officially assumed command of the regiment and the post. He added he was ready to receive any instructions or duties assigned to him. He also began the process of appointing field and staff officers, although it was not filled until November 27. "Order No. 1" also presented the rules and regulations to be followed by the commissioned officers, non-commissioned officers, and the soldiers in general.[84]

During this time Lightburn also wrote James S. Wheat from Point Pleasant stating "another company was day before yesterday mustered into service for my Regiment....making 6 here and two at Charleston. I am informed that there are others in progress of organization. I believe there is an artillery company being raised to be attached to this Regiment provided it can be done." Lightburn added he wished for the commissions of William H.H. Russell as lieutenant colonel and John T. Hall as major in order to assist with drilling. He also wrote: "All things are going right. I have the material for a good Regiment both in officers and men." Lightburn concluded by requesting rifles for two companies – one to scout and one to flank.[85]

Field and Staff

Per Lightburn's request, William H. H. Russell was appointed lieutenant colonel on August 27, from captain of Company F, and John Taylor Hall was appointed major the same day. Hall was born circa 1840 at Point Pleasant in Mason County, (West) Virginia, the son of John Hall, an influential politician in the statehood movement and possibly the wealthiest man in the county. John T. Hall was also the younger brother of James R. Hall, who would later become lieutenant colonel of the 13th West Virginia Infantry and was mortally wounded at Cedar Creek on October 19, 1864. John T. Hall attended the Virginia Military Institute (V.M.I.) and would have graduated with the class of 1863 had he not dropped out due to the war in 1861.

On March 13, James Hall wrote to V.M.I. superintendent Colonel Benjamin F. Smith, requesting he excuse his brother John for receiving demerits for some temper outbursts. His father, John Hall Sr. wrote to the superintendent on March 12, petitioning the colonel to excuse him, citing a concussion sustained at the age of four as the reason his son was prone to such "fits." In April of 1861 the younger John went to Richmond with the corps and trained troops as a drillmaster at the camp of instruction at Liberty Mills near Richmond. According to V.M.I. student records, as the war erupted, John, along with many other cadets, left the school and came to Charleston, (West) Virginia to support Confederate General Henry A. Wise. Reportedly, he was going to join the Confederate army but his father adamantly opposed the idea and refused to allow it. He planned to go to his father's house in Mason County but was "detained and informed that he could not go. He drew a pair of pistols and told those who attempted to detain him that he would shoot the first man who attempted to put a hand upon him. In this way he came through to his father's house and shortly thereafter was made major of the 4th [West] Virginia Infantry."[86]

Philemon Beecher Stanbery, previously described as a 1st lieutenant in Company E, was commissioned adjutant of the regiment August 22.[87] Jesse Vinton Stevens (Stephens), previously described as a 1st and 2nd lieutenant of Company C, was appointed regimental quartermaster on October 18, although his service record states this also transpired on September 1.[88] George Knight Ackley was appointed surgeon August 26. Born September 8, 1831, in Ohio, Ackley was a physician in Racine, Meigs County, Ohio, in 1860.[89]

Charles Augustus Barlow, aka Augustus Charles Barlow, was born January 1, 1825, at Gallipolis, Ohio, and was a physician from Mason County, (West) Virginia, in the 1850 census. He enrolled in the 4th (West) Virginia as assistant surgeon on August 17, 1861, at Point Pleasant. In November he was promoted to major and surgeon of the 8th West Virginia Infantry. He later served as surgeon and assistant surgeon in the 47th Ohio and 62nd Ohio infantry and was brevetted lieutenant colonel.[90]

Barlow would be replaced as assistant surgeon of the 4th West Virginia on November 19, by Dr. John Rush Philson, who was born July 7, 1819, in Adams County, Pennsylvania. At an early age his family moved to Frederick County, Maryland, where he received his early education in community schools. Philson left Maryland in 1839 to settle in Racine, Meigs County, Ohio, where he was an educator (one source says he moved to Meigs County as an agent for wooden wheel clocks). He studied medicine and in 1852 graduated from Starling Medical College at Columbus, Ohio. After briefly going into a medical partnership with Dr. J.B. Ackley, he set up his own practice and "won distinction for his skill in the treatment of diseases."[91]

George Spofford Woodhull was mustered in as regimental chaplain on November 1. He was born July 25, 1829, at Manhattan, New York. Woodhull "graduated from New York University in 1848, with the

Dr. John R. Philson.
Mark Philson Collection.

Martin Van Buren Lightburn.
Terry Lowry Collection.

Greek Honor, and from Princeton Theological Seminary in 1852, and was licensed to preach by the Presbytery of New York the same year." In 1853 he was ordained as an Evangelist by the Presbytery of West Jersey.[92]

Lightburn sent a list of the officers of the 4th West Virginia to James S. Wheat requesting their commissions on August 28. He indicated that Dan A. Smith, 1st lieutenant of Company A, wished to decline his commission and resign because he was in a business partnership with his brother, Captain Thomas Smith of Company C, and they did not wish to split the business relationship. Lightburn added that Lieutenant Smith had been an excellent participant in the organization of the regiment and had served also as his acting quartermaster. Smith resigned on either August 31 or September 1, but his brother did not resign until 1862. Martin Van Buren Lightburn, Colonel Lightburn's brother, was recommended to replace D.A. Smith. Concluding his dispatch, Colonel Lightburn said he also desired, if possible, that a cavalry company and an artillery company be attached to the 4th West Virginia and that rifles be provided for his two flanking companies.[93]

Adolphus De Bussey of Company F also wrote on August 28 that his beloved Captain William H.H. Russell, as previously anticipated, had been appointed lieutenant colonel of the regiment, much to the company's dismay, but he thought Russell was the only man in the regiment capable of filling such a position. He also wrote: "Fifty of our men was taken to Gallipolis to guard stores. They are under the command of Capt. Brown, captain of Co. E. Twelve of us are guarding the commissary apartment [department]." De Bussey added regarding the company: "We have good times and a good deal of fun. The hard times is to come yet, but we are ready for them."[94]

On August 28, Captain James Dayton, Company A (later Company K) wrote a letter to General William S. Rosecrans requesting reinforcements at his post at New Creek. He had reliable information that there were 700 Confederates at Petersburg in Hardy County, and that their cavalry were scouring the county. Besides his own company, it is believed he also had the Ringgold Cavalry with him to protect against the enemy force, but shortly afterward several companies of the 8th Ohio Infantry were dispatched to New Creek, raising the defending force to about 500.[95]

Dayton would also send a telegram to Pierpont on September 4 requesting permission for admission of 110 men to his company as they were anxious to enlist and refused to enlist in another company.[96]

Rumors flew on the night of August 28 at Point Pleasant. 2nd Lieutenant Cincinnatus B. Blake, Company G, wrote: "...our scouts came in with intelligence that two steamboats loaded with secesh were within five miles of this place coming down the Kanawha. Two men came down [and] one run his horse until it fell and the other came in & was given out himself, covered with sweat and dust frightened to death." Captain Welton's Company A was called out to meet the threat and "marched to the Kanawha about a ¼ of a mile before any other Company was ready" before discovering the suspected enemy was actually teams returning from Gallipolis, where they had been sent to draw provisions. Prior to this discovery, however, soldiers at Point Pleasant had run from tent to tent yelling that the enemy was approaching, which caused a major panic, with the men of Company G saying they were going to run for the woods. Blake calmed the men, and Captain Grayum told them he would go to the woods with them if they did not calm down, "damn them."[97]

August 29 found Lightburn at Point Pleasant writing James S. Wheat to request tents for field officers as well as drums and fifes for the regimental band and accoutrements for Captain Henry Grayum's Company. On the 30th, arms arrived at Point Pleasant for Company H, the "Elk River company." This same day Lieutenant Blake, Company G, bragged: "We have a grand time taking secesh. We have taken at least one dozen today, some confined, some let go again." Blake complained that Captain Grayum was not severe enough with the secessionist prisoners.[98]

The last day of August was marked by a measles outbreak at Point Pleasant. Lieutenant Blake wrote: "...it does not go hard with them. Then they report themselves not able to be on duty, we send then straight to the hospital. They do not relish that." Late August also saw the remaining companies of the 4th West Virginia, excepting Dayton's Company A, arrive at Point Pleasant.[99]

Boone Court House
September 1, 1861

In late August, Colonel James V. Guthrie of the 1st Kentucky Infantry, who was in command of the post at Charleston, heard that some four to six hundred rebels were quartered at Boone County Court House, and he decided to send a detachment under Captain Joseph T. Wheeler, Company A, 1st Kentucky, to break up the gathering.

According to Guthrie's account, the detachment consisted of Company A of the 1st Kentucky, Company G of the 26th Ohio, and companies B and D of the 4th West Virginia, who were left at Peytona to scout the area as rear guard and to protect the main force in the event of a retreat. The detachment marched 35 miles over mountains and ravines and arrived on a hill overlooking Boone Court House on Sunday, September 1. They were joined by roughly two hundred men of the Peytona Home Guard, which lacked any officers, so they were placed under Corporal James W. Nowlen, Company A, 1st Kentucky, who was ordered to advance and draw the enemy fire. If successful they were to fall back on the main body.[100]

Although the first part went according to the plan, the home guards refused to fall back, claiming that they had been continually maligned by the area secessionists and now was their chance to show their courage. Captain Wheeler, "finding his plan of flanking the enemy frustrated by the obstinacy of the Virginians," was left with few options. He ordered Company G of the 26th Ohio, under Captain Samuel C. Rook, to lead the advance as they charged down the hill, completely surprising the rebels, who fled in all directions. According to Colonel Guthrie, some 35 of the rebels were killed, and five men were captured. The Union loss was none killed and six wounded, including Corporal James Nowlen, who received a severe breast wound. A Union soldier carrying a small flag was shot through both legs from someone in a house. This so infuriated the Union soldiers they decided to burn

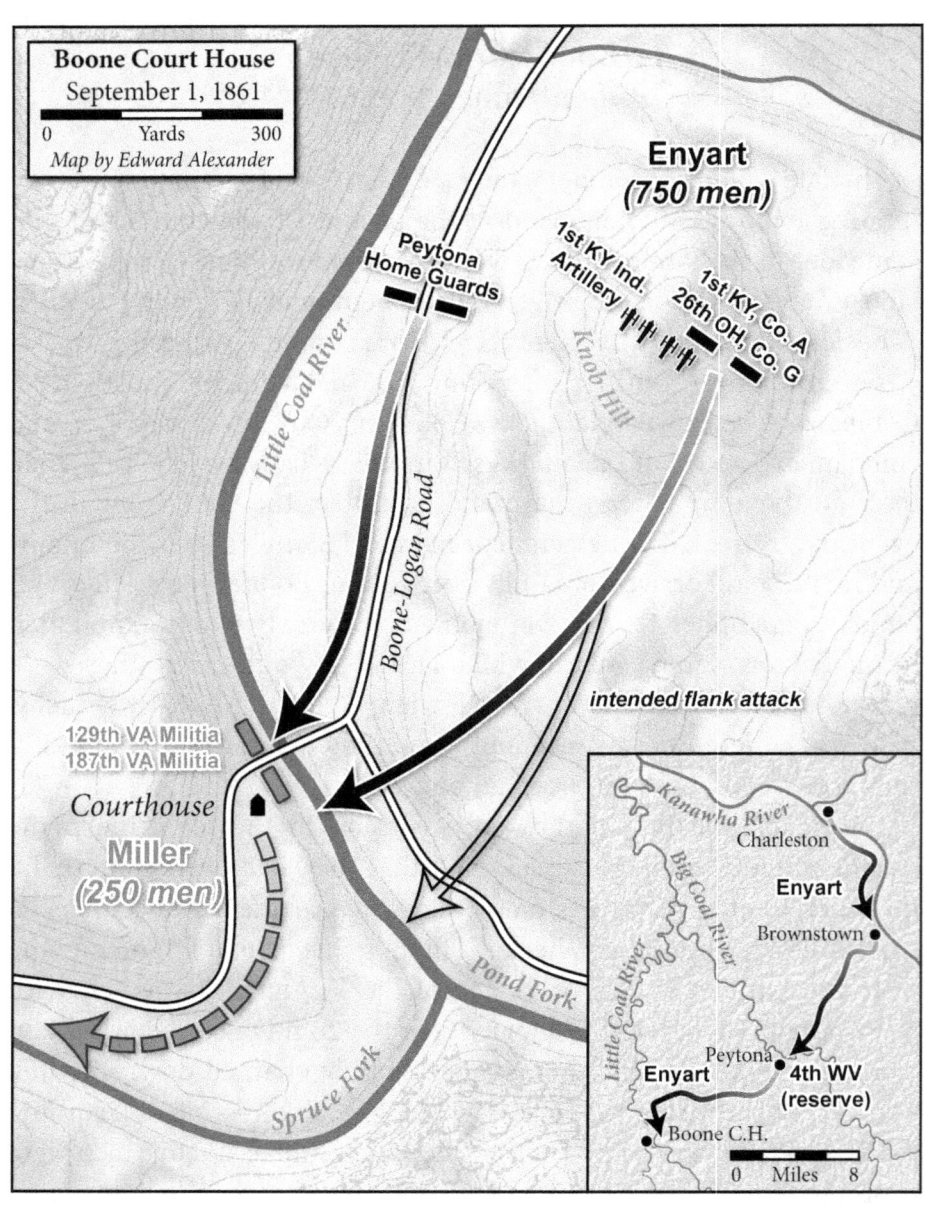

the town to the ground. On the return trip the detachment was met at Peytona by a female home guard unit. The soldiers instructed the women in drill, loaning them their muskets, and then cheered them for their patriotism. Afterward the detachment returned to Charleston.[101]

Although the newspaper claimed Colonel Guthrie submitted this report on the battle at Boone Court House, General Jacob D. Cox filed two separate reports on it and made no mention of the 4th West Virginia, while some contemporary accounts assert the two companies of the 4th West Virginia remained behind at Peytona to guard the road. Perhaps the answer to the question of whether the 4th West Virginia participated in the fight at Boone Court House can be found in the February 16, 1862 letter of Private William V. Brown, Company D, 4th West Virginia, who stated, "we [4th West Virginia] was within six miles" of Boone during the fight. In addition, James B.C. Vale of the company said they went on an expedition to Peytona September 1 and returned to camp September 3.[102]

The Spencer Expedition and Occupation
August 29, 1861 – Early December 1861

During the summer of 1861 the companies of the 4th West Virginia at Point Pleasant became well instructed in tactics and drill and came under strict military discipline. This training helped prepare them for their first active military campaign, the relief of Spencer Court House in Roane County, which began about August 31; although one unidentified member of the regiment, identified only as "Pomeroy," wrote they left Point Pleasant on the morning of the 29th. On this expedition, Lightburn divided the regiment into three active fronts: Spencer, Captain James Dayton's Company in the New Creek area, and the remaining companies in the training camps in the Mason City and Gallipolis vicinity.

Four companies, A (not Dayton's Company), C, E, and F, were ordered to the relief of the Union home guard at Spencer in Roane County, (West) Virginia. Dr. Thomas Barton, Company E, recalled: "... [we] were marched on board a transport, and were soon steaming up

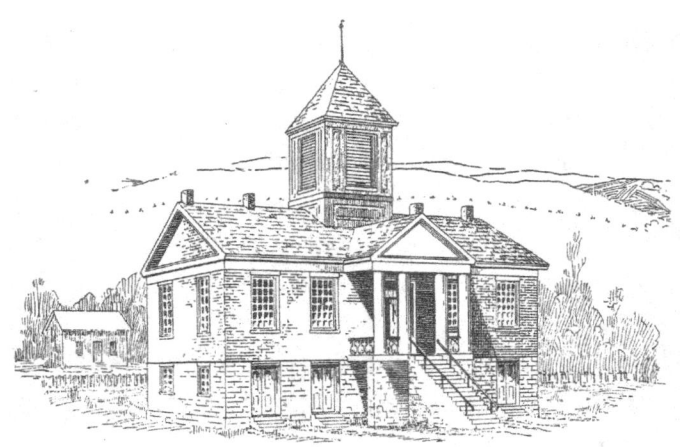

ROANE COUNTY'S FIRST COURT HOUSE.
Built year, 1859.   Destroyed by fire, 1887.
Details in part from an old retouched photograph, and in part fror
memory
The retouched photo shows a slate roof and slated cupola.
The roof was of shingles and the cupola sides were of panelling.

Roane County Court House.
Public Domain.

the Kanawha. The command disembarked at the mouth of Pocatalico [Poca River], marched about eight miles up the river, and bivouacked. This was our first bivouac, and we laid on our arms in line of battle." John G. Farrar, also of Company E, related basically the same information but added: "We marched out [from the mouth of Poca River] about 8 miles and bivouacked. This was our first camp out." The unidentified soldier from Pomeroy, Ohio, said they slept on the ground, with the sky as their tent.[103]

Another soldier of the 4th West Virginia, Corporal George W. Gilliland, Company C, described this first campaign in an 1899 article. Gilliland wrote: "We went up Kanawha to the mouth of Poca and started across the country for Spencer, the county seat of Roane County. The second night we stopped for the night on a hillside where some men had been clearing." The unidentified Pomeroy soldier noted they covered 19 miles the second day. According to Gilliland: "It was very dark and raining very hard. I lay down on some burnt logs on the flat of my back and in the night I turned on my side and got wedged between them and I could not be pulled out. The soldiers had to cut off a little stump on the lower side to let the log roll away and the others held the upper log from rolling until I was freed. The next morning we started for Spencer and arrived there that evening."

The unidentified Pomeroy soldier claimed that on the third day of the trek they marched 23 miles before arriving within two miles of their destination, adding, "...Virginia miles....are one-third longer than our Ohio miles."[104]

The detachment marched on to Spencer, where Captain William Pell's Company of Roane County Home Guard had been besieged by rebel bushwhackers for about three days, in an apparent eleven-day siege, but Pell's men had managed to drive off the rebels before the arrival of the detachment of the 4th Regiment. Dr. Barton suspected the rebels may have actually fled upon learning of the approach of the "Bloody 4th," although one must question where the regiment gained such a name without ever having been in combat. George Gilliland added: "It was at that place that I first saw the blood of a dead soldier. The home guards were guarding the town. One of them was up in the cupola of the courthouse and the Rebels shot him as they entered town. He fell down through the plastering in the floor below. It was a bad sight for a new soldier to see those broken lath with so much blood on them." The casualty was probably Sanford "Doc" Boone of the Roane County Home Guard.[105]

Among the wounded was Private S. Martin, with his arm shot off close to his shoulder on August 31, and Private S. Gibson, shot through the lower jaw on September 9. Both men were members of Captain Lyle Paxton's Company, Roane County Home Guard. A third man, listed only as Weldon, was shot through the breast. All three were in the military hospital at Spencer on September 14. The unidentified soldier of the 4th West Virginia from Pomeroy noted, "There was a man shot out of the cupola of the Court House. Also one shot right here in town. And several wounded."[106]

Private Lewis Love, Company A, while discussing the overwhelming number of bushwhackers and horse thieves in the wild, rugged, mountainous area of Roane County, said: "A day or two after we reached Spencer two messengers were fired upon two miles from town, who were bringing dispatches. One was under lightly and fell as he jumped for the brush. Three rushed on him to get his valuables but the soldier raised up with gun to his face and fired point blank into his breast. I was one of the escorts who took them back to their command. When we reached the battle ground there was a bloody nest of leaves that looked like some man had bled to death. A neighbor said they had carried a man past on a crude litter made of small poles. He supposed the man was dead but asked no questions."[107]

During the 4th West Virginia detachment's first week at Spencer: "...provisions were scarce and there was also much suffering among the soldiers from want of hospital stores. However, in about ten days a train arrived with the necessary and much needed supplies." Sergeant William L. McMaster, Company C, added in a September 17 letter to his father, "We have no mail facilities in this region of the Old Dominion, we have to wait until someone is going through to some point on the Ohio River, and then send our letters by them." He went on to express his opinion of western Virginia, writing: "Western Virginia can brag of good Court-Houses but not of schoolhouses. The schoolhouses are few and far between. But this is a pretty good fruit country; there is splendid peaches and apples in this section, their orchards bear well."[108]

Sergeant Lyman S. White, Company E, had his own views, scribing: "I have seen some hardships. Our Company is continually making forced marches, and scouting over these hills is no easy employment. I am getting so I think nothing of walking 25 miles a day." White would later fall in combat in the Shenandoah Valley in 1864.[109]

Skirmish at Reedy
Early September 1861

Private James F. Stone, Company F, said that after being at Spencer for a few days: "... a detail from Co. F and I think a detail from the other companies was sent with a small wagon train to Elizabeth, after rations. We were fired on out of the brush by some guerillas near what is now known as Kyger, between Spencer and Reedy, but no one was hurt. This was the first I had experienced being shot at." Adolphus De Bussey, also of Company F, wrote from Spencer on the 30th of the incident, stating: "I just returned from Elizabeth today at noon. It is 28 miles from here. It is the second trip we have made since the 23rd, guarding the provision wagons up and back down. On Thursday we had some eight shots fired at us by Secesh in ambush but none of the boys was hurt tho some of them was cut close enough for them to feel the balls....It was about half way between here and the Three Forks of Reedy which is about 10 miles from here...." De Bussey said the following day they marched "through mud and water to our knees all day. We left the [Little] Kanawha yesterday morning. It was very high and oily. Barrels floating thick."[110]

Six companies of the 36th Ohio Volunteer Infantry had also been ordered to Spencer to clear out guerillas. John Palmer of Company G wrote in his diary that on September 1, while en route to Spencer, they got into a small skirmish with some bushwhackers near the Three Forks of Reedy. No casualties were sustained, and the column moved on and arrived at Spencer on the night of September 2. On September 4,

Post-war sketch of the skirmish at Reedy, WV.
Bishop's History of Roane County.

William M. Hovey.
St. Albans Historical Society.

the 36th Ohio, or at least a portion of it, helped escort a supply wagon from Elizabeth and became involved in a small, insignificant skirmish. But on the following day, September 5, the 36th Ohio was attacked near Reedy and, according to John Palmer, a (West) Virginia cavalry officer was wounded in the leg. This was very likely the same skirmish often incorrectly dated as having transpired on September 12, 1863, supposedly at the Duke farm near Reedy in which Colonel Henry Daniel Chapman of the Roane County state troops was wounded. This also appears to be the incident mentioned in the book *The History of Roane County*.[111]

The 36th Ohio remained at Spencer until September 11. The skirmishes they had while near Reedy are probably the same which involved the 4th West Virginia, but Palmer never mentions them.[112]

The remaining days in Spencer for the 4th West Virginia were spent scouting and bringing in many secessionists to take the oath of loyalty. Sergeant William M. Hovey, Company E, wrote, "But few of the prisoners are willing to take the oath of allegiance, and are kept confined."[113]

When the necessary medical supplies arrived at Spencer, regimental surgeon and Meigs County, Ohio, native George K. Ackley established a hospital. Dr. Barton was appointed as acting hospital steward, giving him the opportunity of observing the treatment of gunshot wounds.[114]

Early September proved to be a busy time for the 4th West Virginia. At Spencer, Colonel Lightburn authorized Jesse V. Stevens to acquire all necessary items for the regiment per Quartermaster of Commissary Subsistence and Stores, as well as any items for the sick in the post hospital. Adolphus De Bussey, Company F, said at least some of the regiment departed Spencer on September 6 and were at Spring Creek, about one and a half miles above Burning Springs on the Little Kanawha River in Wirt County, (West) Virginia, and returned to Spencer on the 8th. Back in Kanawha County, according to James B.C. Vale, Company D went on a scout up Coal River on September 5 and returned to camp on the 9th of the month. This was followed on September 12 by Companies B and D of the regiment, which went to

Mud River to reinforce the 1st Kentucky Infantry, although Vale had the measles and did not make the trip.[115]

On September 14, Lieutenant Colonel William H.H. Russell informed General Jacob D. Cox at Gauley Bridge that companies B and D of the 4th Regiment had been stationed at Charleston for nearly two months, denying them, and the regiment as a whole, the opportunity of learning battalion drill from two very experienced drillmasters at Point Pleasant. Russell believed this was detrimental to the regiment and requested Cox return the two companies to Point Pleasant. Russell expanded on this when he wrote Adjutant General H. J. Samuels from Point Pleasant, also on the 14th of September, repeating his message to Cox and adding there were now eight companies mustered in, with Company A comprised of 101 men rank and file; Companies B, C and D with 83 men each; 101 in Company E; 83 in Company F; and 101 in both Companies G and H, for a grand total of 730 men. Russell noted companies G and H only recently mustered in and had not had much opportunity to drill due to constant guard duty at Point Pleasant. Companies A, C, E and F, at Spencer in Roane County since around August 31, were proficient in drill. Lieutenant Colonel Russell went on to discuss the near lack of uniforms and equipment for all of the companies and said companies J (probably I) and K would soon be joining them. In summary, Russell desired that all the companies be posted at Point Pleasant in order to drill in preparation for field service.[116]

Company C briefly left Spencer for a three-day scouting expedition. Their assignment had been to march to "the great bend of Kanawha" where secessionists had killed a number of loyal citizens and mortally wounded by a rifle ball 2nd Lieutenant Ephraim McClaskey, Company K, 3rd West Virginia Infantry (6th West Virginia Cavalry), at Rowles Run in Calhoun County on September 7. McClaskey died the following day. The unidentified soldier from Pomeroy, probably a member of Company C, said they marched 18 miles the first day with three days' rations and advanced four miles the following day. Upon arrival at the designated area, strong but largely unsuccessful attempts were made to locate the guilty parties. The company did find the man who shot McClaskey and shot at him, but he escaped into the brush.[117]

While organizational development continued and camp life became monotonous, Sergeant Columbus Shrewsbury, Company A, wrote to his wife of the recent victory by General William S. Rosecrans at Carnifex Ferry (September 10). He also noted that he and Colonel Lightburn had participated together in some target practice.[118]

Colonel Lightburn wrote James S. Wheat on September 17, only seven days after General William S. Rosecrans and General John B. Floyd had fought the battle of Carnifex Ferry in Nicholas County, noting that he thought the home guard at Spencer was inefficient and should be disbanded. He claimed he could raise two companies there and had already sworn in 35 men as Company A of a new regiment. Lightburn said he had done this in compliance with authorities and that these new men were better than four times that number of home guard. Lightburn offered his opinion that the residents were more interested in a vigilant force which knew the country well.[119]

Sergeant William M. Hovey, Company E, also wrote from Spencer on September 19, "The boys, as a general thing, are well, and not withstanding hardships, are in good spirits, their chief desire being to get a shot at a Secesh."[120]

James B.C. Vale, Company D, reported that on September 22 his company left Charleston on a scout via Peytona in Boone County and up Coal River, the "crookedest river" he had ever seen. He said they waded the river 50 times before crossing over a large mountain, while a cold, steady rain fell. Lacking gum blankets and only partially clothed with government issue, Vale was amazed that the men survived, as most of them had recently had the measles. They eventually arrived at Raleigh Court House as the rain partially turned to snow and sent out pickets. In the morning, scouts reported the approach of Breckenridge's forces, which led Vale's command to return to Charleston, arriving there October 2, at which point Vale saw Colonel Lightburn for the first time.[121]

Late in September Lieutenant Colonel William H.H. Russell mentioned Company H had not yet received arms, accoutrements, or their clothing, excepting one gray shirt per man. Company H was also without tents and cooking utensils. Company G had no blouses or hats, and none of the companies then at Point Pleasant had been issued overcoats, while the field and staff officers were without tents. But Russell was optimistic that these problems could soon be resolved, and the regiment drilled and readied to take the field.[122]

Skirmish at Mill Creek Mountain
September 24, 1861

Captain James H. Dayton's Company A (K) was reportedly involved in another fight near Romney on September 24. Accordingly, a force led by Lieutenant Colonel James Cantwell and his 4th Ohio Infantry, along with a portion of the 8th Ohio Infantry, the Ringgold Cavalry, Company H of the 3rd West Virginia Infantry, and Dayton's company of the 4th West Virginia, totaling about 1,000, attacked a smaller enemy force at Romney and drove them out. Dayton's company was reportedly in skirmish action on Mill Creek Mountain on the morning of this affair.[123]

Battle of Kanawha Gap
September 25, 1861

According to the 1891 memoir of Corporal James B.C. Vale, his Company D and Company B of the 4th West Virginia Infantry accompanied Colonel Abram Piatt and his 34th Ohio Infantry (a.k.a. Piatt's Zouaves) on an expedition to Raleigh in September, which resulted in a battle at Kanawha Gap near Chapmanville in Logan County on September 25. Piatt attacked the crude entrenchments of Colonel James Ward and routed his Logan County Militia, along with the 129th Regiment Virginia Militia under Colonel John Dejernatt. Ward was seriously wounded, losing a thumb and finger, and fractured his arm in addition to a chest wound. Colonel Ward was also captured, then paroled due to the severity of his wound, and never returned to military service. Afterwards Piatt's force returned to the Kanawha

Valley and went into camp at Camp Piatt, a short distance east of Charleston. It is doubtful the two companies of the 4th West Virginia participated as they were posted on rear guard duty at Brownsville during this period. Colonel Lightburn indicated on September 26 that two companies of the 4th West Virginia were ordered to scout Logan County and encountered a large force of Confederate guerrillas there. He wrote, "Roads are hazardous due to 'guerrillas at every turn' and communication was very slow."[124]

Company I

Company I of the regiment was mustered in at Mason City by Major (later brevet colonel) Richard C.M. Lovell on September 27, although many of the men had already mustered in as early as July and August, including 49-year-old Alexander Vance as captain, Calvin A. Sheppard as 1st Lieutenant, and James W. Dale as 2nd Lieutenant. Alexander Vance, father of Captain John L. Vance of Company B, was born January 21, 1812, in Shenandoah County, Virginia. Vance was in the printing and publishing business at Gallipolis, Gallia County, Ohio, in 1850 and was a surveyor living at Gallipolis in 1860. He enrolled in Company I on July 10 and was promoted to captain of the company August 21. In addition to John L. Vance, serving as a captain in the regiment, another son, Reuben, also served with the regiment. After the war Reuben took a dim view of his own service, claiming he felt he had not done enough for his country.[125]

Calvin Alexander Sheppard was born November 9, 1841, and prior to the war was a resident of Gallipolis, Gallia County, Ohio. He joined the company as 1st lieutenant on July 10, 1861, and was mustered September 27, at Mason City. In 1864 he would serve as lieutenant colonel of the 173rd Ohio Infantry.[126] James W. Dale was born May 19, 1839, at Gallipolis, Ohio. He was employed as a day driver in 1860 and enlisted on July 10; Dale then mustered into service on August 22 at Mason City.[127]

Colonel Lightburn, on October 2, ordered Major John T. Hall at Spencer to bring companies A, C, and F to Point Pleasant and to leave

Calvin A. Sheppard.
Terry Lowry Collection.

Captain William R. Brown in command of the post at Spencer. The next day companies B and D, stationed at Charleston, boarded the steamer *Silver Lake* and traveled to Point Pleasant, a distance of 60 miles.[128]

On October 4, Colonel Lightburn wrote General William S. Rosecrans informing him that he had just arrived at Point Pleasant to obtain new shoes for his men at Spencer and that he had now been ordered to move the regiment to Point Pleasant to drill. He also thought Spencer was now relatively calm, and he would remove all but 100 men from that location.[129]

The following day Lieutenant Colonel William H.H. Russell again wrote from Charleston regarding the disposition of the 4th West Virginia, which included five companies at Point Pleasant, four at Spencer, and one company not quite full as it was short about 22 men. He further mentioned the regiment's supply problems, stating they needed overcoats for a full regiment and blankets and knapsacks for two companies. He added that three companies had caps, while six companies had hats, and eighty men had Enfield muskets with the Maynard type lock; 120 had rifled muskets with percussion locks, and there were 534 muskets altered from flintlocks. As to tents, the regiment had 153 small tents with flies, 90 small ones without flies that were used in the three-months service, and 20 wall tents with flies. Additionally, they had a full supply of canteens but needed haversacks for five companies.[130]

On October 8, Francis H. Pierpont, governor of the Reformed Government of Virginia, wrote to General William S. Rosecrans from Wheeling that some 200 rebels were creating havoc in Wirt and Calhoun counties of (West) Virginia and had killed seven Union soldiers and burned an extensive amount of property. Pierpont also indicated that "Lightburn's regiment is full and has four companies at Roane Court House [Spencer]" and requested that the 4th West Virginia be sent to Wirt and Calhoun counties as they were armed and equipped. Pierpont summarily growled, "Let them quarter and feed upon the enemy."[131]

The following day, October 9, General Rosecrans, writing from Mountain Cove in Fayette County, (West) Virginia, sent a telegram

James W. Dale.
Terry Lowry Collection.

to Pierpont at Wheeling, stating, "Have a letter from Col. Lightburn just returned from Roane he thinks the force left there will suffice I will however take further measures." Company E remained at Spencer while companies A, C, and F arrived at Point Pleasant from Spencer on October 10, a distance of some 60 to 70 miles.[132]

The Winfield Expedition
October 10 – October 14, 1861

Company G marched from Point Pleasant to Winfield in Putnam County on October 10 as well, then to Hurricane Bridge on the 13th, and back to Point Pleasant, a distance of 30 miles, on October 14. The expedition to Hurricane Bridge had been initiated to capture a Confederate force that had recently fired upon the steamer *Izetta*. The unsuccessful pursuing force was led by Lieutenant Colonel John Toland and his 34th Ohio Infantry and included companies G and H of the 4th West Virginia. An unidentified member of the 34th Ohio wrote that the companies of the 4th West Virginia "deported themselves through out with great bravery and skill. In Lieut. LeLille [DeLille], a splendid young officer, in one of these companies....Captains Graham [Grayum] and Brunker were the commanders, respectively, of the two companies, and were faultless in the performance of the duties assigned them." The same correspondent said the companies of the 4th West Virginia camped at Winfield (Camp Red House) on the 14th. He stated: "Our encampment is in the center of the village. Our church is given up to the 4th [West] Virginia." In the upper command echelon, the Department of West Virginia was created October 11, with General Rosecrans still in command, but he left his command independent of the Department of Ohio.[133]

Records indicate that Private Elias B. Bell, Company E, of the 4th West Virginia, deserted at Point Pleasant on October 15. According to Senate reports in 1879, 1900 and 1902, he had been wounded in the hand by the accidental discharge of another soldier's gun. The surgeon sent him home on a thirty-day furlough and when he returned his company was leaving for Spencer. Unable to carry a gun he remained at Point Pleasant until June 30, 1862, in charge of the quartermaster stores. Bell's hand was yet in bad condition, prompting the surgeon to recommend amputation, which Bell sternly refused. In response, the surgeon and the colonel approved of a medical discharge.

In September of 1862 Bell enlisted as a private in Company E, 3rd West Virginia Cavalry, and was reportedly honorably discharged from that regiment, although his service records show he deserted at Buckhannon, West Virginia, on September 29, 1863. It would not be until 1879 and later that the charges of desertion were removed from his record, and he obtained an honorable discharge. This accidental discharge of a weapon prompted Lightburn to issue General Order No. 2 at Point Pleasant, stating weapons were to be kept unloaded while in tents, and he also explained the use of weapons by pickets.[134]

Lightburn issued additional orders on September 15, including an announcement of the arrival of Captains Charles E. Means and George W. Palmer, both of the West Virginia State Troops, as drill instructors, and he ordered that they should be obeyed accordingly. General William S. Rosecrans had ordered no further furloughs until countermanded, and no food was to be permitted inside the quarters. Additional orders were issued the following day, including a warning that any officer or soldier found to be drunk would be court-martialed. On October 17, Rosecrans notified his command that any soldier caught destroying the property of private citizens would be dealt with severely and according to the Articles of War.[135]

A false alarm was raised at Spencer on October 20 when rumors spread that a rebel force of 100 men may be headed toward the town. The rebels were headquartered about ten miles from Spencer on the West Fork of the Little Kanawha River. A relief train was sent out immediately from Ravenswood and arrived in the evening, but the rumors proved false.[136]

James B.C. Vale, Company D, recalled that at Point Pleasant they were in barracks fitting churches and other buildings with bunks, performed guard duty, drilled, and were fully clothed and equipped. Vale also noted Lieutenant John Mallernee and Company D guarded a boat going up the Kanawha River on October 21 and returned to Point Pleasant October 23.[137]

Company K

Captain Dayton's Company was supposedly in the Cheat Mountain vicinity during this period but gave no report. As explained earlier, the company originally operated as Captain Dayton's Company Western Virginia Volunteers and Company A. However, another company led by Henry Samuel Welton was mustered in as Company A of the 4th West Virginia on June 17. Adjutant Philemon B. Stanberry stated in October that "I have placed Captain Rockhill's Company, which was Welton's as Company A, and arranged them accordingly to the rank of their former Captains, because Major Oakes mustered Captain Welton's Company A, and they say they were promised that letter by him and are not willing to give it up. According [Accordingly] I suppose Captain Dayton will have to take his position according to Rank elsewhere in the Regiment." As a result, Dayton's Company became Company K, its organization considered as have taken place between June 17 to July 20. Captain James H. Dayton would lead the company, with James J. Mansell as 1st lieutenant and Alpheus Beall as 2nd lieutenant.[138]

Skirmish at Romney
October 26, 1861

At midnight of October 25, Captain Dayton's Company was with a column of troops under the command of Brigadier General Benjamin F. Kelley. His force consisted of some companies of the 3rd and 4th West Virginia Infantries, part of the 7th West Virginia Infantry, nine companies of the 4th and 8th Ohio Infantries, the Ringgold Cavalry, the Virginia Lancers company of cavalry, a small artillery section, and a Maryland militia company, totaling some 3,000 troops. Their intent was to reinforce the line of the Baltimore and Ohio Railroad, but on October 26 the force encountered the enemy near Romney, which resulted in a small action. Among the wounded in Dayton's company was Private Thomas McGinness, who received a gunshot wound of the left foot and in 1862 was discharged for the wound.[139]

During this period in late October, two of the commanding officers of the 7th West Virginia Infantry pleaded with authorities to assign Dayton's Company to them permanently, but the request was denied. The other companies of the regiment remained at either Point Pleasant, Charleston, or Spencer at this time. A proposal to create a Department of the Big Sandy, which would include the 4th West Virginia, was developed by Governor Francis Pierpont on October 29 but not presented to President Abraham Lincoln until a later date.[140]

Colonel Lightburn wrote Adjutant General Samuels from Camp Lightburn on October 30 complimenting Charles E. Means and George W. Palmer, both of the West Virginia State Troops, two men who had been sent to the 4th West Virginia as instructors in tactics, drill, and discipline. Lightburn was highly impressed with them and said if they could remain another month the regiment would be ready to take the field. In fact, he even asked if they might be able to remain on a permanent basis.[141]

On November 1, Captain William R. Brown of Company E was placed in charge of the post at Spencer, "...and the other companies under Col. Lightburn returned to Point Pleasant." As Dr. Ackley accompanied the return of the column from Spencer, Dr. Barton was left as acting assistant surgeon at Spencer, although nothing of serious medical consequence transpired during this period. At least one company of the 11th West Virginia Infantry was formed at Spencer, and the detachment of the 4th West Virginia often had to go to the homes of the volunteers to escort the family members to camp to protect them from local secessionists.[142]

Colonel Lightburn continued to struggle with a supply shortage. He wrote to Adjutant General Henry J. Samuels from Point Pleasant on November 2 that his men needed blouses (sack coats) and overcoats, stressing that "one company are without blouses and if I fail to get them soon the company will be in the hospital." He followed up with a request for 200 blouses, 909 overcoats, and 814 dress coats. Lightburn also noted that "Dr. [Charles Augustus] Barlow has returned. I thought to have written before now in detail but it is probably best that I did not as I was somewhat out of humor at the time. I have no doubt that he thinks the Fraternity got Ackley the choice, but had he not been the choice of the Regiment I should not have made the choice as I did. I hope however the matter is now settled."[143]

Writing General Benjamin F. Kelley from New Creek on November 3, Captain Dayton, commanding Company A (later Company K) of the 4th West Virginia, requested 102 blue caps and 102 gutta percha blankets for his company.[144]

General William S. Rosecrans issued an order on November 6 for Captain Henry Grayum to take his Company G and proceed immediately to Gallipolis to guard government stores until further notice.[145]

Raid on Guyandotte
November 10, 1861

A Confederate cavalry force of about 700 men, under Colonel John Clarkson, attacked a recruiting camp of the 9th West Virginia Infantry at Guyandotte, Cabell County, on November 10. With only some 100 men, the Union soldiers were quickly overwhelmed by Clarkson's troopers, and most of them, along with a number of citizens, were captured and sent on a long march to Richmond for imprisonment. The following day, November 11, as the rebels were successfully withdrawing, a detachment of the 5th West Virginia Infantry and some home guard arrived too late to be of assistance, but they burned most of the town in retaliation for the large number of secessionist citizens. In addition, when news of the raid reached Point Pleasant, Colonel Lightburn sent about 400 men of the 4th West Virginia to Guyandotte, but they did not reach there until about an hour after the Confederates had left on the following day.[146]

Adolphus De Bussey, Company F, participated in the relief column to Guyandotte and described it to his mother, writing, "We was called in ranks at four o'clock Monday morning and marched on the *L. B.*

Empire City and taken to Guyandotte as Jenkins held it with about six hundred of his men. They took the town Sunday night ..." De Bussey continued:

> We reached there in time to see the town burned. A Colonel from Ironton got there with 150 men and run them out and fired the town. Over half the town was burned when we left and I expect the rest was burned last night. There was about 150 soldiers from Maysville had just landed which attacked. Some of their boys killed and taken. They was very wrathy and bound to clean the place out ... you can form an idea of the sight of the flames streaming from the windows and roofs. The men throwing trunks over the riverbank. Women dragging beds and bedding and throwing them over the bank in the greatest confusion. It has turned many a person out of a home.[147]

Lightburn responded to the attack on Guyandotte by sending a telegram from Point Pleasant to Governor Pierpont at Wheeling on November 13, stating: "Send me two 2 pieces of artillery with ammunition. Guyandotte has been taken. Ceredo threatened with three thousand 3000 rebels. Gallipolis and Pt. Pleasant in danger." In another dispatch Lightburn asked Adjutant General Samuels to accept the resignation of 1st Lieutenant John B. Booram, Company H, who had been appointed as recently as August, for health issues that had kept him from performing his duties for some time. Booram had turned in his resignation on November 11, and it was accepted. Lightburn named a replacement and some other changes within the officers of the regiment.[148]

By November 18 all companies of the 4th West Virginia Infantry had moved to Point Pleasant, with the exception of Company G, which was guarding government stores at Gallipolis, and Captain Dayton's Company A (Company K), which remained in the vicinity of Hampshire County. Corporal Clarkson Fogg, Company E, wrote a letter on November 19 describing the conditions at Camp Lightburn, "A submarine telegraph was stretched across the bed of the Ohio River, on Sunday last, at this place, and we now have communication with Ohio and Clarksburg, Virginia, and intermediate points." Fogg added: "Our soldiers have been somewhat disappointed in regard to pay as they have received nothing as yet. Why this delay, I know not. A part of our Regiment have been in the service for nearly 6 months.... We got our winter coats last week. I have more clothing here than I know what to do with ....Company E is quartered upstairs in the Court House and the regimental officers' quarters were in the small room beneath....I spoke in a former letter of the dismissal of Lieut. Bratton [2nd Lieutenant Adam Bratton, Company D], for drunkenness' two of our Corporals in Company E were reduced to the ranks a few days ago for the same offense. These, with the promotion of our 1st corporal, leaves me 3rd Corporal...."[149]

George S. Woodhull was officially appointed regimental chaplain on November 20, while on the 23rd Lightburn wrote Samuels from Point Pleasant stating some men would be discharged on surgeon's certificates. Lightburn also requested 500 forage caps, 600 stockings, and 600 overcoats. The following day John R. Philson was appointed surgeon, while on the 26th Captain Henry Grayum was ordered to take his company to Gallipolis to guard government stores and remain there until further notice.[150]

On the 26th Colonel James Evans of the 7th West Virginia Volunteer Infantry, stationed at Camp Keyes at Romney, wrote Francis H. Pierpont at Wheeling strongly urging him to permanently attach Captain James H. Dayton's Company of the 4th West Virginia Infantry to his regiment. He wisely argued that temporarily attached companies breed jealousies and that Dayton's company had already been serving as a temporarily attached company to the 7th West Virginia Infantry but wished to be a permanent company of the regiment. Evans claimed that Captain Dayton had no desire to be a part of the 4th West Virginia Infantry and believed Dayton would resign before being permanently placed with the 4th. He added that Dayton's men were anxious to become part of the 7th West Virginia and no one in Dayton's company had ever met an officer of the 4th West Virginia. General Benjamin F. Kelley approved of such a transfer, but it never took place.[151]

Meanwhile, Brigadier General William S. Rosecrans reported that the 4th West Virginia was stationed at Summersville and Cross Lanes in Nicholas County on November 29, under command of Colonel George Crook of the 36th Ohio Infantry, but there is no other evidence indicating that the 4th West Virginia was in that area at that time.[152]

As 1861 drew to a close, the soldiers in the 4th West Virginia stationed at Spencer received orders to return to Point Pleasant. During the initial phase of that movement, they were ordered toward Ravenswood in Jackson County by way of Three Forks of Reedy. According to Dr. Barton, "... this was a very disagreeable march, for there was an abundance of rain, and the creeks were swollen to the top of the banks. We marched through the rain and mud, plunged through the streams, being frequently in the water up to our waists. This, however, was only a foretaste of our military experience." Indicative of the hardships of this march was Corporal Clarkson Fogg, who contracted measles on the expedition.[153]

Upon arrival at Ravenswood the detachment of the 4th West Virginia boarded steamers bound for Point Pleasant. John G. Farrar, Company F, wrote: "It rained on us all day. The day we arrived at Ravenswood had to wade swollen stream. We stayed at a church in Ravenswood that night. Next morning took a boat for Pt. Pleasant." Corporal George W. Gilliland, Company C, also recalled the move from Spencer to Ravenswood, writing: "We marched from Spencer to Ravenswood, a distance of 31 miles in one day. I slept in a church there that night. Such a march made us awfully sore, but we ate our piece of hog fat and some crackers and started for Pt. Pleasant."[154]

After arriving at Point Pleasant, the detachment of the 4th West Virginia resumed drilling. James F. Stone stated: "...we remained a while in camp [at Point Pleasant] drilling every day and being trained for real soldiers. Col. Lightburn was a fine drillmaster, and we became a very well drilled organization and won many encomiums by spectators who witnessed our dress parades."[155]

Various field and staff appointments began to take place while at Point Pleasant. Dr. Barton was returned to the ranks, replaced by W.A. Kelloussouski, an excellent pharmacist from Poland, Ohio, as acting hospital steward. John R. Philson, who came to Racine, Ohio, from Maryland in 1839 and practiced medicine with Dr. Jeremiah B. Ackley, was noted for treatment of diseases and was appointed assistant surgeon. George S. Woodhull was made regimental chaplain and announced as such on November 20.[156]

December 1 proved to be a busy day as Colonel Lightburn requested Adjutant General Henry J. Samuels obtain report from Captain James H. Dayton, who was in Hampshire County. General William S. Rosecrans also arrived in camp, and escorted by Colonel Lightburn, left for Wheeling on December 3, the same day Pierpont and Henry J. Samuels presented a request to President Lincoln to create a new military department, the Department of Big Sandy, which was denied.[157]

Move to Ceredo – Fort Lightburn
December 8

Corporal Clarkson Fogg wrote on December 4 that he and 20 men from his company had gone on a two-day trip up the Kanawha River to Cannelton, serving as a guard for the boat delivering garrison equipage, probably to be used at Gauley Bridge. Upon his return to Point Pleasant he once again voiced his views, writing: "We are not paid yet, the paymaster having gone to Gauley. Fifteen of our Co. went with him as a guard....General Rosecrans and Staff arrived here Monday from Gauley and left for Wheeling yesterday," with Lightburn accompanying them. He thought the 4th West Virginia would depart Point Pleasant for a campaign when Lightburn returned, writing, "... appearances seem to include a movement of our Regiment from here within a short time....it is hard to tell where we will go to but I think either toward Gauley or Clarksburg."[158]

Fogg was wrong on both counts. By December 5, Colonel Lightburn had received orders to move the regiment, excepting companies G and K, by government transport just a bit south to Ceredo in Wayne County, which they proceeded to do on December 8. Upon arrival the regiment occupied the former camp of the 5th West Virginia Infantry.

In contrast, on December 6, Private William V. Brown, Company D, claimed it was certain the regiment would move either that day or the next to Parkersburg, and that the 11th West Virginia Infantry would replace them at Point Pleasant. He too was incorrect as Company D and Company G, which had been guarding supplies, moved from Gallipolis, Ohio, on December 8, to Ceredo, along with the other companies that had already made the movement from Point Pleasant, excepting Company K, which remained at Romney and would not arrive at Ceredo until December 29.[159]

William V. Brown described Ceredo as:

> ...a little town, hardly a town at all, containing one large hotel and half a dozen houses and is about two miles from Big Sandy River. We can see into the three states [Virginia, Kentucky, and Ohio] from here. Catlettsburg is in Kentucky on the opposite side of the [Big] Sandy. Ceredo is a nice enough place if only there was enough of it. It is rather too level, inclined to be swampy, has one store, and actually has a post office. Ceredo is 10 miles south of Guyandotte and 12 miles south of Ironton. Louisa is 25 miles going up Sandy on the Kentucky side.[160]

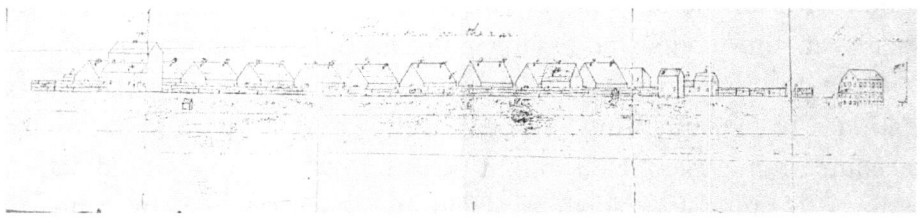

Sketch, probably by Corp. Clarkson Fogg, Co. C, 4th West Virginia Infantry of "Camp Lightburn, seen from the rear - Ceredo House." This was the 1861-1862 winter camp of the 4th West Virginia Infantry at Ceredo, Wayne County. Brian Kesterson Collection.

According to the adjutant general's papers, companies B, C, E, and H departed Ceredo on December 9 for Louisa, Kentucky, and returned December 13.[161]

Writing from Ceredo on December 10, Major John T. Hall of the 4th West Virginia informed his brother, James Hall, at Point Pleasant, to send him oats for horses of the regiment as they had left Point Pleasant without the necessary amount.[162]

At Ceredo the 4th West Virginia built winter quarters and there spent the winter and the early part of spring. John G. Farrar, of Company E, wrote: "We took a boat for Ceredo, Va, about 7 miles below Guyandotte. We staid [sic] at Ceredo that winter and built Fort Lightburn."[163]

In his memoir James B.C. Vale of Company D said the regiment went into camp "just above the mouth of the Big Sandy River....on the bank of the Ohio River north of the Ceredo House." Vale also gave a detailed description of Fort Lightburn:

...on the rising ground southwest of the Ceredo House, it contained perhaps two acres and was oblong from Ceredo House toward Sandy, or rather the long side was fronting the Ohio River. It was made by a double row of logs stacked up as high as a man's head, and the space filled in with earth. Inside this enclosure was built 10 houses in a row, with streets between, and in the rear on next the Ohio River, was 10 more houses for cooking, with wide street between them and the quarters of each company. Still farther and in the rear of the cook's houses was a sink for each company. The Guard House stood near the northeast corner of the Fort, and in the rear of it stood our cannon, frowning at the Virginia hills in our front. Inside the fort we also had a Sutler Shop with Joseph Patten behind the counter. During the winter we stayed here we got our education as soldiers. After the fort was finished a chain guard was continually facing back and forth on top of the works.[164]

Vale also said Company D was designated as a skirmish company at this time and learned the skirmish drill under Lieutenant John Mallernee. Orders were issued at Ceredo on December 10 that until further notice no passes would be issued to cross the lines. Those who did risked being shot by the picket.[165]

The men of the 4th West Virginia would quickly tire of such operations and developed a strong desire for actual combat. James F. Stone said: "Frequently we were taken out on battalion drill with our knapsacks and all of our equipment on our person. We boys thought this quite a hardship but later on in our experience we found our Colonel knew how to make soldiers out of crude material better than we knew." Dr. Barton noted, "There was a battalion drill nearly every day, and the regiment was noted for its fine appearance, noble bearing, and correct military movement." He also mentioned sickness prevailed during this time with pneumonia, bronchitis, typhoid fever, diarrhea, and rheumatism the main culprits.[166]

Colonel Lightburn wrote Assistant Adjutant General Henry Thrall from Ceredo on December 17 requesting Captain Dayton's Company K be sent to Ceredo as they were preparing winter quarters and wished to accommodate Dayton. He also mentioned that he had previously sent four companies of the regiment into Kentucky, although he had not been ordered to do so. Lightburn said he did it as a precaution because he was unaware of the specifics of what was happening around Prestonsburg. In conclusion, he believed he could hold Ceredo against 3,000 rebels if he were given two more pieces of artillery. Private William V. Brown, Company D, confirmed: "...went to building breastworks and will finish them in a couple of days. We have done some tall work here. When we get it done we are going to building quarters, which will take us a week to build." He also confirmed four companies of the 4th West Virginia had been sent to the Big Sandy to reinforce the 5th Kentucky.[167]

An interesting addition to the ranks of the 4th West Virginia came on December 17 when Private Swinfield Hill joined Company C. He was from Yancey County, North Carolina, where in the mountains he had shot and killed a member of the home guard. Apparently in order to escape retribution he joined the 4th West Virginia under the name Winfield Hill. He would die of disease and fever near Vicksburg, Mississippi, in 1863.[168]

Private William V. Brown reported from Ceredo on December 18 that "We have had nice weather ever since we came here, never as nice for this time of year. A person will sweat with his coat off in the daytime."[169]

Colonel Lightburn probably lost the love of some of his command when, on December 24, a day before Christmas, he ordered no more passes would be given due to soldiers overstaying their time on previous furloughs.[170]

Apparently responding to Lightburn's earlier request, Company K of the 4th West Virginia moved from Romney to Ceredo on December 29, a distance of 314 miles.[171]

Dr. Thomas Barton reported that while at Ceredo eight men died from disease, eleven were discharged for disability, one was accidentally shot, and one discharged by civil authority. He added to his summary, writing that up to this point the losses at Point Pleasant had been five deaths by disease, two discharged for disability, and one deserted, making a total loss of 29 of the enlisted men of the 4th West Virginia. At the end of 1861, the 4th West Virginia Infantry consisted of 858 men.[172]

2

1862
On the Edge of Darkness

During the first half of 1862, the 4th West Virginia was tasked to support General Jacob D. Cox's invasion of the New River Valley and an unsuccessful attempt to strike and destroy the vital Virginia and Tennessee Railroad at Central Depot (Radford, Virginia) and Salem, Virginia. While Cox's main force gave battle at Giles Court House (Pearisburg, Virginia), Princeton in Mercer County, (West) Virginia, and Lewisburg, Greenbrier County, (West) Virginia, the 4th West Virginia Infantry remained in the Kanawha Valley with a small number of troops. Their primary roles at this time were guarding Cox's rear and supply line, in addition to scouting and patrolling for bushwhackers and Southern leaning citizens.

After he failed to take control of the New River Valley, Cox drew back to a defensive perimeter on Flat Top Mountain. His line extended to Lewisburg, while Confederates remained south of Flat Top. The resultant stalemate remained until Cox's army was called to Maryland in August 1862. Until then, Cox remained at Flat Top, as the 4th West Virginia Infantry entered the second half of 1862, during which they lost one of their beloved officers to hostile fire. This action was followed by Cox's removal of 5,000 troops from the Kanawha Valley, opening the possibility for Brigadier General William W. Loring to again occupy it for the Confederacy.

Colonel Joseph Andrew Jackson Lightburn was placed in command the District of the Kanawha, with a small force, including the 4th West Virginia, to defend the region. On the first day of January 1862, Colonel Lightburn wrote Henry J. Samuels, Adjutant General of Virginia, stating he had earlier organized a company of 70 men and officers while at Spencer, and that Captain James Dayton's men were now at Ceredo in "good condition," and all was quiet at present. He also noted Colonel William C. Starr was raising a regiment, which became the 9th West Virginia Volunteer Infantry. Lightburn concluded by saying Captain James L. Wallar, Company A, 2nd West Virginia Cavalry, recently had a skirmish with bushwhackers and took one prisoner he would be bringing to Wheeling.[1]

Also on January 1, Lightburn, writing from Ceredo, stated, "My Regt. now is all right and would be pleased if the Inspecting Officer could pay us a visit." Lightburn ordered that all 108 men of Company G return to Ceredo immediately. Camp life continued as usual at Ceredo where on January 7 Adolphus De Bussey thought Company A, 2nd West Virginia Cavalry, would be stationed with them there for the winter. On January 11 the 4th West Virginia Infantry reported 925 men available for duty and 962 rank and file on the muster rolls comprising 10 companies.[2]

William V. Brown, Company D, reported from Fort Lightburn (Ceredo) on January 15 that "Capt. Goodspeed has the mumps, [Lt. John] Mallernee has gone home, and Lieut. Hankinson is in command of Co. D." Brown also wrote about the recent battle of Middle Creek near Prestonsburg in eastern Kentucky, which took place on January 10, 1862. Company G was sent from Ceredo to Louisa on January 9 to reinforce Company H, which was guarding commissary stores, and both companies returned to Ceredo by order of Colonel James A. Garfield, commanding the Sandy Valley expedition. While at Ceredo Colonel Lightburn ordered 1st Lieutenants William C. Bailey and Ephraim C. Carson, along with four privates, to Wheeling, with transportation provided by the 2nd West Virginia Cavalry, to report to Major W.I. Newton for duty on recruiting duty.[3]

Sometime shortly before January 16, Lieutenant Cincinnatus B. Blake of Henry Grayum's Company G, along with two pickets some distance "back of Ceredo," unexpectedly encountered "the notorious Jim Smith" and three of Colonel Albert G. Jenkins' cavalry on their way to the river. Blake fired five shots from his revolver at Smith, one ball hitting in the back and the "other four balls took effect on the body of a scamp by the name of Bing," (probably Francis Marion Bing) formerly of Wayne County. Bing and three others were captured and sent to Wheeling, while it was supposed Smith's wound might be mortal.[4]

Lightburn wrote Adjutant General Samuels from Ceredo on January 16: "I have the honor to say that I am informed by Q.M. [Quarter Master] J.V. Stevens of my regiment that there is a lot of Belgian guns for distribution at Wheeling. If such is the fact I should be please[d] if the Governor chooses to do so to have five hundred (500) sent to my Regt. as the arms now in the hands of five companies a[re] very inefficient being the altered musket and a number of them unfit for service.[5]

Jessie V. Stevens, lieutenant quartermaster of the 4th West Virginia, wrote Governor David Tod of Ohio on January 23 requesting service in an Ohio artillery battery, as he had always favored that branch of service and felt he would see more action than in his position as an infantry staff officer. He also enquired as to raising an artillery company but was apparently told no more batteries were to be raised for Ohio.[6]

Louisa, Kentucky
January 24 – January 29, 1862

Four companies of the 4th West Virginia, B, H, I, and K, went on a 45-mile scout to Kentucky from January 24 to January 29, under command of Colonel Lightburn. The destination was Louisa, where they would help Colonel James A. Garfield with his supplies. Private William V. Brown later reported that these companies were sent to Louisa, Kentucky, to reinforce the Kentucky infantry, although noted

"...they did not have any fight." The companies wanted Company D to go with them to Louisa, but Lightburn said not until they got "new rifles...The Colonel has sent for 600 new rifles, either Enfield with saber bayonet or – I forgot the name of the other gun – Belgian rifles, I believe."[7]

Lieutenant Colonel William H.H. Russell on the 28th ordered Surgeon George Ackley to proceed to Wheeling to "procure drugs and medicine for the Post Hospital as the Post Hospital is destitute of such necessary items."[8]

Fort Lightburn (Ceredo) proved to be an unpleasant location for many of the soldiers. 2nd Lieutenant William Grayum, Company G, brother of Captain Henry Grayum, wrote of Ceredo on January 31, noting: "...of all the dull places I was ever in this is the worst and especially so since the flood for that has cut off the mails until this evening. All we have to do is to wade around in mud. This is a wet swampy place at best but with a thousand men constantly tramping about it is horrible."[9]

A few days later Adolphus De Bussey added to Lieutenant Grayum's description of their camp as he wrote home: "We have a miserable muddy time here. It is the worst winter I ever seen." Grayum added that "Four companies of our regiment have just got back from a scout seventy or eighty miles into Kentucky without meeting any Seccesh," while a few days later De Bussey indicated Companies G and H were on a scout to Big Sandy and expected them back in about three days.[10]

Private John E. Walker of Company E died February 2, 1862, at the Post Hospital from the effects of a fall. In 1899, Corporal George W. Gilliland of Company C offered a different account, however, stating: "...one of our own regiment dug his own grave and [was] buried in it. He was detailed to dig the grave for a young man of the regiment who died and the day he was to be buried his mother came and took the remains home. That evening the grave digger was put in the fly of a tent and the boys would take hold of the edge of it to see how high they could throw him. They tossed him up and when he came down some let go and it broke his spinal column. He lived two days and suffered terribly but was unconscious part of the time. His name was

John Walker." Apparently he was buried in the same grave he had dug for another soldier.[11]

John Farrar of Company E told a slight variation of the story: "Walker and a fellow was scuffling. Walker was throwed against a bunk, his spine was hurt. I think he died the next day....". Clarkson Fogg added to the story, writing: "About thirty-six hours after he was taken ill (during which time it was thought he was taking the fever) he commenced screaming and throwing his hands about him. From that moment he was insensible never speaking. He lived just 24 hours in this situation."[12]

Colonel Lightburn was strictly against alcohol and on February 4 issued a stern warning against smuggling liquor into the garrison or camp, which would result in a court-martial. To emphasize his point, he posted additional regulations against drunkenness.[13]

Not only were the men faced with no alcohol, but they also were preoccupied with the weather, camp conditions, and a possible move for the regiment. On February 10 Sergeant Columbus Shrewsbury, Company A, wrote his wife from Ceredo, "We have no orders to move yet but I don't care how soon we do for we will never be in better trim."[14]

Corporal Clarkson Fogg also wrote from Ceredo: "The weather here has the appearance of winter now – clear and cold without snow. In fact, we have had but 2 inches of snow of any time during the winter, It is likely that we shall remain in this part of Virginia during the summer, that is, within the boundaries of the new department between Kanawha and Sandy."[15]

William V. Brown, Company D, wrote from Fort Lightburn on February 16 that there were rumors in camp that the 4th West Virginia would soon move to Logan Court House. He also mentioned the regiment had just received a new stand of colors: "The Regimental flag (of the 4th WV Regiment) has the Stars and Stripes and a large Eagle in the center with a ribbon in its bill, on the ribbon is to be painted the No. of the Reg't; in the Eagle's claws are the spears and shield; it is a large silk flag and edged with yellow fringe. The National Flag is just a common silk flag with yellow fringe edging."[16]

4th West Virginia Infantry National Flag.
West Virginia State Museum.

Lieutenant Cincinnatus B. Blake, stationed at Louisa, Kentucky, with Company G, wrote that both companies G and H were "Gentlemen Loafers" and were "only stirring enough to jog our stomachs for the next meal." He added they also had captured, shot, or killed various bushwhackers and rebels, and he mentioned that Orderly Sergeant David S. Trobridge (Trowbridge) and he were staying at Squire Savage's boarding house. Blake additionally described Louisa as "a little town lying on Sandy River where the river divides and a part comes from Kentucky and the other from [West] Virginia.... [the] town is partly deserted by the rebel part and the houses have been occupied by soldiery and pretty well torn down, fences torn away, &c. Then there is a class of aristocracy left and good Union [people] too." He boasted not only of his association with that "upper class," but also of his wife's beauty.[17]

On February 25, Colonel Lightburn sent a note of thanks to the ladies of Gallipolis for the supplies and delicacies donated to his post hospital at Ceredo, citing the names of each donor.[18]

Camp rumor then held that another movement was soon possible, and on the 28th William V. Brown suspected the regiment might soon move to either Logan, Lewisburg, or Summersville and that the 9th West Virginia Infantry would replace them at Ceredo. Another rumor emerged at this time that Colonel Lightburn was going to be promoted to brigadier general. Although this eventually proved true, it did not transpire until the following year. Brown also noted the regiment had received 30 or 40 four-horse wagons and four four-horse ambulances, adding fuel to the talk of an upcoming move.

Corporal Clarkson Fogg wrote from Ceredo on March 2: "Gen. Cox telegraphed for Col. Lightburn from Charleston, Virginia, and he is now there. It is reported that our Colonel is to be made a Brigadier General, which may account for his presence being required at Gen. Cox's headquarters." But Fogg was more interested in diseases in the regiment, writing: "There was another of our soldiers died here yesterday, the fifth one since we came here, four of whom were in one company, Co. H from Elk River. It seems strange that there should be so many die in our Regiment, considering how few are in the hospital....the health of some has been improved, while others have sunk beneath the hardships of the soldier's life, and have passed away. There was no Surgeon appointed for our Regiment until it was nearly full, consequently many were admitted who would not otherwise have been. There are about 60 in our Regiment who will probably be discharged for inability, this Spring."[19]

Colonel James A. Garfield, who had been campaigning in the Big Sandy Valley of eastern Kentucky, wrote from Piketon on March 10 that he had two companies of the 4th West Virginia at Louisa but was getting ready to release them. Clarkson Fogg continued in his belief there was a movement underfoot when he wrote on March 11, "The regiment is being placed on a war-footing." Fogg said horses, wagons and mules were arriving from Gallipolis, which led him to think they would participate in an expedition to the Virginia and Tennessee Railroad in mid-April. Such an expedition would be undertaken, but it would be under General Jacob D. Cox and not include the 4th West Virginia. On a positive note, he added the weather was spring-like.[20]

Three officers of Company I of the 4th West Virginia wrote from Fort Lightburn on March 20, thanking the Gallia County Military Commission for supplying the company with "coverlets, socks, etc." The following day the paymaster finally arrived.[21]

General William S. Rosecrans reported to Washington on March 22 the troops under his command in the Mountain Department, which included ten companies of the 4th West Virginia, totaling 868 men, stationed at Ceredo, at the mouth of Twelve-Pole Creek, under command of Gen. Jacob D. Cox. The same day Clarkson Fogg wrote from Ceredo the soldiers were basically happy with General John C. Fremont now commanding their department instead of McClellan and again expressed his suspicion of a movement underway against the Virginia and Tennessee Railroad.[22]

Quartermaster Jessie V. Stevens reported from Ceredo on March 24 that the 4th West Virginia was enjoying good health for the most part, with the exception of the damp climate and some lingering cases of the measles. He added he had been studying the Constitution for the new state of West Virginia and was rather pleased.[23]

On the negative side, the ever-observant Clarkson Fogg wrote on either March 28 or 29 that following payday, "Our camp is filled with peddlers, with bogus jewelry and watches and other trinkets and they find plenty of customers too." He also noted debt collectors lined up outside the paymasters' tent.[24]

The 4th West Virginia Infantry, District of the Kanawha, reported 860 men present on March 30. On the same day Private John Facemyer, Company H, wrote a letter from Ceredo to a friend in Kansas stating, "I am well at present....we have plenty to do here."[25]

The pending movement posited by camp rumors proved true on April 1. John G. Farrar, Company E, recalled his unit moved from Ceredo to Camp Piatt for one or two days, then back to Charleston where they remained until September 1, although that date may not be accurate.[26]

A soldier identified as "M.S." of the 4th West Virginia (probably Milton Stewart) published a list of all monies donated by the enlisted men of each company to be sent home to their families on April 3. A grand total of $26,077.00 was sent, with Captain Rockhill's Company A contributing the most with $3,397.00.[27]

The regiment was yet at Ceredo on April 3 when Clarkson Fogg indicated that the weather was good and that horses and supplies had been arriving from Gallipolis, which again supported the suspicions of the men that they may be on the move in ten days. Regimental chaplain George S. Woodhull wrote on April 5 from a point near Gallipolis to Brigadier General William Kerley Strong at Cairo, Illinois, attesting to the integrity of Private Clark Craig, Company A, 36th Virginia Infantry, Confederate States Army, a resident of Putnam County, West Virginia, who had recently been captured at Fort Donelson, Tennessee.[28]

Still stationed at Ceredo on April 7, Quartermaster Jessie V. Stevens boasted of the good health of the regiment and that "only 12 men have died since muster of the regiments first company." He attributed this to the excellent medical staff of the regiment. Stevens also mentioned that the previous Saturday a detail led by Major John Taylor Hall, comprised of four companies of the 4th West Virginia, went to Catlettsburg, Kentucky, to perform the funeral service of Major William B. Burk of the 14th Kentucky Infantry, who died from disease at Catlettsburg. Burk was buried with full military honors.[29]

It was a busy day as Lightburn confirmed the good health of the regiment, "All quiet and the health of the Regiment passably good." Clarkson Fogg mentioned a false report of Brigadier General John Fremont's arrival at Point Pleasant, and that it had rained on the first day of the first court-martial since the regiment had formed. The general health of the regiment at Ceredo concerned Fogg on April 8 when he wrote of the "monotonous routine of camp duty" and noted: "Good health continues with the exception of now and then a case of fever, Erysipelas, and rheumatism. However, there are many complaining ones who always have something he believes matters, no doubt, to get rid of duty."[30]

Six days later, on the 14th, Private John D. Coates of Company A was discharged, believed to be in the last stages of consumption. Quartermaster Jessie V. Stevens continued with his assessment of the regiment on April 28, writing from Ceredo that the health of the regiment was good and noted "spirits are high, and they are anxious for a fight." He further condemned the recent cowardice of the 53rd Ohio and prayed the 4th West Virginia "will never disgrace itself."[31]

The 4th West Virginia band procured sixteen new instruments at Ceredo on April 15, consisting of "German silver" that cost $800, with more than $500 of the funds raised by officers. The residue was taken from the Regimental Fund, made possible by a tax on the Sutler shop and having their own bakery and making their own bread instead of "pilot bread."[32]

Corporal Purley (Pearley) Bratton and Russ Lowry (likely 24-year-old Corporal Samuel R. Lowry from Athens, Ohio), both of Company D, "last Tuesday" went to Burlington, Ohio, then went about two-and-a-half miles into the country to a Dutch farmer who sold them rot-gut whiskey. Bratton and Lowry got extremely drunk and inquired of a place to spend the night and to get more whiskey. They proceeded about a mile farther to the home of a "Negro wench," where the two were refused entrance but falsely claimed they had a warrant for the arrest of a black man in the house. Thirsting for some liquid spirits they forced their way inside and the woman shot Bratton with a double-barreled pistol. The fired round went through Bratton's pant leg, and she shot him again. Lowry was behind him and attempted to catch him as he fell. The "ball struck Bratton on the left side of the head behind and above the ear and ranged downward." The woman also took a shot at Lowry, who fled looking for a weapon to defend himself with, but eventually he made his way back to camp and informed Captain Goodspeed. Goodspeed and a detail of men, along with a coffin for Bratton, went to Burlington and then to the scene of the crime. The woman was eventually cleared and Bratton charged with being the assailant. His service record states he was killed on April 16 as the result of a drunken riot.[33]

Not everyone was impressed by the 4th West Virginia while at Ceredo, with the April 18 edition of the *Pomeroy Weekly Telegram* indicating the regiment was not fit for fighting. The organ also contained a list of men who "honorably" sent money home to care for their families, totaling $26,077.00. The following day William V. Brown, Company D, reported that, "Co. H went to Wayne C. H. last Monday and Co.'s B and G are going on a scout tomorrow, I think." He added: "We are going to move into tents in a few days, as soon as it stops raining. The tents are nearly all up now. They are putting them up at the bottom below the breastworks and between them and the river....I don't like the looks of this place, it is completely surrounded by swamps and marshes...." Brown closed his letter complaining about the constant rain and snow.[34]

Colonel Lightburn wrote to Adjutant Samuels on April 20 requesting acceptance of a company of home guard, "comprised of the citizens of Tug Fork of Sandy in the upper end of this and the lower end of Logan counties with better arms and ammunition." He believed they could maintain the area better than sporadic details of regular troops.[35]

In another dispatch to Samuels on the same day, Lightburn wrote: "No news here. Some bushwhackers have commenced operations in the upper end of this county which I will attend to shortly as soon as the roads get so we can pack provisions. I had a party at Trout's Hill last week but without success." He also requested new guns for five of the regimental companies as their guns were defective and completely useless.[36]

Sometime around April 23 General Jacob D. Cox began moving his three brigades, with two moving toward Princeton, and the other, under Colonel George Crook, toward Lewisburg and Salem, Virginia. This was part of a Union offensive into the New River Valley, devised during the winter of 1861-1862 by General William S. Rosecrans and President Abraham Lincoln, and now implemented by General John Fremont of the Mountain Department. The mission, although unrealistic, was to capture southwestern Virginia, which contained lead and salt mines essential to the Confederacy, and liberate the Unionists of eastern Tennessee.

The importance of the Virginia and Tennessee Railroad cannot be underestimated. Running from Lynchburg, Virginia, to Bristol, Tennessee, it provided the Confederacy the means to transport large armies and supplies from the Western Theater of war to the Eastern Theater, and vice versa. Two of General Jacob D. Cox's brigades were to advance southwardly and strike the Virginia and Tennessee Railroad bridge at Central Depot (Radford, Virginia), while his third brigade was to move toward Lewisburg and strike the Virginia and Tennessee Railroad at Salem. If successful, these forces were to link up with the Federal troops of James Garfield from eastern Kentucky and Fremont's troops at Staunton, and then converge in eastern Tennessee. The plan was unlikely to succeed but Cox proceeded regardless. While the operations failed in both 1862 and later in 1863, ironically, similar operations occurred in 1864 that achieved brief success.

Cox's men left Fayetteville and were met with slight resistance at Camp Creek; although the first true clash of significance would come at Giles Court House (Pearisburg, Virginia) on May 10, where they were defeated and fell back to Princeton in Mercer County, (West) Virginia, and were again bested in a two-day fight on May 16 and 17. Cox then moved his army to nearby Flat Top Mountain and established a defensive perimeter, which he held until August. Crook, on the other hand, gained a brilliant victory at Lewisburg, but had to end the plan to move to Salem, Virginia, due to the losses sustained by Cox and by General John Fremont at the battle of McDowell, Virginia, on May 8, 1862.

During the New River operation, the 4th West Virginia remained in the Kanawha Valley area protecting Cox's supply line and maintaining a rear guard. As usual, most of their time was spent in the dull daily camp routine and scouting or dealing with bushwhackers and missing their loved ones. According to William V. Brown, two companies of the 4th were sent on a scout on April 27, and on the 28th he wrote: "We received marching orders last night....all the boys are well....Major Hall goes after the two companies sent on a scout the previous day.... Captain Goodspeed says wherever they go will be on a boat. Brown suspected they were going up the Kanawha River." Brown also had a photograph made on that day; Clarkson Fogg corroborated this and mentioned that a photographer was in camp taking pictures. Fogg also commented that there were rumors about the 4th West Virginia being discharged, which were not true. He closed noting the "cool, rainy weather for [the] past week but weather now fair."[37]

Dividing the Regiment
Camp Elk River, Camp Piatt and
Chapmanville (Camp Russell)
May 1, 1862

At the beginning of May an order was issued between General Jacob D. Cox and General John Fremont, commanding the Mountain Department to place four companies of the 4th West Virginia at Charleston, two companies at Camp Piatt, 10 miles above Charleston, and four companies at Chapmanville, on the Guyandotte River, all under the command of Colonel Lightburn, with his headquartered at Charleston.

Corporal James B.C. Vale, Company D, recalled the long-anticipated move out of Ceredo (Fort Lightburn), which began on April 30 and concluded at Charleston on May 1. William V. Brown, also of Company D, in reporting the company arrived at Camp Piatt, a few miles above

Charleston, wrote, "We left Ceredo yesterday about 11 o'clock and got here about noon today, without accident."[38]

Soon afterward, according to Major Benjamin D. Boswell, two companies of the regiment moved to Chapmanville, Logan County, one to Brownstown (Marmet), Kanawha County, and two to Guyandotte in Cabell County. Bosworth added that from May to July nothing of importance transpired except for an occasional brush with bushwhackers.[39]

Private James B.C. Vale, Company D, recalled heading for Chapmanville along the Guyan River on May 3. Dr. Thomas Barton also remembered the movement, writing: "Soon after our arrival at Charleston, two companies under the command of Major Hall, with Surgeon Philson and myself to care for the sick and wounded, were ordered to Chapmanville in Logan County. This place took its name from Mr. Chapman, who was a prominent citizen of that locality, and his residence was used as a hospital and guard house, leaving sufficient room for himself and family. A rude fort was soon constructed. It was built of logs from some old buildings, together with other timber, and contained about half an acre of ground. We had one smooth bore gun, and in the event of danger from Jenkins' cavalry we were to be reinforced by two additional companies, making four in all, that being the largest force at any time at Chapmanville. The rest of the regiment remained at Charleston doing guard and provost duty."[40]

At Camp Piatt, Private Arthur Forbes, Company B, 4th West Virginia, wrote, "I had my pass note to go home down at Ceredo and we got orders to move and Colonel had to stop me and a great many more that [had] their passes ready to go home."[41]

Colonel Lightburn placed Captain William R. Brown in command of all companies of the 4th West Virginia encamped at Elk River at Charleston and announced Captain Alexander Vance would take over duties as Provost Marshall.[42]

Tragedy struck on May 4. Captain George W. Story reported that on the way to Charleston Private Matthew Phelps of Company F accidentally fell overboard and drowned near the mouth of Thirteen-Mile Creek. Story said it happened during the night and Phelps was not missed until the following day. On May 18, Story received a note from D. C. Forbes stating, "Matthew Phelps was found dead in a drift heap, a little above the mouth of Thirteen-Mile Creek, in the Kanawha River, on May 11, and was buried near where he was found, with his pocketbook and personal papers sent home in the hands of R. Harrison of Leon."[43]

At Camp Piatt, William V. Brown, Company D, announced Companies B, C, D, and H were preparing to move from Camp Piatt to Chapmanville, with Lieutenant Colonel William H.H. Russell in command, and the camp to be named after him. Brown added: "We are going to take all the teams in the Regiment but one or two. Five of our Co's are at Charleston now but when we go I suppose two of them will come up here [Camp Piatt]. Co. G is here now; it will stay here too." With Lightburn's headquarters at Charleston and Major John T. Hall in charge at Camp Piatt, Company D awaited the arrival of Enfield rifles before departure for Chapmanville.[44]

Adolphus De Bussey, with the troops at Charleston, wrote a summary of the movement to the new camp, which was roughly ten miles distant: "We left Ceredo Friday at ten o'clock and reached Camp Piatt yesterday morning at seven o'clock, and had been there but two hours when we received orders to return to Charleston. Companies A, F, T, E & H are here [Company I was likely present also]. The other five companies are at Camp Piatt. Our Colonel has been promoted to [Acting] Gen'l and has command of the Kanawha Valley. Russell will be our Colonel. We are encamped the East side of Charleston, across the Elk River, where we will be apt to stay for some time and likely spend the summer here as the Gen'l's headquarters are here. The South dreads the 4th Va. They know too many of them in this part of the country." De Bussey emphasized his point as he spoke of a recent incident where: "Some of our boys were at Malden at a pole and flag raising and a couple of them hallowed for Jeff Davis, and the boys beat them until they are not likely to get over it. We have a pleasant place here. We are camped in a large meadow."[45]

May 4 proved to be a busy day at Charleston, when Colonel Lightburn issued an order to fire a cannon at 9 p.m., signaling all

Negroes, free or not, male or female, to be in their quarters unless they had permission from their masters or employers. Those disobeying were to be turned over to their masters or employers. Lightburn forbid soldiers under his command to harbor or employ slaves except with the permission of the owners and his personal consent.[46]

General Henry Halleck, apparently unaware of where the 4th West Virginia was located, wrote Pierpont on May 5, directing that if the regiment was still in the area, Pierpont was authorized to have them guard the Baltimore and Ohio Railroad. On this same day Companies B, C, D, and K began an expedition to Chapmanville in Logan County, (West) Virginia. The detachment left Camp Piatt, crossed the Kanawha River to Brownstown, where they encamped for the night. Early the next morning they moved rapidly to Coal River, crossed, and pitched their tents about two miles farther on, having marched 15 miles.[47]

On May 7, Companies B, C, and D marched to Little Coal River, crossed at about noon, and ate a quick meal. The march had been over very rough roads, many streams, steep hills, and thick forests. As a result, the supply train carrying them food, guarded by Captain Arza Goodspeed and his Company D, lagged far behind, having to cut roads. They halted at a farm owned by a man known as "Forked John Miller." Eventually the soldiers arrived at Chapmanville, where they learned from locals that a body of Confederates was nearby. Captain James H. Dayton and about 100 men were sent in pursuit but returned empty handed. The following day 1st Lieutenant William L. McMaster, Company C, with 20 men of his company, went in search of the Confederates, and crossed the Guyan River. While they failed to find a large force, they managed to capture some prisoners near Logan, including a man they thought was the acting adjutant of the 129th Regiment Virginia Militia. However, it was actually Captain John Cobert (Covert), the former 129th Regiment quartermaster they captured on May 9, 1862, near Logan. He was identified as a "bushwhacker, not in regular service" and was said to be "Bushwhacking in arms against the U.S." This suggests Cobert had been discharged from the militia by that time and was operating in a partisan–guerilla company. Cobert was taken under guard to the jail at Charleston, where he was held until May 15, 1862, when he was then transferred to Camp Chase, Ohio. He remained incarcerated there until July 3, 1862, and was then sent to Johnson's Island, at Sandusky, Ohio. Cobert was next sent to Vicksburg, Mississippi, on board the government steamer, *Jno. H. Done*, along with 1,103 other men where they arrived on September 20, 1862.[48]

Ironically, James B.C. Vale, Company D, gave a somewhat different version on of the move to Chapmanville, as he claimed the march began on May 4. He said the route would be via Lens Creek, crossing Coal River and camping the first night at Peytona. The second day they moved to near Boone Court House, and the third to Chapmanville. Vale said they arrived at their destination May 8. Their assignment was to go into the mountains to "clean out the guerillas and harass the secesh generally."[49]

Four companies of the 4th West Virginia reportedly departed Ceredo for Camp Piatt on May 7, although some accounts indicate May 8. As previously noted, on Friday, May 9, Captain John L. Vance took about 105 men to Logan Court House in hopes of surrounding a group of Confederates who were reportedly recruiting rebel militia there, but they failed to locate them. The Chapmanville expedition began the return to Camp Piatt on Sunday, and Captain Dayton detailed 40 men to guard the wagon train.[50]

The camp at Charleston was officially designated "Camp Elk River" by Colonel Lightburn, and Philemon B. Stanbury (Stanberry) was designated as acting assistant adjutant general. Their camp was described in a letter written on May 9 by 1st Lieutenant William S. Hall, Company F, who said it was located just outside town and, "I have become acquainted with some very agreeable ladies since we came here and you may rest assured that I am enjoying myself hugely."[51]

Clarkson Fogg was more detailed as he recalled, "Five companies of the 4th left Ceredo a week ago expecting to disembark at Camp Piatt (formerly Camp Enyart)" but instead disembarked at Camp Warren, camp of the 12th Ohio Infantry, two miles above Charleston. The12th Ohio Infantry packed up and left by noon, and the 4th West Virginia stayed two more hours until ordered to make camp at the

Philemon B. Stanbury.
Terry Lowry Collection.

north end of Charleston near the wire suspension bridge spanning the Elk River. Lightburn, the regimental band, and his headquarters staff were stationed at the Elk River camp. Fogg wrote: "Colonel Lightburn is in command of all forces in the Kanawha Valley, as far up as Gauley. Captain Brown being in command there. Capt. A. [Alexander] Vance has been appointed Provost Marshall over in Charleston....Our regiment received 500 Enfield rifles, which are to be given to those companies who heretofore had the old U.S. muskets, five companies having previously been furnished with Minnie [minie] muskets. Our company got the Enfield gun." Corporal Fogg also noted the "Wire Bridge is 450 between towers over which masses of wire are stretched....no support whatsoever between butments [abutments]."[52]

At Chapmanville, Camp Russell remained abuzz with activity on the 9th as 20 men of Company C went on a scout in the morning and captured one bushwhacker. The following day 80 men went on a scout, 20 out of each company, with two days' rations. Captain William Brown observed the "Guyandotte River is the best place for fishing I ever saw, it is clear as a bell, you can see fish two foot long swimming around in it ..."[53]

At 9 a.m. on May 10, Private Robert Fugate, Company A, accidentally shot and killed Corporal William H. Davis of Company F. Fugate had just returned from guard duty with his rifle still loaded. He tried to lower the hammer, but the weapon accidentally discharged, striking Davis, who was standing about 20 yards distant. The rifle ball struck him "between the backbone and left hip, and passed angling through, causing death in about two hours" and then passed through two nearby tents before hitting a wooden box. Both surgeons of the 4th West Virginia were summoned immediately but were unable to save Davis.[54]

2nd Lieutenant Cincinnatus B. Blake, Company G, reported from Camp Piatt on May 12 about the earlier events of the four companies of the 4th West Virginia at Chapmanville, which recently had a skirmish and captured two bushwhackers while two other companies from Charleston went toward Raleigh and joined with Captain Baggs'

Snake Hunters to take 150 bushwhackers prisoner and also killed a few.[55]

Companies B, C, D, and K, under the command of Lieutenant Colonel Russell, were stationed at Chapmanville on May 13, according to a writer identified only as "Milton," who was likely Sergeant Milton Stewart. The battle of Princeton in Mercer County, (West) Virginia took place on the 15th of May and was a defeat for General Jacob D. Cox, who faced Confederates under General Humphrey Marshall. Cox's soldiers fell back to Flat Top Mountain and retained a defensive position at that point for some time afterward, where he maintained communications with Lightburn at Gauley Bridge.[56]

On May 16, Company D's William V. Brown reflected on the recent events at and near Camp Russell, writing of the unsuccessful expedition from Chapmanville to Logan. He mentioned encountering a bushwhacker (guerilla fighter) on the return trip who claimed he was a doctor. Jack Anderson, Company B, would have no part of that tale and "raised his gun and shot him in the side just as he was going to jump a log. He kind of gave a hollow and turned around. Bratton then shot at and hit him in the breast and before he had time to fall Bob Morrow [Private Robert E. Morrow] of Co. B shot him again in the shoulder, the ball ranging upwards and coming out of the back of his head. Any one of them would have killed him; all of them went clear through him. He died in five minutes." The soldiers dug a shallow grave with bayonets, and then told nearby Southern residents to bury him.[57]

Company G remained at Camp Piatt while Clarkson Fogg found time on May 18 to describe Camp Elk River as "one of the most pleasant locations which can be found. Elk River with its green bottoms and hills and clear cool water, is an enviable locality." Fogg said prisoners were coming and going daily, that three companies of the 4th West Virginia were currently present in camp, and that the other two went on a scout in the direction of Spencer and Arnoldsburg for secessionists. He added that apparently the 10th West Virginia Infantry had taken care of the problem, although other troops were moving toward Lewisburg: "The five companies of our regiment who went to Camp

Piatt are scouting the country below or west of the Kanawha. Some of them shot a bushwhacker the other day, who had fired on them across Guyan River, near Chapmanville." Fogg indicated he believed the sentiment in Charleston was mostly "secesh" and noted that he preferred Colonel Lightburn to General Cox, who he thought favored the secessionists.[58]

James B.C. Vale, Company D, recalled his company made a forced march to Charleston from Chapmanville on the 19th and arrived on May 20. The same day, Clarkson Fogg, who was still at Camp Elk River, learned of Cox's defeat at Princeton, which caused fear in the Union camps that the victorious Confederates might be advancing upon the Kanawha Valley. As a result of this, Lightburn hastily ordered the 4th West Virginia companies posted at Spencer and Chapmanville to return to Camp Elk River. Fogg offered a chilling premonition, "There are but about 175 effective men here but we are resolute and the town will soon be laid in ashes before evacuated."[59]

The excitement began to fade on May 21 as Sergeant Columbus Shrewsbury, Company A, wrote from Camp Piatt, "There has been some excitement up here but I suppose not so much as there was at Charleston but it is all quiet at present....I am going to start for the wilderness tomorrow to Chapmanville, Logan County, and I don't like it very well...."[60]

Fogg, still at Camp Elk River, also noted the recent excitement had faded as the alarm was for naught with Cox falling back to a safe position on Flat Top Mountain. A different matter had concerned him as he mentioned a blockade had been established at Charleston to keep check on boats smuggling whiskey, which Lightburn had forbidden.[61]

The battle of Lewisburg in Greenbrier County, (West) Virginia, occurred on May 23, between the Union forces of Colonel George Crook, who was commanding Cox's 3rd Brigade, and Confederates under General Henry Heth, resulting in a decisive Union victory. Meanwhile, James B.C. Vale, Company D, remembered he began the return to Camp Russell (Chapmanville) on May 24 and arrived at that location on May 26.[62]

Camp Piatt was the scene of much activity on May 26, according to 2nd Lieutenant Cincinnatus B. Blake, Company G, who said he and 20 men had just returned from a scout of Logan, "pressed horses, then dashed in and out taking two prisoners." Blake also recalled that the past Saturday there was a false rumor going through the camp that General Cox had been surrounded and defeated by rebels and was attempting to escape from Charleston, which had supposedly flown into a panic, causing Colonel Lightburn to post his men on picket (guard) duty. Blake further wrote that Captain Walter Angelo Powell of the 1st West Virginia Cavalry, a topographical engineer, was supervising Company G, "While a tolerable breastwork was built during the night captains Powell and [Henry] Grayum searched for a good place to fight." Their position was later reinforced by a brass smooth bore cannon and two companies of cavalry.[63]

According to Adolphus De Bussey, on May 31, about 140 rebel prisoners taken at the recent battle of Lewisburg departed Charleston for Camp Chase at Columbus, Ohio. De Bussey recalled, "They was a hard looking set with their butternut brown, and long, tangled hair." Clarkson Fogg confirmed this when he wrote from aboard the steamer *Ben Franklin* at Marietta, Ohio on June 1 that he and 45 men from the 4th West Virginia were returning to Charleston after escorting the Lewisburg prisoners to Camp Chase.[64]

During this period some organizational changes were made. 1st Lieutenant Calvin Shepard, Company I, was appointed quartermaster of the 4th Brigade on June 5, and Master Sergeant Alexander Wartenburg named acting ordnance officer of the 4th Brigade on June 7; although the order was countermanded the following day, and a master sergeant was appointed to each regiment of the 4th Brigade as acting ordnance officer. On June 8 General Cox wrote Lightburn from Flat Top Mountain granting his approval of Lieutenant Colonel Russell's plan to recapture stolen tents and other property from a group of citizens of whose names he acquired.[65]

On June 12, Company D of the 4th West Virginia started up the Guyan River on a scouting mission and passed through Logan, then moved to the headwaters of the Big Sandy River, traversing the Tug

Fork and the "Rough's of Tug Fork," and onto McDowell County Court House, which was then "a hewn log structure." Bushwhackers fired upon Company D from the mountain opposite the courthouse when they arrived but failed to hit anyone and were driven off by a few shots fired in response. James B.C. Vale said this was the "wildest region" of country he had ever seen as he and his comrades moved near the Tazewell County line without further incident. Upon their return, Company D marched through Horse Shoe Bend and went through Logan again, arriving at their camp on June 24.[66]

Lieutenant Colonel Russell wrote from Chapmanville on June 19 that Captain Patrick Brunker's Company H was to report to Major John T. Hall at Camp Piatt and that Brunker had left that morning. Captain Dayton had arrived the previous day from the Logan County area and reported all quiet and that he felt the citizens were mostly loyal and willing to fight the rebels if they were accompanied by soldiers. Russell noted they were having particular trouble in McDowell County out of a Captain Elias V. Harman, Company C, (McDowell Partisan Rangers) Virginia Volunteers, who reportedly stole, threatened, and even killed loyal citizens. Harman apparently had made a particular demand against a Philip Lambert. Lieutenant Colonel Russell ordered Lieutenant John Mallernee to move to McDowell and drive out Harman and his thieves. This was most likely related to the expedition into McDowell County mentioned by James B.C. Vale.[67]

A relaxed atmosphere was described at Camp Elk River on June 22 by Adolphus De Bussey, as he scribed: "We have good times here. The boys are in excellent health. I am learning to play the fife. I will be with the band from this out....I will have an easy time as soon as I get able to play some. I have a nice flute and I intend learning it so that I can make some more pleasant...." He also talked of plans for the regiment to celebrate on July 4.[68]

Writing from Charleston on June 23, Medical Inspector John McCurdy, assistant surgeon, 23rd Ohio Infantry, reported that camp at Charleston where four companies of the 4th West Virginia were located was in excellent condition, providing the "most sanitary and healthy conditions" for the men, noting only eight soldiers were in the hospital and none were seriously ill. He added that the health of the four detached companies at Chapmanville and the two posted at Camp Piatt was in equally good condition.[69]

Major John T. Hall wrote to his mother from Camp Piatt on July 1, stating: "Everything is quiet here as far as I can learn in the country around. [Chaplain] Woodhull passed by a few days ago I suppose on his way to Chapmanville. I suppose he will remain there some time....I am boarding at Mr. Farley's."[70]

On July 4, the 4th West Virginia participated in a large celebration. Leading off the parade was "Col. Lightburn's elegant Band, in a wagon painted in Red, White and Blue....decorated with evergreens....drawn by four splendid iron-greys, discoursing our national airs, in splendid style," followed by long columns of soldiers under Lightburn's command.[71]

Two days later Adolphus De Bussey, who had recently taken up the fife, described the Independence Day affair:

> We had a pretty good time. The ball was opened with the firing of 13 rounds from 'Old Wise' as we call it. It is a six pounder taken from old Wise at the battle of Scary. At nine o'clock we marched over to town and received the representatives consisting of 34 young ladies dressed in robes of white within blue waist and a pink ribbon scarf about the waist. Their heads adorned with wreaths of flowers and evergreen. Each girl carried a Union flag bearing the initials of the names of each and every state. We recrossed the bridge and marched to the old Camp ground [Littlepage estate] about one 4th of a mile from our camp. It was occupied by Wise's troops a year ago after reaching the ground and being seated, having prayer, the Declaration of Independence. Then being read, several speeches being made appropriately on the times and the day at one o'clock. They had recess for dinner. The boys did not fare as well as expected. Many of the citizens dodging to the brush with their baskets....the 1st Colonel seeing this ordered the boys to camp.[72]

De Bussey indicated the day was a disappointment for the 4th West Virginia, but as a member of the band he managed to eat fairly well. He also said there were 1,200 people present and "The girls are as thick here as young toads after a summer shower. The event closed with 34 rounds from 'Old Wise.'" William V. Brown, Company D, viewed the celebration at Camp Russell as uneventful, although he seemed to enjoy the speeches and comic singers.[73]

Brown also mentioned the recent unsuccessful expedition from Chapmanville to McDowell Court House to break up a gathering of General Humphrey Marshall's guerillas. The July 9 edition of the *Gallipolis Dispatch* reported the band of the 4th West Virginia "came down Saturday on the steamer *Victor No. 2*, playing beautifully as they neared the wharf. This band will now rank with the best in the service." Companies B and D went on a scout of Logan County on July 9 and returned on the 10th.[74]

Major John T. Hall wrote Assistant Adjutant General George Ruggles from Camp Piatt on the 10th, tendering his resignation due to the ill health of his father and other family matters. Two days later, on July 12, Colonel Lightburn stated Major John T. Hall had attempted to resign and desired to know if he could have a leave of absence until the resignation was accepted.[75]

2nd Lieutenant C. B. Blake, Company G, wrote from Loup Creek Landing in Fayette County on July 17 that they had just returned from a scout through Summersville, the Yew Mountains, and Cranberry River, where they found the rebel den but no men. He said they were out on the scout for three weeks and four days without tents or a change of clothing and had to carry their food on mules. Blake reported he and 12 men spent one night on Yew Mountain fighting off panthers with torches so as not to alert the enemy by gunfire. In addition, companies B and D left Camp Russell on this same day, July 12, and arrived at Camp Piatt July 19.[76]

The July 24th edition of the *Gallipolis Journal* reported that 20 "villainous bushwhackers" had been captured by the 4th West Virginia and brought to Gallipolis to be transported to Camp Chase, Ohio. The writer stated: "One rascal in the crowd has taken the oath four

Milton Stewart.
St. Albans Historical Society.

times, it is said. They never should have been taken prisoners. All such murderers should be summarily dealt with." Around this same time the *Point Pleasant Register* reported that eight prisoners, all of Logan, had been arrested by Captain John L. Vance and arrived at Point Pleasant, where they were placed in the charge of Captain James H. Dayton. Reportedly all but possibly two were bushwhackers. One of the arrests, of an Ogden Spencer, took place at Logan on July 12.[77]

Governor Pierpont wrote to General Jacob D. Cox on July 25 to quickly reject the resignation of Major John Hall, stating Hall did not understand the effect his resignation would produce. Lieutenant Hankinson and 20 men went on a scout on July 26 and returned the following day. General Cox also wrote Colonel Lightburn on the 27th and told him the 4th West Virginia, along with Lieutenant John Young's Company and a cavalry company, would take care of the Kanawha Valley below Loup Creek.[78]

On July 31 the *Gallipolis Journal* reported that on the previous Saturday Sergeant Milton Stewart, Company K, 4th West Virginia, arrived at Gallipolis with a number of "secesh" prisoners from Charleston, including one particularly "bad man" named Turner. They were lodged in the county jail where "No inmates ever heretofore placed there, were more worthy than these traitors."[79]

Adolphus De Bussey, yet at Camp Elk River, added on July 31 that Company K, 2nd West Virginia Cavalry, arrived the previous day and were going to stay with the 4th West Virginia to serve as scouts and picket outposts. He concluded: "Our two companies that went to relieve the 9th [West Virginia] got back Sunday. They only went to Gauley." Those two companies had been sent to relieve the 9th West Virginia Infantry at Summersville, where Lieutenant Colonel William C. Starr and several of his men were recently captured by Confederates during in a raid. De Bussey concluded that otherwise, "The boys are all well."[80]

Frustrated with Governor Pierpont's refusal to accept his resignation, Major John T. Hall of the 4th West Virginia wrote his father, John Hall, Sr., at Point Pleasant on August 1. The elder Hall was one of the men who helped organize the Reformed Government of Virginia at Wheeling in 1861, and he was a well-known and politically affluent resident of Mason County. Major Hall implored his father to help him obtain a transfer into the newly forming 13th West Virginia Infantry, which his younger brother James R. Hall was helping organize. Hall also wrote: "I will leave for Chapmanville tomorrow. I understand that Capt. Dayton has built a blockhouse at that place."[81]

From August 2 through August 8, Colonel Edward Siber's 37th Ohio Volunteer Infantry and other troops under his command were involved in various operations against Confederate troops and bushwhackers operating in the vicinity of Wyoming Court House. Major Hall departed Camp Piatt on August 2 to take command at Camp Russell in Chapmanville and arrived on the night of August 3.[82]

The next day, Major Hall took 50 men from Companies C and K of the regiment, the only companies then stationed at Chapmanville, on a scout up Guyandotte. At Logan Court House some local women warned Hall they would be attacked within the next ten miles, but he ignored them because Southern citizens pretending to be Unionists had so often lied to them.[83]

From his headquarters at Charleston, Lightburn ordered Colonel Thomas Nutter of the 153rd Virginia (Kanawha) Militia to disarm all disloyal citizens, place the names of the owners on the guns, and send them to Charleston. Lightburn was very detailed as to conditions which warranted such action, including even "Hurrahs for Jeff Davis." Any threats or similar action toward loyal citizens would result in immediate arrest. Ironically, three days later, on August 7, Lightburn countermanded the order and issued another, applying only to armed "marauders and bushwhackers," while disloyal citizens who remained at home "minding their own business" were not to be molested.[84]

At Loup Creek 2nd Lieutenant Cincinnatus B. Blake, Company G, boasted his company's camp at that location was near impregnable and that they had a good route available for retreat if needed. Blake, who clearly disliked his company commander, Captain Henry Grayum, referred to him as their "Old Gum Headed Captain" and called him a "dumb head" for bringing his wife and children into their camp.[85]

The Fight at Beech Creek
and
The Death of Major John T. Hall
August 6, 1862

Confederate Major Vincent Addison "Clawhammer" Witcher commanded the 1st Battalion Virginia Cavalry in 1862 (later became 34th Battalion Virginia Cavalry) and planned to capture Chapmanville. He learned that Major John T. Hall of the 4th West Virginia had taken a detachment of fifty men on an expedition in that area intending to flush out Confederates. On August 6, Witcher took a detachment of 250 men from his battalion and managed to take position in the woods behind Hall's troops at the Kennedy farm at Beech Fork. The Confederates nearly surrounded Hall's men, and opened fire, mortally wounding Major Hall and killing two others. A few Federals were also wounded or taken prisoner, while at least thirty fled to the mountains and escaped, traveling for several days in the wilderness. Witcher was born in Pittsylvania County, Virginia, in 1837, and was an attorney before the war. He had acquired a fierce reputation for savage tactics that often included executing prisoners of war, a cruel practice known as "Witcher's Parole." He later faced court martials for his atrocities including murder, robbing and plundering private citizens, but only received a veritable slap on the wrist.[86]

Corporal George W. Gilliland, Company C, a participant at Beech Creek, left a detailed account, reporting that Major John T. Hall took Companies C and K, 4th West Virginia, from Camp Piatt near Charleston, and marched about 50 miles to Chapmanville, where he selected 50 men and then moved deeper into the mountains. Gilliland wrote:

> In the evening of the second day out we stopped to get something to eat. We had killed a sheep and cooked it in a big iron kettle and had just started to eat when a shower of bullets came whizzing at us killing Major Hall and two of the

Maj. John T. Hall.
Terry Lowry Collection.

soldiers, [Private] Jacob C. Lewberry [Lineberry], [Company C] and [Private] Thomas Lamb [Company K]. We had seven pack horses and mules. The first volley from the Rebels killed them all. This was our first fight. There were forty-eight of us and 250 of the Rebels....That day I took dead aim at Major [William] Straton and when the gun cracked he fell with one arm pretty badly shot. We had to run and 18 of us got away in one squad and nine of us were wounded. I had a bullet put in my left leg and it is there yet [1899]....That night we marched eight miles to Tug River. I carried a comrade by the name of George Edwards across the river on my back. He was shot through the knee. The water came up under my arm and it was quite difficult to ford as it was very rocky. Those that were not disabled, and the Union home guard went back the next day and buried the dead. We were fifteen days in the mountains before we got to any place we knew. We arrived at Louisa, Ky., in the afternoon. The doctor probed my wound and told me to come to the hospital next morning and he would cut the bullet out. I did not go but the next morning four of us started for Catlettsburg in a canoe....[87]

Maj. William Straton mentioned by Gilliland was Lieutenant Colonel Witcher's vice-commander in the 1st Battalion Virginia Mounted Rifles. Sergeant Milton Stewart, Company K, who also participated in the fight at Beech Fork, wrote that Witcher's men quietly dismounted and secured their horses, then crept up a hill into some trees. Once in position, they opened fire on Hall's men. Their first volley did not hit any Federal troops, but severely wounded a small child belonging to the family who owned the land they were on. Gilliand stated that Hall's men immediately ran for their weapons, but the enemy was too well concealed, and Major Hall fell in the third volley, but not before he severely wounded Witcher. Sergeant Stewart ran to Hall's side, who reportedly exclaimed, "Never mind me, fight on boys!" Another version of Hall's last words indicated that he instead yelled, "Never surrender men. Cut your way through."[88]

William L. McMaster.
Terry Lowry Collection.

Stewart continued his description of the fighting after Hall's wounding, stating that he looked around and saw the boys had "retired" except for three, one of whom was severely wounded, and the others who started for the hills were both killed. The rebels began to advance and shot Major Hall two more times; while escaping, a Confederate bullet struck Stewart's gun barrel, glancing off and severely wounding another soldier. He also reported finding the bodies of the two Federal soldiers that Corporal George Gilliand mentioned were killed in the first volley: Privates Lineberry (Lewberry) and Lamb, both of whom were shot in the back.[89]

A recruiting officer from the 8th West Virginia Infantry who had accompanied Major Hall's detachment on the expedition, Captain Andrew W. Gregg, was captured in the fight and taken to a nearby farm house along with Major Hall. The Confederates took Major Hall's boots, hat, blanket, and revolver, and then also plundered the bodies of the dead Union soldiers. Witcher's men also captured Milton Stewart's revolver, as well as that of 1st Lieutenant William L. McMaster of Company C, along with fourteen muskets and all of their food stores, "except for a bag of crackers." Major Hall died about two hours after he was shot. Although he suffered in "intense agony, a groan never escaped his lips and he passed as if going to sleep." Captain Gregg, who was released, walked seven miles looking for a coffin without success. Gregg was later appointed as regimental chaplain in the 8th West Virginia Infantry. The prisoners spent the following day digging a grave with nothing but a piece of a mattock and an old wooden shovel. Stewart was eventually exchanged, and he and the others walked 95 miles in three days to Big Sandy.[90]

Lieutenant Cincinnatus B. Blake, Company G, who did not take part in the debacle at Beech Creek, wrote from Camp Russell, adding what he had learned of the affair by camp hearsay:

They [Confederates] turned off after the Major and came on him in the rear. Our men had taken off their cartridge boxes.... and stacked their arms, and were preparing their supper, some laying down, some cooking and some picking berries....The

Major and two others were killed and three taken prisoners. If the Major had not have got killed they would have whipped them all. The home guards came after them and fired into them & they thought it was some more of our men come up and they ran and left one of our men a prisoner standing. The Major and about six men were all that stood fire....The Major stood his ground and fired off twelve shots from his revolver and three guns that were left. He was shot through five times. One of our Lieutenants, a [William L.] McMaster, was with him and tried to get him away, but he wouldn't run. The Lieutenant did as all Lieutenants would, he ran.[91]

William V. Brown, Company D, although not an actual participant in the expedition, similarly left a detailed summary of what he learned of the action while writing home shortly afterward:

...the men had stopped 30 miles above Logan for dinner and had their guns stacked and their cartridge boxes off, some was asleep, some eating, and some getting dinner, they were surrounded by Cavalry who had followed them all the afternoon before and all the morning and who had come onto them as they were eating dinner. There were four companies of them [Confederates]. They had dismounted and left their horses and surrounded our men on foot, got hold of some of their guns before they knew it. The first our boys knew of it, the secesh fired off two or three guns to attract our boys' attention and when they jumped up and poured in volley after volley. Our boys ran and got their guns, what could, and fired the loads out, and seeing they were surrounded and that the rebels were too many for them, they all broke for the woods and cut their way out except this Major and six more men that stayed with him. The Major was in a house when they were attacked. He ran out and as the rebels were all around him he commenced firing his revolvers off. He fired 12 loads out of his two revolvers and by this time Lt. McMaster and the six I spoke of had got to him and the Lieutenant tried to pull him into an old barn but couldn't do it.[92]

Brown further elaborated:

He, the Major, ran to some guns the boys couldn't get to and commenced picking them up and firing them off. By the time he had fired off the first gun he was wounded twice. When he fired off the second gun he was shot again but he got another and blazed away with it and this time he was shot through the breast, but, after being shot through four times, he raised himself on his knees and got another gun, took aim, and brought his man. The boys, when they saw him fall first, ran to him and wanted to raise him up, but he said, 'Never mind me, boys, fight them!' When the boys found it was all up with the Major they broke for the woods. One of our boys stayed to take care of the Major and the rest of the wounded should there be any, one of their men also stayed. I don't know whether this man has got in yet or not, the last I heard of him he was held as a hostage for one of their men who was taking care of their men. The Major died in about two hours.[93]

Corporal Clarkson Fogg, Company E, also a non-participant in the events, wrote home offering his version:

...our men had halted near a house (which is a scarce thing in that region) to eat their suppers. The men had strayed into a cornfield in rear of the house while the Major and Lieut. McMaster were in the house when the rebs made their appearance. The Major stepped outside the door and commenced firing from his two revolvers, both of which he emptied and was about to fire a rifle, when he fell, wounded, and while Lieut. McMaster was endeavoring to drag him inside the house, received another ball through the body and lived for two hours; two other men were killed and three wounded. Our men could not get to their guns except under a fire from three directions, from three ends of the road and on the opposite side from the house. Only about 10 guns were saved. The men then took to the woods. About 30 arrived here [Camp Elk River] last night [August 16] from Gallipolis, having come into Louisa, about 30 miles up Big Sandy....the rest of them have all arrived at different points except the wounded.[94]

A pair of brothers, Gordon (Grandville) and Patterson Rife (Riffe), previously served with the 129th Regiment Virginia Militia of Logan County. That regiment was largely comprised of Confederate supporters, although it also had a few Union men who left to organize a company of Union home guards when the war began. After the war, both brothers claimed to have been with Major Hall at the time of his death and were likely among the home guards mentioned by Corporal George Gilliand who helped bury the Union dead. When the 129th Militia disbanded in 1862, Gordon and Patterson Rife each enlisted in Company I, 7th West Virginia Cavalry, in March 1864.[95]

Hospital Steward Thomas Barton recollected that Major Hall's "body was recovered and interred at Charleston, and the remains were afterward removed to Point Pleasant." Hall's body was eventually buried in the Hall–Hogg Cemetery north of Point Pleasant. Amidst the grief over Hall's death, Private George W. Edmonds, Company C, was injured by a gunshot wound of the right knee at Beech Creek and treated in the army hospital until December 1.[96]

William V. Brown also took note of Confederate casualties as he claimed "...it is known that Capt. Stratton had a ball put into him at one breast and out at the other and it broke his arm where it came out, and Capt. Witcher, of Guyandotte notoriety, was shot through the thigh. It was said Stratton had died and that they had three or four men killed." Stratton's wound was not mortal, however.[97]

Witcher overestimated the number of Federal soldiers killed as numbering 40, when, in fact, there were only three. His claim on wounded and captured property was a bit more accurate, however. The Federals were convinced Major Stratton was mortally wounded and, although the wound was very serious, Stratton recovered to fight another day. Four days after the tragic death of Major John T. Hall at Beech Creek, Captain James H. Dayton of Company K was promoted to major to fill Hall's office as executive officer. Company G was camped at Loup Creek on August 6, probably yet unaware of Major Hall's demise at Beech Creek. Captain Dayton wrote on August 7 that he now had about 100 men available at Camp Russell at Chapmanville to search for Witcher and sent a request to Camp Piatt for reinforcements. 2nd Lieutenant William Grayum of the company was focused elsewhere as he wrote: "Our pickets shot a teamster last week. He was outside the lines and paid no attention when hailed by the sentinel and of course paid the penalty of his stubbornness with his life. There was a company of the 9th [West] Va. Regiment here until we came and teamsters had run over them as they pleased and boasted they would do the same with us. But the shooting of that man had a good effect on them...."[98]

General Jacob D. Cox's Kanawha Division Ordered to the Eastern Front August 8, 1862

On August 8 General Jacob D. Cox received orders from Major General John Pope to move the greater portion of his Kanawha Division, some 5,000 troops, to the eastern front. This left a minimal number of troops protecting the Kanawha Valley and its vicinity, including the 4th West Virginia. During August 27-30, 1862, Cox's 1st Brigade participated in the Second Battle of Manassas, a.k.a. Bull Run. After a brief tenure in Washington, D.C., the Kanawha Division fought at both the battle of South Mountain on September 14 and the battle of Antietam (Sharpsburg) on September 17, 1862.[99]

At South Mountain, Major General Jesse Reno, who commanded the 9th Corps, was mortally wounded and General Cox was given temporary command of the corps. He resisted this idea, pleading with General McClellan that he was too inexperienced for a corps command, but he was placed under direct supervision of Major General Ambrose

Lt. Charles Holstein.
Richard Wolfe Collection.

Burnside and ordered to take command of the corps. Late in the day, Cox advanced the 9th Corps on Lee's right and nearly overwhelmed the Confederates, until General A.P. Hill's 3rd Corps arrived to reinforce them, forcing Cox to withdraw. Antietam was afterward known as America's Bloodiest Day, with more than 23,000 men killed, wounded, or missing in action. President Abraham Lincoln was so impressed with Cox's aggressive style that he recommended him to Congress for promotion to major general.[100]

On August 8, 1862, at Camp Piatt, William V. Brown, Company D, announced a new addition to the 4th West Virginia, writing:

We are going to have a Battery of Artillery connected with our Reg't. There is to be four guns – six guns make a battery – one of them is at Charleston now, a six-pounder. We brought it from Ceredo with us. It is a gun our men took from old [General Henry A.] Wise, somewhere, we call it the 'Old Blacksnake' because it is painted black I suppose is the reason it was named that. Another one of the guns was to come last night. I believe the other two are to come from Gauley. Charlie Holstein, a Swede, and a private in Co. K has got the appointment of Captain of the Battery. It will take about 100 men to man the Battery and they are to be taken out of the Co's in the Reg't, ten men out of each I suppose.[101]

Brown also mentioned that Governor Francis Pierpont had declined to accept Major Hall's resignation and speculated that it was because he was apparently yet unaware of Hall's death. The situation at Camp Russell intensified on August 9 as Captain Dayton received reliable information he was going to be attacked, and at night he had the wagons loaded and retreated. Eventually Dayton's force met Company F of the 4th West Virginia at Peytona, which had been sent as a reinforcement. Company G and a cavalry company joined them the following day.[102]

General Cox was apparently also unaware of Captain Dayton's actual plight because as of August 10 he incorrectly claimed a detachment of the 4th West Virginia had defeated 150 rebel cavalry in Logan County. In contrast, Lightburn wrote from Gauley Bridge for the troops at Chapmanville, reinforced by two companies, to fall back to Peytona, and if compelled, to fall back to Camp Piatt and hold it at all hazards. Most of these orders were already in motion. Lightburn also ordered Colonel Thomas Nutter of the 153rd Regiment Virginia Militia (Kanawha County) to collect all of his forces and to move immediately to Charleston.[103]

Also on August 10, 4th West Virginia Surgeon George K. Ackley reported he had established a hospital at Guyandotte in "a very large and commodious building" with only one sick man present. Colonel Edward Siber of the 37th Ohio Infantry was at the foot of Guyandotte Mountain on August 11, where he reported the Beech Creek survivors had safely retreated to Peter's Creek, Kentucky. The following day five companies of the 4th West Virginia and the home guard reached Chapmanville and found no enemy present.[104]

During early August 1862, Lieutenant John W. Davis of Company A, 4th West Virginia, brought a portion of the company to Point Pleasant under orders to keep check on any local "secesh" who may be causing trouble. Also, a general muster of the 106th Regiment of Virginia Militia was held at Point Pleasant on August 13; Colonel J.P.R.R. Smith read a "Tribute of Respect" to the late Major Hall of the 4th West Virginia and sent a copy to the 4th regiment.[105]

Lightburn Takes Command
District of the Kanawha
August 17, 1862

Private William Van Brown, Company D, recognized the signs that a large movement was imminent in Cox's Brigade when he wrote from Camp Piatt on August 17: "Cox is ordered to reinforce Pope and will be here tonight with Regt's. I don't know whether we will stay here or not. The Capt. [Arza Goodspeed] said this morning he thought we would leave here before 2 weeks."[106]

Clarkson Fogg wrote from Camp Elk River on August 17 that Colonel Lightburn had been called to Cox's headquarters at Flat Top a week prior and had not yet returned. He added that all of the militia had been called to Charleston, and that he expected Lightburn to be promoted to general. While posted at Camp Piatt on the same date, Brown noted the arrival of several soldiers who had escaped from the earlier tragedy at Beech Creek:

> The men kept coming in one and two at a time for four or five days till about 20 have got in now, I believe, Lieut. McMaster was out about a week, he had a man with him that knew the country and they started in towards Kentucky but they were followed and attacked three times so they had to change their course and in about a week they got to Peytona where they found their Cos....The rest of the boys made their way through to Big Sandy and down it to Catlettsburg, got on a boat there and last night they got to Charleston. Eight of the boys lost their guns. Four or five were wounded but I believe they have all got in. One German in Co. K was wounded in the leg but got away and after traveling several miles he was walking up a path using his gun for a cane, no load in it, when there were about 20 secesh jumped up out of the bushes on the side of the path and told him to throw down his gun, but he just jumped behind a tree, cocked his piece, and hollowed, 'Come on boys, here they are' and every coward of them took to their heels and Dutchy came on into camp. It is a wonder a single one of our men got away.[107]

Colonel Lightburn issued Order No. 41 on August 19 regarding Major Hall's death, requesting all officers of the 4th West Virginia to wear the "usual mourning badge" for thirty days. He also appointed Private Charles Holstein, Company K, in charge of the regiment's artillery. On August 22, Lightburn sent a request to Pierpont recommending various men to be commissioned as officers of the newly forming 13th

Daniel A. Russell.
Terry Lowry Collection.

West Virginia Infantry, which included some of his best officers from the 4th West Virginia. Lightburn stated:

> I desire to recommend as officers for the thirteenth 13th Va Infantry Capt Wm R. Brown 4th Va Infantry for Col. James R. Hall of Point Pleasant for Lieut. Col. Calvin A Sheppard as Major & Lieut CB Blake D.A. Russell and S. Stewart as Capts these are good men I dislike to take them from the 4th 4th but for the benefit of the service I recommend them Wm S Hutchins is wanted as adjt [Adjutant].[108]

In a separate telegram Lightburn further wrote to Governor Pierpont, "I respectfully request that the Head Quarters of the thirteenth 13 regt be at Charleston to enable me to use the 4th in front I can clothe & arm the regt any time it reports for duty."[109]

Clarkson Fogg was in Camp Elk River on August 25 and wrote that Cox's troops were heading east at the "beginning of last week." He also noted Lightburn was at Gauley and Captain William R. Brown of Company E, who was in command of the post at Charleston, might be made either a major in the 4th West Virginia or colonel of the 13th West Virginia. Fogg again speculated that Lightburn would be appointed as brigadier general at the next session of Congress and opined that was because he, unlike Cox, had refused to accept the Fugitive Slave Act, which required Federal troops to return runaway slaves to their owners, and instead protected them. Fogg also mentioned there were four companies of the regiment posted at Chapmanville, three at Elk River, two at Guyandotte, and one at Camp Piatt.[110]

Hospital Steward Thomas Barton summarized on August 25 that up to that point, the regiment had lost five men at Chapmanville, including the three killed in action at Beech Creek, one died from disease, and one deserted. Barton also noted that while at Charleston, the regiment lost 17 men, including three deaths from disease, one accidentally shot, two drowned, two deserted, and nine discharged for disability, making the regiment's total losses to date 51 troops.[111]

On September 7, all state militia in the Kanawha County area, including the 153rd Regiment, were ordered to report to Charleston immediately, and about 200 men arrived at camp on the Elk River within two days. Officers ordered the militiamen to fall into formation, and immediately called out for any "secessionists" to step out of ranks. Fifteen men promptly broke ranks, and a few took the Oath of Allegiance, but others declined, knowing they would be sent to the Confederate army.[112]

Meanwhile at Fayetteville, Companies B, G, and H, which had been sent as relief, arrived to replace Captain Vance's men. Company E, however, soon found themselves entangled in a small skirmish according to John G. Farrar: "One Sunday we got aboard of a boat [at Charleston] and moved to the mouth of Coal River. Remained there until night then started for Mud Bridge Waded Coal River. Next day found Jenkin's cavalry at Mud Bridge. Had a little skirmish. They retreated. That was the first skirmish we had of any notice."[113]

The Kanawha Valley Campaign

The impact of losing more than half of its Union forces had left the Kanawha Valley vulnerable to Confederate attack. Colonel Albert G. Jenkins' 8th Virginia Cavalry and five companies of the 14th Virginia Cavalry intended to exploit the opportunity. Brigadier General William W. Loring ordered Jenkins to create a diversion, as a force of 6,000 Confederates advanced on the Kanawha Valley from Pearisburg, Virginia.

Loring, a native of Wilmington, North Carolina, was known as a hard-edged fighter; he lost his left arm in the Mexican War, and yet continued to lead troops in combat. Jenkins had a promotion to brigadier general pending at Richmond and had only recently resigned his former seat in the Confederate Congress. He soon arrived at Buffalo in Putnam County on September 6, 1862, and occupied the home of Dr. Edward Naret, the former adjutant of the 181st Virginia Militia Regiment, and took a horse and 16 tons of hay for his troopers.

When Dr. Naret later learned one of Jenkins' men drowned crossing the Kanawha River, he was overheard gloating in vengeance.[114]

Governor Pierpont soon learned that Jenkins was back in the Kanawha Valley and telegraphed Colonel Joseph A.J. Lightburn at Point Pleasant, insisting that he send a large force in search of the Confederates. Lightburn was already aware that General Loring was heading toward Charleston, however, and that such a large reconnaissance would leave the region dangerously exposed. He promptly declined Pierpont's request as a result. On the other hand, Lightburn knew he could not ignore Jenkins either and ordered six companies of the 2nd West Virginia Cavalry, under Colonel John C. Paxton, along with three companies of the 4th West Virginia Volunteer Infantry, to find Jenkins. Colonel Paxton's detachment arrived at Coalsmouth at approximately 11 a.m. on Sunday, September 7, and received word that Jenkins was at nearby Hurricane Bridge, some eleven miles away, intending to attack Winfield and Coalsmouth that night.[115]

Skirmish at Coal Mountain

When Colonel Paxton heard that Jenkins was spotted near Hurricane Bridge, he sent Captain Silas H. Emmon's Company K along with Captain John V. Young's Company G, 13th West Virginia Infantry, who were at Coalsmouth, to reconnoiter the situation at Hurricane Bridge. Around 9 p.m. that evening, the Union detachment was moving along the James River Turnpike near the southeastern slope of Coal Mountain and ran into Jenkins' pickets. Although possibly apocryphal, Colonel Jenkins was said to have earlier sent word to Captain Young that he would "eat supper in Coalsmouth or in Hell" that night. After a short skirmish, by 11 p.m. Jenkins' pickets retreated toward their main force that waited further west at the foot of Coal Mountain. Jenkins moved eastwardly up the mountainside, and soon his troopers encountered the Union troops posted along the summit and a ferocious skirmish ensued. Company G lost two men wounded, and two of Jenkins' men were killed. One Union soldier reported they

James H. Ralston.
Terry Lowry Collection.

were "fighting like the devil" but were heavily outnumbered and had to retreat toward Coalsmouth after expected reinforcements never arrived.[116]

The Battle of Fayetteville
September 10, 1862

The Confederates marched from Giles County, Virginia, arriving at Fayetteville on September 10, 1862, where Loring found two Federal regiments waiting. After a brief but intense battle, the Federals withdrew and moved toward Charleston. Lightburn then ordered a general retreat of all Federal outposts from Fayetteville to Charleston with Loring in fast pursuit, burning the Union powder magazines and other military stores left behind along the way. Private Philip Matthews, Company B, wrote on September 13 that the regiment slept in line of battle on some rocky ground, and one of the rocks broke a rib in his right breast. On September 16, Sergeant Major James Hoffersett Ralston was promoted to 2nd Lieutenant of Company E and placed on detached service as Colonel Lightburn's *aide-de-camp*.[117]

The Battle of Charleston:
Lightburn's Retreat

The town of Charleston had roughly 1,500 citizens in 1862. With Major General William W. Loring's force of 5,000 Confederates marching toward Charleston, Colonel Joseph A.J. Lightburn ordered all Union forces in the area to remain on high alert. Loring had orders to create a diversion for General Robert E. Lee's upcoming Maryland Campaign, and in doing so to also capture the salt mines near Charleston. At approximately 1 a.m. on September 13, Lieutenant Colonel William Russell, commanding a small detachment of the 4th West Virginia posted just east of Camp Piatt, received orders to fall back to the camp by daylight and then proceed to destroy the camp and all unnecessary equipages. Afterward, he was to move the detachment toward Charleston and act as the Union rear guard to prevent Confederates from surprising the Federal movement into the city. By eight o'clock that morning, Russell was relieved by the 34th Ohio Infantry near Campbell's Creek.[118]

Private William Van Brown, Company D, wrote that when Lieutenant Colonel Russell's detachment eloped from their outpost toward Camp Piatt, "...we did not know where we were going and did not take a thing with us. We left our knapsacks, overcoats, dress c'ts, [coats] blankets, in fact everything except what we had on....at daylight we were ordered forward, our Reg't bringing up the rear. When we got to Piatt they [Federals] set the barracks on fire and wouldn't let us get anything so we lost all we had." Private James B.C. Vale, also of Company D, echoed Brown's account, grousing: "As we pass back we burn Camp Piatt, our knapsacks were in our quarters, but our officers would not let us leave ranks to get them, so they burned too, trinkets and all."[119]

At approximately 2 a.m. on September 13, the Federals reached Charleston and were posted along the western bank of the Elk River and on the east end of town along the Kanawha River, awaiting the Confederate advance. As General William Loring approached Charleston later that morning, his advance guard made contact with Federal troops on the east end of town along the Kanawha River bank, and the battle began in earnest. Thomas Barton, the hospital steward, recalled that an old smoothbore cannon, along with Colonel Edward Siber's Ohio Battery of howitzers, was placed along a ridge located just east of the James River and Kanawha Turnpike. Colonel Lightburn had earlier warned citizens to evacuate, and many who refused or were unable to make it out in time became trapped under heavy artillery and small arms fire coming from both sides of the river.[120]

Southern supporter Victoria Hansford Teays, at her home in Coalsmouth when the battle began on September 13, could distinctly hear the cannonading and rattle of muskets. In her diary, she recalled panic-stricken Union citizens evacuating:

> Such a sight about me I never saw nor ever expect to see again. The river as far as the eye could reach up and down was covered

with boats of all kinds, large flat boats, jerry boats, jolly boats, skiffs and canoes....When I say the river was covered with boats I mean just what I say, and a person could have almost crossed the river by jumping from one boat to another....I will never forget a woman and a man were on two short pieces of gunnywayles lashed together. A tub sat at one end of it containing their property. The woman sat in a rocking chair at the other end, while the man stood in the middle and paddled them on as best he could. ....all this time the cannonading went on and it was music to us.[121]

The downtown and west end areas in Charleston were severely damaged by artillery, and several buildings were burned in the melee occurring that morning. When General Jacob D. Cox removed the Kanawha Division from the valley earlier in August, they left behind one cannon from each artillery battery in the two brigades comprising the division. One man from each of the remaining regiments was "volunteered" to serve the guns if an attack should occur. Sergeant Charles Holstein, Company K, 4th West Virginia, commanded a detachment of the artillery in the battle. The Union guns were well served, as the artillery firing was described by Thomas Barton as "rapid for the number of guns engaged." After several hours of heavy street fighting, the Federals finally withdrew to the Elk River and crossed a large suspension bridge to the western bank. Once all of the Federals had crossed, they cut the bridge's cables on the west bank, and let it fall into the river to prevent Confederates from pursuing them further. Private William Van Brown, Company D, waited in line along the western bank of the Elk River under artillery fire and observed:

...heavy cannonading and musket fire was kept up for about an hour and then it began to come closer and closer and fire began to break out in several places in town and we knew our men were slowly retreating, but contesting every inch of ground. By this time our heavier cannon on this side of the Elk [western

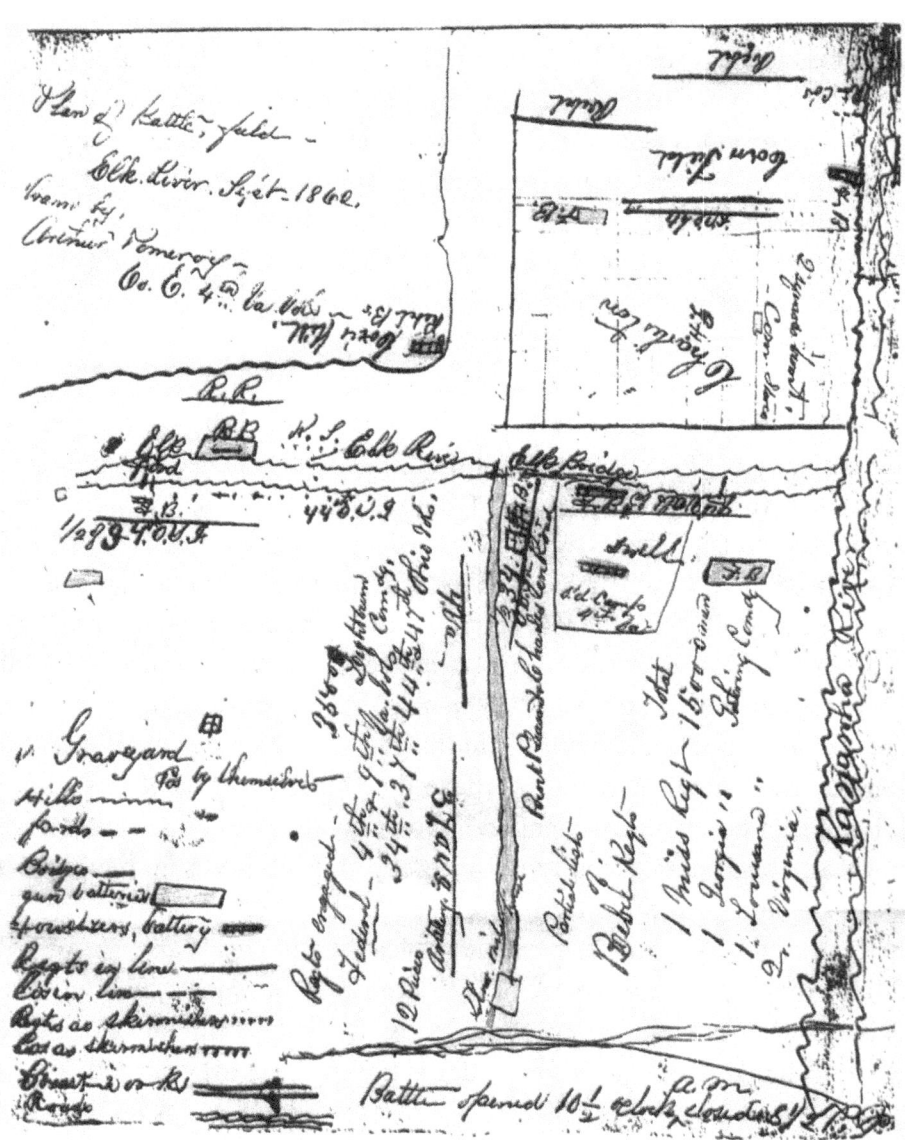

Wartime sketch of the Battle of Charleston
by Private Arthur Pomeroy, Company E, 4th West Virginia Infantry.
Wayne Farley Collection.

bank] had come into action and began to play pretty briskly on the enemy's forces on the opposite side of the Kanawha.[122]

Brown further related that by this time: "...the 37th and 47th Ohio regiments had retreated nearly to the Elk River [bridge] and two rebel Reg'ts were coming down Elk to cut off their retreat. When they [Confederates] came opposite us our Reg't poured a withering fire into them and they broke and ran like white hinds. That saved our two Reg'ts. Several of the 47th [Ohio] told me they would have been cut off in a few minutes in spite of everything, if we hadn't stopped them two Reg'ts."[123]

Private John G. Farrar, Company E, indicated his regiment passed by the 9th West Virginia as they were "fortifying" their position on the riverbank. He wrote: "We could look around the bend in the river and seen the Rebels coming by the thousands. We crossed Elk River on the suspension bridge and went in line of battle.... It was not long until they opened upon us with artillery."[124]

At roughly 11 a.m., Lieutenant Colonel William Russell was ordered to move the 4th West Virginia to the left of the 44th Ohio Infantry along the western bank of the Elk River, leaving two companies posted along the banks of the Kanawha River. He was soon ordered to repost the regiment on the hills north of the Elk River, forming the extreme left flank of the Union lines. Russell deployed Company B, under Captain John Luther Vance, as skirmishers on the bank of the Elk River, exposing them to Confederate sharpshooter fire, which continued until five o'clock that afternoon. Private James Vale, Company D, recalled that Companies B and D were formed as skirmishers, and despite constant harassment from sharpshooters, returned a hot masking fire which "kept up....until evening."[125]

Private William V. Brown observed:

...they fired a volley at us, and as I heard the ball whiz over my head–they fired mostly too high–I instinctively ducked my head Feeling sort of shamed, I looked around at the company, and saw 2/3 of them ducking their heads. This was first fire;

after that there wasn't a man flinched, except one or two cases not worth mentioning.[126]

By 1 p.m., the weather was "clear and hot" along the Elk River according to one Union soldier. Confederate artillery had quickly zeroed in on the Union position, and a heavy artillery duel continued until roughly 5 p.m., with constant and heavy musketry on both sides. Recalling the ferocity of the Confederate artillery that day, Private William Brown further mused:

The rebels planted a battery of 18 pounders on the opposite side of Elk just about a mile from us and the first ball would have moved a row through Company H if they had not got the order to 'lay down.' Then they put the shot and shell to us hot and heavy until we got the order to fall back about 25 yards into the woods where they would not have so good a chance at us, but they still continued to throw their shot at us until Lieut. De Lisle [De Lille] brought his battery to bear on them and the first shot knocked the wheels off one gun. The Rebels had excellent cannoneers....[127]

Sometime before 3 p.m., Cincinnatus B. Blake, leading a detachment from the 4th West Virginia, arrived at Charleston from the upper Elk River, only to learn the regiment was taking heavy fire from Confederate artillery and infantry. Blake testified:

I went in with the rest and stood in the warm[est] part of the fire. We were in the hottest fire below Elk and every time the secesh advanced, we drove them back, but the Elk River was between them and us. They threw shell and round shot pretty lively.[128]

Soon after Lieutenant Colonel Russell took a position on a hill above the Elk River, he spotted a large Confederate force moving into a cornfield across the river. Russell quickly reposted three of his companies behind a fence at the bottom of the hill and moved a 4th company further to the left to a "prominent point within range," but still close enough to receive protection, as the remaining five companies of the 4th West Virginia provided a heavy cover fire. Russell reported that his troops on the hill fired "a few well directed volleys" and "drove the enemy in confusion from the cornfield beyond our range."[129]

Captain John Vance, commanding Company B, observed: "An attempt was made to dislodge my command, and thus open a way across the river. As a consequence, we were engaged almost constantly, and suffered severe loss – three killed and seven wounded. Twice our ammunition ran low. There was no difficulty in getting a supply line the first time, but the second time it proved a difficult task, and it was only found through the persistent efforts of one of the lieutenants of the company."[130]

While the regiment received heavy and incessant artillery fire, with shells bursting "right over our heads," hidden sharpshooters across the river continued to pepper the Federals with musketry. Private Brown stated he saw Confederates firing from houses, behind salt barrels, and "everything that would shelter them."[131]

Private Lewis Love, Company A, indicated that as the battle raged into late afternoon, Union troops were taking more casualties and began to realize the futility of their position: "We did not have a force strong enough to divide....six of our men were killed....another of Mason City had his head cut off by a cannonball. Although he was a member of my company I cannot remember his name."[132]

Shortly after five o'clock that afternoon, Confederate General William Loring concluded he could not cross the Elk River, and Colonel John McCausland, commanding the 36th Virginia Infantry, sent a detachment northward to see if they could locate a suitable spot to cross the river. As the detachment left, Lieutenant Colonel William Russell spotted their movement and sent a company from the 4th West Virginia to harass the scouting party. However, moving under cover of a battery posted on a hill that commanded the Federal position, McCausland's detachment soon located a small ford, possibly at Mink

Shoals, but determined it would be impossible to move the army across and the plan was abandoned.[133]

At that point, Company B had completely exhausted their ammunition, and were relieved by Company D. Private William V. Brown recalled this period as some of the heaviest fighting of the day:

> ...our Company was ordered to reinforce Co. B., and then we were brought under the heaviest fire. We had to go about ¼ of a mile across an open field with bullets flying all around us. At least one [enemy] Reg't gave all their attention to us, but strange to say not a man was hurt. Most of their shots went over us, owing I suppose to their having long range guns, they shot one of Co. E, [Pvt. Joseph Blackburn, Jr.] very near a mile, hit him in the heart. We took Co. B's place and kept up a hot

"Fording the Ohio River - September 13th, 1862 - 34th, 37th, & 44th O.V.I., 4th, 9th & 13th [West] V.V.I. and 2nd [West] V.C."
This image depicts the retreating Federal forces of
Gen. Joseph A.J. Lightburn from the Kanawha Valley.
This would be in the vicinity of present-day Ravenswood,
Jackson County, West Virginia. WV State Archives.

fire until dark. We took advantage of houses, fences, logs, and anything that would cover us. They did the same, they were mostly in houses....Co. B had two killed here and 3 or 4 wounded. We had two men barely scratched, our Company appeared to hold charmed lives. Whenever a man would show himself a second, half a dozen bullets would whiz past his head. They also brought 3 or 4 jackass batteries (8 lb. Mountain howitzer batteries drawn by mules) to bear on us throwing grape, and cannister into the building where we were.[134]

As casualties in the 4th West Virginia mounted, Colonel Lightburn soon realized that Charleston was lost; he ordered Federal troops to begin a general withdrawal toward Point Pleasant. As the Federals left, they burned thousands of dollars in government stores to prevent its capture, and the fires rapidly spread and destroyed several houses and businesses, including the Branch Bank of Virginia, the Southern Methodist Church, and the Kanawha House, presenting a ghastly, near apocalyptic appearance amidst the flames and smoke, with soldiers running through the streets. As Lightburn's troops made their way along the Ohio River toward Point Pleasant by way of Ravenswood, with Confederates rapidly pursing, one soldier described it as "a continual skirmish for fifty miles" under rapid, forced-march conditions. En route on September 16, Sergeant Major James H. Ralston was promoted to 2nd lieutenant and detached as aide-de-camp to Colonel Lightburn; the Union column began to arrive at Point Pleasant on September 17, 1862, and as they filed in, the exhausted soldiers went into camp. After the battle, Captain Lysander Tulleys, Company D, 44th Ohio Infantry, admiringly opined that the 4th West Virginia Infantry had "distinguished itself" at the battle of Charleston.[135]

Exact casualty statistics for the battle of Charleston are impossible to ascertain, as both Lightburn and Loring filed reports incorporating aggregate or total casualties from the entire campaign, rather than specific numbers of killed, wounded, or missing from each battle and skirmish. As might be expected, there are varying numbers found in command reports and individual soldier accounts, although there is some agreement across sources. For example, both Lightburn and Dr. Thomas Barton reflected the 4th West Virginia lost six men killed in action, while the former added that one man deserted during the battle. Soldier accounts, which are often inaccurate, similarly contain divergent statistics, as Sergeant Clarkson Fogg reported on October 15 that the 4th West Virginia lost eight men killed and wounded. He also noted that Private John Turnbull, Company A, was beheaded by a cannonball and was later buried in a meadow. Company B, on the other hand, officially reported two men killed and two more were wounded. Private William V. Brown indicated the regiment lost five men killed in action, with 25 men missing. Private Charles Griffin, Company D, was killed and buried on the Chancy Brooks farm.[136]

Private John G. Farrar wrote that Private Joe Blackburn of Pomeroy, Ohio, was killed in action when he was shot by a Confederate sharpshooter at some 800 yards distance. Blackburn was a baker prior to the war and was baking bread for the regiment on the morning of the battle; he had only been ordered to join the line of battle an hour before he was killed. Afterward, Corporal Britton Cook of Company E was accused of plundering Blackburn's dead body and faced a court martial for allegedly taking a brown pocketbook with a gutta percha strap out of the deceased man's pocket and putting it into his own blouse pocket. Cook was later found innocent when the judge advocate found several conflicting testimonies as to what had actually occurred.[137]

Shortly after Private Joe Blackburn's death, an unidentified resident of Jackson County, "A Virginia Mountaineer," published the following tribute to him in the October 17, 1862 *Pomeroy Weekly Telegraph*:

> When the war cry of liberty rang through our land,
> To arms! Sprang our patriots the foe to withstand.
> On old Charleston height, their entrenchments they rear
> When the army is joined by a young volunteer.
> Tempt not death, cried his friends, but he bade them "good by"
> Saying, "oh, it is sweet for our Country to die."

The tempest of battle now rages and swells,
'Mid the thunder of cannon, the pealing of bells,
And a light not of battle illumes yonder spire,
Scene of woe! Scene of woe! 'tis Charleston on fire;
The Young Volunteer heedeth not the sad cry,
But murmurs, "tis sweet for our country to die."

With trumpets and banners, the foe draweth near,
A volley of musketry checks their career.
With the dead and dying the hillside is strown,
And the shout through our line is, the day is our own.
Not yet! Cries the gallant Lightburn, do they fly,
Stand firm, "Oh, tis sweet for our Country to die."

Now our bayonets are fixed and they rally again!
Stand fast! Cries our Lightburn, while a rebel remains!
The Young Volunteer stood firm on the field,
Reluctant to fly and disdaining to yield.
A shot, ah! – he falls, but his lips latest sigh,
Is, "oh! tis sweet for our Country to die."

And thus Blackburn fell – happy death, noble fall,
To perish for his country at liberty's call.
Should the flag of invasion profane evermore,
The blue of our seas, the greene of our shores;
May the hearts of our Soldiers re-echo that cry;
"Tis sweet, oh! tis sweet for our Country to die."[138]

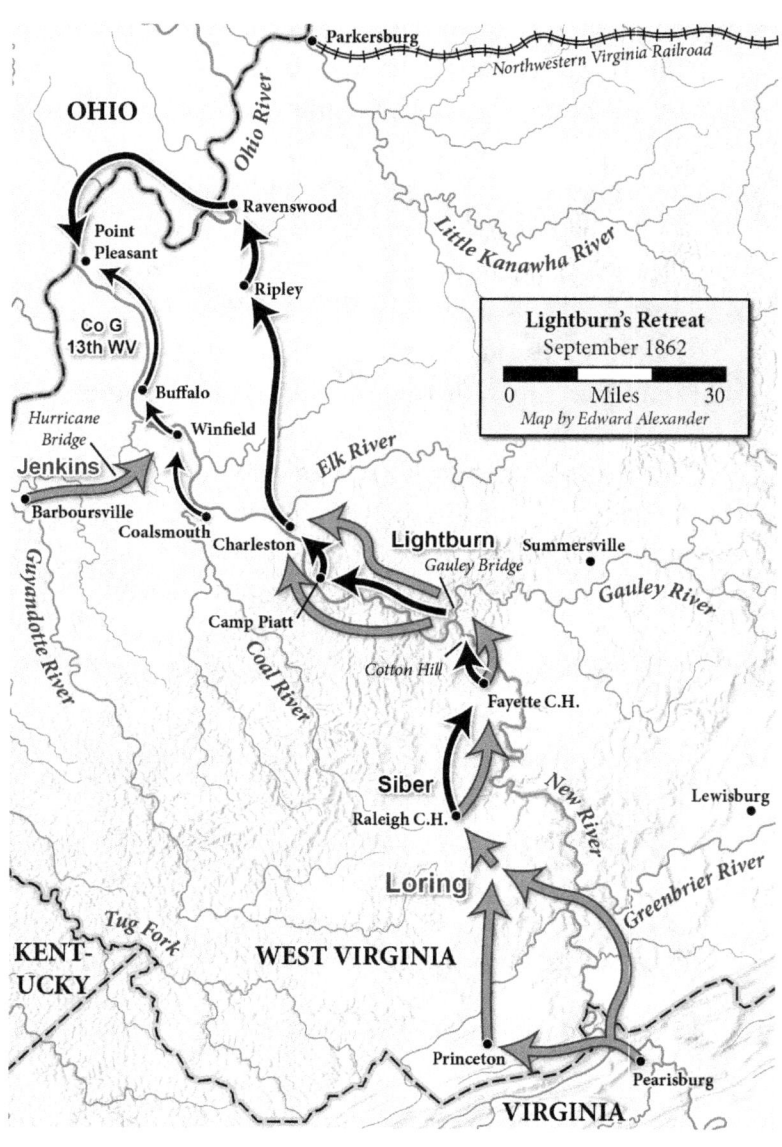

Kanawha Valley Again
Under Confederate Control

Once in control of Charleston, the Confederates quickly seized the *Kanawha Valley Star*, a popular local newspaper. In addition, another newspaper soon emerged, known ironically as *"The Guerilla."* This organ had clear intentions of persuading Union men to side with the Confederacy. The first issue appeared on September 28, describing what Union citizens under Confederate martial law were experiencing:

> During the past few days the Kanawha and Ohio rivers have been full of flatboats....laden with the families of Unionists, who find themselves compelled to flee....fearing the rebel General will carry into execution his recently made threat to hang every citizen "Yankee" he found in the Kanawha Valley.... they are obliged to leave behind them what they depended on to subsistence during the coming winter....most of them have to seek a charitable home among strangers....It is a pitiful sight to see families adrift....to find a home they knew not where- and all because their father or husband would not renounce his allegiance to the Government of his Fathers. The rebels in Western Virginia have declared themselves unsatisfied with anything less than armed resistance to the Federal power on the part of citizens whom they meet in their raids. It will not do to say you have not taken sides with either way, or that your sympathies only are with one side or the other. They demand active participation in their cause, and 'confiscation' robbery and outrage are the punishments for Federalism.[139]

Soon Confederate guerillas began seeking revenge against Union citizens in the area, and Loring's men took dozens of horses and forced eligible males into Confederate service. On the morning of September 29, Colonel Samuel Gilbert's Brigade, comprised of the 4th West Virginia and the 44th and 47th Ohio Infantries, were ordered to prepare three days' rations and be ready to march on a moment's notice, but the movement was suddenly and inexplicably called off. Corporal Clarkson Fogg wrote on the next day from Point Pleasant that the brigade had still not received new knapsacks to replace the old ones they had burned at Camp Piatt when they retreated from the Kanawha Valley. Fogg opined that to adapt to the chilly temperatures in the evening, two men had to share a blanket, which was "fine as long as it does not turn cold or get wet."[140]

General William Loring established his headquarters in the small village of Coalsmouth at the home of Unionist Samuel Benedict, whose son-in-law was John S. Cunningham, the 13th West Virginia Infantry adjutant. Benedict had helped organize the Reformed Government of Virginia, and he helped draft the West Virginia state constitution. Loring found it humorous that he used Benedict's home as headquarters; Benedict, however, was furious but helpless to stop it. Southern residents informed Loring who the local Unionists were at Coalsmouth, and the Confederates targeted the families of Union soldiers. The hardships under an enemy occupying army were once more felt throughout the Kanawha Valley, with shortages of food, clothing, and often medical supplies. With no Federal troops to protect them, Union citizens were afraid to leave their homes, and many simply evacuated the area. Yet, there was still a handful of Union militia companies posted at Buffalo, in Putnam County, pressuring Confederate troops with regular patrols, but the militia men were still raw, disorganized, and poorly armed, rendering them of little effect.[141]

Brigadier General Quincy Adams Gilmore was ordered to replace Colonel Joseph A.J. Lightburn and take command of the Kanawha District on October 2. The next day, General Loring issued a proclamation to the citizens of the Kanawha Valley area, warning them:

> We do not intend to punish those who remain at home as quiet citizens, in obedience to the laws of the land, and to all such clemency and amnesty are declared; but those who persist in adhering to the cause of the public enemy, and the pretended

State Government he has erected at Wheeling, will be dealt with as their obstinate treachery deserves.[142]

On October 9, General Loring learned Union forces had massed some 10,000 soldiers at Point Pleasant, with more on the way, and were planning to regain the Kanawha Valley. Loring wrote to Confederate Secretary of War George W. Randolph, informing him of the Federal build-up, but was only given a thin promise to send more artillery and infantry "when able." Loring prudently decided to plan his withdrawal from Charleston the next day.[143]

Assistant Surgeon John Rush Philson of the 4th West Virginia wrote a letter on October 14 addressed to various ladies and soldier aid groups of Meigs County, Ohio, thanking them for the bountiful supplies for the sick soldiers in the regimental hospital at Point Pleasant. Corporal Clarkson Fogg wrote on October 15 from camp at Point Pleasant that the 44th Ohio had left camp, and he claimed to have overheard captured rebels say one of their regiments, the one posted opposite the 4th West Virginia in the Charleston fight, lost 30 men killed and wounded. Fogg wrote further that the 4th regiment, posted on the upper side of Elk, had lost eight killed and wounded in Charleston battle. Fogg also mentioned that General Robert H. Milroy was recently assigned to command of the department, only "temporarily," with Colonel Lightburn in command of the Kanawha Division. He wrote that the Kanawha Division then consisted of seventeen regiments and pointed out that they had all recently finally received the much coveted supply of "knapsacks, blankets, and clothing...." Fogg lastly noted that with the 44th Ohio Infantry gone, the 1st Brigade then consisted of the 34th and 91st Ohio and the 4th and 13th West Virginia and was commanded by Colonel John T. Toland.[144]

On October 16, *The Weekly Register* reported that on the previous Sunday at Point Pleasant, the 4th and 13th West Virginia Infantries along with the 34th and 91st Ohio Infantries underwent an inspection, and the correspondent opined, "the 4th West Virginia is decidedly the best drilled regiment." Later that month, a scandal occurred when Major Lorenzo A. Phelps of the 5th West Virginia Infantry was a guest at the home of Major James H. Dayton's parents at New Creek. While visiting, Phelps became enamored with the Dayton's young daughter Rebecca and misrepresented himself as a single, religious man, when, in fact, he was married with a family and not religious.[145]

Rebecca fell for it and became infatuated with Phelps, and the next day they eloped together, visiting the towns of Piedmont, Franklinville (Franklin), and Parkersburg. Phelps later threatened to court marital any man who exposed the ruse. His coercive tactics failed, however, and when Major Dayton learned of the deceptive affair with his sister, he was infuriated and tracked Phelps down and shot him in the back. He survived but had severely damaged his reputation; on October 25 he wrote a letter to the editor of *The Weekly Register* from Millersport, Ohio, denying the accusations that he had lied to young Rebecca, hoping he had settled the matter in his favor.[146]

However, on December 16, Major Dayton's father published a detailed letter in the same news organ confirming that the allegations against Phelps were true. Later on August 10, 1863, the hapless Phelps was captured by Confederates at Guyandotte and incarcerated at Macon, Georgia, and he was later sent to Camp Asylum, in South Carolina. Phelps was eventually court martialed for the incident with Rebecca Dayton and was cashiered out of service. After the war, Phelps relocated to California, where he died in 1870 from a self-inflicted gunshot wound.[147]

Kanawha Expedition:
Lightburn's Advance

General Jacob Cox ordered Colonel Lightburn to begin his advance to re-take the Kanawha Valley on October 29 and move toward Buffalo in Putnam County. Lightburn found the Confederates waiting with three pieces of artillery posted in line of battle near Red House, and after a small skirmish, the Southerners retreated toward Charleston. Corporal Clarkson Fogg wrote from camp at Red House the next day that his division was comprised of nine regiments but was sorry to hear that "the band has been mustered out of the service...we are all in fine health and spirits."[148]

On the cold, snowy evening of October 25, General Loring realized he would soon be overpowered and decided to order a general withdrawal from the Kanawha Valley, although it took a few days to organize and execute the retreat. Meanwhile, Major General Jacob Cox arrived at Pocatalico to join Colonel Lightburn on October 27. He immediately sent out scouting parties to Scary Creek in Putnam County and to Tyler Mountain in Kanawha County, located near modern Cross Lanes. On the bitter cold morning of October 28, Loring finally began his retreat from Charleston toward Raleigh Court House in Fayette County.[149]

Late in the afternoon of October 29, Colonel Lightburn's main force arrived at a point two miles from Charleston, and the 37th and 89th Ohio Regiments reached the mouth of the Coal River near Coalsmouth that evening. At 2 a.m. the next morning, Cox's lead elements entered Charleston and discovered that the Confederates had left without a fight. During the next few days, Union troops filled the valley and soon recaptured the numerous salt works in the region. The 8th West Virginia Infantry then had companies spread throughout the Kanawha Valley, with companies posted as far east at Brownstown, near modern Marmet. On the morning of October 30, Corporal Clarkson Fogg indicated that the 1st and 2nd Brigades had both arrived at Charleston, but all were without tents, and Lightburn's troops were living in makeshift shanties comprised of tree branches and blankets or other covering as they might find.[150]

One elderly gentleman in Charleston was so elated to see Union troops in town again, he yelled out to the soldiers marching by, "God Bless you, God bless you, everyone!" and sang the *Star-Spangled Banner* aloud to them. The next day, another excited citizen yelled out to some infantry passing by their home, "By the Blessing of our Heavenly Father our soldiers occupy Charleston again!" Also on October 30, General Cox ordered the large force of Union troops stationed at Guyandotte and Barboursville to reopen communication with Charleston now that the Confederates had withdrawn from the area. The Kanawha Valley was once again in Union hands.[151]

On November 2, Corporal Fogg was encamped seven miles below the Gauley River. He wrote the next evening that the bulk of the regiment had arrived that day and were camped at the Tompkins Farm (Camp Gauley). On November 5, while at the Tompkins Farm, Private William V. Brown reported the weather was crisp and cool, and there was snow on the mountains nearly every morning; fortunately, however, he also noted some tents had arrived to give the men shelter.[152]

Sergeant Columbus Shrewsbury, Company A, further described the camp on November 8 as he wrote: "We are at Gauley yet and likely to stay for the winter if we had good Winter quarters, I would not care so much but we are in our tents yet and it has been snowing for two or three days and makes it disagreeable in tents. There are no rebels near us that we know of." 1st Lieutenant C. B. Blake, Company G, took the description a bit further on November 17, claiming Gauley Bridge was a "God forsaken place" and at least half of his company and regiment were without shirts while those who had them had not been able to wash their garments in almost a month. He said there were not enough tents as there were too many soldiers on the Kanawha to properly supply, and the horses were starving due to lack of hay. "I am getting damned tired of the service, such service as we have."[153]

Sergeant Shrewsbury made an effort to be optimistic about the poor conditions at Camp Gauley, telling his wife on November 19, "... we are expecting to move somewhere but don't know where. I hope they will move us out of this place to a better place. We have had a good Room to work in since we came here." On November 25 he added: "There is some talk about our going out to Fayetteville or the other side of it to stay this winter it is about twelve miles from here. I would no sooner go there than stay here as to places."[154]

Company F was camped about one mile below Gauley River on November 27, placing them in the vicinity of Kanawha Falls, where 1st Lieutenant William S. Hall penned: "How long we are to remain here is more than I can tell. We have heard today however that we are to be ordered to Fayetteville in a few days to go into winter quarters....

we have had a rather hard time of it for the last three months. I have seen the elephant but the elephant didn't see me....we are here almost surrounded by mountains...."[155]

William V. Brown confirmed Hall's description of the camp location, as he said on November 28 they were camped "one and a half miles below the Bridge" at the former camp of the 92nd Ohio Infantry. He felt it was a tolerable good camp and that Lightburn was back in command of the regiment as they were no longer in a brigade. "The boys think there is no such a man as Old Corporal Joe [Lightburn]. His word is law and Gospel with the Reg't. Wherever he leads the 4th will go, you may stake your bottom dollar on that....Our Reg't looks better since Col. Lightburn came back to us; stragglers, Staff officers, orderlies, etc., come in daily. Our Company has increased some; [Lt. John] Mallernee had to come back – he was aide-de-camp to Col. Toland – and 3 of the boys who were at Charleston or somewhere else sick came back today."[156]

The last hostile shots fired in the Kanawha Campaign occurred near Cannelton in late November 1862, when a bushwhacker fired upon Captain Patrick H. Brunker, Company H, with the ball passing through his cap "near the bugle in front" but doing no damage. Around the same time, Private John R. Morford, Company G, 2nd West Virginia Cavalry, received a wrist wound in a skirmish with General Albert G. Jenkins' rear guard near Malden, Virginia.[157]

With the first day of December, musician Adolphus De Bussey, Company F, mused: "The boys are pretty well at present. We are camped one-half mile below the mouth of Gauley close to the falls....I hope we will leave here before long. There is some talk of us going to Piatt to quarter this winter. We are short of tents and the boys are in the rocks and dens. They look like potato hills." According to the regimental order book, Colonel Lightburn was at Fayetteville the same day, probably examining the ground for winter quarters.[158]

Company E arrived at Gauley Bridge on December 4, according to John G. Farrar, Company E, where they found the remainder of the 4th West Virginia and the 12th Ohio Infantry. William V. Brown said they left Gauley in the afternoon and marched to Fayetteville, where Farrar said they "Built winter quarters and never got to go in them."[159]

Sergeant Columbus Shrewsbury was promoted to 2nd lieutenant of Company A on December 5. Though the inclement weather was the main issue on the mind of Clarkson Fogg; he said there had been three inches of snow at Fayetteville, and they were camped on the old battlefield near the fortifications. Private William V. Brown added: "The snow is now about 4 or 5 inches deep and cold as blazes....we are all well in our little tents....Gen. [Eliakim P.] Scammon is commanding here, nobody likes him. The 12th [Ohio] has sworn vengeance against him, say they will kill him the first chance, he is awful tyrannical."[160]

Brown continued his description of activities at Fayetteville on December 14, noting they were building log cabin barracks, but they probably would not be complete until after New Year's. Brown felt all the boys were well except "some of them are grunting [grumbling], including Capt. Goodspeed, Lt. Hankinson, and Ord. Serg. [William L.] Armstrong [Company D]." Brown also indicated the regiment was living in tents on December 21 and described the weather as "cold but tolerable." On December 27 Colonel Lightburn issued an order that gambling was "positively forbidden," which greatly annoyed many of his soldiers.[161]

If there had been any desire among Lightburn's men to leave the "backwoods theater" of the war and enter into major national events, it came on December 28 when the 30th, 37th, and 47th Ohio Infantries, along with the 4th West Virginia, under Brigadier General Hugh Ewing, were ordered out of the District of the Kanawha and sent to General Ulysses S. Grant's command on the Mississippi to participate in the Vicksburg Campaign and join the 15th Army Corps. Only the top-ranking officers knew of their destination for some time, but most of the men were elated just to participate in something they knew had to be of vast importance.[162]

While the 4th West Virginia was posted at Fayetteville, Brigadier General Scammon had Captain John L. Vance arrested on December 29 for intoxication on duty; Vance had alcohol on his breath when he appeared for duty that morning as Field Officer of the Day, which

Scammon would not tolerate under any circumstances. Several officers of the 4th West Virginia petitioned Scammon on Vance's behalf, praising him as a "worthy and dutiful soldier" and mentioned the many friends and influential family Vance had.[163]

Also on December 29, the 4th West Virginia was placed in Colonel Hugh Ewing's Brigade. Ewing was quite familiar with the regiment, having served under General Jacob D. Cox in the Kanawha Valley while commanding the 30th Ohio Infantry as part of the Kanawha Division. Ewing gained notoriety during the Maryland Campaign with Cox, as he led a ferocious charge on Confederates at the summit of South Mountain on September 14, 1862, and was given temporary command of the Kanawha Division when General Cox was placed in command of the Ninth Corps at the battle of Antietam. William V. Brown wrote that the regiment received orders at 11 p.m. that night to pack up and move to Cincinnati to join Ewing with the Army of the Tennessee. John Farrar, Company E, recalled the regiment promptly left Fayetteville, marched to Cannelton, boarded a boat at Brownstown and headed to Charleston on December 30. Arriving there the next day, the regiment continued on a boat along the Kanawha River to Gallipolis, Ohio, changed boats, and moved down the Ohio River toward Louisville, Kentucky, thus ending the second year of the war for the 4th West Virginia.[164]

Library of Congress.

3

1863
From Vicksburg to Missionary Ridge

Looking back on 1863 years later, Hospital Steward Thomas Barton of the 4th West Virginia Infantry recalled: "During the year 1863 the service of the regiment was hard and laborious. They were incessantly marching, fighting, or performing manual labor."[1]

In January 1863, the 4th West Virginia was sent to Mississippi to participate in General Ulysses S. Grant's Vicksburg Campaign, with the regiment serving directly under General William T. Sherman and his Army of the Tennessee. Early in this deployment, they were employed to assist in digging Grant's infamous canal, as well as a canal at Milliken's Bend, Louisiana. In May 1863, the 4th West Virginia participated in two major, but unsuccessful, bloody assaults on a near-impregnable Confederate fort known as Stockade Redan at Vicksburg. There, six men of the regiment earned the Medal of Honor. The actions of the regiment in the May 19 and 22 assaults on Stockade Redan and the siege aftermath played a key role in the eventual surrender of Vicksburg. With no time to rest, the regiment afterward fought at Jackson, Mississippi and participated in the operations against the railroad system between Corinth, Mississippi, and Chattanooga, Tennessee and also drove back a cavalry force at Tuscumbia, Alabama.

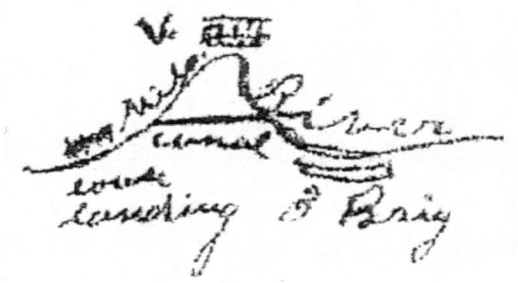

Sketch of Grant's Canal, by William V. Brown.
Brown Family Papers, Ohio. Ohio University Library.

Soon afterward the 4th West Virginia fought on the heights of Missionary Ridge, Tennessee, located near both Lookout Mountain and Chattanooga, then were called west again to help reinforce Knoxville, which was under siege.   With winter approaching, the depleted regiment went into winter quarters at Larkinsville, Alabama, ending the regiment's most violent year of war thus far.

Company A of the 4th West Virginia departed from Camp Piatt on January 1, according to the regimental record of events. Private Lewis Love of the company recalled:

Late in the fall [1862] the 4th West Virginia was sent to Fayetteville where we built winter quarters. I never slept in my shanty but one night. Next morning, we started for Vicksburg to join the army there. We landed in Gallipolis on New Year's Day," where the soldiers bid adieu to their wives and sweethearts. They were yet unaware of their destination and were not permitted to go ashore, but the ladies brought them canteens full of corn liquor. This resulted in numerous drunken soldiers, which the officers ignored. One unfortunate was "a few negroes on board....had to jump overboard to save their lives. One negro was pitched into the wheel from the top of the boat."[2]

Special Order No. 3 was issued on January 2 for the Department of the Ohio and detailed Brigadier General Hugh B. Ewing, then at Cincinnati, to move his brigade, composed of the 30th, 37th, and 47th Ohio infantry regiments, as well as the 4th West Virginia Infantry, from Fayetteville to Louisville, Kentucky. There he was to report to Brigadier General J.T. Boyle, commanding the District of Western Kentucky. On this same day, 2nd Lieutenant Columbus Shrewsbury, Company A, 4th West Virginia, who was aboard the steamboat *Glenwood* at Cincinnati, wrote: "We are laying here on the boat waiting orders. Do not know where we shall go yet. We had a very pleasant trip down. The Boys all in fine spirits singing and cheering all the way down."[3]

Company C arrived at Louisville on January 3, according to the regimental record of events. William V. Brown of Company D said he marched to the commons at the foot of Broadway in Louisville and went into camp, although the regiment was short on tents. Columbus Shrewsbury wrote, "We are now at this place but don't know what route we will go from here." Shrewsbury also observed, "I am glad that we have a new state which will make the property [his farm] more valuable in West Virginia." A number of courts martial also took place within the ranks of the 4th West Virginia while at Louisville in January.[4]

The regiment remained at Louisville until January 7, when Company C shipped aboard the steamer *Aurora*, an event also mentioned by musician Adolphus De Bussey, who wrote, "got marching orders at three o'clock and went on board the *Aurora* and remained there all night." John G. Farrar, Company E, simply wrote, "Boarded another boat–went through the locks of the canal," while Columbus Shrewsbury added, possibly on January 4: "We are under marching orders. Which way we will go I don't know but I think likely the River to Nashville, Tennessee....Yesterday was a very cold day here. The wind blew hard all day which made it very disagreeable to be out in Tents without fire."

William V. Brown bluntly added the regiment left Louisville. January 7 also marked the day Private Joseph Roush of Company C deserted, and he did return to the regiment on April 27.[5]

According to Adolphus De Bussey, the 4th West Virginia was going through the canal at Louisville on January 8 and was near Evansville, Indiana, on the 9th, where he wrote, "The boys are in good spirits." Both Brown and De Bussey said the regiment arrived at Smithland at the mouth of the Cumberland River on January 10. The next day Columbus Shrewsbury reported from Cairo, Illinois: "We are all right. Going down to Vicksburg. The boat will land here a few minutes.... the boat is whistling to land." William Brown, however, said he was on the steamer *Aurora* at Smithland, Kentucky, on January 11 and left the same day. It was at this time that Lieutenant Colonel William H.H. Russell, Major James H. Dayton, and Lieutenant John Mallernee were ordered to make a report of the camp and garrison equipage lost in Lightburn's retreat from Charleston in September 1862.[6]

January 13 found the regiment at Memphis, Tennessee, according to Columbus Shrewsbury, who wrote, "We arrived here today about 11 o'clock and have orders to go down the River farther I suppose to Vicksburg....have had a very pleasant trip so far." Commenting on the situation at Memphis, Shrewsbury noted: "There is two or three gunboats here. They look savage. The rebels came from the other side of the river the other night to this place and stole a steamboat and took her over the river and burned her up....this is a beautiful city principally all brick buildings ..."[7]

The following day the regiment left Memphis for Napoleon, Arkansas, arriving on January 16, where they joined the main fleet heading for Vicksburg. On January 17 Columbus Shrewsbury noted: "Our trip has been a crowded one. There is a good many complaining of colds. We landed here yesterday. When we got here there was thirty-three gunboats loaded with troops. Now I suppose there is between fifty and seventy steamboats with troops. I suppose it will not be long before we strike out for the Rebels somewhere (guess Vicksburg)." Adolphus De Bussey added that the previous three days had been the "coldest" weather ever known in the region and eight inches of snow had fallen 40 miles below Memphis. He also took notice that General William T. Sherman was gathering transports to convey his army.[8]

The 4th West Virginia departed Napoleon on January 19 to Young's Point, Louisiana, having covered 1,400 miles since leaving Fayetteville, (West) Virginia. John G. Farrar, Company E, wrote: "There was about 100 boats loaded left the mouth of White River one morning for Vicksburg. We arrived....on the Louisiana side...." but De Bussey said they landed at Milliken's Bend, Louisiana.[9]

Young's Point, Louisiana
January 21, 1863
Arrival for the Vicksburg Campaign

The Vicksburg Campaign encompassed two major operations, the first from December 29, 1862, to January 11, 1863, and General Ulysses S. Grant's operations against Vicksburg from March 29, 1863, to July 4, 1863. Vicksburg, defended by the Confederate forces of Lieutenant General John C. Pemberton, was the final Confederate stronghold maintaining control of the Mississippi River. The 4th West Virginia moved to Young's Point, Louisiana, on January 21, and was assigned to the 2nd Division, 15th Army Corps. William V. Brown, Company D, recalled they arrived opposite the mouth of the Yazoo River, on the Louisiana side, 12 miles above Vicksburg.[10]

Grant's Canal

Grant's Canal, also known as Williams' Canal, was a military project to divert the flow of the Mississippi River by digging a canal through De Soto Point in Louisiana. This project was intended to provide a means for Union naval forces to bypass the Confederate fortifications at Vicksburg and move past the city unmolested. It was begun in 1862 by Union General Thomas Williams, but following numerous problems, it was abandoned until General Grant resumed the project in 1863. Most people, including Grant, did not have much faith in the idea but persisted anyway. From January 22 to February 7, the 4th West Virginia was camped near Grant's Canal in order to work on it every other day. Hospital Steward Thomas Barton wrote in his autobiography, "Soon after our arrival....the regiment was put on fatigue duty, and the boys did their share in the construction of the canal opposite Vicksburg.... we were placed in the Third Brigade, with the 36th [should be the 30th], 37th and 47th Ohio regiments, commanded by Gen. [Joseph A.J.] Lightburn, who had been promoted to Brigadier-General. The brigade was placed in the second division of the fifteenth army corps, commanded by Gen. W. T. Sherman."[11]

Head of Grant's Canal.
Leslie's Illustrated, March 21, 1863.
Library of Congress.

Paper Collar, Bandbox Soldiers

The 4th West Virginia quickly found themselves the object of ridicule from the battle hardened veterans of the Western Theater. The only West Virginia unit in the XV Corps, when they arrived with neatly fixed kepis and relatively new uniforms it drew the immediate attention and ire of the seasoned western troops, most of whom wore dirty, well-worn uniforms and old black slouch hats. They mercilessly teased the "fresh fish" from the east, knowing they would soon have to prove themselves in battle. Civil War historian Edwin G. Bearss wrote, "The newcomers with their kepis and paper collars are called 'bandbox' soldiers by battered hat-wearing and raggedy-ass Westerners." The western veterans also felt they had been winning fights while the eastern boys had a losing track record, although any doubts that the men in the 4th West Virginia could fight would soon be put to rest forever.[12]

Regimental records indicate that Company C arrived at Young's Point on January 25, which would imply the various companies of the regiment arrived at different times and may have been on separate boats. Private Lewis Love of Company A recalled: "We had a very easy time while sojourning on Young's Point, except when digging the ditch. As we called it. We had no duty to perform except to answer roll-call morning and evening. The rest of the time was spent to suit ourselves. No guard duty at all – the enemy was on the other side of the river, and they could not swim."[13]

Surgeon George K. Ackley requested a discharge on grounds of disability for Lieutenant Colonel William H.H. Russell on January 29, due to Russell's chronic hepatitis and a bone problem. On the same day William S. Hall, Company F, wrote home, "I am very happy to write that I am well and our boys as a general thing are healthy though some of the regiments of our army here are most all sick and dying at the rate of from eight to twelve per day." Hall also wrote about the military situation, noting that "...we are within range of the Rebel guns. They amuse themselves every day by throwing shells at us from their batteries but as yet they have done no damage....we are digging a canal around Vicksburg so that we can pass through with our gunboats and transports." The following day, the 30th, General Ulysses S. Grant accepted Lieutenant Colonel Russell's resignation, and Adolphus De Bussey noted the regiment had been working every day on the canal since arriving at camp: "The Canal is working very slow. It don't cut fast. There is 8 feet of water in it now."[14]

The month of January 1863 ended with Private Arthur Forbes, Company B, 4th West Virginia, dying of disease in camp, while Corporal Clarkson Fogg noted the weather was comfortable, with frost once or twice. He added that troops were arriving daily and there was often artillery skirmishing.[15]

Yazoo Pass Expedition
February 1 – February 3, 1863

During February and March of 1863, the 4th West Virginia continued to assist with the canal. John G. Farrar recalled: "We went to work on the canal. Worked it until they got Negroes enough to fill it from one end to the other." According to Farrar, as a preliminary move to General Grant's Yazoo Pass Expedition, on February 1 "About 400 of us got on a steamer, the *Diligence*, a cotton boat, and went up the river about 40 miles to hunt a route for boats to run through bayous and get below Vicksburg. We started from Milliken's Bend on the morning of 1st of February 1863. Traveled all day, camped that night at Round Bayou close to Richmond, Louisiana. Next morning we got up early so we could make the river below Vicksburg that day. We were getting breakfast before daylight, the Reb's fired a volley at short range, about 75 yards across the bayou, and wounded two of our no. [number] Don't see how it come they did not hit half of us...." The men were nearly surrounded, which compelled the boat's return to Milliken's Bend. On the evening of February 3, the detachment of 400 men boarded a steamer at Milliken's Bend and returned to camp at Young's Point.[16]

The 4th West Virginia ended their work on Grant's Canal on February 7 because the Mississippi River rose, threatening to overflow the canal on the lowlands and forcing the 4th West Virginia to the lower landing at Young's Point. On February 12 Columbus Shrewsbury reflected: "We are laying right across the river from Vicksburg. We can see the Rebels on duty some days. They shoot their cannons at us. We have been digging a Canal changing the course of the River, but I don't think it will do much good. I think it is more to draw their attention of them in that direction while we operate in another." Private Lewis Love of Company A added, "I have always thought that it was only a scheme to deceive the enemy or furnish exercise for the soldiers."[17]

Shrewsbury surmised the plight of the 4th West Virginia on February 16, as he wrote from his post "Opposite Vicksburg." He reiterated his comments from the 12th, further observing: "We are here just across the River from Vicksburg. Can see the Rebels on duty and some days they amuse themselves by throwing shell at us but have done us no damage yet. We are digging a canal to pass around the place which I don't think will ever do any good....We have only lost four men in the Regiment....Several of our officers are on the sick list - J. H. Ralston, Ong, Mansell, Dayton and others but all getting better. Some would like their resignations, but they are not so easily gotten here as in Virginia." Shrewsbury went on to write: "We have had some mud here. It has been raining for several days. The boys was drowned out of their tents night before last. They did not grumble much as the Colonel sent for a Barrel of Whiskey and that dried their feet."[18]

Writing from the lower landing at Young's Point on February 18, William V. Brown cast a dark image of the regiment as he penned: "About half of our Reg't have been sick since we have been here, most of them with the diarrhea, three have died with fever. Our Company has lost one, G. F. Waugh [19-year-old Private George F. Waugh, Company D, died of typhoid fever February 11], he lived at Swan Creek, Gallia Co., Ohio. The health of the regiment is improving now fast."[19]

Brown noted the regiment had previously desired to be moved out of West Virginia but now wanted to go back as "they have seen enough of the elephant....For my part I think I have seen enough." Graphically describing the situation, Brown continued, "I have seen men buried by the hundreds, seen a hole dug 4 feet deep and 6 or 8 men tumbled in like hogs, with nothing on except their clothes, the dirt thrown in on them, and before night the wagons had run over them till they had cut the ground up and their feet were sticking out. It was no uncommon thing when we first came here to see them wheel men off of the hospital boats on a wheelbarrow and dump them into a hole and cover it up and that was the last of them."[20]

By March 1, Brown wanted to resign but no resignations were being accepted at that time. Adolphus De Bussey wrote: "There is nothing doing here at present. They have renewed the work on the canal, they are digging it wider," while Clarkson Fogg observed: "the 'Yankee Ditch' as the rebels call it, progresses slowly, on account of the high water, and wet weather. It will be rendered comparatively useless, in my opinion, from this fact: that the enemy have some of their heaviest guns planted so as to command the mouth of the canal, five or six miles below he city."[21]

Clarkson Fogg and Columbus Shrewsbury both discussed the health and well-being of the regiment on March 2, with Fogg reporting, "Our regiment is very healthy, and we keep the nicest and cleanest camp in the army," while Shrewsbury added: "Our Brigade has the praise of being the best troops here. Our Regiment has the praise of the best here in every respect by every person also said to be the largest Regiment here. We have lost but five men by sickness since we came here."[22]

Death of Corporal William Van Brown

Tragically, Corporal William V. Brown, Company D, who left a detailed chronicle of the regiment in his letters home, came down with a case of smallpox and died on March 8. Brown was promoted to Corporal on November 5, 1862. Before passing, he was moved to the hospital at Milliken's Bend, Louisiana, as they had better medical facilities. On April 19, Brown's close friend and comrade who was with him in his final hours, Private Robert W. Davis, Company D, wrote Brown's mother and told her that when he visited her son, he had the best of care, but his body and face were covered with scabs and sores and Brown had lost his sight, although he retained his rational mind. He added that after Brown died, he "was buried [at] about ten. I am sorry to inform you the way he was buried as he and two others were buried in one grave without any coffin as it could not be helped. There was no tools or lumber to make him a box or anything of the kind so I hope you will not think hard of me as it could not be helped. The only way he could be recognized would be by his blankets that are around him. It would not be safe to send for him as the surgeon in charge says he could not let him go on account of the disease being catching." Private Davis would lose his left arm in the fighting at Vicksburg on June 13.[23]

The Mississippi River rose dramatically on March 9. Captain John Luther Vance was promoted to major of the regiment that day also. Clarkson Fogg lamented: "The canal having been nearly completed, the water at the head, where it had been dammed up, broke through into the canal, and from thence into the bottoms below, which caused the work to be suspended; only a few trees remained in the canal to be removed, and it would have been finished. It was 60 feet wide, and deep enough to float any boat on the river...." Fogg added that "the river continues to rise and would flood Young's Point if not for the levee that was built," and recalled hearing cannonading "below and above on Yazoo River."[24]

Chaplain George S. Woodhull of the 4th West Virginia was appointed chaplain of Ewing's Brigade on March 10, while the next day Surgeon Ackley resigned due to a six-year history of lung disease and cholera. On March 12, Colonel Lightburn requested that Governor Pierpont accept Ackley's resignation and replace him with Dr. John Rush Philson, along with Homer C. Watterman as 1st assistant surgeon. He also requested another assistant surgeon.[25]

Chaplain George Woodhull.
Terry Lowry Collection.

Steele's Bayou Expedition
March 14 – March 27

The Steele's Bayou Expedition, which Lightburn called the expedition to Rolling Fork, took place between March 14 and March 27. It was a joint Union offensive by Major General Ulysses S. Grant's Army of the Tennessee, combining infantry with the naval forces of Rear Admiral David D. Porter's Mississippi River Squadron in the Steele's Bayou region north of Vicksburg. The purpose was to establish protection from enemy fire for Union naval vessels to traverse that area of the Yazoo River and to open a gate to the east of Vicksburg. The initial phase went well, but once in the muddy and curving small canals near their destination, the boats became stuck and were then harassed by rebel gun fire. Porter was on the verge of abandoning his boats when the infantry of General William T. Sherman, which included the 4th West Virginia, arrived and drove off the rebels, giving

Porter time to extricate his boat and return to safety. The expedition proved to be a failure.[26]

Prior to the expedition, the 4th West Virginia underwent a significant organizational change on March 14, when Colonel Lightburn was officially appointed a brigadier general and ordered to report to the Army of the Tennessee. His troops in the 4th West Virginia were joyful at the good news for Lightburn but, at the same time, saddened to lose their beloved commander.[27]

In Lightburn's official report of the expedition, he noted that on the morning of March 17 the 4th West Virginia marched to Young's Point, embarked on the *Silver Moon,* and moved to Eagle Bend. While at Eagle Bend, Private William Lewis Safreed, Company F, 4th West Virginia, who was from the Little Sandy area of Jackson County, West Virginia, wrote in his diary, "Ordered to build a raft to go through a muddy bayou." Clarkson Fogg disputed the departure date, writing that the division left on March 18.[28]

Lightburn's report went on to state they disembarked from the boat on the morning of March 19 and bivouacked on the plantation of Senator William M. Gwinn, a California senator who yet maintained slaves in his home state of Mississippi. None of this activity deterred more organizational changes in the regiment, however, as Major James H. Dayton was promoted to lieutenant colonel of the 4th West Virginia and 2nd Lieutenant William S. Hall was promoted to captain of Company F. Hall, born in April of 1836 in Virginia, was a farmer at Prairie, Kosciusko County, Indiana, in 1860, but was residing at Murraysville, Jackson County, (West) Virginia a year later. He was made 1st lieutenant of Company F, 4th West Virginia, on July 30, 1861.

Capt. William S. Hall.
Courtesy Chris Propes.

James H. Dayton.
Terry Lowry Collection.

Additionally, 2nd Lieutenant James H. Ralston was promoted to 1st lieutenant of Company E.[29]

Lightburn and the 4th West Virginia received orders on March 20 to clean out Muddy Bayou for the passage of flatboats. Lightburn sent nine companies of the 4th West Virginia forward under the command of Lieutenant Colonel James H. Dayton. One company was left behind to do the work at Muddy Bayou, while Dayton's command moved to Black Bayou and disembarked at Hill's plantation.[30]

William L. Safreed, Company F, reported that he was still at Eagle Bend on March 21, and Clarkson Fogg just referred to his location at "Camp above Vicksburg." Fogg went on to relate he had arrived by boat, and commissioners from the "new State" of West Virginia were present, questioning men from the regiment whether or not they thought the new state should be free or remain a slave state. A majority of soldiers from the regiment agreed that West Virginia should be a free state. Also on this date, Governor Francis Pierpont noted he was displeased the 4th West Virginia had been sent south, and Safreed added that Brigadier General David Stuart was not confirmed, so Brigadier General Hugh Ewing became the 2nd Division commander for the present.[31]

Safreed indicated the regiment marched 20 miles, from Eagle Bend to Black Bayou, on March 22 and on the following day, the 4th West Virginia arrived at Hill's plantation. Next the 4th West Virginia was sent to meet and protect the gunboats and troops returning from the Steele's Bayou Expedition. Praise was given to Major John L. Vance of the regiment "who was detained as a field officer in command of the details ordered from each regiment to accompany and guard the stores on the *Silver Wave*. He was of very great service and assistance to me in every way, in embarking and disembarking, distributing, and regulating the distribution of the rations, ammunition, &c. He is very faithful, assiduous, and intelligent officer." Safreed also simply noted, "Marched 7 miles up Deer Creek to meet Gen. Sherman."[32]

Brigadier General Lightburn had assumed command of the 2nd Brigade, 2nd Division, 15th Corps, Army of the Tennessee, and noted in his report the 4th West Virginia moved up the left-hand fork of Deer

Creek, where they met the infantry and gunboats about five miles above Hill's plantation.[33]

On March 24, in connection with Colonel Augustus Parry of the 47th Ohio Infantry, and the 4th West Virginia, the troops moved back toward Hill's plantation. William Safreed said they marched back to Black Bayou, where he went on guard duty as skirmishing persisted throughout the night. Safreed summed up the situation, writing, "We marched in mud up to our ass."[34]

Lightburn said he arrived back at Hill's plantation on the morning of March 25, while Safreed said he was on the captured farm of Confederate General Smith. At 12 a.m. on March 26, the Union troops embarked on the gunboats *Louisville* and *Pittsburg* and headed back to Young's Point.[35]

The 4th West Virginia arrived at Young's Point Bottom on the evening of March 27, thereby ending the Steele's Bayou Expedition. The failure marked Grant's last attempt to attack the Confederate right flank, and he turned his attention to the Confederate left flank. Lightburn suffered no casualties on the expedition, except for a tree limb that fell on the head of the 4th West Virginia's assistant surgeon Dr. John Rush Philson, wounding him severely.[36]

Various members of the 4th West Virginia wrote of the expedition, often with some conflicting views and order of events. Corporal Clarkson Fogg wrote they moved 30 to 40 miles north of Young's Point to Senator Gwinn's plantation and the following day marched across the bayou and then boated to General J. R. Hill's plantation. He noted a few days earlier the gunboats were trapped by Confederate soldiers, where the Sunflower River empties into the Yazoo River above Hillsdale (Haine's Bluff), as the Confederates had obstructed the bayou two miles from where the Sunflower and Yazoo met. Fogg blamed the failure of the naval operation on whiskey and/or liquor given by the operation's planners. Fogg boasted: "Our regiment had the largest number of any in the Division, about 460. We were gone ten days, and in that time there were 3 men died, belonging to the 4th. Inefficiency and recklessness in the Medical Department is one great cause of such fatality among the sick. Fever and diarrhea are the principal diseases, the latter in many cases, assuming a chronic form. My Company has had no deaths since coming South."[37]

William S. Hall, relating his version, said they left Gwinn's plantation at 5 p.m., and then marched two miles and embarked on the steamer *Eagle*. The regiment landed on General Hill's plantation the same evening, then went 23 miles and encamped. The next day, at about twelve o'clock, the command was ordered to advance five miles up the bayou where they took possession of a bridge and held it until General Sherman joined them. The 4th West Virginia encamped for the night on Shelby's plantation "of Uncle Tom notoriety." Hall further wrote, "we lay out in the field without any tents and it rained all night incessantly." The next morning they were ordered back to the river, where they waded back to Hill's plantation in mud and water two feet deep. At Hill's, the men embarked on the gunboat *Louisville* and "after a somewhat tedious and perilous voyage on Black and Steele's bayous" reached the Mississippi on March 27 having been gone ten days.[38]

Hospital Steward Thomas Barton wrote in his autobiography, "I was with the regiment on the Steele's Bayou or Deer Creek expedition, and was left on Steele's Bayou, together with the chaplain, Rev. Woodhull, and a few of the hospital nurses, and some stragglers from the regiment."[39]

The weather was warm, and the river level was falling on March 28 at Young's Point, but tragedy struck the 4th West Virginia on March 30. While the 4th West Virginia was serving in the Vicksburg Campaign, one member, who was left behind in West Virginia, met a tragic end. Private Duckett T. Pritchett, Company I, 4th West Virginia, had apparently deserted or left his company for some reason in 1862 and was now at Point Pleasant awaiting transportation to his regiment. During this time Confederate General Albert Gallatin Jenkins was raiding through the Kanawha Valley and attempted an attack on the Union troops stationed at the Mason County courthouse. Captain John Carter of the 13th West Virginia Infantry had about 60 men from Company E of the 13th West Virginia Infantry and some local militia defending the town. Duckett Pritchett was ordered to assist in holding the line during the assault and was shot in the head and died instantly while defending the courthouse.[40]

Back along the Deep South waterways, Hospital Steward Thomas Barton reflected on the health of the regiment. He recalled on March 31, "Throughout February and March the rain was almost incessant. During part of the time it rained from morning till night....the Regiment lost" 31 men due to sickness while at Young's Point and Milliken's Bend; two at Van Buren Hospital; one aboard a steamer; two at the general hospital in St. Louis, Missouri; and one on the hospital steamer *R. C. Wood.* This added up to a total of 37 from January 20 to the first week in May. Barton wrote: "Several died who were at the convalescent camp at Milliken's Bend, one or two died who had been sent away sick, and four were discharged for disability at these places: at Charleston, West Va., two; at St. Louis, one; at Gallipolis, Ohio, two; at Columbus, Ohio, one; total ten. There were two desertions making a total loss of forty-nine men."[41]

The 4th West Virginia received orders to work on the canal at Milliken's Bend, Louisiana, on April 2. William S. Hall added to Thomas Barton's assessment of the health of the men, writing from Young's Point: "It's becoming very unhealthy here. We have lost two men within the last four days from disease. R. A. Holmes [Private Robert A. Holmes – chronic diarrhea March 18] and William R. Lowe [Private William R. Low–unknown cause March 30 at Milliken's Bend]....We are, however, in as good spirits as could be expected under the circumstances." Hall said all but the sick had gone about four miles to work on the canal at Milliken's Bend and added, "We are having a grand review right in the rear of our camp....General Stewart is reviewing two of his brigades."[42]

William Safreed wrote in his diary that between April 3 and 5 he was in camp, and his company was on brigade guard, while on April 6 he wrote, "In camp doing nothing." Between April 7 and 9 he said he did camp police duty, and on April 7 he wrote from Young's Point: "the boys most all well but nearly all have been sick and four out of our company have died. Their names are Perry Lions [probably Private James P. Lyons, Company G – small pox on March 23 at Van Buren Hospital, Milliken's Bend, Louisiana], Marshall Lions [Private

Marshall Lyons, Company G – chronic diarrhea March 30 at Young's Point], Robert Minor [Private Robert Miner. Company G – chronic diarrhea and remittent fever April 5 at Milliken's Bend] and [Private] George Buck [Company G – chronic diarrhea March 16 at Young's Point]. I feel in hopes that we will have better health now as our camp is dry and cleaner than it was possible to keep when the Regiment was on the Canal below here."[43]

Work on the new canal at Milliken's Bend was the concern of Columbus Shrewsbury on April 8, as he wrote home from Young's Point: "...have commenced digging a new Canal which goes out about twelve miles above Vicksburg and comes into the River about six miles below Vicksburg. It is thought by some that it will do some good." William Safreed confirmed he was working on the Milliken's Bend canal on April 11 and performing camp police duty the following day.[44]

The camp of the 4th West Virginia was besieged by heavy rains on April 12 and 13, and on April 14 the 4th West Virginia was on guard from General Sherman's headquarters to the lower canal. Safreed said he did police duty at General Ewing's on April 20 and noted the 4th West Virginia went to hear a general give a speech on April 21. On the 23rd, Safreed went to Milliken's Bend to help unload a steamboat, and between April 24 and April 26, 100 men from the 4th West Virginia and 100 from the 37th Ohio Infantry were tasked to unload freight from steamboats.[45]

Yet at Young's Point on April 27, Columbus Shrewsbury wrote: "There is an order now to send all sick soldiers to the nearest Hospital to their home that have been sick three months. I have been sick over three months...." The next day William Grayum added: "We are not doing much here and from appearances there is a prospect of this part of the army remaining quiet for some time yet. We expected to move today but the order was countermanded and now it is doubtful if we leave here at all as it will be necessary to keep a strong force in front of Vicksburg to pester the Rebels and keep them in exercise."[46]

During April 1863, the 4th West Virginia took part in expeditions to Steele's and Black Bayou, Mississippi, and on April 30, participated in the feint movement upon Haines Bluff under General William T.

Sherman. Also during April 1863, the 4th West Virginia remained in the 2nd Division with 550 men present for duty. The 2nd Division departed Young's Point on transports early on April 29 and moved to within five miles of Hayne's Bluff to look for the enemy. As part of Sherman's advance guard on April 30, they marched some two to three miles up the river, where "The Rebs threw some shells at us. We fell back to the boats and lay overnight." Clarkson Fogg said the infantry was used only to draw the attention of the rebels as a feint. The 2nd Division then returned to Young's Point on the first day of May.[47]

On May 2, the 4th West Virginia was sent to Milliken's Bend, where on May 3, Clarkson Fogg reported the weather was dry and excessively warm. Columbus Shrewsbury wrote of the recent events in a letter he composed on May 4: "We have moved up above our old camping ground about twenty-five miles. It is a much better place to camp than where we have been. It is not so low or filthy. Our Regiment was out on a scout last week in company with the Gunboats up the Yazoo River. The boats attacked Hayne's Bluff [sic] a very fortified place. The object of the expedition was to draw the attention of the Rebels in that direction while we crossed troops over the River down below the Town."[48]

Between May 5 and May 8, the 4th West Virginia toiled in daily camp life at Young's Point, often performing fatigue and guard duty. Elsewhere, on May 9, Brigadier General Lightburn, in Wheeling per request of General William C. Schenck, complimented Adjutant General H.J. Samuels and the citizens and U.S. soldiers (probably referring to the Jones–Imboden Raid). In addition, Lieutenant Colonel James H. Dayton was commissioned colonel and Major John Luther Vance was promoted to lieutenant colonel of the 4th West Virginia.[49]

Clarkson Fogg reflected upon these promotions, and the health of the regiment, on May 11 as he scribed: "All the regiments of our brigade, except the 30th Ohio, have returned from Milliken's Bend.... General Lightburn will not return to this Department, having been ordered to report to General Ambrose Burnside, so I was told by Col. Dayton yesterday. Our officers are: Col. J. H. Dayton, Lt. Col. [John] Luther Vance [son of Alexander Vance], Maj. A. M. Goodspeed....A

Surgeon, Quarter Master, Major, Captain, two Lieutenants, and an Orderly Sergeant have been appointed for the Negro regiment from the 4th....One of our Company E died the other day, the only one from sickness since the company organized....The health of our regiment is excellent."[50]

Fogg also mentioned seeing "a Negro regiment" from the "4th." He was likely the 2nd Mississippi Infantry (African Descent), which was in the area at that time. That regiment was later re-designated as the 52nd United States Colored Infantry in 1864, and was officered by men from various state regiments, such as Ohio, Illinois, and Indiana, as well as the 4th West Virginia.[51]

Sergeant Major Charles Holstein of the 4th West Virginia, whom Lightburn had placed in charge of all his artillery during the 1862 Kanawha Valley Campaign, was appointed major of the 2nd Mississippi on May 13, 1863. Hospital Steward Thomas Barton recalled that near this time he was appointed surgeon of the 2nd Mississippi, but after a short time, decided not to take the appointment; however, his service record says the recommended appointment was declined by authorities due to "incompetence."[52]

The 4th West Virginia, now under the command of Colonel James H. Dayton, received orders on May 12 as part of the 2nd Division to move to the front with General Lightburn's brigade. As of May 14, the 4th West Virginia had marched more than 100 miles in three days to reach the 15th Corps in time for the assault on Vicksburg, with a census of 550 men present for duty. Joseph Saunier of the 47th Ohio Infantry claimed that on the night of the 13th, five companies of the 4th West Virginia, the 37th Ohio, and a battery from the brigade boarded the *Forest Queen* boat. Their destination, Grand Gulf, was reached on the night of May 14, where Thomas Barton said the town "looked dismal and desolate when we entered it, not a citizen could be seen on the streets....Our brigade remained at this place one day, when we received marching orders, and at once set out for the front." While at Grand Gulf, William S. Hall reported, "The boys are in good health and spirits and eager to get to the front." Hall also complained of the intense heat.[53]

The 4th West Virginia marched 22 miles from Grand Gulf on May 16 and could hear the sounds of the battle at nearby Champion's Hill (Big Black River). The regiment marched an additional 24 miles the following day, again noted by Thomas Barton, who wrote: "On the 17th, we passed to the south and west of Champion's Hill, and crossed Baker's Creek where Pemberton's army crossed on their retreat. We passed through some cleared fields, and saw the ravages caused by the battle. The fences were thrown down and every vestige of vegetation trampled out of existence. On our way through these fields we saw a number of dead horses lying on the ground. Passing through a belt of timber, we saw several human bodies lying by the roadside, and covered with blankets. I suppose these persons were dead....Such scenes as these are sickening....We had a hard march that day, and we went into camp about five miles east of the Big Black River, and about twenty-five miles east of Vicksburg."[54]

Barton further elaborated on May 18, "We were on the march at an early hour, and when near the Big Black, learned that a battle had been fought on the preceding day....We crossed the Big Black on a pontoon, where the battle of the 17th, had been fought....the day was excessively hot....Since the 12th, we had marched about eighty miles in an irregular circle around Vicksburg, and our camp that night was about seven miles east of our starting point." Corporal William L. Safreed, Company F, jotted in his diary: "Came to first battlefield and marched on Rebs fortifications. Battle begins."[55]

Assault on Stockade Redan
and the
Death of Major Arza Goodspeed
May 19, 1863

Vicksburg was surrounded by a massive network of large, earthen forts garrisoned by Confederate Lieutenant General John C. Pemberton, a West Pointer and Mexican War veteran. He commanded the Department of the Mississippi and eastern Louisiana and was now faced with the perilous task of defending Vicksburg from the Union army, which was conglomerated around the city under General Grant. Known among the Confederate high command as an excellent officer and field commander, Pemberton was frequently hampered by conflicting orders from the very outset of the Vicksburg campaign; despite this, he was poised to offer a stubborn defense of the city.

The Confederate position at Vicksburg featured a complex series of forts located along Graveyard Road, the key access route into town. At the apex or center of this network stood a massive, and near impregnable, earthen fortification known as Stockade Redan. In Civil War era engineering parlance, the term redan was used to describe a large, triangular-shaped fort with the point or apex extending forward into the area of battle. This triangular shape allowed occupying troops to fire into the flanks—far left and right sides—of an oncoming army at close range. As such, this massive network of forts became known as the "Gibraltar of the Confederacy." In addition, the Confederates also built a poplar log stockade wall extending across Graveyard Road connecting the lunette, a smaller, half-moon shaped fort located on the left, to the Redan, which was garrisoned by the 27th Louisiana Infantry. Because this position served as the main gatekeeper protecting access into the city, it became the focus of a massive Union assault ordered by Grant on May 19. According to Joseph Saunier of the 47th Ohio Infantry, "This fort [Stockade Redan] was flanked on the right and left by long rifle pits, with a deep ditch next to our lines."[56]

The assault was a bloody and costly failure. General Hugh Ewing reported:

>...at 2 P.M. we charged the works of the enemy in line of battle, the 37th Ohio on the right, the 47th Ohio on the left, the 4th West Va in the center, and the 30th Ohio in reserve. The left of our line under Cols. [Augustus] Parry [of the 47th Ohio] and Dayton reached the enemies entrenchments, and the colors of the regiment waved near them until evening. The right, on account of obstacles, were unable to cross the ravine, but covered the left in its advance position by a heavy fire. Later

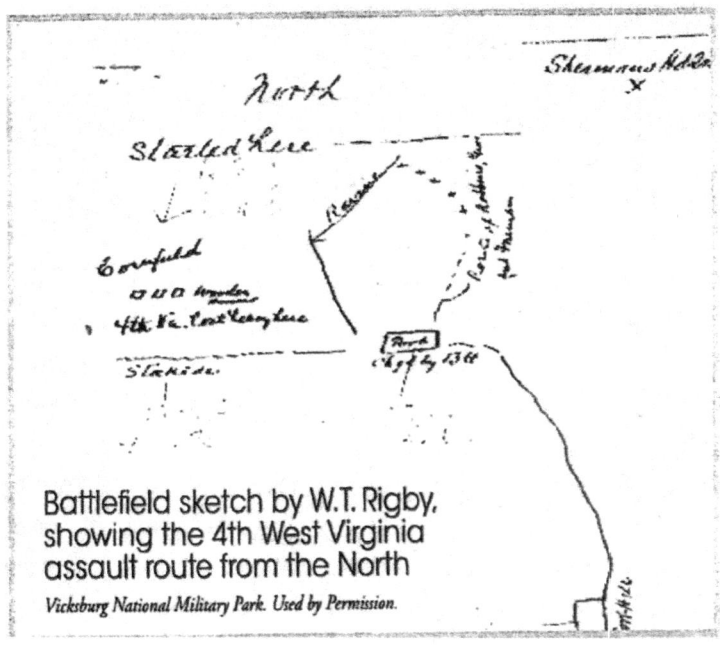

Hand drawn map by Private W.T. Rigby, Co. C, 13th U.S. Regulars
of the 4th West Virginia assault path on Stockade Redan, May 19, 1863.
Vicksburg National Military Park.

Brigadier General Hugh Ewing.
Library of Congress.

the remaining regiments were moved to the left brow of the hill. Prepared on the agreed signal from the brigade on our left to move over the track of the preceding portion of the brigade, and, joining them, renew the assault. I instructed the artillery to open upon the works when our line began to ascend the opposite hill. They, however, opened before the signal was given and the troops, already over, supposed the firing was to enable them to retire under cover, moved back, and the signal not being given, the charge was not renewed. From this to the 22nd my front skirmished along the enemies' entrenchments.[57]

The 13th U.S. Regulars were posted in line of battle to the left of Ewing's Brigade in the May 19 assault, and witnessed the ferocious charge made by the 4th West Virginia. Their attack left a lasting impression on those soldiers, who could vividly recall details several years after the war. Private W.T. Rigby, Company C, 13th U.S. Regulars, witnessed the attack and wrote about it shortly afterward. He described the terrain in front of the Redan where General Francis Blair's Division assaulted the confederate works: "...that the ground in front and on which the action occurred is a succession of hills and ravines covered with thick growth of oak brush and canes, and fallen trees, tops facing us, many of the limbs sharpened and wire strung to strike us about the knees or below and throw us on those sharpened limbs. This impeded our progress...."[58]

Other veterans of the 13th U.S. Regulars who witnessed the charge of the 4th West Virginia left several descriptions now held in the archives of the Vicksburg National Military Park: "Two of Ewing's regiments - the 47th Ohio and 4th West Virginia- rushed forward shouting wildly. Over and through the underbrush they swept. Scaling the steep bluff, Ewing's troops climbed the hillside to within a few yards of the ditch fronting the lunette. But here their surge was stopped by the furious pointblank volleys of the 26th and 27th Louisiana and the 1st Missouri....we witnessed the charge of the 4th Va. There was a gallant line of the Regt [Regiment] when it reached the top of the

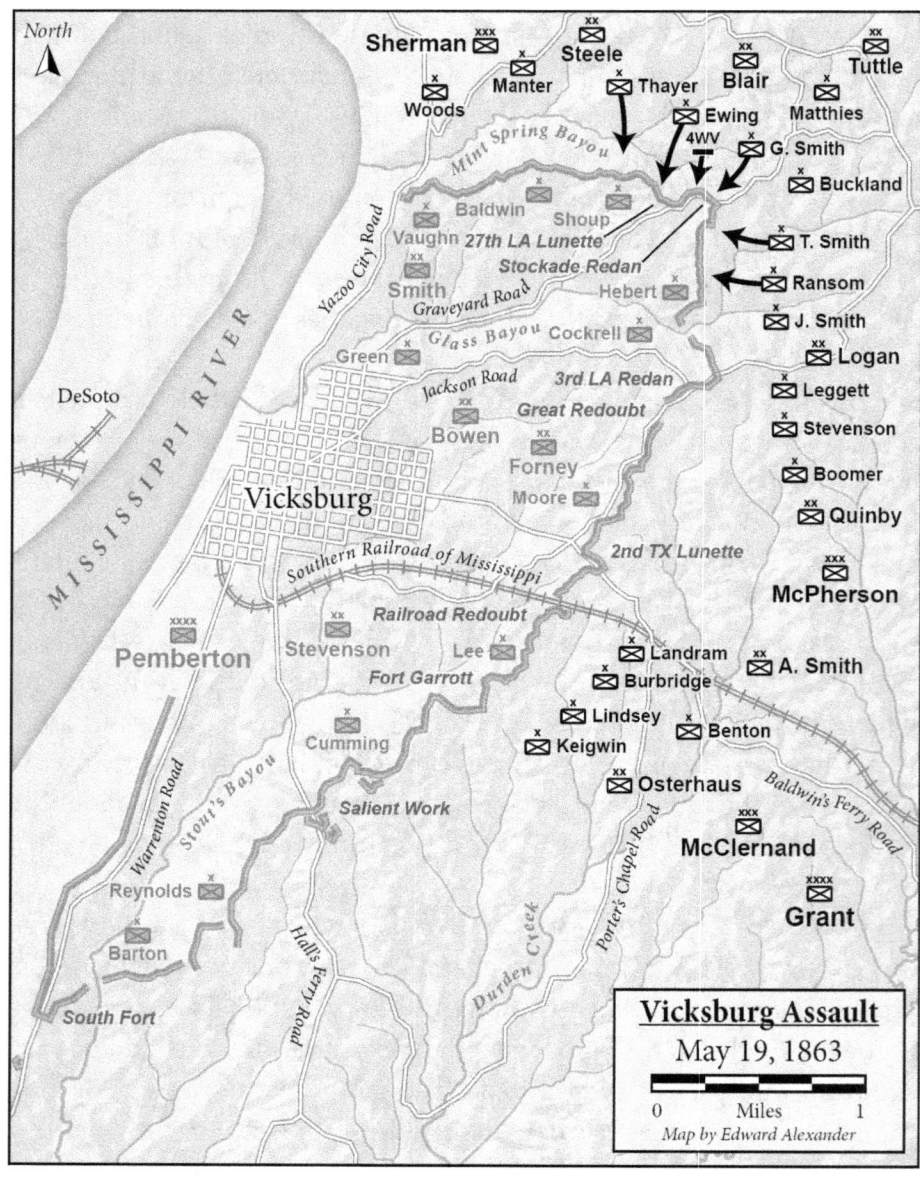

North

Sherman ⊠ Steele ⊠
         Manter ⊠ Thayer ⊠ Blair ⊠   Tuttle ⊠
         Woods   Matthies ⊠
                              Ewing ⊠
                              4WV ┄
                                        G. Smith ⊠
                                        Buckland ⊠
Mint Spring Bayou

            Baldwin ⊠
Vaughn ⊠ Shoup
27th LA Lunette   T. Smith ⊠
         Stockade Redan
Smith ⊠   Ransom ⊠
Graveyard Road   Hebert ⊠
                                        J. Smith ⊠
         Glass Bayou Cockrell ⊠
Green ⊠   Logan ⊠
         Jackson Road 3rd LA Redan   Leggett ⊠
                     Great Redoubt
         Bowen ⊠   Stevenson ⊠
                     Forney ⊠
Vicksburg   Moore ⊠   Boomer ⊠
                                        Quinby ⊠
Southern Railroad of Mississippi
                     2nd TX Lunette
                                        McPherson ⊠
DeSoto
            Railroad Redoubt
Pemberton ⊠ Stevenson ⊠ Lee ⊠   Landram ⊠ A. Smith ⊠
         Fort Garrott   Burbridge ⊠
            Cumming ⊠ Lindsey ⊠ Benton ⊠
                     Keigwin ⊠
         Salient Work   Osterhaus ⊠
                                 McClernand ⊠
Reynolds ⊠   Baldwin's Ferry Road
   Barton ⊠   Grant ⊠
South Fort

MISSISSIPPI RIVER
Yazoo City Road
Warrenton Road
Stout's Bayou
Hall's Ferry Road
Durden Creek
Porter's Chapel Road

Vicksburg Assault
May 19, 1863

0   Miles   1
Map by Edward Alexander

ridge, but it was almost annihilated by an enfilading fire to which they were exposed...."

Another veteran stated: "During the assault of May 19th we saw the 4th Va. Infy Col James Lightburn Com'dg bravely advance with the greatest alacrity and in defiance of obstacles from a small hill on the right of the line but the rebel batteries fire which opened upon them from the fort south of the Stockade seemed to have struck the whole length of the Regiment and they fell back over dead and wounded over the hill in the back ground with a loss of 1/3 Killed and wounded in the unsuccessful charge."[59]

Two of Ewing's other regiments, the 30th and 37th Ohio, were similarly unable to find a way through the timber-strewn Mint Spring Bayou bottom, as the entire brigade was harassed by the fire of General Shoup's Louisiana brigade from Stockade Redan. They soon faltered and had to cease their advance. The 47th Ohio and 4th West Virginia made several attempts to rush the Confederate rifle-pits but were easily repulsed. Like the attacks of Blair's other two brigades on their left, Ewing's assault also stalled.[60]

The 4th West Virginia Infantry suffered immense casualties in the May 19 assault on Stockade Redan. Although the generally accepted official statistic was 156 killed and wounded within ten minutes of the assault order being given, there are variations. "The colors were torn to rags by bullets, both Color Sergeants and all the Color Guard but one, were killed or wounded...." General Lightburn wrote in his official report, "My old regiment suffered terribly in the charge made on the enemies works....Her loss on the first day was 147, including 11 officers." Also, a marker proposed when planning for the national battlefield park indicated the loss at 30 killed and 126 wounded.[61]

Not only are there many different versions of the total casualties, but numerous participants also gave their own personal experiences during the assault, which tend to vary. Perhaps the most intriguing is the death of Major Arza Goodspeed. Captain John Mallernee, who was promoted from 1st Lieutenant on March 14, 1863. reported in the August 20, 1863 edition of the *Athens Ohio Messenger* that the original belief that Goodspeed was taken prisoner "proved sadly untrue on the

Major Arza Goodspeed.
From *History of the Goodspeed Family*,
Volume 1, 1907, by Weston Arthur Goodspeed.

Major Arza Goodspeed.
Terry Lowry Collection.

fall of the city. The remains were found unburied, except by cinder and ashes, but so mutilated by buildings burned over him the identification would have been impossible except for the ring and its initials still on his finger."[62]

Another story passed down through the family of Captain David A. Russell of the 4th West Virginia is that "after the brigade was repulsed some of the wounded men [including Goodspeed] crawled beneath a building or shed which stood somewhere in the area. The building was subsequently set afire by shell-fire and destroyed....Major Goodspeed's remains were never recovered but some of his personal belongs were, among which was his watch. They were returned to his father's family."[63]

Yet another account, published in 1923 in the "State of West Virginia Report of Vicksburg Military Park Commission," reads: "Among the killed was the gallant Major Arza M. Goodspeed, who was killed near an old log house near the enemy's works. Immediately after the assault a Confederate force set the house on fire and later the charred remains of Major Goodspeed was recovered by the men of his regiment." Similarly, an account by a soldier in the 13th U.S. Regulars, who were on the left flank of Ewing's Brigade in General Francis P. Blair's Division, indicated that Major Goodspeed's charred remains were found on May 25 when a truce was called to bury the dead and recover the wounded. While it is not known for certain whether Goodspeed was burned alive, several sources documented that there were numerous fires started the evening of May 19, resultant from the Confederates' torching of the local buildings in the ravines and explosions in order to expose the Union lines at night, enabling their sharpshooters to fire upon them.[64]

Thomas Barton, the regimental hospital steward, wrote in his book in 1890: "He was a brave officer, and killed near an old log house close to the enemy's works. Immediately after the battle a squad of Confederates marched out and set the structure on fire, which in time communicated the flames to the surrounding woods. The charred remains of Major Goodspeed were found near the old log house, together with some articles which belonged to him."[65]

Writing in 1901, Benjamin D. Boswell, Company H, 4th West Virginia, recalled: "My Brigade reached a position so close to Vicksburg about 9 o'clock PM May 18th (dark) that a man within a few feet of me was wounded just at daybreak the morning of the 19th & as soon as we had breakfast we were in position & lay quiet until about 3 PM when we took part in the memorable assault in which my Regiment (4th West Virginia Infantry) lost 134 men out of about 800. I was seriously wounded [in the side] and shortly afterward sent to Young's Point."[66]

In another 1901 letter, Boswell wrote: "The lines were closed around Vicksburg on the morning of May 18th, 1863. The first assault was in the afternoon of the 19th and in it I was seriously wounded. I did not get back to duty until September 20th, 1863." Boswell proceeded to describe the layout of the various Union participants:

> My Regiment was in Ewing's Brigade which was the 2nd Brigade of the 2nd Division, 15th Corps & my recollection is that the 1st Division was between us and the Yazoo. The 1st Brigade of 2nd Division on our right & our Brigade was formed for the assault 4th Virginia [4th West Virginia] on the right–the 47th Ohio on our left. Next 30 and 37 Ohio & Frank DeGrass's Battery of Chicago Artillery [Captain Francis De Grasse's Battery H, 1st Illinois Light Artillery, 3rd Brigade, 4th Division] of Six Parrott Guns was in position about the center of our Brigade in the morning & I think remained there during the day of the 19th. My Regiment went into the assault with 375 men & 24 officers & lost 134 men & 12 officers killed & wounded. The 47 Ohio lost about the same proportion of its strength. The other two regiments did not go in.[67]

Death of Corporal Clarkson Fogg

According to John G. Farrar, "The 4th [West] Virginia lost more on the 19th of May than any other regiment in the Army." Farrar reported eight killed in Company E: Corporal Lewis Johnson who died May 25 of a mortal gunshot wound; Corporal Clarkson F. Fogg; Corporal

Britton Cook who died August 18 of a mortal gunshot wound; Private George W. Willard who died in a Memphis hospital June 9 of a mortal gunshot wound in the neck; Private Gamaliel Bartlett who died of a mortal wound of the leg, but not until September 18; Private Robert Kincade who died October 18 in the Union hospital in Memphis from chronic diarrhea; and Privates William Bell and John Ours. Farrar was mistaken about the last two, however. Bell was killed by a rebel sharpshooter on June 21 while on picket duty at Walnut Hills. The Ours who was killed was Jehu, not John. Wounded were J.S. Coon, John McKee, E.H. Malony, D.A. Russell, J.J.C. Weldon, Wash Rogers, and Samuel Bell. "Perhaps a few others," Farrar wrote, "I don't know how many men the Company had in the fight, not very many though."[68]

Lewis Love, Company A, wrote to the father of Corporal Clarkson Fogg of Company E: "I feel it my pointed duty to write to you on this occasion with the sad intelligence of the Death of one of our bravest boys, your son. He was killed on the 19th while making one of the most gallant charges of the war. In honor to him I must say that he died at his post many of our brave boys fell by his side. Our loss is very great upwards of 150 killed and wounded."[69]

Sometime in the 1890s John L. Vance provided a very different version, recalling: "The lines had been advanced until they were very near each other. At the point where he [Fogg] met his death, they were perhaps not more than 60 feet apart. It was the habit to shout at any and all times and various devices were adapted to cause an enemy to expose himself. One day General Francis Blair commanded the Division–came over to my regiment to take a look at the works. Unguardedly he stepped upon a slight elevation in the rear of the breastworks and instantaneously was fired upon (fortunately without injury) by the Rebels. Fogg called to him, and I pulled him down. It was then that our attention was called to the fact that Fogg had stuck a spade in the top of the earthworks behind which he could take observations and fire. I said to him that it as risky: 'You are liable at any moment to be killed' and Gen. Blair made the same remark. The words had scarcely left our lips when Fogg (who had just fixed his face behind the spade) fell at our feet dead. A Rebel bullet had passed through the spade and penetrated his brain. Even in the midst of the scenes of death that surrounded us, every hour during the siege his sudden taking off was a great shock."[70]

The two accounts of Fogg's death differ immensely, but Love's account was written contemporaneously and corresponds with the official military record, while Vance's was written some 30 years after the war and when he was in bad health. As such, Love's account is likely more reliable. In addition, Vance's account does not sound like it took place during an assault, but at some other date, so it is also possible he had Fogg confused with another soldier.

Captain Daniel Albert Russell, Company E, received a slight wound of the arm. After the war, Florence, the captain's wife, wrote of the event, stating that he had told her about the incident and recalled prior to entering the fray the captain and his tent-mate twisted their blankets, tying them over one shoulder and beneath the other arm placing the knot in front. Early in the advance the captain was hit by a minie ball, which passed through his upper arm, making a large wound. Mrs. Russell further stated he reported being able to continue on, but was later hit a second time, by what he believed was a nearly spent bullet. He was knocked unconscious by the impact or lost consciousness from loss of blood and fell to the ground. He was followed at a short distance by another soldier, David Kincaid (rank unknown). This soldier saw the captain fall, and believing him dead, intended to recover his body at dusk. She further related he said that Kincaid lay down on the ground and kept his head lowered to avoid attracting Confederate fire.

Mrs. Russell continued: "Sometime later Capt. Russell regained consciousness and finding his clothing covered with blood, he believed himself shot through the body. He was able to walk and made his way to a hospital in the rear, where he was treated by a surgeon. They found the second bullet had passed through the knot of the blanket and made a bad bruise but had not broken any ribs. David Kincaid on discovering the Captain gone, was able to make his way safely back to his own lines after dark."[71]

Another member of Company E, Private Gamaliel Bartlett, a 19-year-old boatman from Meigs County, Ohio, was wounded by canister shot in his left leg, which injured his fibula and tibia. He was sent to a hospital in St. Louis and as the days passed, he seemed to be recovering nicely, but then took a turn for the worse and died from the wounds September 18.[72]

Private Samuel R. Lowry (Lowery), Company D, a 24-year-old brakeman from Athens, Ohio, was wounded five times in the assault. Reportedly, "Two bullets took effect in his head, one in the breast, one in the thigh and one in his hand." He would later be transferred to the hospital at Memphis, was honorably discharged, and lived until 1913. Some other injuries from the company were Private Joseph L. Cooper, wounded in the leg; Private Jacob Crossen, who suffered a gunshot wound and was captured but exchanged in June; and Private Robert W. Davis, who lost his left arm.[73]

Corporal William L. Safreed, Company F, wrote, "At ten o'clock a.m. went into battlefield and got my left forefinger and thumb about [shot] off. 19 men killed or wounded in our Company F and 162 in our regiment."[74]

Corporal Robert Henry Sampson, Jr., Company H, a 24-year-old laborer from Kanawha County, West Virginia, was killed in action. According to family history, his two brothers, John and Samuel, who were also in the regiment, knew he had been killed "...but waited for

Robert Henry Sampson, Jr.
Sampson Family History,
West Virginia State Archives.

nightfall to search for his body. Then under the cover of darkness, they began their search. When they found him they took [his] locket from around his neck, and his identification, then they buried him there on the Vicksburg battlefield, where he still remains."[75]

Sergeant John Y. Jarrett, also of Company H, 32-year-old cooper and sawyer prior to the war, was wounded by a gunshot that "struck his thigh on the right side passing through cutting the leaders in two, striking the knee, and producing a very ugly & painful wound, & leaving the ends of the leaders sticking out of the wound, and now from the effects of the wound aforesaid his limb is smaller than the other, and weaker, and pains him always, when the weather is foul, & fails him in walking & working."[76]

Captain William S. Hall, Company F, was slightly wounded in the thigh, while Private Jacob S. Coon, Company E, was wounded in the hand. According to Hospital Steward Thomas Barton: "A few soldiers came to our hospital to have their wounds dressed. Among them was Jacob S. Coon, who had received a gun-shot wound of one of his fingers. I dressed the wound for him."[77]

Private William H. Burdett, age 18, of Kanawha County, (West) Virginia, a member of Company G, was severely wounded in the right shoulder, breast, and right foot, although his compiled service record does not reflect a breast wound. Sent to a hospital at Memphis, he would later return to the regiment at Larkinsville, Alabama.[78]

General Lightburn said Captain Martin V.B. Lightburn of Company A of the 4th West Virginia "was struck three times one shot struck his watch which saved his life his wound was very slight." The watch was apparently torn to pieces by the enemy bullet, thus saving his life. Martin's military records state he was wounded slightly in the breast. General Lightburn also claimed 1st Lieutenant Calvin Luther Lightburn of Company G of the regiment, recently promoted to that rank, "was shot through the clothing." General Lightburn added that he personally "received two shots on striking my sword and another through my coat."[79]

Captain Henry Grayum, Company G, charging at the head of his company, was struck by a musket ball in his left elbow. No bones were broken, but the wound proved quite painful; however, the *Gallipolis Journal* reported on September 17 that Grayum was wounded and had "injured some of the bones."[80]

Adjutant Philemon B. Stanbery , 30 years of age, received a severe wound in the right arm. According to Captain David A. Russell, Stanbery "was wounded early in the attack and went to the hospital." In contrast, Hospital Steward Thomas H. Barton claimed Stanbery was wounded in the head in the May 22 assault, but Stanbery 's official service record states he was severely wounded in the right arm on May 19.[81]

Colonel James H. Dayton "took things as cool as if it had been a battalion drill." An unidentified member of the regiment, who sent a list of the killed and wounded to the *Wheeling Intelligencer* that was published on June 23, stated that Dayton "led the Regiment and I am only doing justice when I say that a braver and more determined man does not live. He evinced the skill of an accomplished officer and won the praise of all. Such man should be rewarded." He added, "The officers and men of the Regiment behaved gloriously, and when the order to charge was given went in with a will. They fully maintained the reputation of West Virginia and have gained a name second to no Regiment in the army of Gen. Grant, but at a terrible loss."[82]

Color bearer Sergeant James C. Neal, Company C, died in the assault. According to General Ewing: "We had our flag up to their works but both bearers were shot, and when they fell back they grabbed up one flag and took it with them, and Cpl. Clendenin fell as though he was dead, and lay until night, when he took the other flag off the field safe. He was promoted the next day to Sergeant."[83]

2nd Lieutenant James W. Dale, Company I, was "struck in the head by a Minnie [sic] ball producing a painful but not dangerous wound." He was also captured and spent about two weeks as a prisoner in rebel hands in the city of Vicksburg before being paroled. He later claimed he witnessed evidence the city would soon fall, and in June he returned to Gallipolis with a "specimen of rebel bread....composed of cornmeal and beans." Hospital Steward Thomas H. Barton claimed Dale "was shot in the foot and taken prisoner," and after being paroled made his way to the convalescent camp at Milliken's Bend.[84]

1st Lieutenant Finley Davis Ong, Company F, was wounded in the thigh and captured. Ong's service record is very confusing and is apparently mixed with that of a younger Finley Ong in the company, who was discharged in September 1863 and soon after died of chronic diarrhea at his home in Jackson County, West Virginia. Making matters even more confusing is a monument with his name and those of a number of other soldiers' names at the Vicksburg National Cemetery, Warren County, Mississippi. It states he was captured December 29, 1862, at the battle of Chickasaw Bayou and died in Vicksburg while still a prisoner of war. This is inaccurate, as the 4th West Virginia did not arrive in Mississippi until early 1863.

Ong's widow's pension file gives both May 19 and May 22 as the date of his death. Reportedly, Ong and 1st Lieutenant James W. Dale were both captured and exchanged the following day. Possibly the best explanation was given in the Ong family history book, which states that on May 19: "He was in command of Company F leading a fierce charge in which 360 of the 800 left in the regiment were killed or wounded. He fell into the hands of the enemy....his leg was amputated above the knee. He was getting along nicely until the 22nd of June,

Lt. Finley D. Ong.
U.S. Army Center
of Military History.

when a shell from the Union battery exploded near his tent, causing him to make a sudden movement, which started a hemorrhage from his wound that soon ebbed his life away. His resting place is among the unknown at Vicksburg."[85]

Sergeant James M. Hodge, Company G, was wounded in the arm and leg. According to a family tradition, Private John Perry Wolfe, Company E, "at Vicksburg in the charge of the fatal triangle another singing messenger of death from the Confederate forts had ploughed a deep furrow across his [Wolfe's] neck." Additionally, Private Michael Richard Jr., Company A, was shot in the right lung. "The incident was often spoke of how the doctor drew a handkerchief through the wound from front to back."[86]

Sergeant John Douglas, Company H, 4th West Virginia, claimed: "On the march from the Gulf to Vicksburg I was overtaken with blindness on May 17, 1863, so that I could not see but poorly in daylight and none after dark. Had to be led by comrades at night, notwithstanding that I went through the 'charge' May 19 in rear of Vicksburg and there received sunstroke which seemed to increase the blindness. The several surgeons of our own and other regiments who examined my eyes said they were injured by fog." His claim was supported by Private Salathiel Jones of the company, who said:

> I never heard him complain until during the Vicksburg campaign. He was said to have a sunstroke about the time of the battle of May 19, 1863. He was brought back to the rear and put in an ambulance. I was then detailed in ambulance corps and saw said Douglas when he was brought back, and he was then unconscious and in a helpless condition, and it was claimed by surgeons he was overcome by heat. He got better after he got over the sunstroke but always had trouble of the head and eyes afterward.[87]

Jones was a nurse at the Chickasaw Bluff hospital around this time, so that may be where Douglas was taken. Douglas eventually recovered and served out the remainder of the war. General Lightburn

Post-war image of John Douglas.
Private Collection.

arrived in time to take the 4th into the battle in the last charge of May 19, with General Hugh Ewing leading two regiments and Lightburn the other wing— Ewing had his sword shot off while "Old Joe" had some holes shot in his clothes. A letter in the Gallipolis newspaper summed up the event in simple terms, "Our boys fought well and have made themselves a good name." Not all members received such plaudits, however, as 1st Lieutenant James H. Ralston, Company E, was reportedly missing or absent on the day of the battle and later requested his resignation, which he stated was due to "family affairs." Colonel Dayton accepted the resignation but called Ralston "strictly incompetent and dissipated," basically charging him with cowardice in the Vicksburg assaults. Lightburn confirmed Dayton's assessment, calling Ralston "useless."[88]

Dr. Thomas H. Barton said the next two days were spent taking care of the wounded. In addition, there was a skirmish along the line on May 20, during which one man in Company G was killed, while a man in Company E was killed on May 21.[89]

One the evening of May 19, the Confederates set fire to several houses and other buildings located near Stockade Redan, in order to light up the area for sharpshooters to better see where Union troops were laying in line of battle. One soldier in the 13th U.S. Regulars recalled seeing a cornfield and frame building on his right, located on the left of Ewing's Brigade. Accounts from the 13th U.S. Regulars also mentioned a stand of colors found near the front of the 27th Louisiana lunette, which several soldiers thought to be the 4th West Virginia flags. They were recovered and returned to the regiment the next morning, May 20, by some soldiers from the 13th U.S. Regulars, with a stern warning, "Here's yer rag back, next time see that you take better care of it."[90]

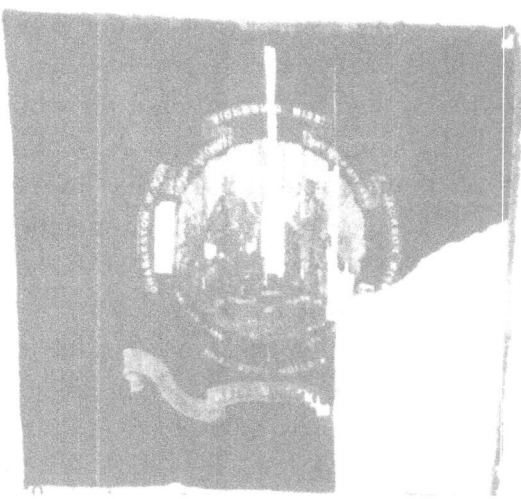

4th West Virginia Infantry Regimental Flag.
West Virginia State Museum.

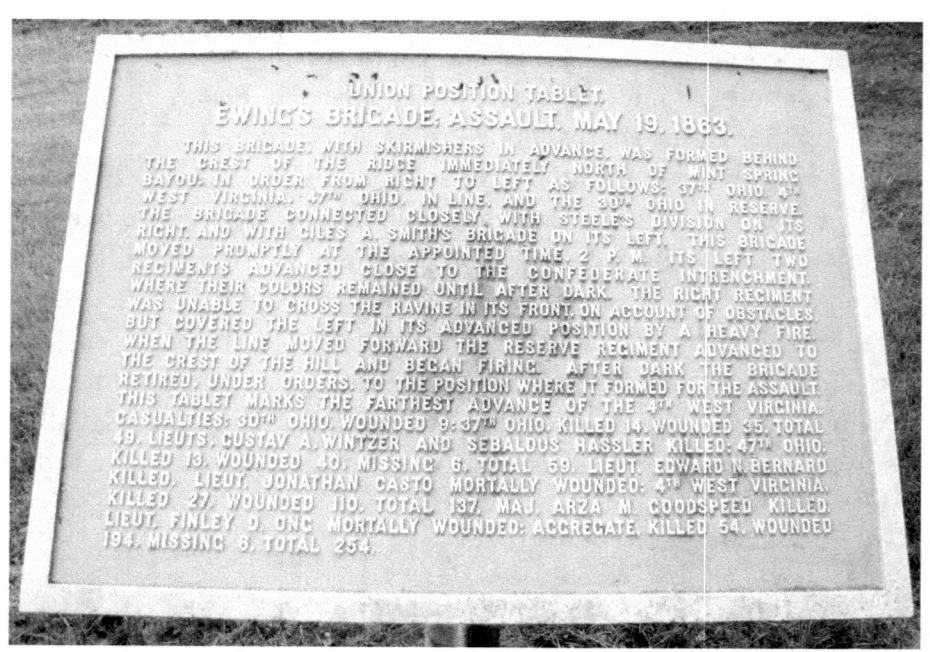

Marker at Vicksburg NPS describing movements of Ewing's Brigade in the May 19, 1863 assault on Stockade Redan. Photo by Richard A. Wolfe.

Close-up of monument to Col. J.A.J. Lightburn, Vicksburg NPS.
Photo by Richard A. Wolfe.

West Virginia monument at Vicksburg National Park featuring the bust of
Major Arza M. Goodspeed. Photo by Richard A. Wolfe.

Vicksburg NPS monument commemorating 4th West Virginia casualties
in the assault on May 19, 1863, including Major Azra M. Goodspeed
and 1st Lt. Findley Ong.
Photo by Richard A. Wolfe.

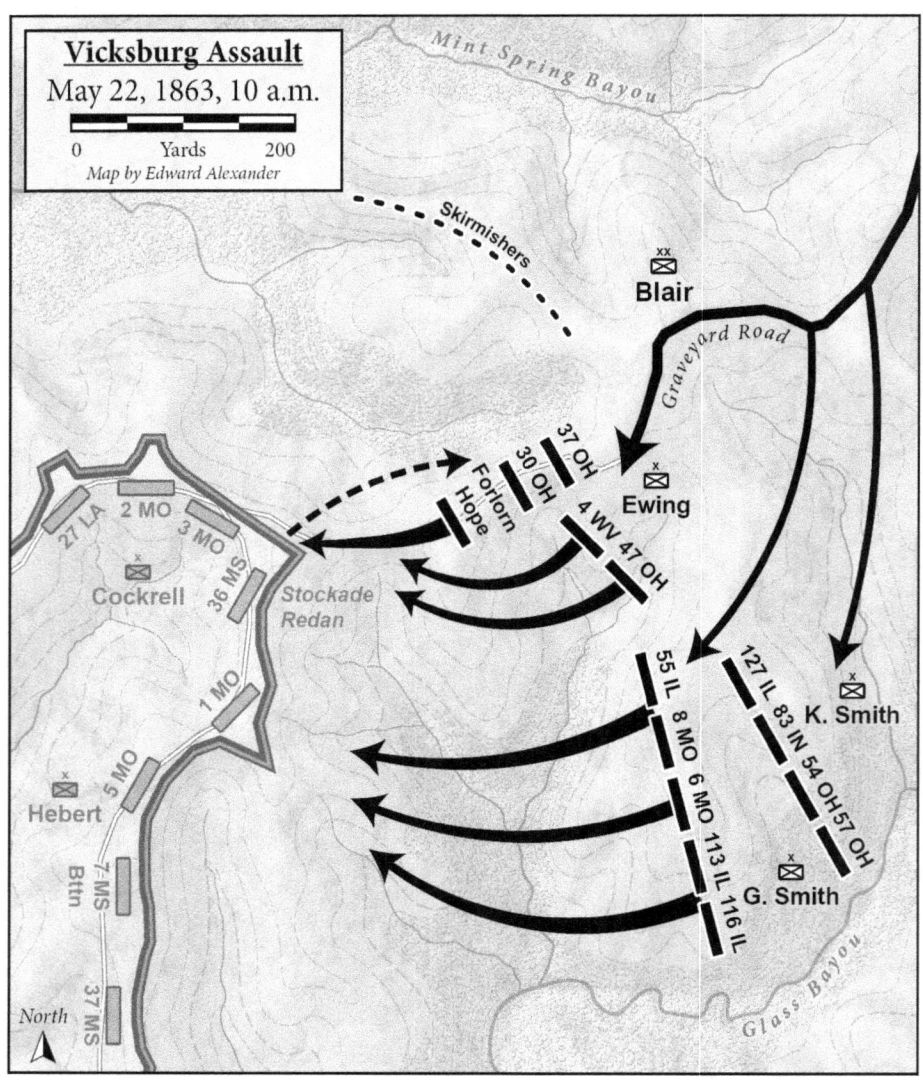

Vicksburg Assault
May 22, 1863, 10 a.m.

0   Yards   200
Map by Edward Alexander

Assault on Stockade Redan
May 22, 1863
"The Forlorn Hope"

General Grant planned a second assault of Stockade Redan on May 22, in which the 4th West Virginia would suffer much less than in the earlier assault; Brigadier General Hugh Ewing's report indicated there were three enlisted men killed, one officer wounded and 15 enlisted men wounded, and one enlisted man missing or captured. Those figures were later echoed in a proposed battlefield marker study at Vicksburg National Park, stating the regiment lost three killed and 16 wounded, for a total loss of 19. General Ewing's brigade was chosen by Major General William T. Sherman to lead the attack, although the 4th West Virginia was placed third in the column due to heavy casualties on May 19. He described the initial movement on that fateful morning, now known as the "Forlorn Hope," as follows:

At 10.04 a.m. of the 22d, a storming party, composed of 50 volunteers from each brigade of the division, bearing the colors of my headquarters, and followed by my troops in column, charged down a narrow, deep-cut road upon a bastion of the enemy's works. They were instructed to bear to the left, and cross the curtain if the ditch at the salient could not be bridged. They made a foot-path at the salient, by which Captain [John H.] Groce, commanding, Lieutenant [George E.] O'Neal, [Private] Trogden, the color bearer, and others, crossing, climbed half-way up the exterior slope, and planted the flag upon it unfurled. The Thirtieth Ohio, next in order, moved close upon the storming party, until their progress was arrested by a front and double flank fire, and the dead and wounded blocked the defile. The second company forced its way over the remains of the first, and a third over those of the preceding, but their perseverance served only further to encumber the impassable way. The Thirty-seventh Ohio came next, its left breaking the column where the road first debouched, upon a deadly fire. After the check, a few passed on, but were mostly shot. They fell back, and, with the remainder of the brigade and division, came over a better route. I formed my troops as they came up on the brow of the hill running from the road to the left, parallel to and 70 yards from the intrenchments. Here we protected our advanced men and wounded until they were gradually withdrawn, and, with a heavy and well-directed sustained fire, covered the after attempt to charge over the intrenchments made down the same road by the brigade of General Mower....[91]

Joseph Saunier of the 47th Ohio further described the assault:

Cannonading and skirmishing commenced at daylight. Our Brigade was marched across the Cemetery [Graveyard] Road by the left flank about one-4th mile, and from there formed an assault on the left face of Cemetery fort [Stockade Redan]. Gen. Sherman had re-connoitered all his front, in person, and had determined upon the points for the second attack. All his batteries were placed in good positions, and orders for the second assault had been given, to be carried out at 10 o'clock. Gen. Sherman was well pleased with our charge of the 19th.[92]

According to Saunier: "A company was detailed as flankers. Some called them sharp shooters and from where they were they could see all that was going on. As the assault was about to be made, our brigade was drawn in line of battle as follows: The 30th Ohio on the right of first line; the 37th [Ohio] on the left of the first line; the 4th West Va. [Virginia] In second line on the right; the 47th on the left second line. The assault, later named the Forlorn Hope, of fifty volunteers from each brigade in the Division. The Forlorn Hope was commanded by six officers; they had in all 150 men."[93]

The Forlorn Hope volunteers knew it was a suicide mission and went into the fight without weapons, fully exposed to Confederate fire. The storming party of 150 men was led by 1st Lieutenant George E.

O'Neal, Company G, 30th Ohio Infantry, 3rd Brigade, 2nd Division, 15th Army Corps, and consisted of a variety of men from the 30th, 37th, and 47th Ohio Infantries, as well as 13 men from the 4th West Virginia Infantry, including Sergeant William Bumgarner (Company A); and privates Joel Parsons (Company B); William Clark and William Hamilton (Company C); Jasper N. North (Company D); John McKee (Company E); William Barringer (Company F); John C. Buckley and John Ullom (Company G); James C. Summers/Somers, (Company H); James Harrison and James Riffle (Company I); and James McGonegal (Company K). Hamilton (face), McKee (head-slight), Buckley (hand), and Riffle (leg) were wounded. Riffle would die from his wound on July 4 or 5. Bumgarner, Barringer, Buckley, Somers/Summers, North and Parsons received the Medal of Honor.[94]

Saunier continued: "Proudly at 10 o'clock A.M. were in line and when the signal sounded, they started on a full run....They carried planks and ladders and other necessary scaling apparatus to bridge the ditch at the Confederate Fort....On they went in a storm of musketry, grape, and canister, but they faltered not, although their ranks were thinned at every step. They kept going forward on the run and gained the ditch at the enemies' fort which was nearly ten feet wide, and seven feet deep. They planted the brigade flag on the side of the fort; here, on account of the shape of the fort they were slightly sheltered above the Confederate works. Our flag floated not a rod from the Confederate lines drawn up to receive them and none of the Confederates dared to take it."[95]

As the wave of infantry from Ewing's Brigade slammed into Stockade Redan, a sergeant from the 37th Ohio Infantry carrying the division flag began waving it and taunting the Confederates. He yelled out, "You sons of bitches surrender this fort!" and the flag was immediately shot to shreds and the sergeant was captured by the defenders from Louisiana and Missouri.[96]

An unidentified postwar account of William Barringer's participation with the storming party, which may be based upon oral tradition or modern interpretation—either way it is otherwise unverified—claimed:

Post-war image. William Barringer.
Charles Haley Collection.

William Bumgarner.
Private Collection.

Post-war image. James C. Summers.
James Cole Collection.

When Grant was besieging Vicksburg in 1863 and was unable to get his troops across the moat in front of the Confederate works, Barringer and six others volunteered to build a bridge across the ditch. After Federal artillery had driven the Confederates back a short distance, these seven men carried timber and planks and threw then across the ditch in the face of enemy fire. The seven men climbed the parapet and spiked 14 Confederate guns on the breastworks. By that time the Confederates had returned to the charge and the men found it impossible to get back to the Union Army. A part of them were killed and others concealed themselves with Rebel uniforms. During the night Barringer and one other got away, rolled a bale of cotton into the Mississippi River, and got on top of it with a board to paddle. Barringer's companion was never heard from again. He [Barringer] paddled and drifted down the river about 10 miles when he was picked up by a Union gunboat. After repeating his story, Barringer was taken before Grant, who recommended him for the medal. [Medal of Honor].[97]

Private Joseph Nicholson, Company C, sustained a musket ball wound to his left leg. The injury was so severe his leg was amputated, or "looped off," just above the knee, and he would be discharged at the hospital at St. Louis on August 4. In 1884 Douglas Bly, manufacturer of artificial limbs, would fit him with an artificial leg. Nicholson's descendants say he walked the remainder of his life with a "peg leg."

Finally, as the heavy fighting tapered off on the evening of May 22, Brigadier General Ewing, who had been at the line of battle all day, observed, "At night, the wounded, dead and colors were brought 70 yard back to the hill, where the brigade remains, intrenching and skirmishing with the enemy." General Ewing also recommended in his report that 1st Lieutenant James H. Ralston, Company E, who had earlier been served as the regimental sergeant major in 1861, be reduced to the ranks for "absence without cause on the day of battle." Ewing does not specify where Ralston was on May 22, nor do his service records, but it is doubtful that he was in the hospital. In his place, Ewing recommended that one of the two men who had saved the regimental colors from being taken by Confederates at Stockade Redan, Corporal Francis M. Clendenin of Company F or Corporal John W. Boley of Company I, be promoted to the rank of lieutenant to replace Ralston. Ewing further reported the total casualties for the 4th West Virginia on May 22 were 24 men killed, and 116 wounded.[98]

1st Lieutenant James H. Ralston was not the only solider to receive reprimands after the assault, as according to William Grayum's June 5, 1863 letter written near Vicksburg: "Our regiment has gained a good name here and Col. Dayton stands high as a good commander and a brave man. But [Lt.] Col. Vance has disgraced himself by his drunkenness on the field of battle. On our last Charge [May 22] he was so drunk that he was staggering around in everyone's way and even mistook the 113th Illinois Regiment for ours and commenced cursing but the officers of that Regiment drew their revolvers and made him crawfish on the double quick." Vance was wounded in the arm, breast and leg.[99]

Adding to Grayum's claims against Vance was an 1876 newspaper article by Private Louis Everett, Company K, who related, "During the siege of Vicksburg the regiment made a charge on the enemy's works, he [Vance] was in such a beastly state of intoxication that he actually cut some of his men, with his sword, and it was finally taken from him by the General commanding the brigade."[100]

Not everyone in the regiments shared Grayum's and Everett's assessment of Vance, however. In 1881, Sergeant Donald McDonald, a veteran of Company A, 4th West Virginia Infantry, wrote in Vance's pension claim that in the assault of May 22: "in charging down the hill there was a great deal of brush and logs. Col. Vance [was] knocked down by some man falling against him –he was hurt very bad and complained a great deal of his side long after. There was no better man in the army than Col. Vance."[101]

In a later letter William Grayum wrote: "In our last charge on their works the Rebels selected our Company for artillery practice and fired Six Solid Shot at us while we were halted waiting orders and didn't hit a man, although they raised the dust around beautifully. The boys stood it nobly and if anything will try a man's nerves, that will. Going ahead is nothing but stopping and standing still under a heavy fire with orders not to fire a gun is hard to stand, and I will never hold our men in such place for the orders of no drunk man living."[102]

William L. Safreed, Company F, reported, "One killed and seven wounded in our regiment today." 2nd Lieutenant Columbus Shrewsbury, Company A, 4th West Virginia, was left at Young's Point in charge of the regimental baggage and about 90 men, due to his weak health. He wrote: "The fight has been going on for six or seven days. I have heard a good many rumors about our Regiment....our Company as far as I have heard have not lost any." Shrewsbury, concerned he was not recovering fast enough from being ill, told his wife: "My hair is coming out. I expect that I will be bald headed."[103]

Another member who missed the two recent assaults due to illness, Private Fernandes Jeffrey, Company K, an 18-year-old from Chapmanville, West Virginia, wrote:

The regiment was cut up very much in making a charge on the rebels breastworks in the two charges. We lost about 200 killed and wounded but I don't know how they came off that well. As to Company K, we had not one killed in our company and severely wounded. I can't give you a full history, but it was a hard fight on the other side of Black River and killed a great many rebels serving them twice as many as them as us. We lost a great many men but not one half what the rebels lost.[104]

On May 23, William Safreed said his men were lying within a couple yards of the enemy fortifications and there was skirmishing along the entire line, yet on the 24th he noted all was quiet along the lines. Safreed's description of some of the troops being within a few yards of the rebels may have been exaggerated. The situation was better described by Lewis Love, Company A, who noted in his account: "Our regiment is laying within 100 yards of the enemies works and while I write the balls are whistling over my head. The enemy is surrounded

Vicksburg, 1863.
Library of Congress.

Assault on Stockade Redan.
Library of Congress.

they cannot get out without breaking our lines which will be hard to do."[105]

The Confederates defending Stockade Redan sent a flag of truce on May 25 requesting permission to bury their dead, while on May 29 there was heavy artillery fire along the line, and the 4th West Virginia was relieved that afternoon and fell back behind the lines. Heavy cannonading continued the next day.[106]

William Grayum, writing from near Vicksburg on June 5, said: "We are having a hot time. There is a continuous roar of musketry and artillery all the time and balls are continually whistling over our heads but as we camped in a deep hollow they can't hurt us much....We were for seven days within one hundred yards of one of their heaviest Forts and had to keep ourselves under cover or get a hole in our hides. We dug rifle pits and fought them in our own way."[107]

The Friday prior to June 11 an incident occurred back in Gallipolis, Ohio, concerning a soldier in the 4th West Virginia. On January 1, 1863, 32-year-old Private James Driver of Company A was detailed from the regiment by General E.P. Scammon to serve as a miner, and as such did not accompany the regiment to Vicksburg. He later became ill and entered the hospital at Gallipolis, but on the Friday in question, he left the hospital and at some point, became intoxicated. In this condition he entered the grocery of a Mr. Hanks on Pine Street and was ordered to leave. Driver refused to depart and a policeman, George Weaver, ordered him to do so. Driver struck at Weaver a few times, which Weaver returned with a pound weight. In an antagonized state, Driver left but threatened to return in an hour and shoot Weaver. Returning to the hospital, Driver obtained his musket and came back to Pine Street, where he found Weaver in the shop door. Driver fired, the ball passing through Weaver's body and killing him within 30 minutes. Weaver left a widow and children with little means of support, while Driver's family in Pomeroy, consisting of two blind children and a feeble wife, were deeply affected by the incident. Driver was placed in jail and eventually given a dishonorable discharge, but later claimed he served until the middle of 1864, including time in the Invalid Corps. His service record shows that he wrote to military authorities throughout 1866

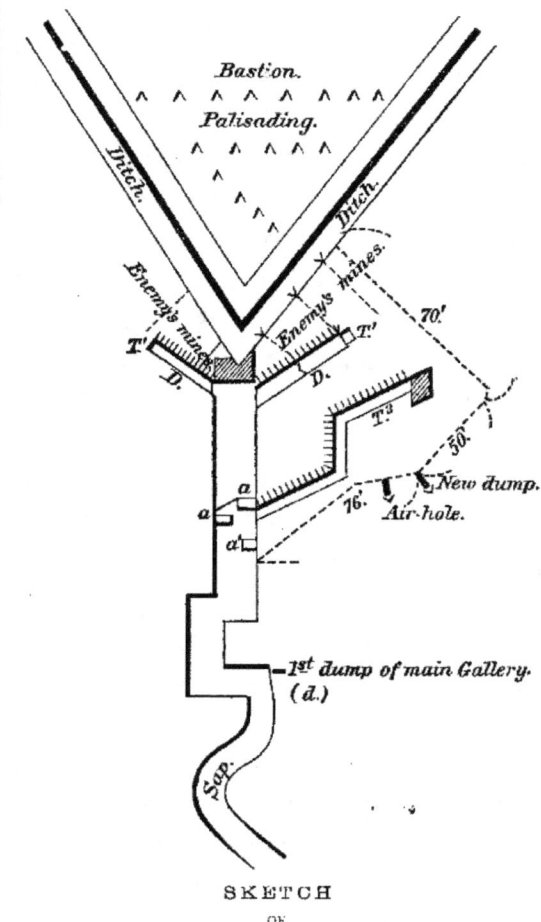

SKETCH
OF
BASTION IN FRONT OF BRIG. GEN. EWING.

OR, Series 1, Vol. 24, Part 2, 191.

hoping to obtain an honorable discharge with no mention of the crime, but in 1899 the authorities supported the dishonorable discharge "due to a crime" he committed.[108]

Meanwhile, the Confederates launched a dual attack on Milliken's Bend and Young's Point on June 7. While the force assigned to attack Milliken's Bend managed to engage Federal soldiers, the column chosen to strike Young's Point met with utter failure in their march and called off their planned assault. Private Robert W. Davis, Company D, suffered amputation of his left arm from a wound received on June 13 and was sent to the general hospital at Milliken's Bend. In the rear of Vicksburg, Private Fernandes Jeffrey, Company K, told his family he had been ill but was almost well, having been tended during his illness by 34-year-old Private John H. Purnell of his company.[109]

One soldier of the 4th West Virginia predicted, "The rebels say that General Starvation has taken command of Vicksburg and they don't appear to like him much." Now stationed at Walnut Hills, Mississippi, in the rear of Vicksburg, General Lightburn wrote a person named George (last name unknown) on June 17, "...we have the city so invested that not even a single individual can escape[.] we have occupied this position for some time[.] our troop are in some places within 75 yards of the enemies works....we have had almost an incessant fire for 25 days and will take Vicksburg....the Boys in the 4th that are left are all well." Lightburn added: "My Brigade is in front and I write this under fire. We have been carrying on war on a large scale and the firing at times is terrific so much so that it would try the nerves of an old soldier."[110]

The regiment remained at Walnut Hills for some time. On the 18th, William L. Safreed returned from convalescent camp and the next day wrote, "we are building a shanty up against the hill side." He also reflected on June 20 that "we went over to the rifle pits. Frank [no last name given] taken sick," and on June 21 Private William Bell, Company E, was killed by a rebel sharpshooter while on picket duty. The regiment continued to remain in camp at Walnut Hills from June 21 to June 23, then guarded the rifle pits on June 24. Finally, on June 25, Safreed wrote that the "great rebel fort" (not Stockade Redan) was blown up by General John A. Logan's force, which produced great cheers as the stars and stripes flew over the fort.[111]

Captain Calvin A. Shepard, at Gallipolis on furlough on June 26, began his return trip to the regiment at Vicksburg, taking with him letters from family and friends of the soldiers. At Vicksburg there was heavy artillery along the line on June 27, and Private Swinfield Hill, Company C, died of disease and fever at Walnut Hills. William Grayum touched upon the health of the regiments, as well as his continued disdain for Lieutenant Colonel John L. Vance, as he wrote from Walnut Hills on June 30: "We have four Reg. crowded into one little hollow not more than 300 yards long and not wide at all. We have a good deal of sickness in the Regiment mainly as a consequence of being crowded too close....Lieut. Col. John Luther Vance, the man of many wounds, has sent in his resignation after receiving a very pressing invitation to do so from his Col. backed by every officer in the Regiment (cause – drunkenness on duty and off duty and in fact all the time)....As to Luther's wounds if you could hear the remarks made by the men about it you would find that they don't believe he was hit at all. They say that he was shot in the neck by a canteen full of Rifle whiskey and I have seen him hit in that way a dozen times myself and I've seen him fall often and it may be that he was hit by shot for there was plenty of them whistling around there and he was in the thickest of the fight all the time." Grayum added: "For two weeks when I was on duty within 100 yards of the enemy works I had but little time for writing. I could not do as Col. Vance did. He went to the hospital or somewhere else [after being wounded on May 22] and staid for two or three days and I presume wrote gassy letters by the dozen."[112]

The 4th West Virginia remained at Walnut Hills and on July 3, according to Grayum, amidst constant annoyance from mosquitos, the Confederates, dirty and ragged, stood on walls and finally came out with a flag of truce to surrender the next day. Grayum added: "This is the 44th day we have been pounding at these infernal fortifications and the loss of life on both sides has been awful. I have seen more men killed in that time than I ever want to again. I have had three men of our company shot by my side and never have had even my clothes touched yet. I have had a shell explode right in front of me and the man behind me was struck on the side and not another man in the Company was hit."[113]

Apparently, many were unaware of the potential surrender, and Captain William Kassak, U.S. Army Engineers, filed a report on July 13, stating: "As I had no miners to spare for these two positions, I called for General Ewing to furnish me 16 men from the 4th West Virginia Volunteer Infantry whom I knew to be old coal miners. These men started two mines on the night between the 3rd and 4th [July], one at Colonel Smith's and the other at Colonel Malmborg's sap." These tunnels were intended to pass underneath the rebel works and blow them up. This assignment proved unnecessary, as on July 4, the national holiday, Vicksburg surrendered. William S. Hall was elated as he wrote: "We are all having a glorious celebration of the 4th of July. It will be a great day in the history of this country." William Safreed recalled that the surrender took place at 10 a.m. Grayum contemplated the future, writing, "we have received no orders yet ....Perhaps we will be stationed here for the rest of our time in the South and I think we have earned the privilege."[114]

The Jackson Expedition
July 5 – 25, 1863

Any notion that the 4th West Virginia would now get some much-deserved rest quickly faded on July 5. By order of General William T. Sherman, who wanted to confront General Joseph Johnston's relief forces, the 4th West Virginia started for Jackson, Mississippi, where they arrived on July 10, and then engaged in operations against the Confederates there until July 19. In an August 23 letter, William Grayum wrote: "I believe I have suffered as much from the heat on the Kanawha last summer as I have here except on [the] march to Jackson. That was awful. I never wish to make such another." William Safreed claimed his division started out for Big Black River in pursuit of General Joseph Johnston's forces.[115]

Only the ill soldiers were left behind at Walnut Hills, where John G. Farrar and Corporal Samuel Curtis of Company E burned and buried the body of Private Joseph B. Price of their company, who had died of chronic diarrhea, on July 10.[116]

In his regimental history, Joseph Saunier of the 47th Ohio wrote that on July 9: "We discovered the enemy was retreating toward Jackson, leaving behind their cattle, hogs and sheep, which were first killed and thrown into the stagnant pools, wherever there was any water to purify, and if possible, make the Yankees sick. The weather was intensely hot and there were several men, horses and mules sunstruck. We skirmished with the enemy a good part of the day."[117]

Private Thomas Carroll, Company A, 4th West Virginia, was wounded in the right arm in the fighting at Jackson on July 11. Sherman defeated Johnston's relief corps at Jackson by July 19, and the federal forces occupied the city. This ended the last Confederate effort to seize Vicksburg.[118]

The 4th West Virginia, together with their fellow regiments, proceeded to the area near Black River and established Camp Sherman on July 25, which they maintained until September 27. William Grayum vividly described their new encampment when he wrote: "Our camp is about ten miles from Vicksburg and four miles from Black River in a grove of beech and oak trees. We have cut out the small trees and have the advantage of both shade and air. The ground is just rolling enough to drain well and taking it all around it is far the best camp we ever had."[119]

1st Lieutenant James H. Ralston, Company E, resigned on July 28 ostensibly due to "family illness," but as earlier noted, Colonel Dayton reported Ralston as "completely incompetent and dissipated," which was supported by General Lightburn, who shared a disdain for Ralston and wrote, "I know him to be useless." The resignation was approved on August 8. In another organizational matter, on July 20, Assistant Surgeon Homer C. Waterman of the 4th West Virginia was approved for a 20-day leave of absence on a surgeon's certificate due to having chronic diarrhea for four months.[120]

Assistant Surgeon Homer C. Waterman.
Private Collection.

The 4th West Virginia "adopted" a new member on August 1, although the person was present with the regiment throughout the Vicksburg Campaign. A former slave named Carolyn/Caroline McCabe became a beloved friend of the 4th West Virginia. In June of 1863 she met Dr. John R. Philson, assistant surgeon of the 4th West Virginia, and worked with him in the regimental hospital. When the regiment later moved to Camp Sherman, she went with Philson and was employed from August 1, 1863, until March 13, 1864, as a nurse for the regiment, paid directly by Philson. Another former slave named Alfred Taylor was employed as a camp servant to Dr. Philson, and he and Caroline later married in Middleport, Ohio, shortly after the end of the war.[121]

According to Private Peter F. Zeis, Company E, 4th West Virginia, Caroline remained with the regiment from Vicksburg to Memphis, then on to Chattanooga, Missionary Ridge, and Knoxville, until about March 1, 1864, when she and Philson, along with many of the regiment, returned to Ohio as veterans. 2nd Lieutenant Robert Dyke, Company C, 4th West Virginia, wrote of Caroline: "Her services were very valuable and highly appreciated by the sick and wounded as she gave every attention as to cleanliness. Ever willing to wait on them at every time and did it cheerfully." She later remained employed by Dr. Philson at Middleport while many of the veterans moved on to the 1864 fighting in the Shenandoah Valley. On or around April 10, 1864, she was employed as a laundress for the 67th U.S. Colored Infantry. In 1893, she filed for a pension as a nurse in the U.S. Medical Department but was denied, due to an army regulation that female nurses working in military hospitals during the war were ineligible for a pension. She died at Middleport, Ohio, in 1905. A number of former members of the 4th West Virginia attended her funeral and were pallbearers.[122]

Between July 25 and September 27, the 4th West Virginia Infantry remained at Camp Sherman, performing the usual camp activities, such as fatigue and guard duty, but were also able to go squirrel hunting. Sickness still prevailed, as evidenced by Private Fernandes Jeffrey, Company K, who died on July 27 of chronic diarrhea. Private Henry H. Dawson, also of Company K, who had been detailed as a cook at the regimental hospital, said that he took care of Jeffrey during his illness. Dawson sent a letter to the father of Fernandes, Milton Jeffrey, in which he stated Fernandes died, "...after a long and lingering disease–I stayed with him during his sickness," at Fernandes' request.[123]

William Grayum wrote on August 5 that General Lightburn was in command of their division, having replaced General Francis Blair, who had been made Military Governor of the State of Mississippi. He also confirmed rumors that the 4th West Virginia desired to return to West Virginia for duty, but such a possibility was yet in the distant future.[124]

The resignation of 1st Lieutenant James H. Ralston, Company E, was finally accepted on August 8—only this time with no mention of his incompetence. On August 23, Grayum wrote from Camp Sherman, "We are having a great deal of ague and diarrhea in camp at present and have lost several men out of the Regiment lately but none of our Company."[125]

Three officers inspecting meat for the regiment on August 25 found the pork was soured and unfit for issue, and a general inspection was made on August 30. Camp duty continued, and on September 7 two members of the regiment transferred to the Signal Corps. On September

10, 1st Lieutenant Alpheus Beall, Company K, was appointed adjutant, while there was a general review of the whole division at Sherman's headquarters on September 19.[126]

Alpheus Beall.
Courtesy of Lt. Eric M. Beall.

A few days prior to September 24, Lieutenant Colonel John L. Vance and 1st Lieutenant William Grayum made a return visit to Gallipolis, as local newspapers lauded the Gallipolis men of the 4th West Virginia. Also on the 24th, Chaplain Woodhull mentioned that Colonel Dayton had told him he was trying to return the regiment back to West Virginia.[127]

The long break ended on September 26, when Colonel Dayton ordered all convalescents of the 2nd Brigade guarding the residences of citizens to report to the brigade as part of a movement to Memphis, Tennessee. John G. Farrar later wrote they moved from Camp Sherman to Vicksburg and then sailed more than 400 miles to Memphis, Tennessee, arriving there October 3.[128]

The new campaign began as the regiment marched for Vicksburg and embarked there on transports, including the ship *War Eagle*, on September 27, and landed about 75 miles above Vicksburg two days later. William L. Safreed recorded they passed Greenville, Mississippi, and Napoleon, Arkansas, on October 1; Helena, Arkansas, the following day; and arrived at Memphis on October 3, where they were encamped until October 8.[129]

Safreed claimed on October 6 they were ordered to be ready to march the following morning at 9 a.m., but on October 7 the order was actually delayed until the next day, according to regimental records. In order to pass the time, Safreed went to the theater in Memphis in the evening. The command was ordered to move the following day, and the 4th West Virginia was to escort the train to White's Station, where the brigade commander met them.[130]

The move eastward to Chattanooga, Tennessee, began at 5 a.m. on October 8 and progressed 16 miles to Germantown, Tennessee that day and another 26 miles to Moscow, Tennessee the following day. The march continued on October 10, covering nine miles to LaGrange, Tennessee, followed by 29 miles to Pocahontas, Tennessee on the 11th, where they remained on the 12th. General Giles Smith took over command of the 2nd Division, 15th Corps, at Clear Creek.[131]

The 4th West Virginia was once more on the march on October 13 and went into camp about four miles after crossing the Hatchee River. An additional 15 miles was covered the next day, and on October 15 the men marched to Corinth, Mississippi, then marched three more miles out on the railroad and camped (The regimental order book states the regiment was at Clear Creek). On October 16, the regiment was in the rear of Corinth, where William Grayum, Company G, who had advanced through the ranks from 2nd sergeant to 2nd lieutenant of his company, was now promoted to captain, as his brother Henry, the former captain, had been promoted to major of the regiment, replacing the deceased Major Goodspeed.[132]

Captain William Grayum.
Terry Lowry Collection.

William Grayum was born September 3, 1821, in Gallipolis, Gallia County, Ohio. He became an expert engineer and sawyer, and as he owned a portable sawmill, he had been detailed by the government to saw lumber at the head of the Kanawha River. He enrolled in Company G, 4th West Virginia, as a 2nd sergeant in December of 1861 and was promoted to 2nd lieutenant of the company on March 19.[133]

The regiment marched eight miles out the Chattanooga Railroad and camped on October 17. Up at 5 a.m. October 18, they passed Burnsville at 10 a.m., and Iuka, Mississippi at 4 p.m. While at Iuka the regimental order book states that orders from headquarters, 2nd Division, Major General Frank P. Blair, Jr.'s Division, 15th Army Corps, named the 4th West Virginia as part of the 2nd Brigade. Commanded by Brigadier General Lightburn, the brigade also included the 30th, 37th, and 47th Ohio Infantries and the 83rd Indiana Infantry. In addition, Sherman's army was named to the Department and Army of the Tennessee. From Iuka, the regiment began to march at 10 a.m. on October 19, marched four miles, and camped near the Memphis and Charleston Railroad.[134]

Operations on the Memphis and Charleston Railroad in Alabama October 20 – 29, 1863

On the march at 10 a.m. on October 20, the 4th West Virginia crossed Bear Creek into Alabama, marched nine miles and camped within one mile of Cherokee Station, where they could hear the sound of General Peter Joseph Osterhaus' men giving battle at nearby Barton Station. The 4th West Virginia moved into camp at Cherokee Station until October 25. The 37th Ohio Infantry relieved the regiment on October 23, and two days later, on the 25th, the 4th West Virginia was ordered to be ready to march at 2 a.m. Before departing Cherokee Station, William Grayum updated the situation as he wrote: "The health of our Company is better than ever before....The Rebel Cavalry are skirmishing every day with our advance but I don't think that their force amounts to much. I suppose that we are to guard and repair this Railroad, up to Decatur, a distance of about 100 miles from here."[135]

Companies D and F of the 4th West Virginia led the advance as skirmishers on October 26 and encountered rebel soldiers at the foot of Olive Hill, driving them back to Tuscumbia, Alabama.[136]

Tuscumbia (Little Bear Creek), Alabama October 27, 1863

The battle of Tuscumbia actually took place about three miles west of the town at Little Bear Creek on October 27. There, Federals engaged the cavalry forces of Major General Stephen D. Lee. During this engagement, a skirmish line of the 4th West Virginia drove the Confederate troopers back a mile across an open field, then the regiment marched to Chickasaw. At a later date Captain William Grayum wrote:

I was taken sick the night before our skirmish but as my Company was one of the four in the advance, I went with them of course. We drove them four miles by the road but I was on the right and made a circuit nearly twice that distance through the woods and brush and I was nearly worn out by the time we got through. Our boys behaved nobly as usual and won the praise of the Division Commander (General Giles Smith) as well as the whole army but Col. Vance will gas enough about it and I will shut up.[137]

The 4th West Virginia marched about seven miles from Cherokee Station toward the Tennessee River and camped on October 30, arriving at Chickasaw, Alabama, on October 31.[138]

November opened with the 4th West Virginia initiating their march at 6 a.m. on the first day of the month, moving eight miles to camp near the Tennessee River—one and a half miles above Eastport, Mississippi—and beginning to cross the river on transports. On the second day of the month, the regiment crossed the Tennessee River and marched by Waterloo, Alabama, to camp about three miles from Chickasaw Landing. The march continued at 7 a.m. on November 3 as they advanced about ten miles up the Tennessee River to camp at Gravel Springs, Alabama.[139]

Companies A and F of the regiment moved in advance as skirmishers on November 4 and covered seven miles to reach Florence, Alabama. They resumed the march at 7 a.m. the following day and covered an additional 12 miles to Clear Creek, Alabama. The regiment was up again at 8 a.m. on November 6, marched 15 miles to Ashmoore Run, Alabama, then resumed the march on November 7, advancing 18 miles to a creek about four miles from Pulaski, Tennessee.[140]

The seemingly endless marching began again at 7 a.m. on November 8, and they passed through Pulaski, Tennessee around 10 a.m., then on to Bradshaw Creek, Tennessee, a total distance of 16 miles for the day. Departing Bradshaw Creek early on November 9, they marched 15 miles and "came up with the 3rd & 4th divisions and camped within one mile of Fayetteville, Tennessee." Starting their march at midnight on November 10, the 4th West Virginia passed through Fayetteville at about 1 p.m., then marched about eight miles and camped.[141]

At 7 a.m. on November 11, the 4th West Virginia marched 15 miles and camped, as Company F was assigned picket guard for the night. The trek continued on the 12th, where the 4th West Virginia marched 14 miles, passing through New Market, Alabama. With little time to rest, the regiment started at 9 a.m. on November 13, marched 14 miles to the Memphis and Charleston Railroad, and went into camp at Paint Creek, Alabama. The following day's march took the regiment 15 miles out the Charleston and Memphis Railroad, where they camped.[142]

As usual, the march resumed at 7 a.m. on November 15 and covered 17 miles, passing through Bellfonte, and they camped outside Stevenson, Alabama. Once again on the move the following day, the regiment covered five miles and stopped for dinner at Stevenson, then marched four miles out the railroad and camped, only to begin again at 10 a.m. on November 17 and march six more miles to Bridgeport, Alabama. On November 18, the regiment finally spent a day resting in camp.[143]

The brief respite ended on November 19, when the 4th West Virginia crossed the Tennessee River on pontoon bridges, then moved ten miles and camped. The march resumed at sunrise on November 20 and took them 18 miles to camp at Lookout Valley, Tennessee. William Safreed wrote in his diary that the 4th West Virginia crossed the Tennessee River on November 21 and then marched two miles to near Chattanooga, Tennessee. The next day, orders were received to be ready to march at midnight.[144]

General Lightburn indicated that the soldiers left camp on the evening of November 23, marched to the Tennessee River, and moved to near Caldwell's at 3 a.m. George W. Gilliland, Company C, confirmed: "We arrived on the night of the 23rd of November....at one-o'clock in the night and by 2:30 o'clock we had a pontoon bridge across the river and our soldiers and artillery started across before daylight. One company of our men went....to the rear of the enemy's picket guard, came down on them and captured them all, 42 in number. Not a gun was fired. We took them completely by surprise." William L. Safreed,

Company F, said they moved about five miles up the Tennessee River and crossed in small boats at about two o'clock at night.[145]

Missionary Ridge, Tennessee
November 24 - 25, 1863

Earlier in October 1863, General Ulysses S. Grant was placed in command of the Union army in the Western Theater. He quickly moved to reinforce the strategically important city of Chattanooga, Tennessee. Located where the Tennessee River flows through the Cumberland Mountains, forming large gaps, it was known as the gateway to the deep South. Chattanooga was a vital railroad hub, connecting to Nashville and Knoxville, as well as south toward Atlanta. The city was also a key manufacturing site for iron. Grant was keenly aware that maintaining control of this area would enable his critical supply lines to remain open, allowing him to sustain extended operations against General Braxton Bragg's Confederates, whom he hoped to soon force back into Georgia by engaging in the battles of Lookout Mountain and Missionary Ridge, fought on the heights above the city. The battle at Lookout Mountain later became known as the "Battle above the clouds" due to the high elevation and steep climb Union soldiers had to make in the attack.[146]

George W. Gilliland, Company C, 4th West Virginia, recalled, "The fighting now began in earnest and on the 24th General [Joseph] Hooker stormed Lookout Mountain on the left of the Confederate line and carried it after a hard fight." Another soldier of the 4th West Virginia claimed that on the evening of November 24 "our Corps" drove back the rebels and occupied the western extremity of Missionary Ridge, a height with a commanding view of Chattanooga and Lookout Mountain. In his official report, General Lightburn wrote that his men crossed the river on pontoon boats on November 24, and that they took position on an elevation near the river and entrenched.

At 2 p.m., they moved out in line of battle for Missionary Ridge and took the first hill without opposition. On the summit of the hill, Lightburn detected it was not the designated hill and ordered Lieutenant

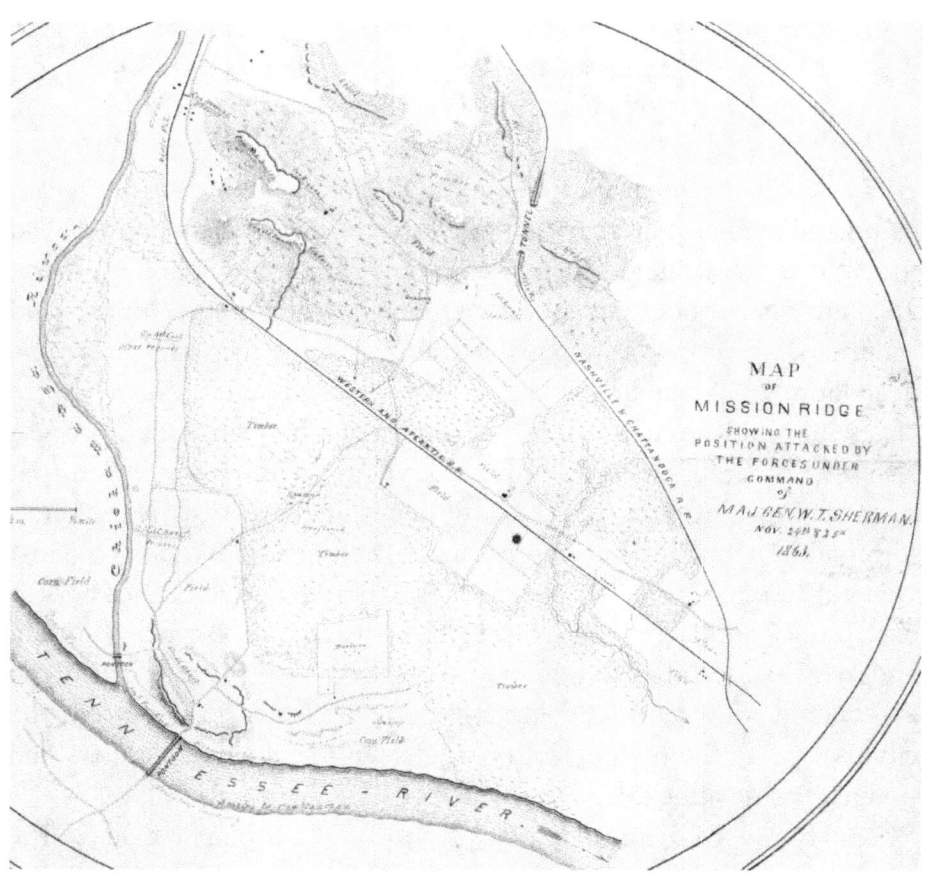

Map of Missionary Ridge showing the position attacked by the forces under
command of Maj. Gen. William T. Sherman, November 24-25, 1863.
Note location of Gen. Lightburn in upper left of map.
Library of Congress.

Colonel Augustus Parry, with his 47th Ohio Volunteer Infantry, to take position on the hill directly in front of Lightburn. On so doing, Parry reported the rebels attacking him from the other side of the hill, as well as rebel artillery from another elevated position on the same hill. Lightburn ordered Colonel Theodore Jones, 30th Ohio Infantry, to reinforce him and ordered Colonel B.J. Spooner, 83rd Indiana Infantry, and Lieutenant Colonel James Dayton, 4th West Virginia, to the same hill, which they were to entrench. He placed Lieutenant Colonel Louis Von Blessing's 37th Ohio on the point of the first hill Lightburn had occupied, facing Chickamauga Creek, to protect Lightburn's left flank and rear. The command remained in this position until the next morning.[147]

William Safreed was brief in his description, saying they started to attack the rebels at 2 p.m. with companies A, B, and F of the 4th West Virginia in advance as skirmishers. They advanced one mile and came upon the rebels in line of battle, drove in their skirmishers, and were relieved and fell back about 6 p.m.[148]

The fighting intensified at Missionary Ridge on November 25, when Lightburn received a verbal order just before 9 a.m. from General Sherman to send forward 200 men to occupy Tunnel Hill. He ordered the 30th Ohio and two companies of the 4th West Virginia, under Captain John L. Mallernee, to take the hill, along with Lieutenant Colonel Parry, 47th Ohio, who was directed to place three companies on the left flank as Colonel Theodore Jones advanced on the hill, which was occupied by Confederates. Lightburn ordered the 37th Ohio forward to support Jones, who advanced, with the 4th West Virginia in reserve, to the first elevation and drove their enemy from the outer works. Jones then moved his skirmishers to within 50 to 75 yards of the interior line and made 20 assaults on the Confederate line, holding his position until sunset, when they were relieved by the 1st Brigade. Lightburn then bivouacked on the entrenched hill that night.[149]

George Gilliland, Company C, 4th West Virginia, who had been assigned to the Pioneer Corps, wrote:

On the 25th the entire Union army advanced on them driving them from the first hill to the second where they were strongly fortified. Myself with others went on the hill to level up the ground to get one of our batteries in position. There were about 20 of us. It was a hot place as iron and lead were flying thick and fast. Two of our boys were killed and six or seven wounded. After we got our cannons in position and the bugle sounded for the pioneers to fall back it made us feel good....After we had taken possession of the first hill our troops and rebels made a charge on each other and met in the hollow. We had the 83rd Indiana, a new regiment, in front and a few of them were killed. They became demoralized and ran. The 4th Virginia and 47th Ohio were ordered to charge. They met the enemy in the hollow coming together clubbed muskets (striking each other with their guns). It got too hot for the Johnnies and they retreated. Their loss was heavy while that of our men was light. Our boys captured several of them and brought them out to our lines on double-quick. Some of them were wounded and some of them unhurt except their feelings at being whipped.[150]

William Safreed added, "at 10 A.M. Company F of the 4th West Virginia charged twice on the reb works without success – heavy loss on our side and fell back." Private John Perry Wolfe, Company E, reportedly, "scaled the gentle slopes of Missionary Ridge with his bayonet."[151]

Post-war image. John Perry Wolfe. Courtesy James C. Cline.

Describing injuries, George Gilliland reported: "One poor fellow was shot in the neck with a grape shot about the size of a hulled walnut. I saw the doctors cut it out and he sat on the ground and gripped beech roots while they were doing the cutting. The doctors could not give him chloroform on account of the clotted blood in his throat, this making him liable to choke to death. He was a corporal of the 30th Ohio and had the everlasting grit." Captain William Grayum, writing from camp near Chattanooga on the 28th but referring to the earlier battle, reflected: "Our loss has been very heavy, but not so heavy as theirs. Our regiment has been very fortunate in having a light loss as far as I have been able to learn. In my own company we have none killed and but two wounded. Sergeant John Greer [earlier shot through the left hand on May 22 at Vicksburg] shot through the [left] foot and [Private] Josiah W. Vance lost an arm (left) at the shoulder [amputated]. Both from Kanawha. [Major] Henry [Grayum] was safe the last time I heard from the field. Although he had been in the hottest of the fight and led the skirmishers of our Brigade – at all times a dangerous position." Grayum continued: "Our men are poorly prepared to bear the winter storms. Many of them are without shoes and nearly all with but one old rag for a shirt. Some with none at all. And no tents–makes our prospects gloomy for the winter."[152]

Casualties for the 4th West Virginia at Missionary Ridge were minimal. According to General Lightburn there were only seven men wounded and none killed, but other estimates have ranged as high as 15 or more. Besides the wounded already noted, 1st Sergeant Josiah Ryan, Company C, was wounded in the foot; Private Peter Hoffman, Company H, fell wounded; and Corporal Leander Harris and Wallace McCully (McCullah), both of Company D, were reportedly wounded, although there is no mention of it on their official service records.[153]

General Lightburn wrote that on the morning of November 26, with the defeated Confederates retreating southward into Georgia, he was ordered to provide his command with three days' rations and at noon march to Chickamauga Station. George W. Gilliland was a bit more detailed as he wrote: "We were ordered to take three days rations in our haversacks and go after them. We again made a charge on them and General [Braxton] Bragg in charge of the rebels started to retreat into Georgia and General Sherman started his army for Knoxville to help General [Ambrose] Burnside's army which was surrounded at that place by the rebels with General [James] Longstreet in command." The regiment marched until 10 p.m. without catching up with the enemy. William Grayum summed up the situation, "Owing to the state of the roads I don't think that we can advance any further South unless we repair the Rail Roads and that is slow work." He added, "We have had no snow or very cold weather yet."[154]

The march continued until roughly 3 p.m. on November 27, and Lightburn camped in the advance about one mile past Chickamauga Station, Georgia, as the pursuing Federals shelled the rear of Bragg's force. The 4th West Virginia reached Graysville Station, Georgia, on November 28 where the regiment "carried rails to burn the railroad." The brigade destroyed the railroad for about one mile below the station, having covered a total distance of 17 miles from Chattanooga. November 29 found the 4th West Virginia on a six-mile march, stopping briefly for the division train to catch up and bring them three days' rations, after which they marched to the railroad and camped at dark.[155]

On November 30, the regiment advanced 17 miles and passed through Cleveland, Tennessee. On December 1, the march began at midnight and took the regiment 11 miles, passing through Charleston, Tennessee, before the men camped at Hiawassee River. The second day of December, the march began at daylight and moved the regiment 24 miles, as they passed through both Athens and Sweetwater, Tennessee. The march was slowed on December 3 as the men had to stop for a bridge to be built, having covered 12 miles to the Tennessee River.[156]

Organizational changes within the 4th West Virginia continued on December 3, as Captain David A. Russell was appointed recruiting officer for the Veteran Volunteer Corps of the regiment. Moving again at about 9 a.m. on December 4, the 4th West Virginia crossed the Tennessee River, and Company F went on picket guard at night. The following day, the regiment marched 15 miles out the Knoxville road and camped, while on December 6 they began at 7 a.m., marched 22 miles, and camped within one mile of Maryville, Tennessee, about 20 miles from Knoxville.[157]

Unable to drive General Ambrose Burnside from Knoxville, and with Sherman's army approaching, Confederate General James Longstreet ended his siege of the city. With Sherman's assistance was no longer needed, he ordered his troops, including the 4th West Virginia, to make an about face early on December 7 and move back to Morando, crossing the river, where they encamped, having covered a total distance of 20 miles. Burnside thanked Sherman for his successful work at Knoxville during the siege. George W. Gilliland added, "When we came within about 15 miles of Knoxville upon the approach of Sherman's army Longstreet raised the siege and started to retreat into Virginia."[158]

Yet again, the 4th West Virginia found itself on the march on December 8, on another road to Tellico, Tennessee, covering 15 miles and wading the Tellico River. They covered an additional 15 miles on December 9, bringing the regiment to the iron works on Tellico River, where they stopped for dinner, then did another about face and marched nine miles down the opposite side of the river. The next day brought another twist, this one resulting in the regiment tramping back to the iron works, where they took the road leading into North Carolina and camped near the Tennessee and North Carolina border. They rested there all day on December 11.[159]

Again retracing their steps, the regiment began to march at 8 a.m. and went back to camp about three miles from the old iron works. Charleston, Tennessee was reached on December 13, after marching 13 miles, followed by 12 miles on the 14th to Connesauga Creek. The incessant marching continued on December 15, passing through Charleston, Tennessee, at approximately 11 p.m. and stopped at 4 p.m. to camp about two miles from Cleveland, Tennessee.[160]

At 9 a.m. on December 16, the 4th West Virginia passed through Cleveland, Tennessee, on a 13-mile march and camped about two miles from Ooltewah Station, Tennessee. The regiment was up early on December 17, marched 18 miles, crossed Chickamauga Creek on a pontoon bridge, and camped two-and-a-half miles from Chattanooga.

On that day, 13 members of the 4th West Virginia, all convalescents, were detailed for guard duty for the 15th Corps.[161]

On December 18, the regiment marched down to the town for three days' rations, then marched "toward the bridge passing the sick and barefoot men going down the river in pontoon boats," some six miles to camp at Lookout Valley. The convalescents were found on December 19 about one-and-a-half miles below Bridgeport, Alabama, as the regiment marched 24 miles and crossed on the pontoons at Bridgeport. The 4th West Virginia found a little rest, as they remained at Bridgeport from December 19 until Christmas Day.[162]

Colonel James H. Dayton claimed he received information on December 20 that men from another regiment would fill up the depleted ranks of the 4th West Virginia, and Sergeant William M. Hovey, Company E, was ordered to Barboursville, West Virginia, on December 23 to accept a commission as a 1st lieutenant in the 13th West Virginia Infantry. While his commission was not official until January 14, 1864, Hovey likely believed the transfer would at last place him closer to home and had no idea what that regiment would face in 1864, when it participated in all major actions during the bloody Shenandoah Campaign, including Lynchburg, Winchester, Kernstown, Fisher's Hill, and Cedar Creek. Hovey would survive unwounded, however, and was eventually promoted to major.[163]

Christmas was spent at Bridgeport, but orders were issued to be ready to march at 9 a.m. the day after the holiday, which the brigade performed. Company F of the 4th West Virginia was left to guard the wagon train. The regiment went into camp at 6 p.m. They moved onward to Stevenson, Alabama, the next morning, and continued another three-and-a-half miles toward the Memphis and Charleston Railroad. There, the regiment was put to work on December 28 making a road out of rails and logs, then camped near the railroad, having covered about three miles.[164]

With winter setting in and 1863 ending, the 4th West Virginia marched three miles to a creek on December 29, where their boats were moored. The march continued on December 30 to about two miles west of Bellfonte, Alabama, where the 1st Brigade camped near the railroad. At this location, the regimental order book listed John L. Vance as commanding the 4th West Virginia.[165]

While camped at Bellfonte on December 31, General Morgan L. Smith complimented the 2nd Division on the recent campaign for their march from Eastport to Tuscumbia. Shortly after the beginning of 1864, the 4th West Virginia went into winter quarters at Larkinsville, Alabama, built winter shanties, and named it Camp Sherman.[166]

4

1864-1865
Into the Shenandoah Valley

From December 8, 1863, through January 8, 1864, the 4th West Virginia Infantry had either been marching or skirmishing, with only five days' rest during that time. For four weeks of that time, they subsisted entirely off the countryside, before finally wintering at Camp Sherman at Larkinsville, Alabama. Hospital Steward Thomas Barton of the regiment remarked, "At this place [Camp Sherman] 'the boys' had an easy time during the remainder of the winter, having nothing but guard duty to perform and an occasional scout."[1]

General Morgan Lewis Smith's entire 2nd Division, which included the 4th West Virginia Infantry, received orders from Major General John Logan on January 7 to move from Scottsboro, Alabama, to Larkinsville on the Memphis and Charleston Railroad, to take charge of all grist and sawmills and to put them in working order. Smith was also ordered to examine Roseburg and Santa creeks to see if pontoons could be taken up either stream.[2]

On January 10, Camp Sherman fell victim to a "Band of Marauders" who were committing depredations outside the immediate camp lines against civilians. The soldiers hoped they were not members of the division. The 2nd Brigade was ordered to investigate and search for these reported thieves, or "marauders" as written in the regimental order book, south of the railroad, while the 1st Brigade looked to the north.[3]

Further orders given on January 11 placed Ewing's 4th Division in charge of guarding the railroad and telegraph line from Scottsboro, Alabama to Stevenson, Alabama. Brigadier General Morgan Smith's 2nd Division was to guard the railroad and telegraph line from the pickets of Ewing on the rail line west of Scottsboro, to Mr. Dodson's plantation about midway between Larkinsville and Woodville.[4]

While on furlough in Gallipolis, Ohio, on February 4, Captain William Grayum gave the *Gallipolis Journal* a list of subscribers of the regiment to the paper, along with cash payment for their subscription renewal. Grayum also mentioned the health of the 4th West Virginia was good while at Camp Sherman, but on the very next day, Sergeant William Henry Reeves of Company I, from Gallipolis, died from chronic diarrhea at Larkinsville, Alabama. His remains were sent home. The only other significant event was at Camp Sherman, where Martin Barringer and Augustus A. Chapman were relieved from duty in the Pioneer Corps, and William Woomer and Joel Parsons were apparently detailed as their replacements.[5]

The 4th West Virginia Infantry underwent a major change on February 11, as noted by Thomas Barton, who wrote: "a part of the regiment enlisted as veterans for three years longer, or during the war; and remained at Larkinsville till the latter part of March. The balance of the regiment was consolidated with the 8th Missouri; that is Company A of the 4th West Virginia was consolidated with Company A of the 8th Missouri, etc." Further details regarding the veterans were given by Lieutenant William Sisson, Company B, who added, "...a trifle over three hundred men, a small regiment, but tried and true." Sisson believed the regiment would probably stop at Gallipolis on the way to Wheeling.[6]

This change in the regiment's organization was confirmed by the February 16, 1864, entry in the regimental order book, which stated 86 members of the 4th West Virginia were assigned by General Sherman to the 8th Missouri Infantry "until the expiration of their term of service." This would keep the non-veterans of the 4th West Virginia, those who had enlisted later in the war than the original veterans, in the South, while the veterans re-enlisted, returned home, and were given a 30-day furlough. The non-veterans who were transferred to the 8th Missouri would accompany Sherman in his campaign from Chattanooga to Atlanta and would be mustered out in July at the expiration of their term of service. This change meant that, in essence, there would be two active 4th West Virginia regiments at the same time, as those serving in the 8th Missouri were still considered members of the 4th West Virginia. The original veterans remaining in the regiment soon found themselves in the bloody Shenandoah Valley of Virginia, while those in the 8th Missouri participated in the battles along Sherman's March to Atlanta.[7]

Still at Larkinsville (Camp Sherman) on February 18, the 4th West Virginia was ordered to report the following day, with three days' rations, to Captain T. Voges, Assistant Quartermaster, 2nd Division, for forage duty.[8]

In compliance with the November 21, 1863 order of the 4th West Virginia, two men from Company A of the 4th West Virginia, Lewis Love and Charles Birch, were assigned to Company H, 1st Illinois Artillery, on February 26, until the expiration of their term of service.[9]

Reportedly, during February of 1864, the 4th West Virginia took part in a raid in northern Alabama, marching about 175 miles.[10]

Re-assignments continued on March 4 when 31 non-veterans of the 4th West Virginia were assigned to the 8th Missouri Infantry. On March 15, following their re-enlistment, the veterans began their movement by rail and river to Wheeling, West Virginia, where they received 30-day veteran's furloughs. The following day, Brigadier General Lightburn, 2nd Brigade, 2nd Division, 13th Army Corps, relieved Acting Assistant Inspector General Benjamin D. Boswell and Martin Lightburn from General Joseph A.J. Lightburn's headquarters, so they could go north with the regiment.[11]

The people of Gallipolis, Ohio, were thrilled with the prospect of their boys returning home. This was evidenced in the March 17 edition of the *Gallipolis Journal*, which reported 23 veterans of the regiment from Gallipolis had re-enlisted and were now referred to as "Veterans." They had been given a furlough until May 3. In addition, Colonel James H. Dayton, yet in command at Larkinsville, reported the remaining veterans of the regiment in the South would probably depart for West Virginia on the evening of March 17, with the caution, "any man drunk, a straggler, or bad behavior will be arrested and left behind."[12]

In the latter part of March, the non-veterans were consolidated with the 8th Missouri Infantry, then continued to serve under General Sherman until their enlistments expired around July 20, 1864. The 8th Missouri served in the Army of the Tennessee, 1st Division, 1st Brigade, under Brigadier General Giles A. Smith, while Brigadier General Lightburn would command the 2nd Brigade, 2nd Division, Army of the Tennessee.[13]

Major General John A. Logan, 2nd Division, Army of Tennessee, at Huntsville, Alabama, on March 18, ordered the 4th West Virginia Veteran Infantry to report to the superintendent of the recruiting service for the State of West Virginia for a 30-day furlough, and at the expiration of the furlough, to report to the commanding officer of the 2nd Division in the field.[14]

About March 20, the veterans reached Louisville and left in the evening on a steamer for Wheeling, where they arrived on March 22 according to James Farrar. He wrote that the citizens and Governor Arthur I. Boreman gave the regiment a grand reception party, from which they departed for their homes on their 30-day furlough. This account is disputed by a regimental history of the 7th West Virginia Infantry, which stated that on March 26 the steamer *Express* tied up at the wharf at Moundsville, Marshall County, West Virginia, and a large detachment of "Veterans," including some members of the 4th West Virginia, debarked and were placed under the immediate command of a captain of the 7th West Virginia. This was followed by a host of festivities for the soldiers during the day. It is possible the 4th West Virginia divided into two different boats and arrived on different days.[15]

The regiment remained in Gallipolis and its vicinity from April 20 to May 2. On April 26, Lieutenant Colonel John L. Vance sent Captain Calvin Shepard to Wheeling to manage financial and other logistical business of the regiment.[16]

The 4th West Virginia veterans returned to duty on May 1, were ordered to the Department of West Virginia, and then placed in the 2nd Brigade, 1st Infantry Division, under Brigadier General J.C. Sullivan, in the Provisional Brigade commanded by Colonel Joseph Thoburn, along with the 1st, 12th, 14th and 15th West Virginia Infantry Regiments.[17]

The regiment took a boat to Parkersburg and from there took the railroad to Martinsburg. On May 4, the 4th West Virginia was assigned to participate in operations against Lynchburg, Virginia. However, according to James Farrar, the veterans reported back from their furloughs to Gallipolis, were ordered up the Ohio River to Parkersburg, then to Clarksburg, and then to Weston, where they remained for two weeks. They were then ordered back to Clarksburg to participate in General David Hunter's Raid on Lynchburg, Virginia.[18]

The May 5, 1864, edition of the *Gallipolis Journal,* apparently unaware of the regiment's new assignment, reported the 4th West Virginia were collecting again for another campaign but were unaware of where they would be sent. The general desire of the regiment was to be sent up the Kanawha to defend their homes.[19]

Confusion reigned on May 6 as General Henry Halleck told Governor Boreman that if the 4th West Virginia were still in West Virginia, he was authorized to organize and employ them to guard the Baltimore and Ohio Railroad. Colonel Nathan Wilkinson of the 6th West Virginia Infantry, commanding a brigade at this time, wrote General Franz Sigel, stating he was informed the 4th West Virginia had left Gallipolis for Parkersburg that morning, and the commanding officer of the 4th would report to him. Wilkinson, at New Creek, told General Benjamin F. Kelley that the 4th West Virginia had been assigned to him and would report the following day. Kelley responded by telling Wilkinson to tell the 4th West Virginia to remain at Parkersburg for the time being.[20]

Major General William T. Sherman.
Library of Congress.

The confusion continued on May 7 as Kelley told Boreman he had ordered the 4th West Virginia to Clarksburg and for the 4th West Virginia to send two companies, along with a squad of Captain Thomas Maulsby's Battery with one gun, to Weston for protection.[21]

While the 4th West Virginia remained at Parkersburg on May 9, on the 13th, Colonel Nathan Wilkinson told Kelley the regiment had arrived at Clarksburg and he had sent the two detachments to Weston.[22]

Resaca, Georgia
May 13 -15, 1864

The non-veterans (8th Missouri Infantry) left Larkinsville on May 1 for service as mounted infantry in the advance of Colonel James McPherson in General Sherman's advance to Atlanta. One of the earliest clashes the 4th West Virginia fought in on this campaign was at Resaca, Georgia, on May 13. Corporal George Gilliland wrote in 1899:

On the seventh of May Sherman started his army after the enemy. They were commanded by General [Joseph] Johnston. We drove them down to Resaca where they made a stand. They were extremely well fortified at that place and our men made an open charge on them but were repulsed with the loss of a great many. You could see many dead soldiers on the battle ground that had on the blue. The way iron and lead flew it seemed for a while [there] would be none left. I was close by General [Judson] Kilpatrick when he was wounded. He was shot through the thigh. His aid-de-camp helped him off his horse and sent a messenger after a doctor. One of our doctors dressed his wound and he begged them to put him in the saddle as he wanted to command his men, but the doctor would not allow it for he said he would bleed to death if he did. They took him to the rear. He was a brave little fellow.[23]

The battle, fought between May 13 and 15, was described further by Gilliland, as he wrote: "On the 15th our troops made another charge and again were repulsed with a heavy loss of men. Sherman then moved his army around to the left and went after them again. This time they had to retreat and fall back to Dallas [Georgia]."[24]

Meanwhile, the re-enlisted veterans of the 4th West Virginia were yet at Clarksburg on May 16 when Captain William Grayum, Company G, wrote: "We are again under marching orders and I suppose that this time we will go to Martinsburg with the six Companies that are here. The other four are at Weston and Glenville." Grayum assumed, "We travel on the Rail Road and it is easier than tramping through the mud, although we may have enough of that to do yet."[25]

This period was marred by confusing and alternating versions of locations, numbers, and dates regarding the 4th West Virginia. General Franz Sigel was at Martinsburg on May 17, where he ordered General B.F. Kelley to send him the 4th West Virginia. Kelley told him three companies of the 4th West Virginia were currently scouting in Lewis and Gilmer counties, and he had ordered the rest to Martinsburg as requested. On May 20, Kelley wrote Sigel from Cumberland, Maryland that the 4th West Virginia, minus the three companies in Lewis and Gilmer, had passed through on the night of May 19, and the lieutenant colonel commanding the regiment had said that in lieu of the hard service in the southwest, the War Department had ordered them back to West Virginia to guard the railroad. Kelley asked if he could use the regiment, having been reduced to about 300 men, to guard the railroad and his communications line.[26]

As the two different incarnations of the 4th West Virginia Infantry, the veterans and the non-veterans, continued to operate on separate fronts, General Kelley wrote to General Sigel on May 21 he would relieve the four companies of the regiment in Lewis and Gilmer counties "as soon as practicable" and have them rejoin their regiment. The following day, Lieutenant Colonel John L. Vance handed Sigel the order to relieve the four companies of the regiment and Vance would take command of the detachments.[27]

On May 21, Major General Franz Sigel was removed from command; he would soon be replaced with Major General David Hunter, per Special Order No. 105. Hunter, a West Point alumnus, became acquainted with Abraham Lincoln in 1860 while stationed at Fort Leavenworth, Kansas. Hunter was a strong abolitionist and achieved notoriety in 1862 when he issued his own Emancipation Proclamation in three Southern states; however, it was immediately rescinded by President Lincoln, who had not yet released his own. Not yet under Hunter, the 4th West Virginia was reassigned to the 1st Infantry Division, commanded of Brigadier General Jeremiah C. Sullivan.[28]

Dallas, Georgia
May 24 – June 4, 1864

The non-veterans of the 4th West Virginia (8th Missouri Infantry) advanced southward from Resaca to Dallas, Georgia, where fighting took place between May 24 and June 4, with the heaviest fighting between May 25 and 28. According to Corporal George Gilliland: "Here Johnston made another stand and it was hard fighting from the 25th to the 28th when he started to retreat again and Sherman's army after him. It was continuous fighting every day until Johnston's army reached Kennesaw Mountain, which place was strongly fortified."[29]

Private George W. Gandee, Company F, 8th Missouri Infantry (formerly with the 4th West Virginia), was killed in action on May 27 at Dallas. The battle raged on May 28, and on May 29 Private John C. Dawson, Company D, 4th West Virginia (8th Missouri), was captured.[30]

With General Hunter yet to take command, General Sigel, still operating out of Martinsburg in the Shenandoah Valley on May 31, assigned 130 men from the 4th West Virginia, along with detachments from other regiments, to escort and guard a wagon train.[31]

Map of Hunter's Lynchburg Campaign.
Library of Congress.

Piedmont (New Hope), Virginia
June 5 – 6, 1864

General David Hunter clashed with General William "Grumble" Jones at Piedmont (New Hope), Virginia, on June 5 – 6. Colonel James H. Dayton led a detachment of the 4th West Virginia in the fight as part of the infantry under General Jeremiah C. Sullivan, 2nd Brigade, with Colonel Joseph Thoburn commanding. Thoburn's report of the battle stated the 4th West Virginia guarded the wagon train. General Jones was killed in the battle, after which the Confederates retreated.[32]

In the pre-dawn darkness of June 10, Colonel Augustus Moor of the 28th Ohio Infantry assembled a force to escort northward the prisoners captured at Piedmont. This group included most of the 28th Ohio, a small detachment of the 4th West Virginia Infantry, and a mounted escort from the 1st Veteran Cavalry. Battery G, 1st West Virginia Light Artillery, provided support.[33]

The Lynchburg Campaign
June 14 – 22
and the
Battle of Lynchburg, Virginia
June 17 - 18

Between June 14 and 22, the 4th West Virginia, 1st Division, 2nd Brigade, under Colonel Joseph Thoburn, participated in Major General David Hunter's Lynchburg Campaign and were commanded by Colonel Dayton. The 4th West Virginia reportedly lost two killed and ten wounded. Hunter's Lynchburg Raid culminated in the battle of Lynchburg on June 17-18. On the latter date, the 4th West Virginia was detached from Joseph Thoburn's brigade to support a battery on the extreme left of the Union line. Private William M. Shannon, Company G, was wounded in action and left in the field hospital at Lynchburg, where he was captured. He was later exchanged and taken to the hospital at Annapolis, Maryland, where his leg was amputated above the knee.[34]

Finding Confederate defenses at Lynchburg too strong to assault, Hunter's army retreated and literally staggered back into West Virginia and the Kanawha Valley. The exhausted and hungry soldiers included the veterans of the 4th West Virginia Infantry, many of whom suffered from piles (hemorrhoids) and heatstroke, as well as the usual cases of disease and diarrhea. On the retreat Private Samuel Sampson, Company H, 4th West Virginia, "contracted a severe cold. This odd cold left him with a persistent ache in his legs and lower back. Near the end of the return march, Samuel broke down. This was also due somewhat to a severe lack of food, and a long hard march. He was put on a wagon" for the remainder of the return. He also suffered from piles on the march.[35]

During the retreat from Lynchburg, Lieutenant Colonel John L. Vance met one Dr. Perrin Gardner of Gallia County, Ohio, on the march from Staunton, Virginia, to Charleston, West Virginia. The doctor later recalled Vance was terribly fatigued and complained of great suffering from the wound he had received at Vicksburg.[36]

John F. Stone, Company F, reflected: "In all my four years' experience as a soldier this trip to or within sight of Lynchburg, Virginia was the most trying. It was a long tedious march ..."[37]   William Grayum wrote from the steamer *Nettie Sarputec* on the Kanawha River on July 3:

We arrived at Gauley Bridge last Wednesday tired out and starved out, dirty and ragged. I succeeded in bringing all my men through but one – William Shannon, who was shot through the knee at Lynchburg [and] was left in charge of the surgeon in the field. For the first time in my life I have seen men starved to death. We had some green regiments with us that had never seen any service but guarding Rail Roads and of course they suffered more than our veterans did....We were seven days without bread. All we had was a little poor beef.[38]

Captain William S. Hall developed piles (hemorrhoids) from overexertion and suffered from heat exhaustion. Sergeant David Gatchell, Company F, confirmed in Hall's pension application that he saw Hall's piles during the Lynchburg retreat and that they were the worst he had ever seen, and Hall was barely able to walk so he assisted him as much as possible.[39]

Battle of Kennesaw Mountain, Georgia
June 27, 1864

While the Lynchburg Campaign transpired in the Shenandoah Valley, the non-veterans operating with the 8th Missouri Infantry continued to move south with General William T. Sherman as he chased General Joseph Johnston, who took up a commanding defensive position north of Atlanta on Kennesaw Mountain, Georgia. According to George W. Gilliland:

Kennesaw Mountain which place was strongly fortified. Between the 15th of June and the 2nd of July Sherman made several attempts to force them out of that stronghold but failed with the loss of many men. One of the rebels came running over to our lines and we supposed he was running to desert the rebel army but he came right up to our flag and tore it down. It was a very foolish trick as our men shot him to pieces. At the same time they made a charge on our works and our soldiers made a charge on them and that was what you might call a genuine battle when the two forces came together. Many a soldier fell to rise no more in this world. Besides the killed our men brought out twenty-two hundred of them as prisoners.... Sherman then moved his army around to the rear of the enemy and made a charge on them. They again started to retreat. They retreated across the Chattahoochee River and within the lines of Atlanta.[40]

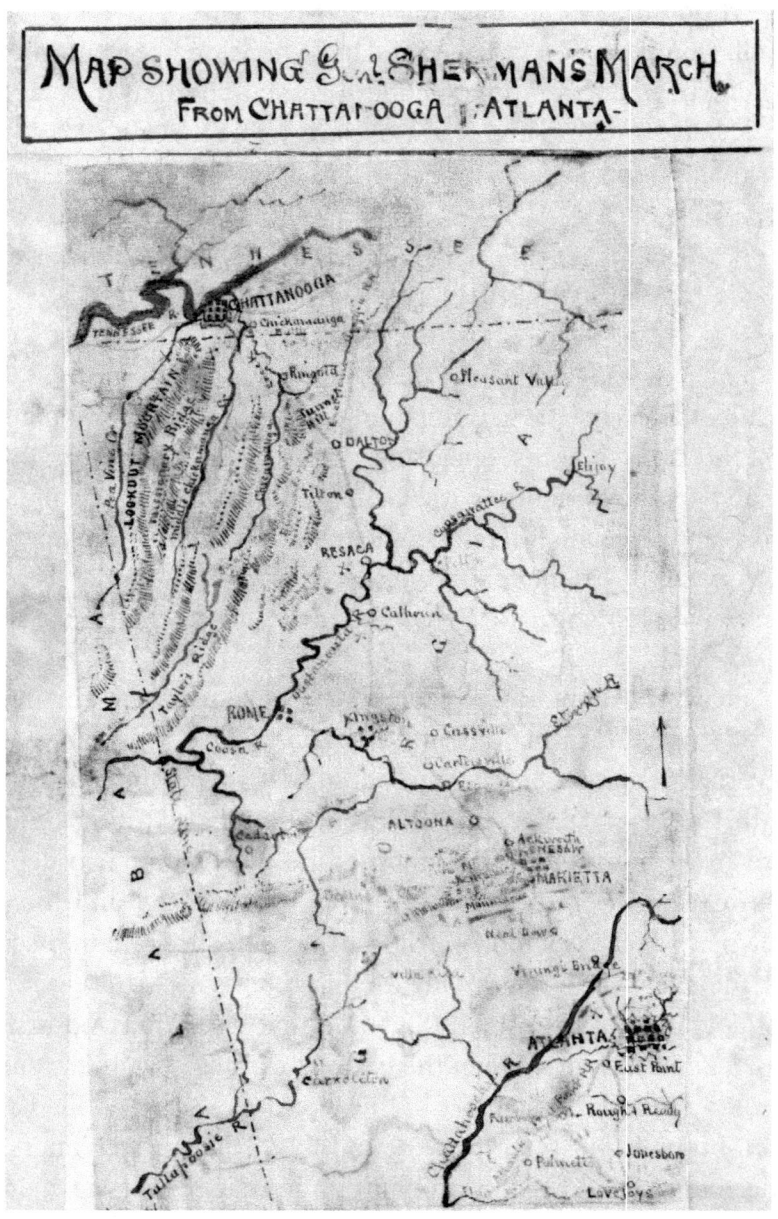

Atlanta Campaign showing Rebel Defenses. Map by Robert Sneeden.
Library of Congress, used with permission from
Virginia Museum of History and Culture.

The 4th West Virginians consolidated with the 8th Missouri remained at Marietta, Georgia, until their time of enlistment had nearly expired. They then took a train north to Wheeling, West Virginia. George Gilliland further wrote:

My time expired when I arrived in this city [near Atlanta]. We left them [Sherman's army] and started back to Chattanooga and in a freight car just below Resaca the rebels had put in a torpedo under the road and our train ran on it [probably late June] and the engine, tender and two freight cars were upset. It was quite an explosion. It tossed us around pretty lively for a little while. Old Colonel Jones was in one car and it threw him out and he lit on a rail pile badly hurt."

Gilliland added:

There was a fine house upon the raise and we went up and found the tools with which the rebels had done their digging under the house. We went to go into the house and there were two women there. The younger one met us at the door with a revolver and said she would shoot the first Yankee that would step in the door. One of our boys snatched the revolver from her and in a short time that house was burned to the ground. By this time another engine had been procured. We fixed the road so we could get over and then we went on to Chattanooga.[41]

Another version of the train episode appeared years later, written by an unidentified author, found in the Vicksburg Military Park booklet celebrating the dedication of the 4th West Virginia monument at Vicksburg. In this account, the train accident was said to have occurred somewhere between Dallas and Calhoun, Georgia. The date for the accident has been stated as June 27, but that would be unlikely as that is the date of the battle at Kennesaw Mountain.[42]

Thomas Barton summarily concluded: "No further accident occurred, and they reached Wheeling in safety. They went into camp on Wheeling Island, where they remained till the latter part of August, and were mustered out of the service...."[43]

The 4th West Virginia veterans continued their service in the Shenandoah Valley; Colonel James H. Dayton was mustered out at the expiration of his term of service on July 4, 1864, and command of the 4th West Virginia Infantry fell to Lieutenant Colonel John L. Vance. He arrived at New Creek on July 6 by order of General J.C. Sullivan, and on the 8th, according to James B.C. Vale, Company D of the 4th West Virginia was mustered out by 1st Lieutenant W.G. Fitch, United States Army.[44]

On July 11, Colonel Joseph Thoburn wrote in his journal that he had arrived at Martinsburg at 10 in the morning with the 1st, 4th, and 12th West Virginia Infantries, 2nd Maryland Home Brigade, and the 2nd Maryland Eastern Shore.[45]

On July 16, 1864, Major General David Hunter ordered Brigadier General George C. Crook to take field command of troops in the Department of West Virginia. On July 18, Crook then ordered Colonel Joseph Thoburn to take command of the 1st Division, which was then consolidated with remnants of the 3rd Brigade of the 2nd Division, increasing the 1st Division strength to approximately 6,000 troops. At that time, the 1st Division was comprised of two brigades; Colonel George D. Wells commanded the 1st Brigade: 34th Massachusetts, 5th New York Heavy Artillery, 116th, 123rd, and 170th Ohio, while Colonel William G. Ely had the 2nd Brigade: 18th Connecticut, 2nd Maryland (Eastern shore), 4th and 12th West Virginia.[46]

Snicker's Ferry (Cool Springs), Virginia
July 18, 1864

The next significant action involving the 4th West Virginia Infantry was the July 18 battle of Snicker's Ferry, also known as Snicker's Gap or Cool Springs. In this engagement, while holding the right flank, the regiment lost four officers wounded and 30 enlisted men killed or wounded. A correspondent identified as "J.A.W.," thought to be Private Joseph A. Walsh, Company K, noted that the entire command, under

Colonel Joseph Thoburn, crossed the Shenandoah River at Snicker's Ford, about a mile from Snicker's Gap. The 1st Brigade, under Colonel George D. Wells, was in the advance, followed by Colonel Thoburn with his 2nd Brigade and the 3rd Brigade led by Colonel Daniel Frost, which brought up the rear. Skirmishers were immediately sent forward as the division crossed the river at 3 p.m. and formed with the 1st Brigade on the left, the 3rd Brigade holding the center, and the 2nd Brigade holding the right. This position was held for the next hour without any sign of the enemy. At this point, the enemy was discovered massing on the right. To counter this movement, the 4th West Virginia was sent to the extreme right and formed on the crest of a small ridge running parallel to the river. A strong force of dismounted cavalry was placed as skirmishers, "to protect the battleline" even farther to the right and in advance of the 4th West Virginia.[47]

While the regiment was forming line of battle, a strong Confederate force appeared in their front along the skirt of a dense wood. As the Federals prepared to launch an assault, another large body of Confederates moved to the right within three hundred yards of the Charles Town turnpike, placing them in an excellent position to attack the Federals. The Confederates attacked en masse, driving off the dismounted cavalry, who did not fire a shot. Immediately Colonel John L. Vance moved two companies of the 4th West Virginia to the right to protect his exposed flank. But the Confederates had already advanced, and taking position behind a stone fence that ran at right angles with the Federal line, began pouring a deadly enfilading fire into the Union right and front. A Union soldier succinctly stated, "...here it was that all our loss occurred."[48]

Early news reports claimed 1st Lieutenant George A. Scott, Company F, "an efficient officer and perfect gentleman," was killed. In reality, however, Scott recovered and died in 1913 in Colorado. George F. Stone of Company F of the 4th West Virginia succinctly opined, "And I want to tell you that was a nasty little fight." In addition, he indicated that Sergeant Finley D. Chalfant lost a leg; his service records indicate that he was "severely wounded in the side" and left on the field. Private Daniel Forney McNeer was wounded badly but recovered and died in

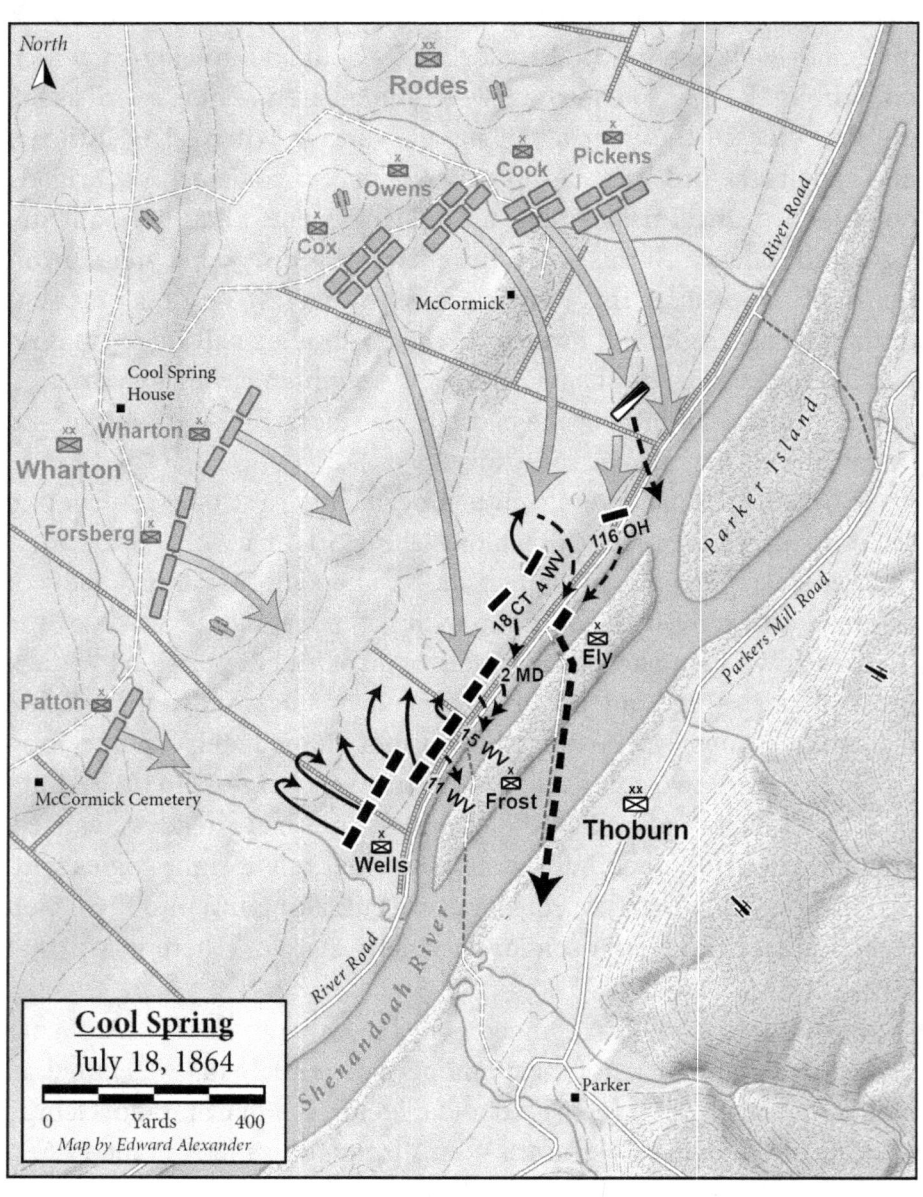

North

Rodes

Pickens

Cook

Owens

Cox

McCormick

Cool Spring
House

Wharton

Wharton

Forsberg

116 OH

18 CT 4 WV

2 MD

Ely

Patton

15 WV

McCormick Cemetery

11 WV Frost

Thoburn

Wells

Parker Island

River Road

Parkers Mill Road

River Road

Shenandoah River

Parker

Cool Spring
July 18, 1864

0   Yards   400
Map by Edward Alexander

Huntington, West Virginia, in 1923. Also wounded was Private David Hamilton, who received a severe shoulder wound from a conical ball, and "others of our company...."[49]

Private Joseph Walsh of Company K also noted that at this location Captain William S. Hall, Company G, was wounded slightly in the side (Not listed wounded in his official record); Captain Calvin A. Shepard, Company I, severely in the heel; and 1st Lieutenant Michael Christopher, Company H, severely in the leg.[50]

Lieutenant Colonel Vance realized the position was untenable and ordered the men to quickly fall back to a stone fence located about 50 yards to their rear and upon the riverbank. The dismounted cavalry rushed across the river, and it was suspected that many of them drowned. At the stone fence, Vance rallied the 4th West Virginia and other soldiers and was able to check the enemy assault. But the enemy on the far right was seen on the riverbank threatening to advance. At this critical point Colonel James Washburn and his 116th Ohio Infantry arrived and checked the enemy. Although it was thought Washburn may have been killed, he was seriously wounded but did survive. The 4th West Virginia and the 116th Ohio held the stone fence until dark, when they withdrew across the river under the cover of darkness. Many members of the 4th West Virginia believed they could have held the position at the fence all night, and Lieutenant Colonel Vance requested permission to do so but was denied.[51]

Lieutenant Colonel Vance, by this time in the war, had earned a reputation for efficiently and safely bringing his men from a battlefield. When crossing the Shenandoah River, he chose a few men and sent them to a small island in the middle of the river, and repeated the process until all were across. The colonel was the last to cross. An unidentified newspaper correspondent wrote: "The heroic conduct of Col. Vance in the trying ordeal cannot be too highly extolled. He labored incessantly to beat back the insolent foe and after having accomplished his object was the last man to cross the river."[52]

A member of the 12th West Virginia Infantry, also in the fight, later wrote of a particularly sad irony he observed:

One of the especially sad and lamentable results of this fight was, that some members of the 4th West Virginia Infantry whose time had expired were killed in it. They had been waiting before starting home until a sufficiently strong force should be going to the rear to make it safe for them to start. In the meantime, this Snicker's Ferry fight came on, and the 4th boys being plucky fellows generally, these discharged men said that they would not stand back while their comrades were going into a fight, and so some of the poor fellows were killed with discharges in their pockets. [53]

John Farrar also gave a detailed account of the fight at Cool Springs:

We followed the Rebel army around through Snicker's Gap, forded the Shenandoah River at Snicker's Ferry. There was just one way you could ford without going in over your head. The river was wide and deep. Gen. [Jubal] Early's Army was waiting for our Army to cross. He was behind a lot of timber, had set a trap for us. It took a long time for our division to cross. When we got across Gen. [Jeremiah C.] Sullivan sent the 4th [West] Va. [Virginia] on the skirmish line under [Lieutenant] Col. Vance. In a short time the Rebs showed themselves. They came marching in line of battle in front and on both flanks up the river and down the river. The General ordered us not to fire. Said they was our own men. A lot of them had captured a lot of our clothing sometime before & was wearing it, but we could see a lot dressed in the gray. They come within 4 or 500 yards and some of the boys began to fire at them. Gen. Sullivan rode out and threatened to shoot the first man that fired.[54]

Lieutenant Colonel Vance told Sullivan it was the enemy and asked him if he could not see the gray uniforms. Farrar continued: "Our fellows all began to shoot, didn't pay any attention to his [Sullivan] orders. The Rebel Army kept coming on closing up their ranks. Then another line of battle showed themselves, their reserve. They had our little Army completely surrounded. Except the ford, it was important to get away. They kept coming on, never paid any attention to our skirmish line firing on them. After they got pretty close they raised the Rebel yell and come on a charge. We had to get back to a stone fence where the rest of the Army was. They charged on the stone fence 5 or 6 times."[55]

As night fell, the Federals fell back across the river while the Confederates continued to pour volleys into them. John Farrar said the enemy suffered immense losses in their front, writing: "They was laying piled up in some places across one another. Our regiment had 120 men in the fight, lost 30." Farrar also noted that when his regiment fell back to the stone fence, the dismounted cavalry went into a panic, thinking it was "every man for himself," and broke for the river. As many as 30 men were said to have drowned and a few others were shot while crossing.[56]

Battle of Winchester, Virginia
(Second Kernstown)
July 24, 1864

The 4th West Virginia Infantry was at Cedar Creek, Virginia, on July 22, the same day as the battle of Atlanta, Georgia. On July 24, the regiment was engaged in battle near Winchester, Virginia, in an action known as Second Kernstown or Second Winchester. Colonel Joseph J. Thoburn indicated that at Kernstown, his division, including the 4th West Virginia Infantry, was posted on the far right or western flank. Colonel William G. Ely reported the 1st and 4th West Virginia Infantries were placed at the main fortification in support of a section of artillery, where the two remained until the artillery left. Afterward, the regiments were ordered to follow their brigade. Colonel Thoburn initially believed he had lost "a great many" men captured, but the records only showed six men missing or captured, along with four enlisted men killed, 11 wounded, and two officers wounded at Kernstown.[57]

John Farrar of Company E of the 4th West Virginia recalled that the Confederates initially formed for an attack on Crook but fell back when he accepted the challenge: "On Sunday morning....they marched out to attack us....Crook ordered all of the troops to fall in and started out to give them battle. They commenced to fall back without fighting scarcely any." Eventually the rebels, who outnumbered the Federals, halted to fight. Lieutenant Colonel Vance informed the 4th West Virginia to stick together because if one were to be captured, they would all be captured. Farrar wrote: "They would make a charge on our regiment sometimes but we would make it so hot for them that they began to be very careful how they advanced on us. Sometimes they would be on our flank and would fire end ways on the regiment."[58]

Farrar further wrote: "Our orderly sergeant Lyman S. White of Pomeroy got killed that day. [Corporal] Edgar C. Brown, [Company E], got wounded in the side. Lost 3 in our small company. Don't know how many the regiment lost, think about 35 or 40." The 4th West Virginia next moved to Harpers Ferry, where on July 28 they spotted signal flags indicating the army was preparing to move.[59]

As of July 31, Colonel Joseph Thoburn commanded the 1st Division, which was comprised of two brigades, with the 4th West Virginia placed in Colonel William Ely's 2nd Brigade, along with the 18th Connecticut Infantry, 2nd Maryland (Eastern Shore), 1st West Virginia Infantry (Battalion) and 12th West Virginia Infantry.[60]

During August of 1864, Chaplain George S. Woodhull was officially absent with leave to preserve the regimental books and papers by order of Brevet Major General George Crook. John Farrar related that the regiment spent time unsuccessfully chasing after General John McCausland, and also sadly recalled having recently witnessed his first army execution, a member of the 23rd Ohio Infantry, at Frederick, Maryland.[61]

The 4th West Virginia Infantry next moved northwardly in the Shenandoah Valley on August 6 and, according to Farrar, "Marched so we could form a line of battle on short notice." The first night was spent in camp at Berryville, Virginia.[62]

The 4th West Virginia again camped near Snicker's Ferry on August 9, with Lieutenant Colonel John L. Vance in command. With their time of service nearing expiration, Vance sent Captain David A. Russell, Company E, along with ten enlisted men from Companies E and F to Wheeling to arrange the muster out of the veterans of the 4th West Virginia who had not re-enlisted. Russell returned and said he was able to procure the muster out for men in Company E, but not Company A, as that procedure required an officer of the specific company mustering out of service. Captain Russell also reported that immediately afterward, he applied to the adjutant general at Wheeling for all men whose terms of service had expired, or were about to, and the veterans to be mustered out of service.[63]

Cedar Creek, Virginia
August 12 – 13, 1864

The 4th West Virginia fought on the skirmish line at Cedar Creek, Virginia, on August 12 and 13. James F. Stone, Company F, fondly recalled that on August 12: "... he [Lieutenant Colonel John L. Vance] was only a few rods from me on the skirmish line the twelfth day of August, 1864 when I was wounded [by gunshot]. I shall always remember how nice he was to me after he knew I had been injured. Col. Vance was always alert to see that his regiment was treated right in rations and clothing."[64]

On August 16, the headquarters of the 4th West Virginia Infantry, 2nd Brigade, 1st Division, Department of West Virginia, was at Strasburg, where Chaplain George Woodhull wrote West Virginia Governor Arthur I. Boreman that his commission paper and trunk, as well as much of the officers' luggage, had been destroyed during the retreat of General Sigel "last month." Woodhull also sent by a Mr. Hornbrook "a rebel flag captured by Sergeant John W. Boley, Company I, at Staunton to be preserved at the Capitol."[65]

On August 26, Company F of the 4th West Virginia Infantry was discharged while on the field, and about the last of August, the non-veterans, who had been encamped on Wheeling Island since returning from Georgia, were also discharged and received their final payoff and bounty.[66]

Lieutenant General Ulysses S. Grant placed all Union forces in the Shenandoah Valley, including those in the Department of West Virginia, under the command of Major General Philip Sheridan on August 31; at that time, the 4th West Virginia remained in the 1st Division, under Colonel Joseph Thoburn, while the 2nd Division was placed under Colonel William Ely.[67]

Berryville, Virginia
September 3, 1864

The 4th West Virginia fought again on September 3 at the battle of Berryville, where they were posted along the Winchester Pike about an hour before sunset as the Confederates were advancing. General George Crook reported that the greater portion of Thoburn's Division was on the right of the pike, and when Confederates of Brigadier General Joseph B. Kershaw's Brigade of Georgians "...made a furious charge...driving his two or three left regiments in great disorder, and compelling me to use [Colonel Isaac] Duval's division to check and drive him back, and retake the position lost by these regiments." Crook noted he intended to place Duval's troops on the extreme left, which he speculated "...would have unquestionably resulted in the capture of the attacking rebel force." Sergeant John C. Buckley, Company G, who was later awarded the Medal of Honor for his bravery at Vicksburg on May 22, 1863, was captured at Berryville, and he was "struck on the knee by a piece of shell or they never could have taken him. Near Richmond he escaped by jumping from the cars and took 17 days to get back through the lines to his regiment."[68]

One newspaper claimed Lieutenant Colonel John L. Vance was wounded at Berryville, although neither his pension file nor his official service record reflect such information.[69]

On September 12, those members of Company I who had not re-enlisted received orders that their term of service would officially end on September 27. Led by Lieutenant Edward H. Trickle, they traveled to Wheeling and were mustered out. On the same day, Lieutenant Colonel Vance was detailed for recruiting service, and Captain Benjamin Boswell, Company H, became the regimental commander.[70]

Captain Benjamin D. Boswell.
Oregon State Archives.

Third Battle of Winchester, Virginia
September 19, 1864

The marching and fighting did not cease for the 4th West Virginia, as they were again heavily engaged under Captain Benjamin Boswell at the Third Battle of Winchester on September 19. Brigadier General George Crook, commanding the Army of West Virginia, reported that Colonel Joseph Thoburn's 1st Division was posted on the far right of the 19th Corps, facing the Confederate extreme left in the Confederate line of battle, while the 2nd Division, under Colonel Isaac Duval, was posted further to the right "for the purpose of swinging around the left flank of the enemy." Just as Duval's Division had wheeled around to the right, coming in sight of the Confederate skirmishers, Thoburn suddenly ordered a charge, "driving the enemy's right back in confusion to their final position." Duvall immediately reacted and ordered a charge on the Confederate flank, where they found him "posted behind a stone wall with his left flank resting on an almost impassable morass, named Red Bud Run..." Colonel Isaac Duval was wounded in this engagement, and command of the 2nd Division divulged upon Lieutenant Colonel Robert S. Northcott.[71]

John Farrar, Company E, wrote: "We had orders to move at daylight....They attacked first. We marched up the Opequon where the Harper's Ferry & Winchester Pike crossed the Opequon. The 6th Corps had got in the fight in the morning and was getting the worst of it. They fell back about 2 miles. We crossed over and formed in line and advanced. They opened fire on us. Gen. Crook ordered us to charge. We broke their line and they started in a run. The cavalry charged on the left and it was a general stampede. We followed them, pushed them through Winchester and up the valley."[72]

Sometime in the weeks following September 22, a squad of the 4th West Virginia was on the skirmish lines all day until 11 p.m., in the vicinity of Cedar Creek, when a comrade was wounded. They left him with a haversack containing their only food rations and had to move on to the next position in the firing line, being in the immediate presence of the enemy. Later that night, after being relieved from duty, the squad went through camp searching for their wounded comrade, calling out his name, but could not locate him. Colonel Joseph Thoburn, who was sitting next to a campfire beside the road, heard the soldiers, who explained their situation to him, in particular their lack of food. Thoburn calmy directed them, "Set down here and eat your supper," displaying one of the many reasons he was held in such high esteem by his troops.[73]

Captain William S. Hall, Company F, later wrote that on September 26, "There was a military commission appointed to consolidate the regiment but two of the officers comprising it are severely wounded and besides we are in the midst of a campaign that may last two or three weeks yet."[74]

The depleted and exhausted ranks of the 4th West Virginia Infantry were next encamped at Harrisonburg, Virginia, on September 28, where General Crook announced on October 3 that "the original term of service for the organization of the 4th West Virginia having expired, and it not being a veteran organization, the re-enlisted men and recruits, numbering 321, will be organized into three companies and a detachment of 27 men. Ten officers were announced for the new organization and the organization of the companies would be performed by Colonel J. Thoburn, 1st West Virginia Infantry, 1st Division."[75]

4th West Virginia Veteran Battalion
October 8, 1864

With the remnants of the regiment near Woodstock, Virginia, on October 8, General Crook ordered Lieutenant Colonel John L. Vance to Wheeling to be mustered out of service, as the 4th West Virginia was not able to produce enough men to be considered a regiment and therefore was not entitled to a field officer. In essence they became the 4th West Virginia Veteran Battalion.[76]

On the night of October 10, some brigade clothing was stolen due to the failure of Corporal Abraham Friedline, Company D, to properly follow procedure and guard it. This transpired at Fisher's Hill, Virginia. Six days later, October 16, while at Winchester, Colonel William B. Curtis, Headquarters, 2nd Brigade, 1st Infantry Division, Army of West Virginia, issued Special Order No. 2, reducing in rank Corporal Friedline, Company D, then also designated as part of the 4th West Virginia Veteran Battalion, for failure to properly guard supplies of uniforms when some of the clothing was stolen on his watch.[77]

The regiment was at Martinsburg on October 12 and then moved to Cedar Creek October 15, where they went into camp with the 1st and 12th West Virginia Infantry Regiments and were ordered to guard a wagon train taking rations to Martinsburg.[78]

Colonel William. B. Curtis, 12th West Virginia Infantry, announced on October 16 he was placed in command of the 1st Brigade, which included the 4th West Virginia; two days later, a wagon train guarded by a detachment of soldiers from the 4th West Virginia Veteran Battalion arrived at Winchester.[79]

Cedar Creek, Virginia
October 19, 1864

Early on the morning of October 18, at 4:30 a.m., Major General Jubal Early's Confederates executed a daring surprise attack on General George Crook's Army of West Virginia—then with only 4,000 effective troops available—which was posted inside a series of earthen works located near the Winchester Turnpike, on the left of the 19th Corps. The Confederates attacked with ferocity and stealth, rapidly breaching the earthworks, leaving the Federals overwhelmed, and resulting in what amounted to a stampede, rather than an orderly retreat. A dense, gray shroud of smoke quickly covered the field, making visibility poor, and according to Crook, greatly aggravated the already panic-stricken soldiers under his command to the degree that a "great deal of confusion prevailed" for nearly an hour. Crook's 1st Division was led by Colonel Joseph Thoburn, who was mortally wounded in the attack, and the 2nd Brigade was led by Colonel William B. Curtis of the 12th West Virginia Infantry. The 4th West Virginia was still commanded by Captain Benjamin Boswell, Company H, who was the last officer to command the 4th West Virginia in the war.[80]

Benjamin Dempsey Boswell was born September 10, 1837, in Wayne County, Indiana, although the 1850 census lists him as then residing at Letart, Meigs County, Ohio, and his birth state as Iowa. He was the son of John Boswell, a physician practicing in Meigs County, and Mary Smith, both of whom were Ohio natives. A Boswell family history record states he resided at Union, Wayne County, Iowa in 1856. His parents also relocated to Iowa per the 1860 census, although he is not listed as residing with them. Boswell enlisted on August 11, 1861, and was appointed as 1st Sergeant in Company I.[81]

John Farrar recalled the chaos: "...before daylight we heard heavy firing up the valley, whole volleys of artillery. We started with the train for the front. We commenced meeting the wounded and stragglers, settlers, Negroes and everybody that could get away. They said they had been attacked before day and was all cut to pieces." Once Major General Philip Sheridan arrived from Winchester later that morning, he ordered the brigade to halt the wagon train and move to the front, "We had to get between the Rebel cavalry and our train." Farrar further observed, "This was the last fighting our regiment done," and added, "We moved back to Stephenson's Depot and from there to Cumberland, Maryland." According to family history, Private John P. Wolfe, Company F, had "a ball pierce his left hand" at Cedar Creek, but did not seek medical treatment. [82]

On the march from Snicker's Ferry to Cedar Creek, Captain William S. Hall continued to suffer intensely from piles and heat exhaustion, which he had acquired during the retreat from Lynchburg to Charleston. Concerned that someone may think he was feigning the symptoms, Hall made a point to write that Lieutenant Colonel Vance, who had already been mustered out of service, had previously confirmed that he suffered from those conditions.[83]

Captain William Grayum wrote from Newtown, Virginia, on October 27: "Our regiment is consolidated into a Battalion of three Companies and I am retained in command of one of them. I would not have acted the calf as some officers did if I should be kept in the Army for ten years. Col. [John L.] Vance and [Major] Henry Grayum have both gone home to be mustered out. Neither of them wanted to leave but we are not allowed a field officer. Lieut. [James W.] Dale and [John N.] Dean will both go out soon. [Charles B.] Malone, [James M.] Hodge and [John] McDonald stay with us....Our regiment was not engaged in either of the late battles here and I am sure not sorry of it. I have seen enough of my men killed and wounded this summer." Note that John Farrar's memoir, along with other sources including General George Crook's official reports, contradict William Grayum's claim that the 4th West Virginia was not in "the last battles" in the Shenandoah Valley.[84]

November began with the 4th West Virginia Battalion at Cedar Creek, then at Newtown on November 4, where Corporal Matthew S. Glover, Company B, was killed in an attack on a wagon train by Colonel John S. Mosby's men. While stationed at Middletown, Corporal Glover was ordered with eight men to go to Newtown, a distance of about seven miles, to guard a wagon that was sent after rations. On the way, the guard was attacked by Mosby's men. Private George W. Davis, Company B of the 4th West Virginia, was one of the guards, and he thought, but was not certain, that the order to guard the wagon had been given by Colonel Thomas M. Harris of the 10th West Virginia Infantry. Glover is believed to be the last member of the 4th West Virginia killed by hostile fire in the war. The same day that Glover was killed, Lieutenant William L. McMaster was ordered to Wheeling to procure the books and records of the regiment.[85]

General Philip Sheridan announced on November 15 that all passes to Winchester were canceled excepting those with prior approval, and on November 17 he officially redesignated his command as the Army of the Shenandoah and renamed their current encampment at Cumberland, Maryland as Camp Russell. On November 19, General B.F. Kelley sent a telegram to Colonel James Dayton, then at Moundsville, West Virginia, advising him that the 4th West Virginia was no longer under his command.[86]

2nd West Virginia Veteran Infantry Formed

During November 1864, the 4th West Virginia veterans were ordered to muster out of service. Due to a large number of discharges, casualties, and illnesses thinning the ranks of the regiment, General George Crook issued an order on December 1 stating he planned to consolidate the 1st and 4th West Virginia Infantries into one regiment. On December 3, Captain William Grayum wrote from Stevenson's Depot, speculating on the impending changes:

We are living pretty rough. We have no tents and have to build little shantys to stay in and it is so uncertain how long we will stay in any place that we don't take much pains with them and of course are not very comfortable....I have heard today that our Regiment is to be consolidated with the first Virginia Infantry [1st West Virginia Infantry] but I hope that is not the case for I would rather remain as we are.[87]

Final Reorganization

Despite Grayum's apprehension, on December 5 an order from Colonel Thomas M. Mahaley stated that the remaining troops of the 4th West Virginia were thereafter consolidated into "Battalion 4th West Virginia Veteran Volunteer Infantry," consisting of three companies and a detachment. The first company, designated as Company A, would be composed of former Companies C, I and 26 men of Company H, with Captain Benjamin Boswell, 1st Lieutenant James W. Dale, and 2nd Lieutenant William R. Malone as officers. Company B was to consist of Companies A, B, D, and 21 men from Company E, and officered by Captain William Curtiss, 1st Lieutenant William L. McMaster, and 2nd Lieutenant John McDonald. Companies K and G and 31 men from Company F were to be consolidated into Company C, commanded by Captain William Grayum, 1st Lieutenant C.L. Lightburn, and 2nd Lieutenant James M. Hodge. The battalion would be rounded out by a detachment formed by the residue of companies E, F, and H, with 2nd Lieutenant John A. Dean in charge.[88]

The reorganization was finalized on December 6, 1864, wherein General George Crook ordered that the consolidated 1st and 4th West Virginia Infantry Regiments would henceforth be known as the 2nd West Virginia Veteran Volunteer Infantry, with Lieutenant Colonel Jacob Weddle of the 1st West Virginia Infantry commanding the battalion and Captain Benjamin Boswell of the 4th West Virginia as vice-commander. The 2nd West Virginia Veteran Infantry was then placed under the overall command of General Benjamin F. Kelley, under whom it served until the close of the war.[89]

On December 21, at Cumberland, Lieutenant Colonel Weddle formally requested West Virginia Governor Arthur I. Boreman to commission Captain Benjamin Boswell as a major in the 2nd West Virginia Veteran Infantry. Also on that date, James F. Stone, formerly of Company F, 4th West Virginia, mentioned in a letter home that he thought the late Company C had remained as Company C of the 2nd West Virginia Veteran Infantry, though he was in error; rather, the remnant of that company was placed in Company A.[90]

The 2nd West Virginia Veteran Volunteer Infantry was permanently detached from the Army of West Virginia on December 19. On December 26, William Grayum penned a letter at Cumberland, Maryland, a new location he found quite agreeable. He wrote: "We were ordered to join the balance of the Regiment here and I presume that we will remain here this winter. We found quarters partially built and moved into them and waiting lumber to finish them. It has been very cold here and moving was a rough job....This town is a nice place."[91]

Lt. Col. Jacob Weddle.
Private Collection.

1865
Four Months to Home

The 2nd West Virginia Veteran Volunteer Infantry was at Cumberland on the first day of January 1865, with the exception of Company E at South Branch Bridge and the Baltimore and Ohio Railroad, also ordered to Cumberland for garrison duty.[92]

Private William P. Mowery (Mowry), Company C, 2nd West Virginia Veteran Infantry, was killed on January 1 when he was accidentally "shot by a comrade" at Cumberland and died there in the U.S. General Hospital. Mowery previously served in the 4th West Virginia Infantry.[93]

Four men of the 2nd West Virginia Veteran Infantry were assigned to recruiting service for the regiment on January 26, while on February 3 Private George Nagle, Company C, 2nd West Virginia Veteran, formerly a member of Company F, 4th West Virginia, died of apoplexy in the regimental hospital at Cumberland.[94]

While at Cumberland on February 14, Major Benjamin D. Boswell charged 2nd Lieutenant Samuel Mellon (Melon), Company G, 2nd West Virginia Veteran Infantry, with being intoxicated while on duty as Officer of the Day, alleging he was completely incapable of performing his duties and had given the countersign to an unauthorized private. Mellon was convicted and cashiered out of service by general court martial on March 31, 1865.[95]

Generals George Crook and Benjamin Kelley Kidnapped

On the night of February 22, Generals George Crook and Benjamin F. Kelley were asleep in their quarters at a hotel, when at 3 a.m., a band of Confederate partisans dressed as Union soldiers, from the infamous McNeill's Rangers, under Captain John H. McNeill, kidnapped them. This organization was formally sanctioned as a Partisan unit under the Partisan Act of 1862 by the Confederate government, and was one of only two such units allowed to continue service when the Act was

Maj. Gen. George C. Crook.
Library of Congress.

Brig. Gen. Benjamin F. Kelley.
Library of Congress.

repealed a few days earlier, on February 17, 1864. The Rangers quietly crept into the city and captured Federal pickets without firing a shot. Moving swiftly, the Rangers stealthily moved to the hotel, slipped upstairs, and found the generals' doors unlocked; they quietly nudged them awake. Both were quickly captured without making a sound and taken to horses waiting on the street below. Oddly, none of the other hotel guests or other Union soldiers were aware of the Confederates' presence until they were safely out of town. Before eloping, however, the Rangers raided the telegraph office and destroyed the instruments, and captured several horses, including General Kelley's mount known as "Philippi." It wasn't long until Union troops discovered the missing generals, and a detachment was hastily sent in hot pursuit of the Confederates. Along the way, they discovered pieces of a letter addressed to General Crook, which he had torn and dropped every mile or so, so that the Union soldiers would know in which direction they were taken.[96]

James F. Stone, formerly of Company F of the 4th and now with Company C of the 2nd West Virginia Veteran, recalled the eventful night, "...I with about 40 others of our Regiment was in that town [Cumberland] the night Generals Crook and Kelley were captured by McNeil and his gang."[97]

With the exception of Company C, on the night of February 22, the 2nd West Virginia Veteran was ordered to move by rail to New Creek, West Virginia, to garrison the town. Company B was at South Branch Bridge and the Baltimore and Ohio Railroad. The regiment was ordered back from New Creek to Cumberland on March 31.[98]

Lincoln Assassinated

On April 14, President Abraham Lincoln was assassinated at Ford's Theatre in Washington, D.C. James F. Stone of Company F recalled: "We were in Cumberland at the time of the assassination of President Lincoln. I well remember the sorrow it brought to all the soldiers when they heard the sad news." William Grayum also elaborated on the loss on April 22, "The murder of the President is about all that is talked or thought about here and a stranger is closely watched and if he bears the least resemblance to Boothe [*sic*] he is arrested and made to give an account of himself."[99]

As the last few months of the war slowly passed, news of General Robert E. Lee's surrender to Lieutenant General Ulysses S. Grant at Appomattox Court House began to dwindle into camp, as the 2nd West Virginia Veteran remained at Cumberland. On June 2, William Grayum felt rather pessimistic as to being discharged anytime soon, however, and opined, "Our prospects for getting discharged look a little dark just now but still we hope to get home this summer." Four days later, on June 6, the 2nd Veteran West Virginia Infantry moved by rail from Cumberland to Grafton, Taylor County, West Virginia, a distance of 100 miles, with instructions to be distributed in West Virginia for the purpose of "restoring law and order."[100]

During their final weeks of service in June 1865, Companies A and B were posted at Weston, while Companies C and I were at Parkersburg; meanwhile, Companies D, F, and H were encamped at Bulltown, with Company E posted at Grafton, and Company G at Glenville. The situation remained fluid, as on or about June 10, the regiment was ordered to move to Clarksburg and then proceed to the Kanawha Valley. However, consistent with the classic military truism, 'hurry up and wait,' further orders were received directing the regiment to remain at Clarksburg and prepare to muster out of service.[101]

As such, the move from Grafton to Clarksburg, a distance of 22 miles, did not actually begin until June 19. On July 16, the 2nd West Virginia Veteran Infantry was formally mustered out of service. The regiment then traveled to Wheeling by train on July 18, arriving there the next day. After receiving pay, and copies of their discharge papers, the regiment disbanded. The Civil War service of the 4th West Virginia Infantry was officially over.[102]

Two days later, on July 24, Private William Clark, Company C, 2nd West Virginia Veteran (formerly 4th West Virginia), murdered 55-year-old Henry J. Jackson, a resident of Ritchie County, in Point Pleasant. Reportedly Jackson, armed with a Bowie knife, ordered Clark off his property, and Clark responded by shooting Jackson dead. Jackson's wife Lydia offered a $1000 reward for the arrest of Clark. Jackson was buried in Ritchie County, West Virginia.[103]

Summary Service Record

According to Frederick Dyer's *A Compendium of the War of the Rebellion,* during its service the 4th West Virginia Volunteer Infantry lost three officers killed and 80 enlisted men killed or mortally wounded, and two officers and 156 men died by disease, for a total of 241. This figure does not include wounded in action or accidentally wounded, resignations, medical discharges, and other contributing factors. The 2nd West Virginia Veteran Infantry as a whole lost a total of 17 men to wounds and disease.[104]

Major Benjamin Boswell accurately reported that the 4th West Virginia traveled more distance than any other regiment from the thirty-fifth state during the war, making them not only the most traveled West Virginia regiment, but also the only Mountaineer regiment that fought in both the Eastern and Western Theaters of war. Six members of the 4th West Virginia received the Medal of Honor for gallantry at Vicksburg in May 1863.[105]

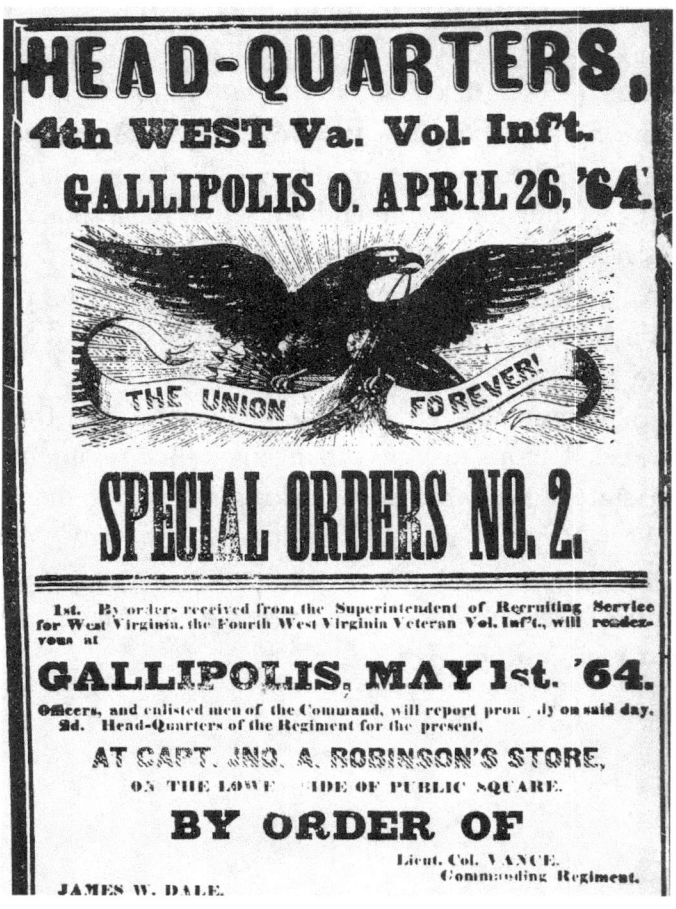

Recruiting Broadside.
Courtesy of Gallia County Historical Society.

5

Anecdotes, Oddities, and Curiosities

A notice appeared in the September 21, 1865, edition of the *Gallipolis Journal* requesting former members of the 4th West Virginia Infantry meet at Point Pleasant on September 27 for "important matters." The notice had originally been composed and signed by former members John L. Vance, Henry and William Grayum, and James W. Dale at Gallipolis on September 13, 1865, which is confusing as a veteran's reunion of the 4th West Virginia Infantry was held at Point Pleasant on September 27, 1865, led by former members Alexander Vance and James H. Ralston. Many of the area veterans attended.[1]

The next reunion of the 4th West Virginia Infantry was held in late 1867 at Aleshire's Hall in Gallipolis. The event was poorly attended due to transportation problems caused by low water. Another reunion of the 4th West Virginia Infantry was in the process of being organized by former member Captain D.A. Russell in November of 1868 at Pomeroy, Ohio. General Joseph A.J. Lightburn was invited but could not attend. In the years to follow, many of the former members of the 4th West Virginia Infantry became scattered throughout the country, and some opted to "forget" as much as possible related to their time as soldiers.

Many of the veterans interested in revisiting their days as warriors and fellowshipping with their comrades began to attend the much larger Grand Army of the Republic reunions or those of the Society of the Army of West Virginia. During the September 1908 reunion of the Society of the Army of West Virginia in Huntington, West Virginia, the original drum of the 4th West Virginia Infantry was used at the head of the parade by the drum corps. The drum was reportedly made at the beginning of the Civil War and caried by the regiment from Memphis to Vicksburg to Missionary Ridge, and beyond.[2]

A CONFEDERATE YANKEE

John Lacey Mallernee of Company D of the 4th West Virginia Infantry served briefly in Company C, 3rd Ohio Infantry during 1861, (3 months regiment), and served in the army until a few years after the war ended. He later moved to Fayetteville, Tennessee, where during the 1870s he promoted a new washing machine that sold for thirty cents. Later he was employed as a surveyor for the railroad at McMinnville, Tennessee, and died on August 19, 1883, in Fayetteville, Tennessee. His widow passed away December 22, 1927, and in her obituary, John Mallernee was identified as a "Confederate" soldier. There is no evidence that he was a Confederate soldier, however, although apparently no one ever questioned it. His widow, Mrs. Mallernee, received Federal pension.[3]

A WELL TRAVELED MAN

James Calvin Summers, Company H, 4th West Virginia Infantry, was from Elkview, Kanawha County, West Virginia. He was a member of the storming party now known as the "Forlorn Hope" during the May 22, 1863, assault on Stockade Redan at Vicksburg, for which he later received the Medal of Honor. Summers served throughout the war and died in 1927 at the age of 89 and was buried in an obscure family plot in Elkview. In 2019 his body was reinterred to the Donel C. Kinnard Memorial State Veterans Cemetery at Institute, West Virginia, and he was given full military honors. The new gravestone acknowledges him as a Medal of Honor recipient. Indeed, a well-traveled man from West Virginia's most traveled Union regiment.[4]

PLAYING WITH FIRE

Lieutenant Colonel William Henry Harrison Russell of the 4th West Virginia, resigned from the regiment due to poor health at the beginning of the Vicksburg Campaign and eventually returned to New York City, where he found employment as a clerk in the legal profession. While so engaged he was involved in something of a scandalous romance with a judge's daughter-in-law, which so infuriated the barrister that Russell feared for his life and left town. In 1876, Russell moved to Los Angeles, California, where he eventually became an attorney. He also utilized his military experience and reorganized the struggling National Guard of Southern California, which under his leadership led to the creation of the Seventh Regiment of the southern California National Guard, in which he advanced to the rank of colonel. Russell's health began to fail in the early 1890s and he moved north to Sacramento, California, where he died in 1898.[5]

Benjamin Dempsey Boswell served throughout the war with the 4th West Virginia Infantry and was Vice-commander of the 2nd Veteran West Virginia Infantry. He remained in the Union Army after the war, and while on extended leave from the 11th Infantry Regiment in 1873, was hired by Oregon State University to teach military science at Corvallis State Agricultural College, the first active duty U.S. Army officer to teach military science at a land grant school in the West. Boswell was named Professor of Military Science in 1878; afterward, he and his wife purchased the Boswell Mineral Springs Resort in 1887. The main building was destroyed by fire in 1901. Boswell died in Oregon and is buried as a member of the 14th U.S. Infantry in the San Francisco National Cemetery.[6]

MYSTERIOUS INSOMNIAC IN THE RANKS

A thirty-six-year-old veteran ostensibly associated with the 4th West Virginia Infantry, identified only by the surname Saunders, is said to have never slept, according to a July 13, 1877, article in a Lebanon, Missouri news organ, *The Rustic*. The article claimed that during the war, several soldiers and officers of the regiment were so stumped by his apparent lack of need to sleep, that they arranged multiple covert shifts to monitor him day and night in a vigilant effort to catch him sleeping, but to no avail. The article indicates several soldiers even paid Saunders to replace them while standing picket (Guard) duty at night, knowing he would not fall asleep and get them in trouble. While modern medical research would likely rebut this account as impossible, *The Rustic* claimed that in 1863, the sleepless fellow identified only as Saunders went to Philadelphia to be examined by expert physicians about his condition, but after a month of intensive examinations, were left baffled as to why he could not sleep and discharged him. Whether it was discharge from service or the hospital remains unknown as records do not specify. We cannot be certain as to the full identify of Saunders, although there was a Musician in Company G named Jesse C. Saunders; yet, according to the regimental muster rolls, he died from chronic diarrhea on June 29, 1863, at a hospital in St. Louis, Missouri. He was later interred at the National Cemetery in St. Louis, with a military headstone marker. Further complicating matters, his death certificate is not signed by a physician, bearing only an "X." There are certain factors suggesting the Saunders cited in *The Rustic* is the same person as the Musician Jesse C. Saunders of Co. G, including both were in the 4th West Virginia, with birthdates in 1841, and were native Ohioans; however, this is circumstantial at best. With the lack of viable evidence to corroborate this fascinating, but ambiguous account, we are left to speculate, begging the questions of whether or not it was really the same Jesse C. Saunders, and did he really die in June 1863? The possibilities are endless, yet it remains a mystery to date.[7]

SUTLERS

During the Civil War, merchants known as Sutlers usually followed the armies selling textile and other goods, often at exorbitantly high prices. The sutlers were appointed by the Secretary of War for no more than three years, to sell various necessities and luxury items, usually working out of the back of a wagon or setting up a tent in camp. Each regiment was authorized to have one sutler and were decidedly a for-profit operation. Sutlers accepted cash, but due to a shortage of coins and large gaps in pay cycles, they developed a private form of currency known as Sutler tokens that soldiers could use on credit until pay day. These tokens were generally a small, thin metal disc, with the regiment and value in goods stamped on it, as well as the die striker (maker) and location of the token creator. Various period documents list Joseph Patten of Athens County, Ohio, as the sutler of the 4th West Virginia Infantry, probably for the first two years of the war. No evidence has yet been found to indicate he went south with the regiment to Vicksburg in 1863. Being from Athens, Ohio, indicates he may have had a connection with Company D of the regiment. Private coinage became illegal on April 22, 1864, when Congress passed a law making the use of such tokens or devices not created by the government used as currency a crime. Below is an example of Sutler tokens used by soldiers in the 4th West Virginia.[8]

4th West Virginia Sutler Token.
Private Collection.

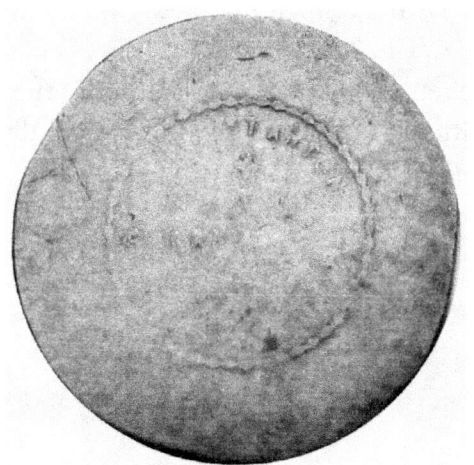

Obverse, 4th West Virginia Sutler Token.
Private Collection.

The West Virginia State Museum at Charleston, West Virginia, has a display featuring the Civil War cartridge box of Lt. Col. James R. Hall of the 13th West Virginia Infantry, brother of Major John Hall of the 4th West Virginia. Major Hall was killed in action in August of 1862 in McDowell County, West Virginia. There is a hand-written inscription on the inner flap stating the box was presented to Lt. Col. Hall by the sutler(s) of the 4th West Virginia, and Joseph Patton's name is listed. There appears to be another name, but it is illegible, but appears to be Samuel Keenan of the 13th West Virginia. Although it is not stated, it is highly probable this was actually Major John Hall's cartridge box, retrieved from his body, and presented to his brother James as a memorial. Courtesy West Virginia State Museum.

The metal numeral '4' uniform attachment or device is about the same size as the West Virginia medal given to the state's Union veterans shortly after the war. Very little is known about the device except it apparently was given to or bought by officers only, as there are a number of photographs of officers wearing it. (For an example, see image of Col. Dayton on back cover) The device has a pin attachment on the back side where the name of the soldier can also be found. The particular one in the photo here belonged to James Summers, but he was not an officer therefore it must have been given to him by the actual owner. The actual purpose of the device and when they were issued is unknown.

6

4th West Virginia Infantry Monument at Vicksburg

The 1921 session of the West Virginia Legislature created a commission to erect a monument and position markers on the Vicksburg National Battlefield Park. The idea originated at a 1919 Encampment where a committee was formed to procure funding from the West Virginia Legislature for the monument and markers. The bill was introduced by Department Commander W.T. Cox, a member of the House of Delegates from Wirt County, but Cox died while the bill was in committee and no further action was taken in 1919.

At the 1920 Encampment, the Committee explained Cox's death had delayed their proposal and the Committee continued to work on the project. The bill was reintroduced in 1921 and $7500.00 was secured, and West Virginia Governor Ephraim P. Morgan officially named the members of the Committee, which included two veterans of the 4th West Virginia and the Vicksburg Campaign, Phillip H. Elliott of Graham's Station, Mason County, West Virginia, and Henry Clay Rowley of Ravenswood, West Virginia. The project was further delayed when Rowley died November 21, 1921. In the meantime, negotiations were made with Roy Sears of Sears Monument Company of Charleston, West Virginia, to produce the monument and markers.

The commission decided to place a bronze bust of Major Arza Goodspeed of the 4th West Virginia, killed in the May 19 assault on Stockade Redan, along with four markers designating the trench line of the 4th West Virginia (this trench is yet visible), the camp of the regiments, and the two assaults. The monument and markers were dedicated November 14, 1922, with all committee members present as well as Roy Sears.

The dedication ceremony also included the Women's Relief Corps and the Ladies of the G.A.R. (Grand Army of the Republic). In 1923, the state of West Virginia printed a "Report of the Vicksburg Military Park Commission" relating all of the details of the project and statements from various persons involved in it. The booklet contains a brief history of the 4th West Virginia Infantry, a roster of the regiment, and a fold-out color map of the Vicksburg battlefield showing the location of the markers. The booklet contains some errors, including stating Major John Hall was a West Point graduate (he attended Virginia Military Institute for two years) and that the Confederate partisan commander Colonel Vincent "Clawhammer" Witcher was killed at Beech Creek in August 1862, when in fact he survived the war.

Dedication of the Arza Goodspeed monument
at Vicksburg National Battlefield. Credit: Vicksburg National Battlefield.
Left to Right:
1. unknown female
2. Hugh Martindale, Adjt. & Q.M Gen., represented G.A.R. Dept of W.Va.
3. William Kelly, represented West Virginia Governor,
was 2nd Lt. and Post Q.M. 13th Maine Infantry
4. Phillip H. Elliott, 4th West Virginia Infantry
5. Dr. J.J. Morgan, 4th West Virginia Infantry
6. Mrs. H.S. White, Sec. of Vicksburg Military Park Commission and
President Ladies G.A.R. Dept. of W.Va.
7. Roy Sears, Sears Monument, Charleston, WV
8. H.S. White, Chairman, Vicksburg Military Park Commission
All others are unknown.

Appendix A

Company Rosters
West Virginia Adjutant General's Report
December 31, 1864
4th Infantry Regiment

Record of Captain M. V. Lightburn's Company "A," 4th West Virginia Volunteer Infantry, showing the changes in said Company from the date of organization to the date of muster-out on the 4th day of July 1864, by W. G. Fitch, 1st Lieut. U. S. A. Compiled from the muster-out rolls.

Names.	Rank.	Age.	Mustered in.	Remarks.
Welton, Henry S.	Capt.,	38	June 17, 1861	Resign'd Sept. 1, '61.
Rockhill, Tilton B.	"	53	Sept. 2, "	Appointed Sept. 1, '61. Resigned Nov. 30, '62.
Lightburn, M.V.	"	23	Nov. 30, 1862	Pro. Cap. Nov. 30, '62.
Smith, ----	1st Lt.,	30	June 17, 1861	Res. Sept. 1st, '61.
Sayre, John J.	1st Lt.	26	Jan. 1, 1863	Pro. Serg't Aug. 31, '61. Pro. Lt, Nov. 30, '62.
Davis, John W.	2d Lt.	26	June 17, 1861	Res. Dec. 5, '62.
Shrewsberry, Col'bs	2d Lt.	30	Jan. 1, 1863	Ap'ted Com. Serg't Aug. 31, '61. Pro Lt. Dec. 5, '62. Res. May 26, '63.
Bumgarner, Wm.	Serg't	24	June 17, 1861	- - -
Swilling, Francis	Serg't	22	June 17, "	- - -
French, Robert	Corp'l	41	17, "	- - -
Flitcher, Adam	"	19	17, "	- - -
Carroll Thomas	"	23	17, "	Wounded at Jackson, Miss., July 11, '63.
Ross, Joseph G.	"	23	17, "	- - -
Mason, John	"	34	17, "	- - -

Cowey, Thomas	"	19	17, "	-	-	-
Hall, William C.L.	"	21	17, "	-	-	-
Elliott, Joseph	Mus'n	21	17, "	-	-	-
Bailey, James E.	Priv.	22	17, "	-	-	-
Beach, James	"	21	17, "	-	-	-
Circle, Charles E.	"	24	17, "	-	-	-
Crabtree, Charles	"	36	17, "	-	-	-
Circle, Noah	"	28	17, "	-	-	-
Circle, John	"	24	17, "	-	-	-
Driver, James	"	33	17, "	-	-	-
Evans, John	"	24	17, "	-	-	-
Edwards, Thomas	Priv.,	25	June 17, 1861	-	-	-
Fugate, Robert	"	26	17, "	-	-	-
Fowler, Jesse	"	18	17, "	-	-	-
French, George M.	"	20	17, "	-	-	-
Fry, Gideon	"	19	17, "	-	-	-
Gibbs, Michael	"	19	17, "	-	-	-
Gamble, William W.	"	18	17, "	-	-	-
Gwynn, Amos	"	30	17, "	-	-	-
Gibson, John W.	"	20	17, "	-	-	-
Harrison, Henry	"	35	17, "	-	-	-

Hardy, James	"	23	17, "	-	-	-
Hughes, Morgan	"	32	17, "	-	-	-
Ilderton, Mark	"	40	17, "	-	-	-
Jones, William	"	23	17, "	-	-	-
Knapp, John	"	22	17, "	-	-	-
Keith, William A.	"	18	17, "	-	-	-
Love, Lewis	"	28	17, "	-	-	-
Mitchell, William	"	33	17, "	-	-	-
Martin, John	"	24	17, "	-	-	-
Miller, Andrew	"	28	17, "	-	-	-
Miller, Henry	"	28	17, "	-	-	-
Oliver, David	"	22	17, "	-	-	-
Powell, John	"	24	17, "	-	-	-
Parry, David	"	33	17, "	-	-	-
Parker, Michael	"	33	17, "	-	-	-
Parry, Matthews	"	28	17, "	-	-	-
Ritz, George	"	22	17, "	-	-	-
Rickford, Michael	"	23	17, "	Wounded at Vicksburg, Miss., May 19th, '63.		
Roberts, John	"	22	17, "	-	-	-
Rollison, Isaac	"	20	17, "	-	-	-
Robinson, John	"	30	17, "	-	-	-
Stevens, John	"	23	17, "	-	-	-

Severance, Henry	"	21	17, "	-	-	-
Turner, Henry C.	"	22	17, "	-	-	-
Turner, De Witt	"	20	17, "	-	-	-
Thomas, Henry	"	28	17, "	-	-	-
VanMeter, John W.	"	18	17, "	-	-	-
West, William	"	28	17, "	-	-	-
Recruits.						
Arnold, George G.	"	27	Oct. 10, 1862	-	-	-
McLaughlin, John	"	24	10, "	-	-	-
Quigley, Owen	"	30	10, "	-	-	-
Rodgers, John	"	36	10, "	-	-	-
Whitney, James		18	10, "	-	-	-
Veterans.						
McDonald, John	Serg't	26	June 17, 1861	Re'enlis'd Jan 21, '64		
McDonald, Donald	"	23	17, "	"	Jan 21, "	
Pascoe, Thomas	"	23	17, "	"	Jan 21, "	
Carney, Samuel E.R.	Corp'l.	24	June 17, 1861	Re'enlis'd Jan 21, '64		
Avery, Robert	Priv.,	30	Jan. 1, 1862	"	Feb 12, "	
Bumgarner, Calvin	"	24	June 17, 1861	"	Jan 21, "	
Clendenen, Joseph	"	23	17, "	"	Jan 1, "	

Goodrich, Marcus	"	31	17, "	"	Jan 21, "
Icenhower, Thos. J.	"	21	17, "	"	Jan 21, "
Lavender, Wm. H.H.	"	23	17, "	"	Jan 21, "
Lewis, Isaac N.	"	27	17, "	"	Jan 21, "
Roy, William H.	"	26	17, "	"	Jan 1, "
Smith, William J.	"	22	Aug. 19, "	"	Jan 1, "
Webster, Samuel	"	27	June 17, "	"	Jan 1, "
Discharged.					
Burrows, Daniel	"	23	17, "	Disch'd Jan. 18, '62.	
Benton, William	"	32	17, "	"	Oct. 14, "
Collins, Richard	"	32	17, "	"	Aug. 19, '63.
Cutchall, George	Corp'l,	30	17, "	"	Jan. 18, '62.
Dickens, William	Priv.,	24	17, "	"	Aug. 1, '63.
Engelman, William	Serg't	35	17, "	"	Mar. 15, '62.
Gaskins, John R.	Priv.	21	17, "	"	Feb. 23, "
Jones, James	Corp'l,	31	17, "	"	July 1, '63.
Hardy, Luke	Serg't,	34	17, "	"	April 1, "
Loyd, David	Priv.,	31	17, "	"	Jan. 16, "
Lightburn, Calvin L.	Priv.	20	Oct. 10, 1862	"	Aug. 28, "

Richardson, H.S.	"	21	June 17, 1861	" Jan. 1, '62.
Rodgers, Charles	"	28	17, "	" Jan. 1, "
Robinson, Charles	"	23	-	-
Shoemaker, Joseph	"	23	June 17, 1861	" Mar. 11, "
Transferred.				
Spencer, Albert	Mus'n	19	17, "	Transferred to Co. "H," Mar. 10, '62
Killed in Action.				
Campbell, Alexander	Priv.,	22	17, "	Killed in action at Charleston, Va., Sept. 13, '62.
Turnbull, John	"	38	17, "	Killed in action at Charleston, Va., Sept. 13, '62.
Latham, Sumner H.	"	21	17, "	Killed in action at Vicksburg, Miss., May 19, '63.
Ritz, Peter	"	18	17, "	Killed in action at Vicksburg, Miss., May 19, '63.
Randall, John	"	18	17, "	Killed in action at Vicksburg, Miss., May 22, '63.
Died of Disease.				
Kneff, Joseph	Corp'l	29	17, "	Died July 16, '63, at Walnut Hills, Miss.
Williamson, Lewis	Priv.,	22	17, "	Died at Ceredo, Va., May 2, '62.
Wilson, Huston	"	21	17, "	Died at Young's Point, La., March 11, '63.

Young, John II	"	20	Oct. 10, 1862	Died at Young's Point, La., Feb'y 2, '63.
Deserted.				
Burgess, Lewis	Priv.,	21	10, "	Desert'd Dec 18, '62
Evans, John D.	Corp'l,	27	June 17, 1861	" Dec. 18, "
Ray, Robert	"	35	17, "	" Dec. 18, "
Hardy, Joseph	Priv.	18	17, "	" Dec. 18, "
Williams, William	"	27	17, "	" Dec. 18, "
Kern, Jacob	"	34	17, "	" Aug. 10, '61
Slosher, Martin	"	22	24, "	" Aug. 10, "
Williams, Talesian R.	"	30	Sept. 1, "	" Sept. 30, '62

Aggregate ..... 117 men.

Record of Capt. Barlow W. Curtiss' Company "B," 4th Regiment W.Va. Infantry Volunteers, showing the changes in said Company from the date of organization to the date of muster-out on the 5th day of July 1864, by Lieut. W. G. Fitch. U.S.A. Compiled from the muster-out rolls.

Names.	Rank.	Age.	Mustered in.	Remarks.
Vance, John L.	Capt.,	23	Mar. 16, 1863	Promoted to Major Jan. 30. '63, vice Dayton, pro. to Lt. Col; pro. to Lt. Col., vice Dayton, promoted Col.
Curtiss, Barlow W.	"	24	Mar. 26, "	Pro. 1st Lt. from 2d Lieut., Sept. 30, '62, vice Bailey, res'd; pro. to Cap. Jan 30, '63, vice Vance pro. to Maj.
Bailey, William C.	1st Lt.,	27	July 5, 1861	Resigned, Sept. 30, '62.
Sisson, Wm. H.H.	"	20	Mar. 26, 1863	Pro. to 2d Lt, from Ser., Sep. 30, '62, vice Curtiss, pro. to 1st Lt.; pro. to 1st Lt. Jan 31, '63, vice Curtiss, pro. to Capt.
Wartonburg, Alex'r	2d Lt.,	23	Mar, 1, "	Pro. to 2d Lt. from Ser. Maj., Jan. 30, '63, vice Sisson pro. to 1st t.
Young, John	Serg't	42	July 5, 1861	- - -
Dabney, James	"	21	5, "	- - -
Anderson, Thomas	Corp'l	38	5, "	- - -
Calloway, Eli	"	43	5, "	- - -
Chapman, Wm. H.	"	23	5, "	- - -
Gillis, Thomas	"	39	5, "	- - -
Wolf, Mallory	"	20	5, "	- - -

Bails, Hugh	Mus'n	21	5, "	-	-	-
Stover, James L.	Wag'r	21	5, "	-	-	-
Anderson, David R.	Priv.	38	5, "	-	-	-
Allinder, Samuel	"	32	5, "	-	-	-
Atkinson, Samuel	"	33	5, "	-	-	-
Atkinson, Thomas	"	30	5, "	-	-	-
Brabbin, Robert	"	30	5, "	-	-	-
Childs, Richard C.	"	26	5, "	-	-	-
Crossley, Thomas	"	28	5, "	-	-	-
Crago, George R.	"	24	5, "	-	-	-
Dawalt, Henry	"	42	5, "	-	-	-
Gould, Stephen	"	22	5, "	-	-	-
Greenlee, Charles	"	23	5, "	-	-	-
Gwinn, Ahaz S.	"	19	5, "	-	-	-
Hardey, Robert	"	27	5, "	-	-	-
McNamee, B.P.	"	24	5, "	-	-	-
Morrow, Gideon	"	18	5, "	-	-	-
Mathews, Philip	"	29	5, "	-	-	-

Natross, Martin	"	26	5, "	-	-	-
Parsons, Joel	"	21	5, "	-	-	-
Potts, William	"	43	5, "	-	-	-
Rayburn, Gilbert	"	21	5, "	-	-	-
Whorley, James M.	"	26	5, "	-	-	-
Williams, Gideon H.	"	18	5, "	-	-	-
Recruits.						
Bails, Joseph	"	26	Aug. 11, 1861	-	-	-
Bowden, Charles L.	"	18	Sept. 16, 1862	-	-	-
Bowden, Alonzo S.	"	17	16, "	-	-	-
Bowden, Rolands A.	"	15	16, "	-	-	-
Childers, Jerome	"	20	16, "	-	-	-
Eades, James	"	20	16, "	-	-	-
Eades, Joseph	Priv.	24	Sept. 16, 1862	-	-	-
Veterans.						
Greenlee, Easton	Serg't,	25	July 5, 1861	Re-enlisted as Vet. Vol., Jan. 20, '64		
Gardner, Hugh T.	"	22	5, "	"	"	"
Mitchell, Philip	"	29	5, "	"	"	"
Glover, Mathew S.	Corp'l	21	5, "	"	"	"
Atkinson, Edw'd M.	"	31	5, "	"	"	"

Blackburn, Jas. A	"	18	5, "	"	"	"
Bails, John	Priv.	20	5, "	"	"	"
Blackburn, Jas. M	"	18	5, "	"	"	"
Blake, James T.	"	25	5, "	"	"	"
Cubbage, Lewis P	"	18	5, "	"	"	"
Collins, Harrison	"	22	5, "	"	"	"
Davis, George	"	21	5, "	"	"	"
Goodrich, Lewis	"	26	5, "	" 1, '64.	"	Jan.
Gardner, John H.	"	22	5, "	" 20, '64.	"	Jan.
Hedrick, Henry D	"	23	Nov. 1, "	"	"	"
Inman, Bazaliel	"	36	19, "	"	"	"
Kinser, John	"	23	July 5, "	" 1, '64.	"	Jan.
Morrow, John T.	"	20	Oct. 10, "	" 20, '64.	"	Jan.
Morrow, William T.	"	22	Nov. 26, "	"	"	"
Moler, James	"	20	July 5, "	"	"	"
Missell, Thomas	"	41	5, "	"	"	"
Pursinger, Joseph B	"	18	5, "	"	"	"
Pontser, Joseph	"	24	Nov. 1, "	"	"	"
Roach, William	"	21	July 5, "	"	"	"

Roberts, James	"	22	5, "	"	"	"
Roberts, Andrew	"	18	5, "	"	"	"
Shephard, James R.	"	25	Oct. 25, "	"	"	"
Sines, William	"	28	July 5, "	"	"	"
Workman, Joshua L.	"	19	Feb. 11, 1862	"	"	"
Discharged.						
Alexander, Saml. C.	Serg't	25	Oct. 15, 1861	Discharged at Gallipolis, O., Feb. 20, '63.		
Blackburn, M. W.	Corp'l	30	July 5, "	Discharged at Gallipolis, Ohio, Ap. 15, '62.		
Hall, William L.	Serg't	44	5, "	Discharged at Gallipolis, Ohio, Oct. 15, 62.		
Hart, Alonzo	Priv.	27	5, "	Discharged at Camp Sherman, Mississippi, Sept. 4, '63.		
Johnson, James	"	22	5, "	Discharged at Ceredo, W. Va., Ap. 15, 62.		
Patterson, Carey E.	"	23	5, "	Discharged at Camp Sherman, Mississippi, Sept. 26, '63.		
Redmond, Arthur	"	41	5, "	Discharged at Ceredo, W. Va., Ap. 15, 62.		
Sheline, Michael	"	19	5, "	Discharged at Ceredo, W. Va., Ap. 15, 62.		
Snyder, John	"	18	5, "	Discharged at Ceredo, W. Va., Ap. 15, 62.		
Died.						
Sheline, Samuel	"	22	Oct. 10, "	Killed in action at Charleston, Va. Sept 13, '62.		

Wallace, George M.	"	21	July 5, "	Killed in action at Charleston, Va. Sept 13, '62.
Bradley, John L.	"	25	5, "	Died of disease near Black River, Miss., Aug., 1863.
Childers, George W.	"	20	5, "	Died of disease at Mill. Bend, La., April 5, '63.
Childs, George C.	"	18	5, "	Died of wounds received at Vicksburg, Miss., July 6, '63.
Childs, William H.	"	22	5, "	Died of wounds received at Vicksburg, Miss., June 25, '63.
Forbes, Arthur	Priv.	34	July 5, 1861,	Died of disease near Vicksburg, Miss., Jan. 31, '63.
Hart, Columbus	"	27	5, "	Died of disease at Young's Point, La., March 20, '63.
Hall, Robert E.	"	18	5, "	Died of disease at Vicksburg, Miss., July 12, '63.
James, John T.	"	39	5, "	Died of disease at Cairo, Ill., March 16, '63.
Mass, Andrew J.	"	22	5, "	Died of disease at Memphis, Tenn., Oct. 8, '63.
Morrow, James J.	"	23	5, "	Died of disease at Chapmansville, Va., July 11, '62.
Plants, Jacob	"	25	5, "	Died of disease near Memphis, Tenn., June 15, '63.
Runnion, Reuben	"	18	Nov. 23, 1861	Died of disease at Ceredo, Va., Jan. 25, '62.

Tillis, David	"	18	Nov. 26, "	Died of disease at Young's Point, La., May 21, '63.
Williams, Enoch	"	17	Sept. 29, 1862	Died of disease at Gallipolis, Ohio, Oct. 22, '62.
Transferred.				
Smith, Thomas V	"	20	July 5, 1861	Transf'd to V.R.C. Oct. 1, '63.
Stover, William P	"	24	25, "	" " " "
Wilson, Alonzo	Serg't	24	5, "	Transferred to 8th W.V. Inf. To receive promotion.
Deserted.				
Aldridge, D. B. F.	Priv.	23	Feb. 19, 1862	Deserted at Ceredo, Va., Mar. 28, '62.
Morris, John R.	"	29	July 5, 1861	Deserted at Charleston, Va., Aug. 25, '64.
Morrow, Robert E.	"	33	5, "	Deserted at Gallipolis, Ohio, Jan. 2, '63.
Neville, Charles	"	21	5, "	Deserted at Brownstown, Va. Jan. 1, '63.
Smith, William	"	19	5, "	Deserted at Camp Sherman, Miss., Aug. 15, '63.

Aggregate ..... 105 men.

Record of Captain Barney J. Rollin's Company "C," 4th Regiment West Va. Infantry Volunteers, showing the changes in said company from the date of organization to the date of muster-out on the 6th day of July 1864, by W. G. Fitch, 1st Lieutenant, U. S. A. Compiled from the muster out rolls.

Names.	Rank.	Age.	Mustered in.	Remarks.
Smith, Thomas J.	Capt.	36	July 5, 1861	Res'd Nov. 20, 1862.
Rollins, Barney J.	"	40	Feb. 28, 1863	Promoted from 1st Lt. to Cap. Nov. 20, '62.
McMaster, Wm. L.	1st Lt.	24	28, 1863	Promoted to 2d Lt. from Ser't, Sept. 1, 1861; pro. to 1st Lt., Nov. 20, 1862.
Stevens, Jesse V.	2d Lt.	34	July 5, 1861	Pro. 1st Lt. and Reg. Q. M. from 2d Lt., Sept. 1, 1864.
Dyke, Roberts	2d Lt.	21	Jan. 1, 1863	Promoted to 2d Lt. from 1st Serg't, Nov. 20, 1862.
Ryan, Joseph	1st Ser	24	July 5, 1861	Pro. to 1st Serg't from Serg't, Nov. 20, '62; wounded at Missionary Ridge, Tenn., Nov. 25, 1863.
Ryan, Thomas	"	22	5, "	- - -
Davis, James	"	18	5, "	- - -
Hallan, James	Corp'l	21	5, "	- - -
Love, James L.	"	18	5, "	- - -
Cain, Hugh	"	27	5, "	- - -
Collins, Thomas, Sr.	Priv.	43	5, "	- - -
Collins, Thomas, Jr.	"	18	5, "	- - -
Conway, Henry	Priv.	32	July 5, 1861	Wounded at Vicksburg, Miss., May 19, 1863.

Cradle, Casper	"	22	5, "	-	-	-
Cart, Crawford C.	"	38	5, "	-	-	-
Curtis, John	"	23	5, "	Wounded at Vicksburg, Miss., May 19, 1863.		
Curtis, Thomas	"	31	5, "	-	-	-
Carsey, William	"	44	5, "	-	-	-
Crawford, Samuel	"	18	5, "	-	-	-
Dunn, Patrick	"	23	5, "	-	-	-
Eoff, Hiram	"	18	5, "	-	-	-
Enochs, Enoch	"	24	5, "	-	-	-
Gillillan, George W.	"	18	5, "	-	-	-
Hart, James	"	42	5, "	-	-	-
Hallan, Patrick	"	29	5, "	-	-	-
Klingensmith, David	"	20	5, "	-	-	-
Love, Christopher C.	"	20	5, "	-	-	-
Merril, Luther	"	36	5, "	-	-	-
Musgrove, James	"	40	5, "	-	-	-
Manaise, Patrick	"	25	5, "	-	-	-
McIntire, Edward	"	19	5, "	-	-	-

McAtomney, Henry	"	34	5, "	-	-	-
Roush, Eli	"	18	5, "	-	-	-
Roush, Gilbert	"	18	5, "	-	-	-
Roush, Joseph	"	23	5, "	-	-	-
Stanford, Bernard	"	36	5, "	-	-	-
Shaffer, Michael	"	23	5, "	-	-	-
Thomas, Calvin H.	"	23	5, "	-	-	-
Terril, Franklin	"	28	5, "	-	-	-
Terril, John	"	25	5, "	-	-	-
Vains, Hugh	"	33	5, "	-	-	-
Recruits.						
Baldwin, Isom	"		Jan. 26, 1862	-	-	-
Barker, Isaac	"		Dec. 20, "	-	-	-
Canterberry, S.H.	"		20, "	-	-	-
Gates, Augustus	"		Oct. 13, "	-	-	-
Hudson, John J.	"		Dec. 20, "	-	-	-
Hayden, William	"		20, "	-	-	-
Ryan, Richard	"		Aug. 23, 1861	-	-	-
Ward, James	"		23, "	-	-	-
Veterans.						
Glenn, William	Serg't	21	July 5, 1861	Re-enlis'd Jan. 20, '64		
Hudson, Preston A.	"	22	5, "	"	Jan. 20, "	

Higginbothem, John	Corp'l	18	5, "	"	Jan. 20, "
Sampson, John	"	23	5, "	"	Jan. 20, "
Edmonds, William	"	18	5, "	"	Jan. 20, "
Carey, Daniel	"	18	5, "	"	Jan. 1, "
Fulmer, Ralston	Mus'n.	21	5, "	"	Jan. 20, "
Nease, Elijah	"	18	5, "	"	Jan. 20, "
Bowers, George	Priv.	28	5, "	"	Jan. 1, "
Clark, William	Priv.	19	July 5, 1861	Re-enls'd Jan. 20, 64	
Curtis, Michael	"	28	5, "	"	Jan. 20, "
Crough, Thomas	"	18	5, "	"	Jan. 20, "
Carsey, George W.	"	18	Aug. 28, "	"	Jan. 20, "
Corcoran, James	"	27	July 5, "	"	Jan. 20, "
Collins, Enoch A.	"	25	5, "	"	Feb. 24, "
Davis, Elwood	"	18	5, "	"	Jan. 20, "
Elliott, John	"	18	5, "	"	Jan. 20, "
Freed, Jacob	Priv.	23	July 5, "	Re-enls'd Jan. 20, 64	
Hamilton, William	"	18	Dec. 12, "	"	Feb. 12, "
O'Brian, Alfred F.M	"	18	July 5, "	"	Jan. 20, "
Oliver, John T.	"	20	5, "	"	Jan. 20, "
Pinick, John T.	"	22	5, "	"	Jan. 20, "
Porter, James L.	"	20	5, "	"	Jan. 20, "
Shirley, Benj. F.	"	22	5, "	"	Jan. 20, "
Smith, George H.	"	19	5, "	"	Jan. 20, "
Terril, Daniel	"	18	5, "	"	Jan. 20, "

Townsend, Geo. W.	"	19	5, "	" Jan. 20, "
Discharged.				
Edmonds, George W.	Corp'l	18	5, "	Dis. Jan 23 '64 for dis
Buckley, Richard	Priv.	42	5, "	" Mar 23 " "
Collinson, Alfred	"	28	Aug. 29, "	" Jan 6 " "
Dunn, Michael	"	34	23, "	" Jan 21 '63 "
McCart, Edward	"	24	July 5, "	" Mar 8 " "
Minns, Thomas	"	43	5, "	" Sept 24 '62 "
Nicholson, Joseph	"	25	Aug. 29, "	Discharged Aug. 11, '63. Wounded at Vicksburg, May 19, '63
Townsend, Solomon	"	25	Feb. 26, 1862	Dis. Jan 7, '63 for dis
Williams, Caleb	"	19	July 5, 1861	" Sep 24 " "
Martin, John A.	"	36	5, "	Dis. April 15, '63, to accept Com. 2d Lt, in 13 Va Reg't.
Transferred.				
Ralston, James H.	1st Ser	24	5, "	Pro. Serg't Major & transf'd to Non. Com. Staff Aug 18, '62
Wartenburg, Alex	"	25	5, "	Pro. Serg't Major & transf'd to Non. Com. Staff, Sept 16, '62
Blankenship, Levi	Priv.	22	5, "	Trans. to Co. "H," Feb. 15, '62
VanMeter, Jacob	"	28	5, "	Trans. to V.R. Co. Oct. 17, '63

Killed.				
Neal, James C.	Serg't	28	5, "	Killed in action at Vicksburg, May 19, 1863.
Faughner, Michael	Priv.,	26	Aug. 23, "	Killed in action at Vicksburg, May 19, 1863.
Lewberry, Jacob C.	"	22	Dec. 12, "	Killed in action at Beech Creek August 6, 1862.
McAllister, John	"	26	July 5, "	Killed in action at Vicksburg, May 22, 1863.
Quinn, Joseph	"	22	5, "	Killed in action at Vicksburg, May 19, 1863.
Died.				
Porter, Nicholas	Corp'l	22	5, "	Wound'd at Vicks'g May 19, '63.
Conley, Patrick	Priv.,	26	5, "	Di'd at Wal't Hills May 25 '63
Canterberry, John	"	18	Oct. 13, 1862	Died Feb. 23, '63, at Youngs Pt.
Hill, Swinfield	"	26	Dec. 12, 1861	" May 9, " "
McManns, Thomas	"	25	Aug. 23, "	Drowned in Ohio River, near Burlington, O., Aug. 18, '62.
Workman, Amos	"	32	Oct. 13, 1862	Died Aug 19, '63, at Camp Sherman, Miss.
Workman, James	"	34	Dec. 20, "	Died July 8, '63, at St. Louis.
Deserted.				
Barker, Cumberland	Priv.	20	Dec. 20, 1862	Deserted Jan 1, '63, at Brownstown, Va.
Hamilton, Alexand'r	"	23	July 5, "	Deserted Oct. 15, '62, at Point Pleasant, Va.

Holston, John	"	19	-	-
Smith, Eli	"	19	Sept 20, 1861	" Oct. 20, '62, at Pt Pleasant
Trotter, Thomas	"	25	Aug. 29, "	" Oct. 15, '62 at "

Aggregate ..... 108 men.

Record of Capt. John L. Mallernee's Company "D," 4th Regiment West Virginia Volunteers, (three years' service,) showing the changes in said company from the date of organization to the date of muster-out, on the 8th day of July 1864, by W. G. Fitch, 1st Lieut., U. S. A. Compiled from the muster-out rolls.

Names.	Rank.	Age.	Mustered in.	Remarks.
Goodspeed, Arza M.	Capt.,	21	July 8, 1861	Promoted to Major from Capt., Mar. 14, '63.
Mallernee, John L.	"	21	May 16, 1863	Promoted to Capt. from 1st Lt., Mar. 14, '63.
Hankinsson, Geo. W.	1st Lt.	24	16, "	Pro. from 1st Ser. to 2d Lt., Oct. 25, '61. Pro. to 1st Lt., Mar. 14, '63.
Bratton, Adam	2d Lt.,	43	July 8, 1861	Assigned to duty as 2d Lt., but never commissioned.
Dean, John N.	"	22	May 16, 1863	Promoted from 1st Serg't to 2d Lt., March, 14, '63.
Conner, Milton	Serg't	20	July 8, 1861	Appointed 1st Serg't, March 14, '63.
Grimes, William	"	21	8, "	" Serg't, " 14, "
Wolf, Joseph	"	24	8, "	" " Feb. 20, '62.
Young, John	"	28	8, "	" " Mar. 14, '63.
Havner, James	Corp'l	22	8, "	Reduced from Serg't to Corp'l, Feb. 28, '62.
Tremain, David C	"	19	8, "	- - -
Harris, Leander	"	20	8, "	- - -
McCully, Wallace	"	19	8, "	- - -
Cottrill, Henry	"	19	8, "	- - -

King, Joshua R.	Mus'n.	21	8, "	- - -
Bobo, Isaac	Priv.,	24	8, "	- - -
Baninger, Leon. H.	"	20	8, "	- - -
Cline, George	"	18	8, "	- - -
Cooper, Joseph L.	"	22	8, "	- - -
Crasson, Jacob	"	18	8, "	Wounded at Vicksburg, Miss., May 19th, '63.
Cottrill, Thomas	"	22	8, "	- - -
Davis, Robert W.	"	22	8, "	Lost left arm from wounds received at Vicksburg, Miss., June 13, 1863
Gaskill, Jacob	"	22	8, "	- - -
Goff, Robert	"	28	8, "	- - -
Hiem, Adam W.	"	22	8, "	- - -
Knowlton, Oliver L.	"	18	8, "	- - -
Lowery, Samuel R.	"	24	8, "	Wounded in the face, breast and hand at Vicksburg, Miss., May 19, '1863.
Lowery, William	"	26	8, "	Reduced to the ranks from Sergeant, Feb. 20, '63.
McLain, John B.	"	18	8, "	- - -
McLaughlin, John	"	19	8, "	- - -
McKitrick, Malan L.	Priv.,	21	July 8, 1861	- - -
Naff, John	"	22	8, "	- - -

Name	Rank	Age		Remarks
Stewart, James A.	"	19	8, "	- - -
Smith, John G.	"	22	8, "	Reduced to ranks from Serg't, Mar. 4, 1864.
Williams, John W	"	28	8, "	- - -
Wallace, George	"	18	8, "	- - -
Young, Robert	"	28	8, "	- - -
Veterans.				
Irwin, James H.	Serg't	26	8, "	Re-enl'd Jan. 21, '64
Savage, Thomas H	Corp'l	22	8, "	" 21, "
Vale, James	"	20	8, "	" 21, "
Friedline, Abraham	"	21	8, "	" 21, "
Knight, Newman D.	Mus'n	21	8, "	" 21, "
Dean, William C.	Wag'r	20	8, "	" 21, "
Buckley, Henry A	Priv.	26	8, "	" 21, "
Bradshaw, John W.	"	19	8, "	" 21, "
Bratton, Caleb	"	19	8, "	" 21, "
Beckley, Wallace	"	18	8, "	" 21, "
Baker, George W	"	19	8, "	" 21, "
Courtney, Nathan W.	"	21	8, "	" 21, "
Glenn, Alexander	"	21	8, "	" 21, "
Graham, Perry	"	19	8, "	" 21, "

Goddard, Jefferson	"	19	8, "	"	21, "
Goddard, Joseph	"	19	Oct. 25, "	"	21, "
Housen, George	"	22	July 8, "	"	21, "
Hicks, Robert	"	19	8, "	"	21, "
Kisterson, John W.	"	21	8, "	"	21, "
Lewallen, Jeremiah	"	19	8, "	"	21, "
Lane, Francis M.	"	20	Jan. 29, 1862	"	21, "
Mace, Jesse T.	"	19	July 8, 1861	"	21, "
Martin, Josephus	"	30	8, "	"	21, "
Pullins, Addison	"	21	8, "	"	21, "
Royston, Steph. W.	"	19	8, "	"	21, "
Smiley, Ezariah	"	20	8, "	"	21, "
Witten, Samuel R	"	19	8, "	"	21, "
Wooley, Jefferson	"	19	8, "	"	21, "
Discharged.					
Coates, John	"	23	8, "		Discharged Mar. 10, '62; disability
Howell, Edmund	"	42	8, "	" "	Oct. 16, '62.
McCole, William	"	37	Jan. 29, 1862	" "	July 27, '63.
Armstrong, Wm. L.	"	24	July 8, 1861	"	Sept. 4, " "
Wood, George	"	18	8, "	"	Feb. 5, '64. "

Prisoners of War.				
Dawson, John C.	"	19	8, "	Taken prisoner at Dallas, Ga., May 29, '64.
Killed in Action.				
Goff, Sylvester	"	20	8, "	Killed in action at Vicksburg, Miss., May 22, '63.
Funk, Christian	"	19	8, "	Killed in action at Vicksburg, Miss., June 2, '63.
Died.				
Bosman, William	Priv.,	21	July 8, 1861	Died at Pt. Pleasant, Va., Oct. 31, '61
Goddard, William J.	"	18		" " Oct. 23, "
Bice, Rollin	"	26	8, "	" Ceredo, Va., Jan. 31, '62.
Bratton, Purly A	Corp'l	23	8, "	" Burlington, O., Ap'l 15, '62, of wounds received in a riot.
Gabriel, Abram B	Serg't	24	8, "	Died at Charleston, Va., Nov. 4, '62.
Waugh, George F	Priv.	19	Jan. 28, 1862	" Youngs Pt., La., Feb. 21, '63
Brown, William V.	Corp'l	19	July 8, 1861	" Milliken's Bend, La., Mar. 8, '63.
Yonkie, Lewis	Priv.	26	8, "	Died at Milliken's Bend, La., Ap. 2, '63.
Dickson, James W.	"	23	8, "	Died at Milliken's Bend, La., May 1, '63.
Bobo, Ambrose	"	20	8, "	Died at Vicksburg, Miss., July 25, '63.

Crossen, William H.	"	19	8, "	Died at Vicksburg, Miss., Aug. 5, '63, of wounds received May 19, '63.
Shirkey, Arthur	"	26	8, "	Died at Memphis, Tenn., Oct. 1, '63.
Vale, Samuel M.	"	19	Jan. 24, 1862	Died at Albany, O., April 12, 1864
Transferred.				
North, Jasper N.	"	19	July 8, 1861	Transf'd to V.R.C.
Deserted.				
Howard, John	"	29	8, "	Deserted at Mason City, Va., July 10, 1861.

Aggregate ..... 90 men.

Record of Captain Daniel A. Russell's Company "E," 4th West Virginia Volunteer Infantry, showing the changes in said Company from the date of organization to the date of muster-out on the 20th day of July 1864, by W. G. Fitch, 1st Lieut. U. S. A. Compiled from the muster-out rolls.

Names.	Rank.	Age.	Mustered in.	Remarks.
Brown, William R.	Capt.,	36	July 22, 1861	Pro. to Colonel 13th W.V. Inf. Sept. 16, '62.
Carson, Ephraim C.	"	29	22, "	Pro. from 2d to 1st Lt., vice Stanbery , app'd Adj't, Aug. 22, '61; to Capt. from 1st Lt., vice Brown to Col. 13th Va., Sept. 16, '62; res'd Jan 5, '63.
Russell, Daniel A.	"	21	Mar. 26, 1863	Pro. from 1st Ser. to 2d Lt. vice Carson pro. to 1st Lt.; from 2d to 1st Lt. vice Carson to Capt., Sept. 16, '62; to Capt., vice Carson res'd, Jan. 5, '63.
Stanberry, Phil. B.	1st Lt.,	29	July 22, 1861	Appointed Adj't of the Reg't, Aug. 22, '61.
Ralston, James H.	"	25	Mar. 16, 1863	Pro. from Ser. Maj. to 2d Lt., vice Russell pro. to 1st Lt., Sept. 16, '62; from 2d to 1st Lt. vice Russell to Capt., Jan. 5, '63; res'd Sept. 6, '63.
Mallory. Edward	"	20	Feb. 6, 1864	Pro. from 1st Ser. to 2d Lt., vice Ralston pro. to 1st Lt., Jan. 5, '63; from 2d to 1st Lt., vice Ralston res'd, Sep. 6, '63.
Dawson, Thomas H.	Serg't	24	July 22, 1861	- - -

Snowden, George	"	22	22, "	Pro. to 2d Lt. 13th W.Va. Inf. Oct. 16, '62.
Story, Samuel S.	"	24	22, "	- - -
Cable, Abner H.	"	25	22, "	Not mustered out with Co.
Phelps, Oliver	Corp'l	18	22, "	Pro. to 2d Lt., 9th W.V. Inf. March 9, '62.
Bell, Charles L.	Priv.,	21	July 22, 1861	- - -
Hovey, William M.	"	19	22, "	Pro. to 1st Lt. 13th W.V. Inf., Dec. 19, '63.
Davis, James H.	Mus'n,	24	22, "	- - -
Atkinson, Charles W.	Priv.	18	22, "	- - -
Ables, James M.	"	19	22, "	Not mustered out with Co.
Bell, William G.	"	18	22, "	- - -
Banks, John	"	22	22, "	Not mustered out with Co.
Bush, James W.	"	20	22, "	- - -
Curtis, Abner	"	26	22, "	- - -
Crough, Michael	"	40	22, "	- - -
Davidson, William	"	22	22, "	- - -
Davidson, John	"	18	22, "	- - -
Ginter, William	"	27	22, "	- - -
Garmar, Emanuel	"	21	22, "	- - -
Henke, Christian F.	"	19	22, "	- - -

Hudnley, James M.	"	22	22, "	Missing since Nov. 1, '63. Supposed to be prisoner of war.
James, John	"	36	22, "	- - -
Kemp, Joseph	"	23	22, "	- - -
Lallance, Adam	"	30	22, "	- - -
Layne, Pleasant G.	"	25	22, "	Not mustered out with Co.
Lowrey, George E.	"	23	22, "	- - -
McGraw, Reuben	"	26	22, "	- - -
McKee, John	"	26	22, "	- - -
Plants, Christian	"	29	22, "	- - -
Pomeroy, Arthur	"	18	22, "	- - -
Roberts, Franklin	"	18	22, "	- - -
Rose, Asa C.	"	22	22, "	Not mustered out with Co.
Soulsby, Mathew	"	20	22, "	" " " " "
Standly, John V.B.	"	21	22, "	- - -
Sergeant, Charles B.	"	19	22, "	Not mustered out with Co.
Tucker, William H.	"	37	22, "	- - -
Torrence, Lewis W.	"	22	22, "	Missing since Nov. 1, '63. Supposed to be prisoner of war.
Williamson, Hen. C.	"	19	22, "	- - -

Williamson, Wm.	"	18	22, "	Not mustered out with Co.
Welden, John J.C.	"	19	22, "	Wounded in left arm in battle at Vicksburg, Miss., May 19, 1863.
Wollahan, Richard	"	35	22, "	- - -
Recruits.				
Cable, William B.	"	19	Oct. 16, 1862	- - -
Ours, John	"	21	16, "	- - -
Pauley, James	"	28	16, "	- - -
Nicholas, Willis W.	"	18	Mar. 8, "	- - -
Zeise, Peter F.	"	20	Sept. 1, 1861	- - -
Veterans.				
White, Lyman S.	Serg't	18	July 22, "	Re-enlisted at Vet. Vol., Jan. 21, '64
Bell, Samuel	"	27	22, "	" " "
Cooper, Lewis O.	"	18	22, "	" " "
Curtis, Samuel	Corp'l	21	22, "	" " "
Brown, Edgar C.	"	20	22, "	" " "
Carsey, Martin V.	Priv.	25	July 22, 1861	Re-enlisted at Vet. Vol., Jan. 21, '64.
Coon, Jacob S.	"	18	22, "	" " "
Curtis, Hiram	"	18	22, "	" " "
Deiker, Job	"	28	22, "	" " "

Elliott, Philip H.	"	20	22, "	"	"	
Farrar, John G.	"	19	22, "	"	"	
Hasselton, Albert I.	"	18	22, "	"	"	
Kinkead, David	"	20	22, "	"	"	
Love, William	"	18	22, "	"	"	
Murrey, Melvin	"	18	22, "	"	"	
McGoffie, James	"	39	22, "	"	"	
Neuse, George W	"	18	22, "	"	"	
Parsons, Aaron	"	24	22, "	"	"	
Robb, James M.	"	18	22, "	"	"	
Runnion, James E	"	18	22, "	"	"	
Rodgers, Washington	"	28	22, "	"	"	
Shaffer, Benjamin F.	"	20	22, "	"	"	
Wells, William F.	"	19	22, "	"	"	
Whetstone, Sam'l H.	"	18	22, "	"	"	
Williard, Francis M.	"	24	22, "	"	"	
Wolf, John	"	21	22, "	"	"	"

Discharged.				
Chase, James P.	"	19	22, "	Dis'd at Gallipolis, O., Sept. 27, '62, by reason of disability.
Coon, Josiah	"	19	22, "	Dis'd at Gallipolis, O., Sept. 18, '62, by reason of disability.
Davis, David	"	27	22, "	Dis'd at Charleston, Va., Feb. 3, '63, by reason of disability.
Hayman, Franklin	"	28	22, "	Dis'd at Camp Sherman, Miss., Sep. 22, '63, by reason of disability.
McGraw, Samuel P.	"	28	22, "	Dis'd at Ceredo, Va., March 6, '62, by reason of disability.
McGraw, Burnell	"	24	22, "	Dis'd at Charleston, Va., Ap'l 3, '63, by reason of disability.
Roush, Peter	"	23	22, "	Dis'd at Gallipolis, O., Nov. 1, '62, by reason of disability.
Williamson, Ed. S.	"	18	22, "	Dis'd by civil authority, Feb. 3 '62.
Ward, Peter	"	28	22, "	Dis'd at Gallipolis, O., Sept. 22, '62, by reason of disability.
Killed.				
Bell, William	"	18	22, "	Killed in action at Vicksburg, Miss., June 21, '63.
Blackburn, Joseph	"	19	July 22, "	Killed in action at Charleston, Va., Sept. 13, '63.
Fogg, Clarkson	"	21	22, "	Killed in action at Vicksburg, Miss., May 19, '63.

Ours, Jehu	"	22	22, "	Killed in action at Vicksburg, Miss., May 19, '63.
Died.				
Johnson, Lewis	Cor'pl,	23	22, "	Died June 25, '63, from wounds rec'd in action at Vicksburg, Miss., May 19, '63.
Cook, Britton	"	30	22, "	Died June 18, '63, from wounds received in action at Vicksburg, Miss., May 19, '63.
Burtlett, Gamaliel	Priv.,	19	22, "	Died Sept. 18, '63, from wounds received in action at Vicksburg, Miss., May 19, '63.
Banks, William	"	18	22, "	Died in Regt'l Hosp'l Aug. 11, '63, of Chronic Diarrhea.
Price, Joseph R.	"	18	22, "	Died in Regt'l Hosp'l July 10, '63, of Chronic Diarrhea.
Kinkead, Robert	"	24	22, "	Di'd in Union Hosp'; Memphis Tenn., Oct. 18, '63, of Chronic Diarrhea.
Roush, John	"	34	22, "	Died in Van Buren Hosp'l, La., Ap'l3, '63 of Ch'nic Dirrhea.
Roush, Isaac	Priv.	24	July 22, 1861	Died in Regt'l Hosp'l Aug. 11, '63, of Chronic Diarrhea.
Willard, George W.	"	22	22, "	Died June 9, '63, from wounds rec'd in act'n at Vicksburg, Miss., May 19, '63.

Walker, John E.	"	20	22, "	Died in Regt'l Hosp'l, Feb. 27, '62 fr'm wounds rec'd by a fall
Transferred.				
Trickle, Edward H.	Corp'l	25	22, "	Transf'd to Co. 'I,' Nov. 10, '61
Barton, Thomas H.	Priv.,	32	22, "	Pro. to Hosp'l Steward, Dec. 1, '61.
Deserted.				
Bell, Elias	"	20	22, "	Des. at Pt Pleasant, Oct. 15, '61
Chase, Cyrus S.	"	18	22, "	" at Gallipolis, O., Jan 1, '63.
Shibler, Samuel	"	22	22, "	" at Gallipolis, O., Jan 1, '63.

Aggregate ..... 106 men.

Record of Captain Daniel A. Russell's Company "E," 4th West Virginia Volunteer Infantry, showing the changes in said Company from the date of organization to the date of muster-out on the 20th day of July 1864, by W. G. Fitch, 1st Lieut. U. S. A. Compiled from the muster-out rolls.

Names.	Rank.	Age.	Mustered in.	Remarks.
Russell, Wm. H.H.	Capt.,	21	July 30, 1861	Pro. Lt. Col. Sep 1, '61
Story, George W.	"	35	Sept. 1, "	Appointed Capt. Sept. 1, '61, vice Russell pro. Lt. Col. Res. Jan 5, 63
Hall, William S.	"	30	Mar. 26, 1863	Pro. from 1st Lieut., Jan. 5, '63, vice Story resigned.
Ong, Finley D.	1st Lt.,	39	-	Pro. from 2d LT., Jan. 5, '63, vice Hall pro. Capt. Died a pris'ner at Vicksburg, May 22, '63, of wounds rec'd in battle of Walnut Hills, May 19, '63.
Scott, George A.	"	18	-	Pro. from 1st Serg't to 2d Lt., vice Ong, pro. 1st Lt., Jan. 5, '63, pro. to 1st Lt., May 22, '63, vice Ong, died of wounds.
Jeffrey, John E.	Serg't	26	July 30, 1861	- - -
White, John L.	Corp'l	34	30, "	- - -
Sines, Josiah	"	21	30, "	- - -
Wood, Byron G.	"	19	30, "	- - -
DeBussey, Adolphus	Mus'n	38	30, "	- - -

Tidd, Charles T.	"	18	30, "	- - -
Barringer, Martin L.	Priv.	21	30, "	- - -
Ball, Joseph F.	"	19	30, "	- - -
Boso, Sylvester G.	"	18	30, "	Right hand disabled from gunshot wound rec'd in battle of Walnut Hills, May 19, '63.
Boyce, Jesse T.	"	18	30, "	- - -
Bowen, Ezra	"	28	30, "	- - -
Fellows, John W.	"	21	30, "	- - -
Ferrell, Major E.	"	20	30, "	- - -
Hoselton, Thomas	"	18	30, "	- - -
Irwin, Isaac	"	28	30, "	- - -
Massingham, Wm.	"	22	30, "	- - -
Parker, Freeman S.	"	20	30, "	- - -
Polk, Gideon	"	20	30, "	- - -
Priddy, William B.	Priv.,	18	July 30, 1861	- - -
Rowley, Henry C.	"	19	30, "	- - -
Rand, Kinsey	"	20	30, "	- - -
Swearingen, John	"	18	30, "	- - -
Woomer, William T.	"	21	30, "	- - -
Wood, Horace T.	"	18	30, "	- - -

Recruits.				
Cornell, David R.	"	19	Oct. 11, 1862	- - -
Holmes, Amos H.	"	20	Dec. 7, 1861	- - -
Morehouse, William	"	21	Jan. 15, 1862	- - -
Ramsey, William	"	32	Aug. 18, 1861	Trans. from Co. H, 4th W.V. Infy, Sept. 1, '62.
Sayres, Isaac	"	18	-	- - -
Young, Charles	"	34	Aug. 15, 1862	- - -
Veterans.				
Bloomfield, Allen	Serg't	22	July 30, 1861	Re-enlis'd Jan 24, '64
Raridon, Samuel	"	28	30, "	" Jan. 24, "
Gatchel, David	"	36	30, "	" Jan. 24, "
Chalfant, Finley D.	"	18	30, "	" Jan. 24, "
Wood, William	Corp'l	20	Aug. 23, "	" Jan. 24, "
Duffey, William J	"	20	July 30, 1861	" Jan. 24, "
Jackson, Leonard N.	"	18	30, "	" Jan. 24, "
Barringer, Wm. H	Priv.,	19	30, "	" Jan. 24, "
Birch, John D.	"	25	Jan. 6, 1862	" Jan. 24, "
Flowers, John	"	26	Oct. 17, 1861	Re-enlis'd Jan 24, '64
Griffith, Charles	"	28	Aug. 18, "	Re-enlis'd Jan. 24, '64. Trans. from Co. H, 4th W.V. Infy, Sept. 1, '62.
Hamilton, David	"	36	July 30, "	Re-enlis'd Jan 24, '64

Morehouse, Josiah P.	"	23	30, "	" Jan. 24, "
Murray, L.M.D.	"	18	30, "	" Jan. 24, "
Nesmith, William H.	"	19	30, "	" Jan. 24, "
Nagle, George	"	25	30, "	" Jan. 24, "
McNeer, Daniel F	"	19	30, "	" Jan. 1, "
Ong, William	"	19	30, "	" Jan. 24, "
Priddy, John W.	"	20	30, "	" Jan. 24, "
Robinson, Allen	"	20	Sept. 27, "	Re-enlis'd Jan. 21, '64. Trans. from Co. I, 4th W.V. Infy, March 1, '64.
Ray, Samuel	"	18	July 30, "	Re-enlis'd Jan 24, '64
Smith, Daniel K.	"	18	30, "	" Jan. 24, "
Safreed, William L.	"	18	30, "	" Jan. 24, "
Safreed, Benjamin F.	"	19	30, "	" Jan. 24, "
Stone, James F.	"	18	30, "	" Jan. 24, "
Sayres, Daniel	"	19	30, "	" Jan. 24, "
Vankirk, John	"	42	30, "	" Jan. 24, "
Whetzel, Ezekiel C.	"	18	30, "	" Jan. 24, "
Whetzel, Francis M.	"	20	30, "	" Jan. 1, "
Wolf, Isaac	"	21	Nov. 30, "	" Jan. 24, "

Discharged.				
McKinley, Kelotus	Serg't,	22	July 30, "	Discharged at Camp Sherman, July 27, '63, to rec. pro. as 2d Lt. in Miss. Col. Reg't.
McMillan, Charles M	Corp'l	21	July 30, 1861	Discharged at St. Louis, Mo., April 22, '63, by reason of loss of left leg.
Robinson, William	"	26	30, "	Discharged at Charleston, Va., June 21, '62, on account of disability.
Davis, Samuel F.	Priv.,	19	30, "	Discharged at Ceredo, Va., April 15, '62, on account of disability.
Gilpin, Joseph		18	30, "	Discharged at Pt Pleasant, Va., Nov. 27, '61 on account of disability.
Hague, McDonald De	"	19	30, "	Discharged at Jackson, Miss., July 17, '63, on account of disability.
Harless, John C.	"	32	30, "	Discharged at Charleston, Va., June 2, '62, on account of disability.
Laughlin, Robert	"	34	30, "	Dis. at Charleston, June 2, '62, to receive pro. as Lt., in 9th W.V. In.
Richardson, Ralph	"	42	30, "	Discharged at Camp Sherman, Miss Sept. 4, '63, on account disability.

Reed, Columbus	"	24	30, "	Discharged at St. Louis, Mo., Sept 1, '63, by reason of loss of left leg.
Smith, William	"	33	30, "	Discharged at Charleston, Va., June 2, '62, on account of disability.
Stevens, William	"	18	30, "	Discharged at St. Louis, Mo., Sept. 16, '63, on account of disability.
Savage, William	"	18	30, "	Discharged at Louisville, Ky., Jan. 7, '63, on account of disability.
Watkins, Thomas	"	42	Oct. 24, 1862	Discharged at Louisville, Ky., Feb. 18, '63, on account of disability.
Woomer, Emanuel	"	18	July 30, 1861	Discharged at Charleston, Va., June 2, '62, on account of disability.
Killed.				
Dennis, Morris	Corp'l.	23	30, "	Killed in action at Vicksburg, Miss., May 19, '63.
Davis, William	"	21	30, "	Accidently shot at Charleston, Va., May 10, '63.
Booth, James J.	Priv.,	19	30, "	Killed in action at Vicksburg, Miss., May 19, '63.
Gandee, George	"	18	30, "	Killed in action at Dallas, Georgia, May 29, '63.

Merriman, James	"	18	30, "	Killed in action at Vicksburg, Miss., May 19, '63.
Walker, John	"	28	Aug. 18, "	Killed in action at Vicksburg, Miss., May 19, '63.
Died.				
Mills, Marion M.	Serg't	24	30, "	Died of Chronic Diarrhea, at Portland, Ohio, July 29, '63.
Ong, Finley J.	Corp'l	21	30, "	Died of Chronic Diarrhea, at home, Jackson, Co., Va., Sept. 1, '63.
Boyce, Sanford	Priv.	19	Nov. 10, "	Died of Fever, at Gen. Hospital Charleston, Va., Nov. 12, '62.
Barnes, Wesley	"	23	July 30, "	Died of Congestion of Brain, at Gen. Hosp. at Gallipolis, O., Dec. 6, '61
Brooks, Josiah T.	"	28	30, "	Died of Pneumonia, at Gen. Hosp'l at Gallipolis, O., July 2, '64.
Carpenter, Jeremiah	"	27	Oct. 21, "	Died of Chronic Diarrhea, at Camp Sherman, Miss., Sept. 23, '63.
Davis, Jacob	"	31	July 30, "	Died of Chronic Diarrhea at home, Apple Grove, O., Sept. 28, '63.
Holmes, Robert A	"	18	Dec. 2, "	Died of Chronic Diarrhea at Gen. Hosp'l, Youngs Pt., Mar. 18, '63.

Low, William R.	"	20	June 18, 1862	Died of Chronic Diarrhea at Gen'l Hosp'l, Young's Pt., Mar. 30, '63. Trans. from Co H, 4th W.V. Infy, Sept. 1, '62.
Priddy, George W	"	19	July 30, 1861	Died of Typhoid Fever, at Regt'l Hosp'l, Ceredo, Va., Feb. 23, '62.
Raridon, William	"	18	30, "	Died of Lung Fever, at home, Jackson co., Va., June 6, '62.
Phelps, Mathew	"	19	30, "	Drowned May 4, '62, in Kanawha River.
Savage, James	"	19	30, "	Died of Chronic Diarrhea, at Walnut Hills, Miss., July 22, '63.
Whittlesy, Joseph H.	"	18	Dec. 10, "	Died at Gen. Hosp'l, Gallipolis, O., May 22, '64.
White, Benjamin F.	"	21	30, "	Died of Consumption, at home, Jackson Co., Va., Aug. 10, '62.
White, John W.	"	18	30, "	Died of Chronic Diarrhea, at Memphis, Tenn., June 21, '63.
Transferred.				
Barnes, James M.	"	24	30, "	Trans. to Signal Corps, Sept. 7, '63.
Boggs, Levi J.	"	41	Aug. 18, "	Trans. from Co. H, 4th W.V. Infy, Sept. 1, '62. Trans. to Invalid Corps Sept. 1, '63.

Deserted.				
Slater, Joseph	Corp'l	18	July 5, "	Des. at Ceredo, Dec. 14, '61.
Davis, George W.	Priv.,	27	Aug. 19, 1862	Trans. from Co. H, 4th W.V. In. Sept. 1, '62. Des. at Fayetteville, Va., Dec 17, '62.
Wallace, William	"	13	July 30, 1861	Des. at Pt. Pleasant, Oct 2, '62.

Aggregate ..... 107 men.

Record of Captain William Grayum's Company "G," 4th Regiment West Va. Infantry Volunteers, (three years' service), showing the changes in said company from the date of organization to the date of muster-out on the 24th day of August 1864, by Henry C. Peck, 1st Lieut., 14th U.S. Infantry. Compiled from the muster out rolls.

Names.	Rank.	Age.	Mustered in.	Remarks.
Grayum, Henry	Capt.,	40	Aug. 11, 1861	Pro. to Major May 19, 1863.
Grayum, William	"	31	Oct. 16, 1863	Pro. from Serg't to 2d Lt., Jan 5, '63. Pro. From 2d Lt. to Capt. May 19, '63.
De Lille, John	1st Lt.,	36	Aug. 11, 1861	Resig'd Nov. 30, '62.
Blake, Cincinnatus B	"	30	11, "	Pro. from 2d Lt. to 1st Lt. Nov 30, 1862. Resig'd April 3, '63
Lightburn, Calvin L	"	20	-	Pro. from Private to 1st Lt., April 3, 1863.
Haskins, James P.	Serg't	30	Aug. 11, 1861	- - -
Greer, John T.	"	21	11, "	Wounded in left hand May 22, '63, at Vicksburg. Wounded in left foot Nov. 25, '63, at Mission Ridge.
Trowbridge, David S	"	26	11, "	- - -
Johnson, Walter	Corp'l	25	11, "	- - -
Adams, John H.	Priv.,	18	11, "	- - -
Bailey, Caleb	"	24	11, "	- - -
Bailey, Martin	"	19	11, "	Wounded in right hand, May 22, 1863, at Vicksburg, Miss.
Burditt, William H.	"	18	11, "	Wo'ded in shoulder, also right foot, May 19, '63, at Vickb'g.

Chapman, Charles	"	20	11, "	Wounded in left arm, also left leg, May 19, '63, at Vicksburg
Dailey, John J.	"	30	11, "	- - -
Harrison, Lowell	"	23	11, "	Wounded in right hand May 23 '63, at Vicksburg. Missing in action July 23, '64, at Winchester.
Huffman, Samuel	"	25	11, "	- - -
Johnson, Harvey	"	20	11, "	- - -
Johnson, Jonathan L	"	28	11, "	- - -
Knapp, Mores	"	19	11, "	Wounded in neck, at Snicker's Ford, July 18, 1864.
Lemley, Jacob W.	"	22	11, "	- - -
Oliver, Samuel	"	19	11, "	- - -
Pullens, William	"	23	11, "	- - -
Roger, Edward K.	"	18	11, "	- - -
Shannon, John D.	"	23	11, "	- - -
Sayres, John W.	"	17	11, "	- - -
Wolf, John	"	25	11, "	- - -
White, John	"	21	11, "	- - -

Recruits.				
Caldwell, Wm. H.	"	27	Oct. 15, 1862	Not mustered out.
Chapman, George W.	"	28	Dec. 5, 1861	" " "
Chapman, A.A.	"	18	Oct. 16, 1862	Not mustered out. Wounded in left side at Vicksburg May 22, 1863,
Hilburn, William	"	39	Mar. 30, 1864	Not mustered out.
Malone, Charles B.	"	25	Oct. 16, 1862	" " "
Trobridge, John	"	23	April 4, "	" " "
Vance, Josiah W.	"	27	Oct. 16, "	Not mustered out. Wounded in left arm, Nov. 25, '63, at Mission Ridge.
Veterans.				
Hodge, James M.	1st Sgt	21	Aug. 11, 1861	Re-enlis'd Jan. 20, '64
Buckley, John C.	"	19	11, "	" Jan. 20, "
Avery, James A.	Corp'l	18	11, "	" Jan. 20, "
Hobb, Thomas D.	Corp'l	26	Aug. 11, 1861	Re-enlis'd Jan. 20, '64
Garard, Walter	"	22	11, "	" Jan. 20, "
Caldwell, James R.	"	19	11, "	" Jan. 20, "
Chapman, Hentz J.	"	24	Oct. 5, "	" Jan. 20, "
Enochs, Columbus	"	18	Aug. 11, "	" Jan. 20, "

Ullom, John	"	18	11, "	"	Jan. 20, "
Ripley, Orville C.	Mus'n.	22	11, "	"	Jan. 1, "
Dawson, Albert	Wag'r	25	11, "	"	Jan. 20, "
Brown, Charles W.	Priv.,	22	11, "	"	Jan. 1, "
Banks, George W.	"	18	11, "	"	Jan. 20, "
Chapman, A.A.	"	27	11, "	"	Jan. 20, "
Coats, George W.	"	18	11, "	"	Jan. 1, "
Downs, Robert O.	"	16	Oct. 7, "	"	Jan. 20, "
Davis, Elias	"	18	Aug. 11, "	"	Jan. 1, "
Dunlap, John	"	26	Oct. 24, "	"	Jan. 20, "
Edler, George W.	"	23	Aug. 11, "	"	Jan. 20, "
Fillinger, Henry	"	19	11, "	"	Jan. 1, "
Flesher, George W.	"	19	11, "	"	Jan. 20, "
Gerin, John	"	21	11, "	"	Jan. 20, "
Hannon, Thomas F.	"	22	11, "	"	Jan. 1, "
Johnson, William	"	22	11, "	"	Jan. 20, "
Jenkins, Daniel P.	"	20	11, "	"	Jan. 20, "
Kitterman, Isaac	"	22	11, "	"	Jan. 20, "
Miller, Henry	"	18	11, "	"	Jan. 1, "

Mowry, William P.	"	23	11, "	" Jan. 1, "
Pigman, Martin	"	22	11, "	" Jan. 20, "
Peas, Thomas J.	"	23	11, "	" Jan. 1, "
Pierson, James M.	"	20	11, "	" Jan. 20, "
Shannon, William M.	"	21	13, "	" Jan. 20, "
Wallace, Thomas H.	"	19	11, "	" Jan. 1, "
Wolf, Joseph H.	"	18	Aug. 11, 1861	Re-enlis'd Jan. 1, "
Discharged.				
Switzer, Daniel W.	Serg't,	25	11, "	Dis'd Sept. 1, '63, at Camp Sherman, Miss., disability.
Brannon, George	Priv.	44	Oct. 16, 1862	Dis'd Feb. 20, '63, at Gallipolis for disability.
Caldwell, John H.	"	18	Aug. 11, 1861	Dis'd Aug. 1, '63, at St. Louis, Mo., for disability.
Downs, William	"	39	11, "	Dis'd Nov. 16, '62, at Gallipolis, O., for disability
Forbush, James J.	"	32	11, "	Dis'd Oct. 17, '62 at Gallipolis, O., for disability
Fry, Henry J.	"	19	11, "	Dis'd April 12, '62, at Gallipolis, O., for disability.
Flesher, Andrew C.	"	20	11, "	Dis'd Feb. 20, '62, at Ceredo, Va., for disability
Fillinger, Francis M.	"	19	11, "	Dis'd March 16, '62, at Ceredo, Va., for disability

Gales, George W.	"	20	11, "	Dis'd Aug. 3, '63, at Camp Dennison, O., for disability
Haskins, Charles	"	18	11, "	Dis'd July 30, '63, at Camp Sherman, Miss., for disability
Knuckles, Joel	"	18	11, "	Dis'd March 16, '62, at Ceredo, Va., for disability
Lane, George W.	"	21	11, "	Dis'd Sept. 1, '63, at Camp Sherman, Miss., for disability
Moore, Thomas C.	"	22	11, "	Dis'd April 13, 1863, at Young's Pt., La., for disability
Nichols, Wm. T.	"	18	11, "	Dis'd Oct. 15, '62, at Gallipolis, O., for disability
Newman, Albert	Priv.	22	Aug. 11, 1861	Dis'd Mar. 16, '62, at Ceredo, Va., for disability.
Winters, Jackson A.	"	31	11, "	Dis'd Oct. 18, '62, at Gallipolis, O., for disability.
Died.				
Kassmol, John	Corp'l	21	11, "	Killed in action, May 20, 1863, at Vicksburg, Miss.
Elliot, Martin S.	"	21	11, "	Died May 28, '63, at Milliken's Bend, La.
Saunders, Jesse C	Mus'n	20	11, "	Died June 29, 1863, at St. Louis, Mo.

Angel, Hezekiah	Priv.,	31	11, "	Killed in action, May 19, 1863, at Vicksburg, Miss.
Backus, Franklin E.	"	23	11, "	Died Aug. 19, 1864, at Wheeling, W.Va.
Buck, George	"	18	11, "	Died March 16, '63, at Young's Point, La.
Crouch, Gilbert	"	20	11, "	Died Dec. 6, 1863, at Gallipolis, O
Farley, Charles W	"	24	11, "	Died Aug. 24, 1863, at Camp Sherman, Miss.
Farley, Merida	"	22	11, "	Killed in action, May 19, 1863, at Vicksburg, Miss.
Hellerman, Mad. R.	"	20	11, "	Died April 7, '64, while at home on furl'h, at Hanover, O.
Howard, Joshua W.	"	32	11, "	Died March 13, '64, at St. Louis, Mo.
Jacobs, Levi L.	"	27	11, "	Died Feb. 23, '64, at Louisville, Ky.
Livisay, William	"	18	11, "	Killed in action, May 19, 1863, at Vicksburg, Miss.
Lyons, James P.	"	19	Dec. 27, 1862	Died Mar. 23, '63, at Milliken's Bend, La.
Lyons, Marshal	"	18	Aug. 11, 1861	Died March 30, '63, at Young's Point, La.
Lewis, Henry	"	20	11, "	Died Sept. 15, '61, at Pt. Pleasant, Va.
Minor, Robert	"	27	11, "	Died April 4, '63, at Young's Point, La.
Pratt, Ezra	"	18	11, "	Died Sept. 2, '63, at St. Louis, Mo

Powers, Ezekiel	"	23	11, "	Died Sept. 29, '63, on Hospital Steamer R.C. Wood.
Sands, William	"	31	11, "	Died June 12, '63 of wounds received in action at Vicksburg, May 19, 1863.
Turner, John W.	"	26	11, "	Died March 7, 1864, at Memphis, Tenn.
Wright, Gad	"	26	11, "	Died Sept. 29, 1863, on the Hospital Steamer R.C. Wood.
Waugh, Charles C.	"	25	11, "	Died March 12, 1863, on Hospital Steamer R.C. Wood.
Transferred.				
Gibbs, Henry S.	Serg't	25	11, "	Trans. to Regl Band, Nov. 20, 1861.
Malone, William R.	"	21	11, "	Trans. by reason of promot'n to 2d Lt. of Co. H, Nov. 30, '62.
Bailes, Joseph	Priv.	26	11, "	Transferred to Co. "B," Dec. 31, 1862.
Davis, Henry C.	"	23	11, "	Trans. to Signal Corps, 15th A.C., Sept. 15, 1863.
Reeves, William H.	"	20	11, "	Transferred to Co. "I," Sept. 1, 1863.
Stover, William P.	"	24	11, "	Transferred to Co, "B," Dec. 31, 1862.

Deserted.				
McCoy, Clark A.	"	29	11, "	Deserted June 20, 1862, from Camp Piatt, Va.

Aggregate ..... 115 men.

Record of Capt. Benj. D. Boswell's Company "H," 4th Regiment West Virginia Volunteers, (three years' service,) showing the changes in said company from the date of organization to the date of muster-out, on the 8th day of July 1864, by W. G. Fitch, 1st Lieut., U. S. A. Compiled from the muster-out rolls.

Names.	Rank.	Age.	Mustered in.	Remarks.
Brunker, Patrick H.	Capt.,	28	Aug. 18, 1861	Resig'n accepted Jan. 5, 1863.
Boswell, Benj. D.	"	23	-	Pro. from 1st Ser. in Co. "I" to 2d Lt., Nov. 11, 1861; pro. 1st Lt., Dec. 8, 1862.
Booram, John B.	1st Lt.	40	Aug. 18, 1861	Res'd Nov. 11, 1861.
Donnelly, H.F.	"	22	-	Appointed to 2d Lt. Aug. 18, 1861; pro. to 1st Lt. Nov. 11, 1861; Resigned Dec. 8, 1862.
Christopher, Michael	"	28	Mar. 26, 1863	Pro. from 1st Ser. to 2d Lt., Dec. 8, 1862; pro. 1st Lt., Jan. 5, 1863.
Malone, William R.	2d Lt.,	21	Jan. 1, 1863	Trans. from Co. "G," Jan. 5, 1863.
Jarret, John Y.	Serg't,	32	Aug. 18, 1861	Wounded in the thigh at Vicksburg, Miss., May 19, '63.
Hammoe, Perry	"	20	18, "	Wounded in the leg at Vicksburg, Miss., May 19, 1863.
Allen, William A.	Priv.,	43	18, "	- - -
Buckner, John R.	"	23	18, "	- - -
Burges, Amos	"	20	18, "	- - -

Blackwell, Louis Y.	"	27	18, "	- - -
Collins, Jesse	"	36	18, "	- - -
Crouch, Thomas A.	"	21	18, "	- - -
Ferril, Squire	"	21	18, "	Wounded in hand, July 18, '64, Snicker's Gap, Va.
Griffith, John P.	"	23	18, "	- - -
Hays, David A.	"	26	18, "	- - -
Hammoc, Lewis A.	"	29	18, "	- - -
Hoffman, Peter	"	21	18, "	Wounded Nov. 25, '63
Hacker, George W.	"	19	18, "	- - -
Jones, Salathiel	"	27	18, "	- - -
Jones, James P	"	20	18, "	- - -
Jarrett, John H.	"	18	18, "	- - -
Jacobs, William	"	21	18, "	- - -
Light, Elijah	"	34	18, "	- - -
Matheny, Sam'l D.	"	18	18, "	- - -
Matheny, Edmund P.	"	18	18, "	- - -
Patridge, Sol. M.	"	27	18, "	- - -
Pauley, Oscar F.	"	22	18, "	- - -
Page, James M.	"	18	18, "	- - -
Page, Charles H.	"	21	18, "	- - -

Pence, Henry	"	22	18, "	-	-	-
Rucker, Joel F.	"	25	18, "	-	-	-
Somers, James C.	"	22	18, "	-	-	-
Spencer, Albert	"	19	18, "	-	-	-
Wiseman, Augustus	"	22	18, "	-	-	-
Young, Franklin D.	"	23	18, "	-	-	-
Recruits.						
Kennedy, David M.	Corp'l	19	Sept. 1, 1862	Not mustered out.		
Carr, William	Priv.	19	June 5, "	"	"	"
Facemyer, John	"	21	Dec. 18, "	"	"	"
Hammoc, Andrew J.	"	22	Sept. 13, "	"	"	"
Jarrett, Harrison	"	26	13, "	"	"	"
Osburn, David	Priv.,	34	Sept 13, 1862	Not mustered out.		
Rucker, Wesley	"	30	May 26, "	"	"	"
Reed, Thomas	"	21	Sept. 13, "	"	"	"
Reed, Alexander	"	36	13, "	"	"	"
Reynolds, Arch C	"	22	Ap'l 5, 1864	"	"	"
Veterans.						
Davis, James V.	1st Ser	20	Aug. 18, 1861	Re-enl'd Jan. 20, '64		
Capers, Marshal	Serg't	24	18, "	"	Jan. 20, "	
Douglas, John	"	35	18, "	"	Jan. 20, "	
Selby, Adrian C.	Corp'l	18	18, "	"	Jan. 20, "	

Montandum, Chas. I.	"	22	22, "	"	Jan. 20, "
Hall, Perry C.	"	19	18, "	"	Jan. 20, "
Reynolds, Presley V	"	23	18, "	"	Jan. 20, "
Young, John M.	"	20	18, "	"	Feb. 22, "
Hoak, Jacob C.	Mus'n.	32	18, "	"	Jan. 20, "
Anderson, James M	Priv.,	20	18, "	"	Jan. 20, "
Booker, William I	"	28	18, "	"	Jan. 20, "
Burgess, Anthony	"	18	18, "	"	Jan. 20, "
Blankenship, Levi	"	22	-	"	Jan. 20, "
Cart, Richard D	"	41	Aug. 18, 1861	"	Jan. 20, "
Cart, William	"	40	18, "	"	Jan. 20, "
Drake, Lorenzo D	"	20	Dec. 31, "	"	Jan. 20, "
Hoffman, Adam	"	22	Aug. 18, "	"	Jan. 20, "
Kalussowski, W.A.	"	25	18, "	Re-enlisted Jan. 20, 1864; dis'd by order Sec. of War to enlist as Hosp. Steward. U.S.A.	
Koontz, Elihu P	"	28	22, "	Re-enlis'd Jan. 21, '64	
Wastin, Samuel	"	35	18, "	"	Jan. 20, "
Newhouse, Henry A	"	22	18, "	"	Jan. 20, "
Newhouse, Benj.	"	23	18, "	"	Jan. 20, "

Sampson, Samuel	"	18	18, "	" Jan. 20, "
Smith, John	"	26	18, "	" Jan. 20, "
Smith, Squire	"	20	18, "	" Jan. 20, "
Strickland, John	"	22	18, "	" Jan. 20, "
Strickland, Wm. W	"	35	18, "	" Jan. 20, "
Tawney, David J	"	29	Dec. 31, "	" Jan. 20, "
Vance, John	"	22	Aug. 18, "	" Jan. 20, "
Discharged.				
Young, Lewis A	Serg't	39	18, "	Dis'd June 3, '62, at Charleston Va., for disability.
Strickland, Ephraim	Mus'n	27	18, "	Dis'd June 3, '62, at Charleston Va., for disability.
Botkins, Columbus	Priv.	64	18, "	Dis'd Aug. 13, 1863, at Camp Dennison; disability
Copen, William	"	21	18, "	Dis'd June 3, '62 at Charleston, Va., for disability.
Hall, William	"	21	18, "	Dis'd Mar. 4, '64, at Cincinnati, O.; leg amputated.
Neely, Richard	"	45	18, "	Dis'd June 3, '62 at Charleston, Va., for disability.
Rucker, John	"	30	Aug. 18, "	Dis'd June 3, '62 at Charleston, Va., for disability.
Sigmore, Edward W.	"	30	Dec. 20, 1862	Dis. May 2, '63 at Columbus, O., for disability.

Wiseman, James	"	45	Aug. 18, 1861	Dis'd June 3, '62 at Charleston, Va., for disability.
Transferred.				
Ryan, Richard	Corp'l	35	Aug. 18, 1861	Trans. to Co. "C," Jan. 1, '62
Boggs, Levi J.	Priv.,	41	18, "	" Co. F, Sept. 1, "
Dunn, Michael	"	38	18, "	" Co. C, Jan. 1, "
Davis, George W	"	27	Oct. 6, 1862	" Co. F, Sept. 1, "
Fackner Michael	"	28	Aug. 18, 1861	" Co. C, Jan. 1, "
Griffith, Charles P	"	28	18, "	" Co. F, Sept. 1, "
Low, William R	"	20	Oct. 16, 1862	" Co. F, Sept. 1, "
Mathews, John C	"	22	Aug. 18, 1861	" V.R.C.
McMannas, Thomas	"	22	18, "	" Co. C, Jan. 1, '62
Rumsey, William	"	32	18, "	" Co. F, Sept. 1, "
Smith, William J	"	19	18, "	" Co. A, Jan. 1, "
Smith, Clark	"	26	18, "	" V.R.C.
Ward, James	"	22	18, "	" Co. C, Jan. 1, '62
Walker, John	"	28	18, "	" Co. F, Sept. 1, "
Walton, Richmond	"	22	18, "	" V.R.C.
Young, Charles	"	34	Oct. 16, 1862	" Co. F, Sept. 1, '62

Died.				
Bradbury, Curtis	1st Sgt.	19	Sept. 27, 1861	Died of wounds rec'd in battle, June 3, '63, at Walnut Hills.
Vance, William	"	22	Aug. 18, "	Died June 12, '63 at Young's Point, La.
Bastic, James	Cor'pl,	24	18, "	Died at Memphis Hospital
Hall, Samuel	"	29	18, "	Killed at Vicksburg, May 19, 1863.
Sampson, Robert	"	28	18, "	Killed at Vicksburg, May 19, 1863.
Burges, George	Priv.,	22	18, "	Died Feb. 15, 1864, at Larkinsville, Ala.
Blackwell, C.C.	"	26	Dec. 31, "	Died April 19, 1863, at Young's Point, La.
Cobb, Silas	"	34	Aug. 18, "	Died June 6, 1863 at Milliken's Bend, La.
Erno, Charles	"	29	18, "	Died July 1, 1863, at Young's Point, La.
Given, Andrew J	"	26	18, "	Died May 7, 1863, at Milliken's Bend, La.
Hill, William V.	"	19	18, "	Died Dec. 16, '61 at Ceredo, V.
Hammoc, Martin	"	48	18, "	Died at Charleston, Va. Date unknown.
Hundley, Aaron	"	18	18, "	Died Mar. 23, '63 at St. Louis.
Hammoc, John C	"	27	Oct. 16, 1862	Died at Memphis, June 13, '63, of wounds received in battle.

Judy, Harrison	"	27	Aug. 18, 1861	Died May 13, '63, at Charleston Va.
Kennedy, A.S.	"	26	18, "	Killed at Vicksburg, May 19, 1863.
Kennedy, Robert M	"	21	18, "	Died May 24, 1863, near Vicksburg.
McGuire, John	"	24	18, "	Died Dec. 27, 1861 at Point Pleasant, Va.
Neeley, William	"	19	18, "	Died June 28, '63 at St. Louis.
Newhouse, Michael	"	35	18, "	Died May 30, 1863, at Millikins Bend, La.
Osburne, George W	"	23	Oct. 16, 1862	Died at Young's Point, La.
Slack, Benjamin F	"	18	16, "	Died April 15, 1864, at Charleston, Va.
Spencer, Robert H	"	23	Aug. 18, 1861	Died April 7, 1863, at Van Buren Hospital, La.
Slack, William G	"	20	18, "	Died May 1, 1862, at Charleston, Va.
Vance, Richard	"	36	18, "	Died Aug. 27, 1863, at Camp Sherman, Miss.
Young, Samuel H	"	19	Oct. 16, 1862	Died at St. Louis.

Deserted.				
Cobb, William W	"	42	Aug. 18, 1861	Des. June 15, '62, at Charleston Va.
Casey, Elisha	"	19	18, "	Des. Dec. 31, 1862 at Camp Piatt
Ferrell, Isaac	Priv.		-	Des. Sept. 10, 1862, at Gauley, Va.
Morris, Josephus	"	35	Aug. 18, 1861	Des. Sept. 1, 1862, at Charleston Va.

Aggregate ..... 130 men.

Record of Captain C. A. Shephard's Company "I," 4th West Virginia Volunteer Infantry, showing the changes in said Company from the date of organization to the date of muster-out on the 3d day of October 1864, by Lieut. Henry C. Peck, 14th U. S. Infantry. Compiled from the muster-out rolls.

Names.	Rank.	Age.	Mustered in.	Remarks.
Vance, Alexander	Capt.	9	Aug. 22, 1861	Res'd Feb. 16, 1863.
Shephard, Calvin A.	"	20	Ap'l 2, 1863	Pro. from 1st Lt. Feb. 16, '63; severely wounded at Snicker's Gap, July 20, '64.
Dale, James W	1st Lt	22	2, "	Pro. from 2d Lt., Feb. 16, '63; Severely wounded at Vicksburg, May 19, 1863
Trickle, Edward H	2d Lt	25	Mar. 1, "	Trans. from Co. "E," and appointed 1st Ser. Jan. 1, 1862; pro. from 1st Ser. Feb. 16, '63
Rupe, Matthias C	Serg't	36	Aug. 22, 1861	- - -
Shank, William	Corp'l	41	Sept. 27, "	- - -
Harris, William	"	36	27, "	Severely wounded in arm in action at Vicksburg, Miss., May 19, 1863.
Fife, George A	Priv.	37	Aug. 22, "	- - -
Frasure, Andrew F	"	19	Sept. 27, "	Severely wounded in arm in action at Vicksburg, Miss., May 19, 1863.
Kimberling, Wm.	"	19	Aug. 22, "	Detached in Van Buren Hosp., La., April 20, 1863.

Lane, Washington	"	22	Sept. 27, "	- - -
Porterfield, John	"	25	27, "	Missing since Nov. 2, '63. Supposed to be prisoner of war.
Sharp, Arnold C	"	41	Aug. 22, "	Sent home by Captain Vance, Sept. 1, 1862, and discharge sent for. Neither man or papers have been heard from since. Lives in Mason, Co., Va.
Springer, Albert	"	41	Sept. 27, "	- - -
Recruits.				
Burditt, Eli	"	23	Oct. 16, 1862	Not mustered out.
Cantree, Abner	"	23	16, "	" " "
Brown, Jonathan	"	20	Mar. 12, 1863	" " "
Fisher, Emerson	"	18	Oct. 16, 1862	" " "
Coughenour, Lewis	"	18	16, "	" " "
Legg, Francis M.	"	18	16, "	" " "
Legg, William H.	"	18	16, "	" " "
Shriver, Gotleib	"	20	16, "	" " "
Williams, William N	"	18	16, "	" " "
Witherow, Lewis M	"	31	16, "	" " "

Veterans.				
Boley, John W	Serg't	24	Sept. 27, 1861	Re-enl'd Jan. 21, '64
Kite, James	"	23	Aug. 22, "	" 21, "
Scantlin, Hannibal	Corp'l	18	Aug. 22, 1861	Re-enl'd Jan. 21, '64
Gillilan, William	"	43	22, "	" 21, "
Hill, Benom C	"	21	Sept. 27, "	" 1, "
Clutter, John L	"	23	Aug. 22, "	" 21, "
Nichols, Wm. H	"	21	22, "	" 1, "
Burd, Jesse	Mus'n	22	Sept. 27, "	" 21, "
Lewis, Isaac N	"		-	Re-enlisted Jan. 21, '64. Trans. from Co. "A," Jan. 21, 1864.
Arbaugh, Alex	Priv.	24	Aug. 22, 1861	Re-enl'd Jan. 21, '64
Barney, Sylvanus	"	15	Sept. 27, "	" 21, "
Bonham, Jasper	"	18	27, "	" 21, "
Canterbury, Lewis R	"	18	Aug. 22, "	" 1, "
Cox, James R	"	19	Sept. 27, "	" 21, "
Cort, Frederick	"	21	27, "	" 21, "
Clark, Townsend	"	23	Aug. 22, "	" 21, "
Duncan, George W	"	19	Sept. 27, "	" 21, "
Deen, Thomas	"	26	27, "	" 1, "
Dodson, Philip	"	26	27, "	" 21, "
Entsminger, Joseph	"	20	Aug. 22, "	" 21, "

Hall, Thomas	"	25	Sept. 27, "	"	21, "
Halfhill, John W	"	18	Feb. 28, 1862	"	21, "
Kite, Abner	"	20	Aug. 22, "	"	21, "
King, Ephraim	"	19	Oct. 31, "	"	21, "
Millstead, James H	"	24	Aug. 22, "	"	1, "
Phelps, Samuel	"	23	Sept. 27, "	"	Feb. 15, "
Pearse, Levi	"	19	27, "	"	Jan. 21, "
Scantlin, John	"	21	Aug. 22, "	"	21, "
Sayre, Daniel W	"	18	22, "	"	1, "
Slaughter, L.D.	"	19	22, "	"	1, "
Searles, Benj. F.	"	31	22, "	"	21, "
Searles, Daniel	"	18	Sept. 27, "	"	21, "
Discharged.					
Asbury, Abraham	"	43	27, "	Dis'd for disability, Ap'l 14, '62, at Ceredo, Va.	
Bruce, John	"	40	27, "	Dis'd for disability, Ap'l 14, '62, at Ceredo, Va.	
Craig, John	"	23	27, "	Dis'd for disability, Mar. 10, '63, at Gallipolis, O.	
Gordon, Alexander	"	22	27, "	Dis'd for disability, Ap'l 14, '62, at Ceredo, Va.	
Haly, Solomon	"	41	27, "	Dis'd for disability, Ap'l 14, '62, at Ceredo, Va.	
Higginbotham, J.M.	Corp'l	56	27, "	Dis'd for disability, Jan. 14, '63, at Louisville, Ky.	

Jones, Hezekiah	Priv.	42	Aug. 22, "	Dis'd for disability, Oct. 16, '62, at Pt. Pleasant, Va.
Needham, Alfred	"	24	Sept. 27, "	Dis'd for disability, Ap'l 14, '62, at Ceredo, Va.
Perkins, George	Mus'n	54	27, "	Dis'd for disability, June 11, '63, at Walnut Hills, Miss.
Riddle, Moses A	Priv.	37	Aug. 22, "	Dis'd for disability, Nov. 21, '61, at Pt. Pleasant, Va.
Taylor, Charles B	"	18	Dec. 31, "	Dis'd by civil authority, Feb. 5, 1862, at Ceredo, Va.
Vance, Reuben A	Serg't,	18	Aug. 22, "	Dis'd for disability, Sept. 1, '61, at Harper's Ferry, Va.
Vanderbilt, John	Priv.	21	22, "	Dis'd for disability, Ap'l 14, '62, at Ceredo, Va.
Wine, James	"	38	Sept. 27, 1861	Discharged for disability, Oct. 18, 1862, at Gallipolis, O.
Transferred.				
Boswell, Benjamin D.	Serg't,	24	Aug. 22, "	Transfer'ed to Co. H, Dec. 9, '61
Bradbury, Curtis	Corp'l	19	Aug. 22, 1861	Trans Co. H, Jan. 1, '63
Flowers, John	Priv.,	24	Oct. 31, "	" Co. F, Mar. 1, '64
Higginbotham R.L.	"	18	Sept. 27, "	" Co. C, Mar. 1, "
Koontz, Elihu P	"	26	27, "	" Co. H, Feb. 1, "

Montandon, C.L.	"	22	Aug. 22, "	" Co. B, Sept. 1, '63
Martin, Thomas	"	39	Sept. 27, "	" Inv. C, Oct. 17, "
Mangus, Chester B	"	18	Oct. 16, 1862	" Inv. C.
Rommey, George W	"	27	Aug. 22, 1861	" Inv. C, Sept. 27, '63
Robinson, Allen	"	18	Sept. 27, "	" Co. F, Mar. 1, '64
Williams, Tallison R	"	28	27, "	" Co. A, Jan. 1, '62
Died.				
Burcham, George	"	26	Aug. 22, "	Died of Disease, April 2, '63, in Gen. Hospital, St. Louis.
Butcher, George	"	18	22, "	Killed in action at Vicksburg, Miss., May 19, '63.
Boyce, David	"	44	Sept. 27, "	Died of disease, Sept. 9, '63, at Lawson Hospital, St. Louis.
Burditt, William C	"	19	27, "	Died May 31, '63, at Memphis, from wounds received at Vicksburg.
Clendinen, F.M.	Serg't,	18	27, "	Killed in action at Snicker's Gap, Va., July 20, '64. Was a Vet. Vol.
Cort, John	Priv.,	18	27, "	Died of disease, June 29, '63. In Regt'l Hosp., Walnut Hills.
Corbean, William	"	32	27, "	Accidentally killed, Sept. 13, '62, at Camp Sherman, Miss.

Coulter, Andrew W	"	18	Oct. 31, "	Died of disease, Sept. 16, '63, in Hospital, St. Louis.
Deen, Seth	"""	27	Sept. 27, "	Killed in action at Vicksburg, Miss., May 19, '63.
Free, William D		25	27, "	Died of disease, March 1, '63, at Gen. Hospital, St. Louis.
Flowers, Arthur	"	21	Oct. 31, "	Died of disease, June 29, '63, at Van Buren Hospital, La.
Halfhill, Benjamin	Serg't	20	31, "	Killed in action at Vicksburg, Miss., May 19, '63.
Hughes, Elijah	Priv.	18	Sept. 27, "	Died Aug. 2, '63 at Memphis from wounds received at Vicksburg.
Harrison, James	"	23	27, "	Died of disease, Sept. 19, '63 in Hospital at Centralia, Ill.
Jeffers, David	"	29	Oct. 31, "	Died of disease, Nov. 27, '63, in Hospital, at New Albany, Ind.
Lewis, Andrew F	"	19	31, "	Died of disease, Aug. 9. '63, in Hospital, St. Louis.
Long, Hugh	"	22	Aug. 22, "	Died of disease, Feb. 13, '62, at home neat Point Pleasant, Va.
Lake, Daniel A	"	18	22, "	Killed in action at Vicksburg, Miss., May 19, '63.

Messick, John C	"	18	Sept. 27, "	Killed in action at Vicksburg, Miss., May 19, '63.
Prichett, Duckett	"	30	27, "	Killed in action at Point Pleasant, Va., March 31, '63.
Phelps, Elisha	"	36	27, "	Died of disease, Sept. 1, '63 at Reg'l Hospital, Camp Sherman, Miss.
Riffle, Joseph A	"	20	Aug. 22, "	Died June 7, '63, from wounds rec'd in action at Vicksburg, Miss.
Riffle, William	"	23	22, "	Died July 5, '63, from wounds rec'd in action at Vicksburg, Miss
Reeves, William H	Serg't	20	11, "	Died of disease, Feb. 5, '64, in Regtl Hospital, at Larkinsville, Ala.
Safford, Philip C	Priv.	18	Ap'l 30, 1862	Died of disease, May 4, '64, in Gen'l Hospital, at Gallipolis, O.
Strickland, Jacob	"	27	Oct. 16, "	Died of disease Aug. 19, '63, in Reg'tl Hospital, Camp Sherman, Miss.
Snyder, George L	"	24	Sept. 27, 1861	Killed in action at Vicksburg, Miss., May 19, '63.
Workman, Rhodes	"	34	Aug. 22, "	Died of disease, May 23, '64 at Van Buren Hospital, La.
Woodall, James	"	23	Sept. 27, 1861	Died of disease, Dec. 8, '61, at Point Pleasant Hospital, Va.

Williams, John W	"	27	Oct. 16, 1862	Died of disease, April 1, '63 at Young's Point, La.
Deserted.				
Brown, Andrew J	"		-	Des. in act'n at Charleston, W.Va, Sep. 13, '62. Serv'g in co. E 13 Ify.
Benson, John H	"	20	Feb. 28, 1862	Deserted at Charleston, Va., May 17, '62.
Everton, Daniel	"	23	Sept. 27, 1861	Des. at Pt. Pleasant, Va., Oct. 8, '62
Shafer, John J	"	27	27, "	Des. at Mason City, Va., Sept. 27, '61

Aggregate ..... 115 men.

Record of Capt. James J. Mansell's Company "K," 4th Regiment West Virginia Volunteers, (three years' service,) showing the changes in said company from the date of organization to the date of muster-out, on the 20th day of July 1864, by W. G. Fitch, 1st Lieut., U.S.A. Compiled from the muster-out rolls.

Names.	Rank.	Age.	Mustered in.	Remarks.
Dayton, James H.	Capt.,	24	July 20, 1861	Pro. Major Aug 1, '62
Mansell, James J.	"	32	Aug. 10, 1862	Pro. from 1st Lt. to Captain, Aug. 10, 1862.
Beall, Alpheus	1st Lt.,	21	10, "	Pro. from 2d Lt. to 1st Lt., Aug. 10, 1862.
Clice, Enoch	"	20	Feb. 6, 1864	Pro. from 1st Ser. to 2d Lt., Aug. 10, 1862.
Cogan, John W.	Serg't,	25	July 20, 1861	- - -
Holstine, Charles	"	24	20, "	Pro. from Ser. to Major in 2d Miss Col. Reg., June 20, '63.
Stewart, Milton	"	19	20, "	Pro. from Ser. to Capt. in 13th W.V. Reg. Inf., June 17, '62
Ayres, Ezekiel	Priv.,	27	20, "	Wounded at Vicksburg, Miss., May 19, '63.
Cogan, Daniel S.	"	21	20, "	Wounded at Vicksburg, Miss., May 19, '63.
Crawford, James S.	"	25	20, "	Wounded at Vicksburg, Miss., May 19, '63.
Danner, Martin	"	23	20, "	- - -
Grim, William R.	"	34	20, "	- - -
Griffin, Patrick	"	21	20, "	- - -
Griffin, Michael	"	19	20, "	- - -

Jones, James	"	24	20, "	-	-	-
Longley, John	"	22	20, "	-	-	-
McGunigal, James	"	22	20, "	-	-	-
Meek, John	"	18	20, "	-	-	-
Murry, David	"	19	20, "	-	-	-
McMullen, Angus	"	26	20, "	-	-	-
Mayhew, John W.	"	18	20, "	-	-	-
Nolen, Martin	"	26	20, "	-	-	-
O'Neal, Hugh	"	30	20, "	-	-	-
Purnell, John	"	24	20, "	-	-	-
Rankin, John	"	22	20, "	-	-	-
Riley, James	"	27	20, "	Wounded at Vicksburg, Miss., May 19, '63.		
Stickley, James W.	"	25	20, "	-	-	-
Stickley, David T.	"	20	20, "	-	-	-
Spiker, Isaac	"	23	20, "	-	-	-
Smelt, Andrew	"	19	20, "	-	-	-
Sonenburg, Louis	"	27	20, "	-	-	-
Talford, John	"	28	20, "	-	-	-
Watkinson, Joseph	"	19	20, "	-	-	-

Recruits.				
Mullen, William	1st Ser	36	25, "	App'd Ser. Maj. from 1st Ser., Sept. 22, 1863. Not mustered out; time not out.
Clice, John P.	Serg't	22	24, "	Not mustered out.
Michael, James H.	"	24	Aug. 29, "	" " "
Fry, Joseph F.	Corp'l	21	Oct. 24, "	" " "
Longley, George	Priv.,	18	Aug. 25, "	" " "
McDonald, Peter	"	32	5, "	" " "
McKinsey, Henry C.	"	19	28, "	" " "
Powers, John	"	21	Sept. 10, "	" " "
Reitzel, Jacob H.	"	21	10, "	" " "
Hunley, Silas	"	18	Nov. 1, 1862	" " "
Owens, George	Priv.	18	Sept. 1, 1862	Not mustered out.
Riffe, Grandville	"	24	1, "	" " "
Veterans.				
Hartley, John C.	1st Sgt	24	July 20, 1861	Re-enlis'd Jan 21 '64
Cogan, Joseph M.	Ser'gt,	18	20, "	" Jan. 21, "
Hackette, Wm. T.	Corp'l,	24	20, "	" Jan. 21, "
Betz, Anthony	"	28	20, "	" Jan. 21, "
Liller, Sandford S.	"	19	20, "	" Jan. 21, "

Walsh, Robert R	"	19	20, "	"	Jan. 21, "
Brooks, Geroge S	Mus'n,	21	20, "	"	Jan. 21, "
Walsh, Joseph	"	23	Nov. 7, "	"	Jan. 21, "
Boyd, Franklin I	Priv.,	22	Aug. 28, "	"	Jan. 21, "
Baker, James H	"	19	July 20, "	"	Jan. 21, "
Brooks, Sol. C.	"	23	20, "	"	Jan. 1, "
Buckbee, William P	"	19	Aug. 19, "	"	Jan. 21, "
Clark, William A	"	23	July 20, "	"	Jan. 21, "
Carney, Michael	"	22	20, "	"	Feb. 17, "
Dickerhoof, Jos. L.	"	27	Aug. 16, "	"	Jan. 1, "
Dawson, Henry H.	"	21	29, "	"	Jan. 1, "
Everetta, Louis	"	21	July 20, "	"	Jan. 21, "
Feevay, Frederick	"	10	20, "	"	Jan. 21, "
Feevay, August	"	25	Aug. 25, "	"	Jan. 21, "
Knight, William H.	"	21	July 20, "	"	Jan. 21, "
Knight, James P	"	18	20, "	"	Jan. 21, "
Liller, John C.	"	21	20, "	"	Jan. 21, "
Miller, Henry T.	"	21	Sept. 20, "	"	Jan. 21, "

Metts, Charles O.	"	20	Aug. 25, "	" Jan. 21, "
McGuire, Joseph	"	22	July 20, "	" Jan. 21, "
Paris, James	"	21	Sept. 20, "	" Jan. 21, "
Rector, James L	"	19	July 20, "	" Feb. 17, "
Snider, William	"	25	20, "	" Jan. 21, "
Taylor, Robert	"	19	20, "	" Jan. 21, "
Discharged.				
Liller, William W	Serg't,	35	20, "	Dis'd June 25, '63; disability.
Crow, Nathan	Priv.,	23	20, "	" Mar. 28, '62, "
McGinnis, Thomas	"	20	20, "	" Nov. 15, " "
Murphy, John	"	24	20, "	" Feb. 18, " "
Metts, George	"	33	20, "	" Nov. 15, " "
Eisentrout, Charles	"	25	20, "	Dis'd Oct. 22, '63, on account of wounds received at Vicksburg, May 19, '63.
Thomas, Alfred	"	32	20, "	Dis'd Jan 7, '63; disability.
Killed in action.				
Carney, Thomas	"	20	20, "	Killed in action at Vicksburg, Miss. May 19, '63.
Lamb, Thomas	"	23	20, "	Killed in act'n at Beech Creek, Logan, Co., Va., May 6, '62.

Died.				
Broadwaters, Joseph	Priv.	23	20, "	Died July 4, '63, at Memphis, Tenn.
Canfield, Thomas	"	37	20, "	Died June 25, '63, at Memphis, Tenn., of wounds received May 19, '63.
Critzburg, Christian	"	33	20, "	Died July 30, '63, at St. Louis.
Coleman, Daniel	Priv.	21	July 20, 1861	Died Mar. 17, '63, at Millikin's Bend.
Floyd, John	"	35	20, "	" Ap'l 1, '62, at Frostburg, Md.
Hudson, William	"	48	20, "	" Dec. 23, " Greenspring, Va.
Hendrickson, Jas. H.	"	18	20, "	" Mar. 5, " Millikin's Bend.
Jeffries, Fernando	"	18	Aug. 1, 1862	" July 27, '63, near Vicksburg, Miss.
Lohr, John	"	21	July 20, 1861	Died Ap'l 12, '63, at Millikin's Bend, La.
Miller, Moses	"	25	20, "	Died Jan. 23, '63, on board steamboat.
McKinsey, Geo. W.	"	22	20, "	Died Jan. 12, '64, at Larkinsville, Ala.
Moore, William	"	38	20, "	Died Sept. 1, '63, at Piedmont, W.Va.
Newman, Henry C.	"	20	20, "	Died Aug. 27, '63, at Camp Sherman, Miss.
Poehm, Charles	"	34	Aug. 25, "	Died Oct. 29, '63, at Webster Hosp., Tenn.

Riley, James H.	"	21	July 20, "	Died Sept. 27, '61, at New Creek Va.
Sigler, Jacob	"	20	20, "	Died Mar. 7, '63, at Millikin's Bend, La.
Sigler, John	"	23	20, "	Died Dec. 7, '63, at Nashville, Tenn.
Wilson, William K	"	32	Oct. 24, "	Died Feb. 5, '63, at Young's Pt., La.
Transferred.				
Critzburg, Casper	"	45	July 20, "	Trans. to V.R.C., at Memphis, Oct. 8, '63.
Hunsley, Chris	"	19	Dec. 20, 1862	Trans. to V.R.C., at Memphis, Oct. 8, '63.
Deserted.				
Dodson, Daniel V	"	20	July 1, 1862	Des'd Aug. 1, '62, at Chapmansville, Va.
Feevay, Samuel	"	20	Aug. 27, 1861	Ordered to his Co. Jan. '63, and never arrived.
Montgomery, John	"	22	July 20, "	Ordered to his Co. Jan. '63, and never arrived.
Ross, Joseph W	"	38	20, "	Des'd Jan. 7, '63 at Louisville, Ky.
Water, John	"	24	20, "	Des'd Jan. 1, '63, at Kanawha Valley, Va.
Shaw, George	"	28	20, "	Des'd April 20, '62, at Ceredo, Va.

Aggregate ..... 110 men.

Appendix B

Images Gallery
4th West Virginia Infantry

John D. Birch, Co. F. Courtesy Brian Abbott.

Sylvester G. Boso, Co. F. Private Collection.

Edgar C. Brown, Co. E. Meigs County Historical Society.

William P. Buckbee, Co. K. Terry Lowry Collection.

William H. Burdette, Co. G. Courtesy John Snodgrass.

Crawford Cart, Co. C. Courtesy C.C. Cart.

Richard C. Carte, Co. H. Courtesy Claudio Cooper.

Charles E. Circle, Co. A. U.S. Army Military History Education Center.

Lt. Enoch Clice, Co. K. Terry Lowry Collection.

Lt. Enoch Clice, Co. K. Terry Lowry Collection.

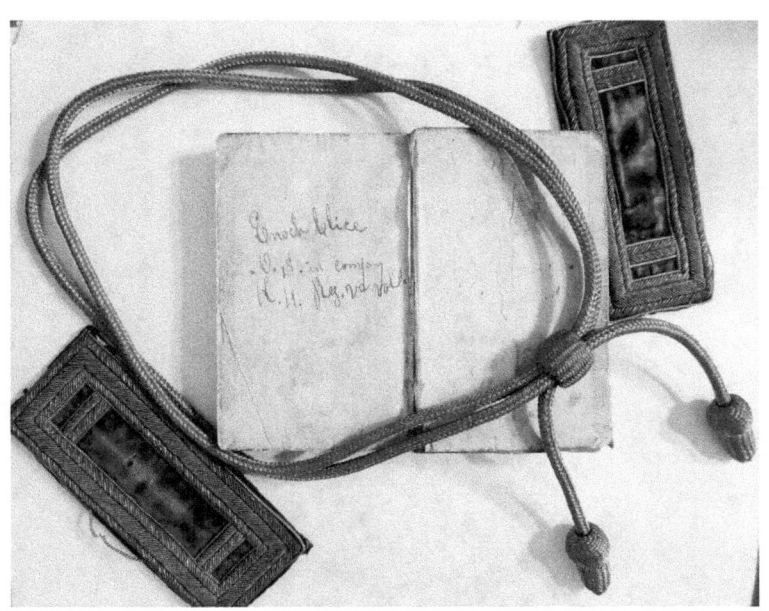

Lt. Enoch Clice's hat cord, shoulder straps, and journal.
Terry Lowry Collection.

David R. Cornell, Co. F. Courtesy Brian Abbott.

Samuel Curtis, Co. E. West Virginia Regional History Collection,
West Virginia University Library.

James V. Davis, Co. H, and wife.
U.S. Army Military History Education Center.

Lt. John Nicholson Dean, Co. D. Private Collection.

Patrick Dunn, Co. C. Courtesy Kevin Martin.

Columbus Enoch, Co. G. Courtesy Richard Wolfe.

Ahas S. Gwinn, Co. B. Private Collection.

Easom Greenlee, Co. B. Terry Lowry Collection.

Christian F. Henke, Co. F. Terry Lowry Collection.

Leonard N. Jackson, Co. F. Courtesy Brain Abbott.

Calvin Luther Lightburn, Co. G. Courtesy Richard Wolfe.

George E. Lowry, Co. E. Courtesy *Civil War Times Illustrated.*

William H. Nesmith, Co. F. Courtesy Jamie Buckner.

John Ours, Co. E. Courtesy Richard Wolfe.

Charles Henry Page, Co. H. Courtesy Craig Mueller.

John Porterfield, Co. I. Terry Lowry Collection.

Benjamin F. Shaffer, Co. E. William T. Shaffer Collection.
U.S. Army Military History Education Center.

Marcus B. Wells, Co. B. Terry Lowry Collection.

Orville C. Ripley, Co. G, Musician. Private Collection.

George Snowden, Co. E. St. Albans Historical Society.

Alonzo Wilson, Co. B. West Virginia State Archives.

Notes

Chapter 1

1. Records of the Colonial Militia through World War I; United States War Department. *War of the Rebellion Official Records of the Union and Confederate Armies.* (Washington, D.C.: Government Printing Office, 1901), Series 3, Vol. 1, 431. (hereafter cited as OR).

2. Egan, Michael. *The Flying Grey Haired Yank*, 21-24. (hereafter Egan).

3. Ford, Frederick. "Riddled With Bullets", *National Tribune.* June 3, 1886.

4. Gibbs, Mildred C. *Mason City: W. Va.: The History of the Town.*

5. West Virginia Adjutant General's Papers 1861-1865, AR 382, Box 12, 4th West Virginia Infantry, Folder 14, Regimental History by Benjamin D. Boswell. West Virginia State Archives. (hereafter Boswell, 4th West Virginia History)

6. Union Militia Records, West Virginia Adjutant General's Papers 1861-1865, AR 373, Box 11, Folder 2, West Virginia State Archives. (hereafter WV AG Union Militia); Wallace, Jr. Lee A. *A Guide to Virginia Military Organizations 1861-1865*, 255-256. (hereafter Wallace)

7. *Ibid.*

8. Maxwell, H. & Swisher, H.L. *The History of Hampshire County*, 33-34; Civil War Widows Pensions, Record Group 94, West Virginia, James H. Dayton, April 7, 1892, Application No. 546411. National Archives; Compiled Service Records, Union Regiments, Record Group 94, M508, Roll 115, Letter signed by Capt. James Dayton, Company A, 4th Virginia, August 28, 1861, National Archives (hereafter CSR); See also: Civil War Widows Pensions, RG 94, West Virginia, James H. Dayton, April 7, 1892, Application No. 545411. National Archives; Kooken, Tom. "Formation of Company K, 4th West Virginia Infantry." Unpublished Manuscript. Online: http//:www.rootsweb.com. (hereafter Kooken, Formation of Company K, 4th West Virginia)

9. WV AG, 4th West Virginia, Folder 1.

10. *Ibid.*

11. *Ibid; Gallipolis Dispatch June* 11, 1862.

12. The Seventh United States Census: 1850: Record Group 29; National Archives, Washington, D.C. (hereafter 1850 US Census); The Eighth United States Census: 1860: Record Group 29, National Archives. (hereafter 1860 U.S. Census)

13.   Records of the Adjutant General's Office, Record Group 94. Book Records of Volunteer Union Organizations, 4th West Virginia Infantry, Regimental Consolidated Morning Report & Order Book. National Archives, Washington, D.C. (hereafter 4th WV Regimental Records, Order Book, Morning Reports); WV AG Union Militia; Records of the Adjutant General's Office, Record Group 94. Book Records of Volunteer Union Organizations, 13th West Virginia Infantry, Regimental Consolidated Morning Report & Order Book, National Archives, Washington, D.C. (hereafter 13th WV Regimental Records, Order Book, Morning Reports)

14.   4th West Virginia Regimental Records.

15.   Love, Lewis. "Company A, 4th West Virginia Infantry." (1899) Monograph, *Camp Fire*, (Pomeroy, OH: The Meigs County Pioneer and Historical Society, 1995, Vol. 1,(25), 13-14. (hereafter *Camp Fire*)

16.   Evans, Nelson W. *A History of Scioto County, Ohio Together With A Record of Southern Ohio.* (Portsmouth, OH: Nelson W. Evans, 1903) (hereafter Evans, History of Scioto County, Ohio); "Colonel Vance Dead", *Gallipolis Daily Tribune*, June 11, 1921. Vol. 31; John L. Vance, U. S. Pension File, Application No. 263447, November 27, 1878 (Invalid); Application No. 1175848, June 28, 1921 (Widow), Record Group 15, T289, Roll 600, National Archives; (hereafter J.L. Vance Pension File) CSR, RG 94, M508, Roll 122, National Archives. (hereafter J.L. Vance CSR)

17.   Everett, Louis, "Vance's Army Record," *Jackson Standard*, September 21, 1876, Vol. 32(38).

18.   1860 U.S. Census; WV Adjutant General Papers, AR 452, Box 12, Muster Rolls, 4th West Virginia Infantry, WV Archives; *Annual Report of the Adjutant General of State of West Virginia for the year ending December 31, 1864.* (Wheeling, WV: John F. Dermont, Publisher, 1865), 79. (hereafter WV AG Report 1864)

19.   *Ibid.* 1860 U.S. Census.

20.   *Pomeroy Weekly Telegraph, July 19, 1861, Vol.4(29).*

21.   1860 U.S. Census; CSR, RG 94, Captain Thomas J. Smith, M508, Roll 121, National Archives; Gilliland, *Camp Fire.*

22.   Rollins Family History: Unpublished Manuscript. Typescript of original in Terry Lowry Collection. Courtesy Barney Rollins; 1860 U.S. Census.

23.   *Ibid.*, U.S. Census; CSR, RG 94, Jesse V. Stevens, M508, Roll 121, National Archives; Ancestory.com

24.   Gilliland, George W., *Camp Fire.* "Letters from Volunteers." (hereafter Gilliland)

25.   Vale, James B. C. Journal. 1891. Company D, 4th West Virginia Infantry. Civil War Manuscripts, A&M 3593, West Virginia Regional History Center, West Virginia University Library, Morgantown, West Virginia. (hereafter Vale)

26.   Walker, Charles M. *History of Athens County, Ohio.* (Cincinnati, OH: Robert Clark & Co., 1869); Personal Correspondence: Terry Lowry with David Maggio and Joe Geiger January 18, 2007.

27.   1860 U.S. Census; CSR, RG 94, John L. Mallernee, M508, Roll 119, National Archives.

28.   *Ibid.,* U.S. Census; CSR, RG 94, Adam Bratton, M508, Roll 114, National Archives.

29.   *Ibid.,* U.S. Census; CSR, RG 94, George Hankison, M508, Roll 117, National Archives.

30.   Brown Family Collection, 1843-1866. MSS018, William V. Brown Letters, Company D, 4th West Virginia Infantry. Ohio University, Alden Library, Athens, OH. (hereafter William V. Brown Letters)

31.   Vale.

32.   William V. Brown Letters.

33.   Vale.

34.   William V. Brown Letters.

35.   WV AG Union Militia, Folder 9.

36.   Kooken, Formation of Company K, 4th West Virginia.

37.   *Whitney, Carrie W. Kansas City, Missouri: its history and its people.* Vol. 2. (Chicago, IL: S.J. Clarke Publishing, 1908). (hereafter Whitney, *Kansas City History*); CSR, RG 94, M508, Roll 115, National Archives.

38.   Ancestry.com.

39.   1860 U.S. Census; WV AG Report 1864, Company K, 4th West Virginia, Alpheus Beall, 101.

40.   WV AG Union Militia, Kanawha County, AR 373, Box 12, Folder 1. Lightburn's correspondence as militia and volunteer officer. WV State Archives.

41.   Biography of William R. Brown, Sons of Union Veterans of the Civil War. https://suvcw.org/past/cwrbrown.htm. (hereafter Brown Biography)

42.   Ancestry.com; Findagrave.com.

43.   1860 U.S. Census.

44.   *Pomeroy Weekly Telegraph*, July 12, 1861, Vol. 4(28); Barton, Thomas H. *Autobiography of Dr. Thomas H. Barton including a History of the 4th Regt. West Va. Vol. In'fy.* (Charleston, WV: West Virginia Printing Company, 1890). (hereafter Barton)

45.   *Ibid.*

46.   Farrar, John G., *Personal Account of the Civil War. February 14,* 1895. Original copy was found pasted in the family bible belonging to Joseph T. Farrar, John's younger brother. John wrote to the account for him "according to agreement." Farrar told his younger brother, "I will try and give a partial account of my services in the Army as near as I can remember. I did not keep a memoranda." (hereafter Farrar Memoirs)

47.   Stone, James F. *Company F, 4th West Virginia Volunteer Infantry.* (Ravenswood, WV: J.F. Stone Newsprint, 1914). (hereafter Stone)

48.   *Ibid.*

49.   Lewis Love, *Camp Fire*

50.   *Grand Army of the Republic, Department of Ohio Records*, Vol. 1, Call No. MSS-715, Ohio State Archives & Library, Columbus, Ohio. (hereafter GAR Ohio Records)

51.   Fogg, Clarkson. Corporal, Company E, 4th West Virginia Infantry. Transcribed copies of Civil War Letters 1861-1865, Civil War Artificial Collection, MS 79-18, Series 1, No. 74, West Virginia State Archives, Charleston, WV. Courtesy Brian Kesterson, Vienna, WV. (hereafter Fogg Letters)

52.   1850 U.S. Census; CSR, RG 94, William H. Russell, M508, Roll 121, National Archives; Ancestory.com; Russell's Obituary: *The Capital*, September 3, 1898, 3.

53.   De Bussey, Adolphus. Company F, 4th West Virginia Infantry, Civil War Letters, Collection number A&M 3296, West Virginia Regional History Collection, WVU Library, Morgantown, WV. (hereafter De Bussey Letters)

54.   1860 U.S. Census.

55.   Hall, William S. Civil War Letters. Civil War Collection, (Artificial), MS79-18, No. 64, WV State Archives. (hereafter William S. Hall Letters)

56.   Ong Family History. Unpublished manuscript. Courtesy Richard, Shepard, Boerne, TX. Terry Lowry Collection; 1860 U.S. Census. (hereafter Ong Family History)

57.   WV AG, 4th West Virginia, Folder 38.

58.   *Ibid.*

59.   Stone.

60.   Grayum, William. Company G, 4th West Virginia Infantry. Letters 1862
– 1865. 4th West Virginia Infantry File, Vicksburg National Battlefield Park
Archives, Vicksburg, Mississippi. (hereafter Grayum Letters)

61.   1860 U.S. Census; CSR, RG 94, John Delille, M508, Roll 115, National Archives.

62.   *Ibid.*, U.S. Census; Hardesty, H. H. *History of Gallia County, Ohio.* (Chicago, IL:
H. H. Hardesty & Co., Publishers, 1882), 41. (hereafter Hardesty, History of Gallia
County)

63.   Blake, Cincinnatus B. Letters. Company H, 4th West Virginia Infantry, August
30, 1861. (hereafter Blake Letters)

64.   Foreman, William. *Camp Fire, Vol. 1, 11.*

65.   Gilliand, *Camp Fire.*

66.   *Ibid.*, Lewis Love, *Camp Fire*; Farrar Letters.

67.   Vale.

68.   William V. Brown Letters.

69.   *Ibid.*

70.   *Ibid.*

71.   De Bussey Letters.

72.   Taylor County Historical and Genealogical Society. *A History of Taylor
County, West Virginia.* (Parsons, WV: McClain Printing Company, 1986).
(hereafter *History of Taylor County*); "A Fight Near Grafton: Twenty-one Guerillas
Killed." *Wheeling Intelligencer*, August 15, 1861, Vol. 10(10); *Wheeling Intelligencer,*
August 16, 1861, Vol.10(11); *Jackson Standard*, August 22, 1861, Vol. (13).

73.   *Ibid.*

74.   *Ibid.*

75.   Kooken, *History of Company K, 4th West Virginia Infantry.*

76.   *The Hancock Jeffersonian*, August 16, 1861. *Vol. 4(11).*

77.   Warner, Ezra. *Generals in Blue.* (Baton Rouge, LA: University of Louisiana
Press, 2006). (hereafter Warner, Generals in Blue); Cook, Roy Bird. "Joseph
Lightburn." *West Virginia History.* Vol. 15, (October 1953); Cook, Roy Bird.
Joseph Andrew Jackson Lightburn." *West Virginia History.* 15 (October 1953);
Farnsworth, Ronald. "Joseph Andrew Jackson Lightburn: Gallant Soldier and

Christian Minister." *West Virginia Review,* (May 1938); Lightburn, Joseph A. J. *U.S. Army Generals' Reports of Civil War Service 1864-1887.* Washington D.C.: The National Archives Microfilm Publications M1098, 1980; Lightburn, Joseph A.J. Wartime Misc. Correspondence 1861-1865. West Virginia Adjutant General Papers, 4th West Virginia Infantry, AR 452, Boxes 12, Folders 1 & 9. West Virginia State Archives, Charleston, WV; Cressman, Frances Lightburn. *Joseph Andrew Jackson Lightburn, Union Brigadier General and a Baptist Pastor, or "Here by a Quarter of an Inch."*(Jane Lew, WV: Frances Lightburn Cressman, 2001); Cressman, Francis Lightburn. *Kanawha Valley Campaign of 1862.* (Jane Lew, WV: Frances Lightburn Cressman, 2001); Lowry, Terry. *The Battle of Charleston and the 1862 Kanawha Valley Campaign.* (Charleston, WV: 35th Star Publishing, 2016). (hereafter Lowry, *Battle of Charleston*)

78.   *Ibid.*

79.   1860 U.S. Census.

80.   www.findagrave.com; 1860 U.S. Census; WV AG Papers.

81.   *Ibid*; CSR, RG 94, Henderson F. Donnally, M508, Roll 116, National Archives.

82.   De Bussey Letters.

83.   Francis H. Pierpont Civil War Telegrams. Regional History Center, West Virginia University, Morgantown, WV. (hereafter Pierpont Telegrams, WVU Library)

84.   4th WV Regimental Order Book; WV AG 4th West Virginia, Folder 1. WV Archives.

85.   *Ibid.*, Folder 1.

86.   Hall, John Papers. Transcriptions of original copies of letters by Major John T. Hall, 4th West Virginia Infantry, held in Heidi Klein Collection. Original letters held in William Matthews Collection, Huntington, WV. Terry Lowry Collection. Used with permission of Heidi Klein and William Matthews. (hereafter John T. Hall Letters); Hall, John T. Student File, Virginia Military Institute, Archives and Records, Preston Library, Lexington, Virginia; Miller, Edward A. *VMI Men Who Wore Yankee Blue,* 6-7.

87.   CSR, RG 94, Philemon Stanberry, M508, Roll 121, National Archives.

88.   CSR, Jesse V. Stevens.

89.   1860 U.S. Census; CSR, RG 94, Dr. George Ackley, Surgeon, M508, Roll 113, National Archives.

90.   1860 U.S. Census; CSR, RG 94, Charles Barlow, M508, Roll 113, National Archives; Ancestory.com; Ohio Roster Commission. *Official Roster of the Soldiers of the State of Ohio in the War of the Rebellion 1861-1865*. (Akron, OH: Werner Company, 1893). (hereafter Roster of the Soldiers of the State of Ohio)

91.   Larkin, Stillman C. *The Pioneer History of Meigs County*. (Columbus, OH: The Berlin Printing Company, 1908). (hereafter Larkin, History of Meigs County); Ervin, Edgar. *The Pioneer History of Meigs County, Ohio to 1949 including Masonic history of the same period*. (Pomeroy, OH: Meigs County Pioneer & Historical Society, January 1949).

92.   Woodhull, Mary G. Francis B. *Woodhull Genealogy: The Woodhull Family in England and America*. (Philadelphia, PA: Henry Coates & Co., 1904). (hereafter Woodhull & Woodhull, The Woodhull Family)

93.   WV AG, 4th West Virginia, Folder 1.

94.   De Bussey Letters.

95.   Kooken, History of Company K, 4th West Virginia Infantry.

96.   Pierpont Telegrams, WVU Library.

97.   Blake Letters, August 30, 1861.

98.   *Ibid*; WV AG Papers, 4th West Virginia, Folder 1; 4th West Virginia Regimental Book.

99.   Ibid., Blake Letters; 4th West Virginia Regimental Book.

100.   "Late from the Kanawha: The Fight at Boone." *Gallipolis Journal*, September 12, 1861. Vol. 26(43), 4; "Late from the Kanawha: The Fight at Boone. *Cleveland Morning Leader*, September 6, 1861, Vol. 15(211), 2; Graham, Michael B. *The Coal River Valley in the Civil War*. (United Kingdom: History Press, 2014), 51. (hereafter Graham); Cox, Jacob Dolson. *Military Reminisces of the Civil War*, Vol.1. (Whitefish, MT: Kessinger Publishing, 2004 Reprint, Original 1900), 35; OR Supplement Vol. 51, 465, 468, 472; Jeffrey A. Hill. *The 26th Ohio Veteran Volunteer Infantry: The Groundhog Regiment*. (Bloomington, IN: Author House Publishing, 2010), 52. Note that in addition General Jacob D. Cox's memoirs failing to mention the 4th West Virginia as a battle participant at Boone Court House, the 26th Ohio regimental history simply does not mention them at all. Cox specified it was the 1st Kentucky Infantry and two companies of the Peytona Union home guards who attacked the Confederates.

101.   *Ibid.*

102.   *Ibid;* William V. Brown Letters; Vale.

103.   Barton; Farrar Memoirs.

104.   Gilliland, George W. *Camp Fire;*" Letters from Volunteers." *Pomeroy Weekly Telegraph, September 27, 1861, Vol.4(39).*

105.   Bishop, William H. *History of Roane County, West Virginia: From the Time of Its Exploration to A.D. 1927.* (Spring Valley, NY: Apple Manor Press, 2007; Original published by W.H. Bishop, 1972); (hereafter Bishop, *History of Roane County*) Barton; Gilliland, *Camp Fire.*

106.   WV AG 4th West Virginia, Folder 1; WV AG Union Militia, Box 22, Folder 17 Captain Lyle Paxton's Company Muster Roll; Letter from unidentified 4th West Virginia Soldier, *Pomeroy Weekly Telegraph*, September 29, 1861.

107.   Love, Lewis. *Camp Fire.*

108.   Barton; *Pomeroy Weekly Telegraph, October 4, 1861, Vol.4(40).*

109.   White, Lyman S. "Letter from Spencer, Va." *Pomeroy Weekly Telegraph, September 13, 1861, Vol.4(37); CSR, RG 94, Lyman S. White, M508, Roll 122, National Archives.*

110.   Stone, *Company F, 4th West Virginia Infantry*; De Bussey Letters.

111.   Kemper, Lester L. The Salem Light Guard: Company G, 36th Ohio Volunteer Infantry. (Chicago, IL: Adams Press, 1973); (hereafter Kemper) Bishop, History of Roane County.

112.   Kemper.

113.   Hovey, William H. "Letter from a Volunteer," *Pomeroy Weekly Telegraph, September 27, 1861, Vol.4(39).*

114.   Barton; CSR, RG 94, Thomas H. Barton, M508, Roll 113, National Archives.

115.   4th West Virginia Consolidated Morning Report & Order Book; De Bussey Letters.

116.   4th West Virginia Regimental Papers; WV AG, 4th West Virginia, Folder 1.

117.   CSR, RG 94, Ephraim McClaskey, M508, Roll 60, National Archives; Letters from Volunteers." *Pomeroy Weekly Telegraph, September 27, 1861, Vol.4(39).*

118.   Shrewsbury, Columbus. Letters. Company A, 4th West Virginia Infantry. A&M 3216. Roy Bird Cook Collection, West Virginia Regional History Center, West Virginia University, Morgantown, WV. (hereafter Shrewsberry Letters)

119.   WV AG, 4th West Virginia, Folder 1.

120.   *Pomeroy Weekly Telegraph, September 27, 1861.*

121.   Vale.

122.   WV AG, 4th West Virginia, Folder 9.

123.   Mellott, David W., and Mark A. Snell. *The Seventh West Virginia Infantry: An Embattled Union Regiment from the Civil War's Most Divided State."(Lawrence, KS:* University Press of Kansas, 2019). (hereafter Melott and Snell, *7th West Virginia*)

124.   Vale; Moore, Frank. *The Rebellion Record – A diary of American Events.* (New York, NY: G.P. Putnam, 1862); WV AG Papers, AR 452, Box 12, 4th West Virginia, Folder 9. WV State Archives.

125.   Findagrave.com; Ancestory.com; 1860 U.S. Census; McDougal, Henry Clay. *Recollections 1844–1909. (Kansas City, MO:* Franklin Hudson Publishing Co., 1910). (Contains detailed post-war account of Reuben A. Vance of the 4th West Virginia Infantry); CSR, 129th Regiment Virginia Militia, RG 94, M324, Roll 1056, National Archives.

126.   Ancestory.com; 1860 U.S. Census; CSR, RG 94, Calvin A. Sheppard, M508, Roll 121, National Archives.

127.   *Ibid.*

128.   WV AG, 4th West Virginia, Folder 1.

129.   *Ibid.*

130.   4th West Virginia Regimental Papers.

131.   Pierpont Telegrams, WVU Library.

132.   *Ibid.*

133.   "Our Camp Correspondence From the Kanawha: Operations of the Piatt Zouaves." *Cincinnati Daily Times,* October 21, 1861, Vol. 41; OR, Series 1, Vol. 5, 625.

134.   CSR, RG 94, Elias Bell, M508, Roll 113, National Archives; U.S. Records of the 56th United States Congress, Vol. 31; *U.S. Statutes at Large of the United States of America, from December 1899 to March 1901, and Recent Treaties, Conventions and Executive Proclamations, and the Concurrent Resolutions of the Two Houses of Congress.* Vols. 31 & 32, (1900-1901), 56th & 57th Congress. (Washington DC: U.S. Government Printing Office, 1901-1902). Library of Congress; 4th West Virginia Consolidated Morning Report and Order Book.

135.   *Ibid,* 4th West Virginia.

136.   De Bussey Letters.

137.   Vale.

138.   WV AG, 4th West Virginia, Folder 1; Kooken, History of Company K, 4th West Virginia.

139.   hereafter Melott and Snell, *7th West Virginia; Wheeling Intelligencer, October 25, 1861, Vol.19(54)*.

140.   *Ibid.*

141.   WV AG, 4th West Virginia, Folder 1.

142.   Barton.

143.   WV AG, 4th West Virginia, Folder 1.

144.   *Ibid.*

145.   4th West Virginia Regimental Papers.

146.   *Gallipolis Journal*, November 14, 1861, Vol. 26(52); *Gallipolis Journal*, November 28, 1861, Vol. 27 (2); WV AG, 4th West Virginia Infantry Order Book; WV AG, 4th West Virginia, Folder 1.

147.   De Bussey Letters.

148.   *OR, Series 1*, Vol. 5, 674-675; WVU Library; WV Adjutant General Papers, 4th West Virginia Infantry, AR 452, Box 12, Folder 1, West Virginia State Archives, Charleston, WV; CSR, RG 94, John B. Booram, M508, Roll 114, National Archives.

149.   Fogg Letters; CSR, RG 94, Clarkson Fogg, M508, Roll 114, National Archives; WV AG Papers.

150.   *OR, Series 1*, Vol. 5, 674-675; WVU Library; WV General Papers, 4th West Virginia Infantry, AR 452, Box 12, Folder 1, West Virginia State Archives, Charleston, WV; CSR, RG 94, John B. Booram, M508, Roll 114, National Archives.

151.   WV General Papers, 7th West Virginia Infantry, AR 382, Box 15, Folder 1, West Virginia State Archives, Charleston, WV.

152.   OR Series 1, Vol. 5, 670.

153.   Barton; Fogg Letters; Ancestory.com; 1860 US Census.

154.   Farrar Memoirs; Gilliland.

155.   Stone.

156.   Barton; *Op. cit.* CSR, Thomas H. Barton; CSR, Woodhull.

157.   WV AG, 4th West Virginia, Folder 1.

158.   Fogg Letters.

159.   William V. Brown Letters; WV AG Papers.

160.   *Ibid.*

161.   *Ibid.*

162.   Hall, John T. Letters.

163.   Farrar Memoirs.

164.   Vale.

165.   *Ibid.*

166.   Stone, *Company F, 4th West Virginia Infantry.*

167.   William V. Brown Letters; WV General Papers, 4th West Virginia Infantry, AR 452, Box 12, Folder 1, West Virginia State Archives, Charleston, WV.

168.   CSR, RG 94, Swinfield (Winfield) Hill, M508, Roll 117, National Archives; Personal Correspondence Terry Lowry with Dallas Hill regarding Swinfield/ Winfield Hill, 2005; U.S. Pension Files Index, 1861-1865, Swinfield (Winfield) Hill, Company C, 4th West Virginia Infantry, Application No. 178795, August 20, 1869, RG 15, T289, Roll 600, National Archives.

169.   William V. Brown Letters.

170.   4th West Virginia Consolidated Morning Report and Order Book.

171.   *Ibid.*

172.   Barton.

Chapter 2

1.   4th West Virginia Regimental Papers.

2.   4th West Virginia Order Book; Pierpont-Samuels Telegrams, WV Archives.

3.   *Ibid.*, 4th West Virginia Regimental Book; William V. Brown Letters.

4.   *Gallipolis Journal*, January 16, 1862, Vol. 27(9).

5.   Pierpont-Samuels Telegrams, WV Archives.

6.   GAR Ohio Records, Vol. 1.

7.   William V. Brown Letters.

8.   Pierpont-Samuels Telegrams, WV Archives

9.   Grayum Letters.

10.   De Bussey letters. Note this statement is a bit confusing, as it is not clear if Grayum was speaking of the recent expedition to Louisa or a new movement.

11.   Fogg Letters, March 11, 1862. Gilliland, William, Campfire Letters.

12.   *Ibid.*, Farrar Memoirs.

13.   4th West Virginia Order Book.

14.   Shrewsbury Letters.

15.   Fogg Letters.

16.   William V. Brown Letters, February 16, 1862.

17.   *Spared and Shared 22*, Category Archives: 4th West Virginia Infantry, February 15, 1862 letter of Cincinnatus B. Blake.

18.   Lightburn, Joseph A. J., "For the Gallipolis Journal", *Gallipolis Journal*, March 6, 862. Vol. 27(16).

19.   William V. Brown Letters; Fogg Letters, March 2, 1862

20.   *Ibid.*, March 11, 1862; OR, Series 1, Vol. 10, 32. Colonel James Garfield's report on action at Pound Gap, KY.

21.   *Gallipolis Journal*, March 27, 1862. Vol. 27(19).

22.   *OR, Series 1*, Vol. 5, 27-28: Rosecrans report to Fremont; Fogg Letters, March 22, 1862.

23.   Stevens, Jessie V., "Letter from the 4th Virginia Regiment," *The Weekly Register*, March 27, 1862, Vol. 1(4).

24.   Fogg Letters, March 28 or 29, 1862.

25.   History Happens, "Civil War Letters April 13-14, 1862", Online.

26.   Farrar Memoirs, September 1, 1862.

27.   Milton Stewart Letter. *Gallipolis Journal*, April 10, 1862. Vol. 27(21).

28.   Fogg Letters, April 3, 1862; Woodhull Letters, April 5, 1862; Craig Family Scrapbooks, 1861-1865. Civil War Manuscripts, Sc86–201. West Virginia State Archives, Charleston, WV.

29.   Stevens, Jessie V. "Letter from the 4th Virginia Regiment," *The Weekly Register*, April 10, 1862, Vol. 1(6). Burkee's military records indicate he died April 15, 1862,

after the article was published; hence, there is possibly a misprint of dates in the original letter or error in the time frame cited.

30.   WV AG Lightburn Letters; Pierpont-Samuels Telegrams, WV State Archives; Fogg Letters, April 8, 1862.

31.   William V. Brown Letters; Stevens, Jesse V. "Letter from the 4th Virginia Regiment," *The Weekly Register,* April 24, 1862, Vol. 1(8).

32.   Fogg Letters, April 15, 1862.

33.   William V. Brown Letters, April 19, 1862; CSR, RG 94, Samuel R. Lowry, M508, Roll 118, National Archives. Wounded on May 22, 1863 (some records say May 19) charge at Vicksburg, in the throat, breast, and hand and hospitalized at Memphis, and later sent to the army hospital at Gallipolis, Ohio afterward, until July 1864 when he mustered out of service

34.   *Pomeroy Weekly Telegraph*, April 18, 1862. *Vol.5(15);*William V. Brown Letters, April 19, 1862.

35.   Pierpont-Samuels Telegrams, April 20, 1862, WV State Archives.

36.   *Ibid.*

37.   William V. Brown Letters, April 27 or 28, 1862; William V. Brown Letters, April 27, 1862; Fogg Letters, April 28, 1862.

38.   Vale Letter, April 30, 1862, or May 1, 1862; William V. Brown Letters, May 1, 1862.

39.   WV AG 4th West Virginia, Folder 14. Boswell, History of the 4th West Virginia.

40.   Vale.

41.   Forbes, Arthur. Letter from Camp Piatt, Red House, Virginia, May 3, 1862. Original in private collection of Mae Persinger, Nitro, WV. (hereafter Forbes Letter).

42.   4th West Virginia Order Book.

43.   *Pomeroy Weekly Telegraph*, May 30, 1862. *Vol.5(21)*. Story's papers and pocketbook are held the private collection of R. Harrison, of Leon, WV.

44.   William V. Brown Papers, May 4-5, 1862.

45.   De Bussey Letters.

46.   4th West Virginia Regimental Order Book.

47.   *Ibid.*; William V. Brown Letters, May 5, 1862; Governor Francis H. Pierpont, Executive Papers, 1861-1865. Accession 36928, Box 6, Folder 3, H. Halleck to Pierpont Telegram, May 5, 1863. Library of Virginia, Richmond, VA.

48.   *Ibid.*, Brown, 4th West Virginia Order Book; CSR, RG 109, Roll 1056, National Archives. Note the Prisoner Rolls cited in CSR are from Camp Chase Register No. 1, 1862, page 40; Vicksburg Roll 27, Sheet 28.

49.   Vale.

50.   "Accidentally Shot." and Letter from Milton Stewart. "For the Journal" *Gallipolis Journal,* May 22, 1862. Vol. 27(27).

51.   William S. Hall Letters, May 9, 1862.

52.   Fogg Letters, May 9, 1862.

53.   William V. Brown Letters, May 9, 1862. Chapmanville is on the Guyandotte River and was possibly Ballardsville on the map Brown was looking at.

54.   *Op. cit. Gallipolis Journal,* May 22, 1862.

55.   Blake Letters, May 12, 1862.

56.   *Gallipolis Journal,* May 15, 1862. Vol. 27(6).

57.   William V. Brown Letters, May 16 1862.

58.   Fogg Letters, May 18, 1862.

59.   Vale.

60.   Shrewsbury Letters, May 21, 1862.

61.   Fogg Letters, May 21, 1862.

62.   Vale.

63.   Blake Letters, May 26, 1862.

64.   De Bussey, May 31, 1862; Fogg Letters, June 1, 1862.

65.   4th West Virginia Order Book, June 5-7, 1862; WV AG Papers, AR 452, Box 12, 4th West Virginia Infantry, WV Archives.

66.   Vale.

67.   *OR, Series 1,* Vol. 12, Part 3, 412.

68.   De Bussey Letters, June 22, 1862.

69.   WV AG, 4th West Virginia, AR 382, Box 30, Misc. Records, Folder 8. Letter from John McCurdy, Assistant Surgeon. 23rd Ohio Infantry, Medical Inspector at Charleston, June 23, 1862.

70.   John T. Hall Letters.

71.   "The 4th at Charleston." *The Weekly Register,* July 10, 1862, Vol. 1(18).

72.   De Bussey Letters, July 6, 1862.

73.   *Ibid.* William V. Brown Letters, July 9, 1862.

74.   William V. Brown Letters; *Gallipolis Dispatch,* July 9, 1862; Vale.

75.   Major John T. Hall to Assistant Adjutant General George Ruggles, July 10, 1862. CSR, RG 94, M508, Roll 117, National Archives. (hereafter John T. Hall CSR)

76.   Blake Letters, July 17, 1862; Vale.

77.   *Gallipolis Journal,* July 17, 1862, Vol. 27(34); *The Weekly Register,* July 16, 1862, Vol. 1(19); CSR, Citizens File, RG 109, Ogden Spencer, M346, Roll 970, National Archives.

78.   John T. Hall CSR; Vale.

79.   *Gallipolis Journal,* July 31, 1862, Vol. 27(36); *The Weekly Register,* July 31, 1862, Vol. 1(21).

80.   De Bussey Letters, July 31, 1862.

81.   John T. Hall Letters, July 31, 1862.

82.   William V. Brown Letters, August 3, 1862.

83.   *Ibid.,* August 4, 1862.

84.   WV AG Papers, Union Militia, Kanawha County, 153rd Regiment, AR 373, Box 10, Folder 9, WV State Archives. Letters from J.A.J. Lightburn to Captain Thomas Nutter, August 4&7, 1862.

85.   Blake Letters, August 7, 1862.

86.   *OR, Series I,* Vol. 12, Part 2, 115-116; Fogg Letters, August 17, 1862. Colonel Edward Siber's OR Report skirmish near Chapmanville, including death of Major John T. Hall. Witcher evidenced a propensity toward violence even before the war, however, as in February 1860 he was involved in a shooting at Franklin County, Virginia Court House during the divorce trial of a female family member that resulted in the deaths of two brothers and one of his cousins. Not surprisingly, Witcher later entered politics after the war, and ran for the Virginia House of Delegates, but failed to be elected.

87.   Gilliland, Camp Fire.

88.   Stewart, Milton, Co. K, 4th Va. Infantry. "Murder of Major Hall", *The Weekly Register*, August 28, 1862, Vol. 1(25).

89.   *Ibid; Wheeling Intelligencer*, August 18, 1862. Vol.10(306).

90.   *Ibid.*, Stewart. CSR RG 94, M508, Roll 0074, National Archives.

91.   Blake Letters, August 7-8, 1862.

92.   William V. Brown Letters, August 1862 (otherwise undated)

93.   *Ibid.*

94.   Fogg Letters, August 17, 1862.

95.   Adjutant General's Papers, West Virginia State Service Commission, 1901, Ar402-403, Logan County, Gordon and Patterson Riffe, WV State Archives; CSR, 129th Regiment Virginia Militia, RG 109, M324, Roll 1056, National Archives; CSR, 7th West Virginia Cavalry, RG 94, M508, Roll 0080, National Archives.

96.   Barton; U.S. Senate Records, No. 1216: 57th Congress, First Session.

97.   William V. Brown Letters, August 17, 1862.

98.   William Grayum Letters, August 6, 1862.

99.   *OR, Series 1*, Vol. 12, Part 3, 551; 582; 619; Lightburn Letters September 1862; Blundon & Matthews Family Papers, Edgar Blundon Civil War Diary and letters, typescript, 1861-1920, Letter from September 5, 1862, West Virginia Civil War Manuscripts Collection, Ms 89-94, Folder 1, WV State Archives. Cole, Scott. *34th Battalion Virginia Cavalry.* (Lynchburg, VA: H.E. Howard, 1993), 26-27.

100.   *OR, Series 1,* Vol. 12, Part 3, 407; 534; 540; 543; 567; 570; 577; 619; 629; 698-699; 712; 722; 726; also Part 1, 738; 742; 754; Part 2, 405-411; OR, Series 1, Vol. 19, Part 1, 419; 424-426; 427-431; 458-474; Cox, *Military Reminisces of the Civil War.* Vol. 1, 77-79; 80-81; 96-98; 114-115; 118-122.

101.   William V. Brown Letters, August 8, 1862.

102.   *Ibid.*, August 9, 1862.

103.   WV AG Papers, Union Militia, 153rd Regiment, Kanawha County, AR 373, Box 12, Folder 9, WV State Archives. (hereafter 153rd Militia Files, WV Archives)

104.   George K. Ackley, CSR RG 94, M508, Roll 0113, National Archives; William V. Brown Letters, August 11, 1862.

105.   *The Weekly Register*, August 14, 1862, Vol. 1(23); *The Weekly Register*, August 21, 1862, Vol. 1(24), 1.

106.   William Van Brown Letters, August 17, 1862.

107.   Fogg Letters, August 17, 1862; William V. Brown Letters, August 17, 1862.

108.   4th West Virginia Order Book; Pierpont Telegrams, WVU.

109.   *Ibid*, Pierpont.

110.   Fogg Letters, August 25, 1862.

111.   William V. Brown Letters, August 29, 1862.

112.   153rd Militia Files, WV Archives; Fogg Letters August 30, 1862.

113.   Farrar Memoirs, September 8, 1862.

114.   Robinson, James I., Jr. (Ed.). *Soldier of Southwestern Virginia: The Civil War Letters of Captain John Preston Sheffy.* (Baton Rouge, LA: Louisiana State Press, 2004), 77-84; *Journal of the Congress of the Confederate States of America*, 1861-1865, Vol. 5. (Washington DC: Government Printing Office, 1905), 340-341; Lowry, *Battle of Charleston*, 77-78.

115.   Lightburn Letters, September 1862; Lowry, *Battle of Charleston*, 84-86; Diary of Sarah Francis Young 1861-1862. Diary, September 7, 1862; Typescript. West Virginia Regional History Collection, Roy Bird Cook Collection, Call No. AM 1651, West Virginia University Library. Morgantown, WV. OR, Series 1, Vol. 12, Part 2, 756-764; *Weekly Register*, September 18, 1862, & January 22, 1863; Jack L Dickinson *16th Virginia Cavalry.* (Lynchburg, Virginia: H.E. Howard, 1989), 9-10; 109; OR, Series 1, Vol. 19, Part 1, 1058-1060; Griffith, 49-52; Joseph J. Sutton. *History of the 2nd Regiment, West Virginia Cavalry Volunteers.* (Huntington, West Virginia: Blue Acorn Press, Reprinted 1992; Original publication 1892), 59-61.

116.   Ibid., Sarah Francis Young Diary. *OR, Series 1*, Vol. 12, Part 1, 759-764; 13th West Virginia Infantry Field History, Part 1.

117.   Pension Papers, Philip Matthews, Company B, 4th West Virginia Infantry, Application No. 182647 (Invalid), April 4, 1873, CSR, RG 15, T289, Roll 59/3891, National Archives. Note: Theodore Lang indicated the date was October 2, 1863.

118.   *The Weekly Register*, September 18, 1862, Vol. 1(27), 2 and October 9, 1862, Vol.1(29).

119.   William V. Brown Letters, September 13, 1862; James Vale Diary.

120.   Roy Bird Cook. "The Civil War Comes to Charleston." *West Virginia History*, Vol. 23(2), (January 1962), 153-167; Letter from unidentified Union soldier from

Ohio written on September 18, 1862 from Gallipolis, Ohio. *Cincinnati Daily Commercial,* October 5, 1862, Vol. 46(244); *OR, Series 1,* Vol. 19, Part I, 1057-1090; Cook, 153-167; Barton.

121.   Diary of Victoria Hansford Teays, Boyd Stutler Collection, MS78-1, Series 1, No. 8, July 1861, WV Archives; William D. Wintz. *Civil War Memoirs of two Rebel sisters.* (Pictorial Histories Publishing, Charleston WV, 1989), 25-26.

122.   William V. Brown Letters, September 13, 1862; Lowry, *Battle of Charleston,* 218; Barton.

123.   *Ibid.*

124.   Lowry, *Battle of Charleston,* 200-201; Farrar Memoirs, February 14, 1895.

125.   *The Weekly Register,* October 9, 1862, Vol. 1(29); Vale.

126.   William V. Brown Letters, September 13, 1862.

127.   *Ibid.*

128.   Blake Letters, September 11, 1862.

129.   *Ibid.; The Weekly Register,* October 9, 1862.

130.   Chamberlin, W.H. (Ed.). *Sketches of War History 1861-1865: Papers Prepared for the Ohio Commandery of the Military Order of the Loyal Legion of the United States 1890-1986,* Vol. 4. "The Retreat of Union Forces from the Kanawha Valley in 1862." by John L. Vance, 4th West Virginia Infantry. (Cincinnati, OH: Robert Clark Co., 1896). (hereafter Chamberlin/Vance)

131.   *Ibid.,* Chamberlin/Vance.

132.   Lewis Love, *Camp Fire.* An Account of the battle of Charleston, Vol. 1.

133.   Lowry, *Battle of Charleston,* 224.

134.   *Ibid.;* William V. Brown Letters, September 13, 1862.

135.   Roy Bird Cook. "The Civil War Comes to Charleston." *West Virginia History,* Vol. 23(2), (January 1962), 153-167; Letter from unidentified Union soldier from Ohio written on September 18, 1862 from Gallipolis, Ohio. *Cincinnati Daily Commercial,* Vol. 46(244) October 5, 1862; *OR, Series 1,* Vol. 19, Part I, 1057-1090; Cook, 153-167; Lowry, 224.

136.   *OR, Series 1,* Vol. 19, Part 1, 1058-1059, 1070-1071; Barton, 86; Lowry, *Battle of Charleston,* 227-230.

137.   *Ibid.,* Farrar Memoirs; Lowry; WV AG Papers, 4th West Virginia, AR 382, Misc. Records, Court Martials, Folder 21, WV State Archives; Barton, 86.

138.   *Pomeroy Weekly Telegraph*, October 17, 1862, Vol. 5(41).

139.   *The Guerilla*, Vol. 1(2), September 28, 1862; Pierpont Telegraphs, J.A.J. Lightburn to F. Pierpont, September 19, 1862, WVU Library; *OR, Series 1*, Vol. 19, Part 1, 1057-1090; 13th West Virginia Field History, Part 1.

140.   Fogg Letters, September 30, 1862.

141.   Lowry, *Battle of Charleston*, 292-293; *The Guerilla*, October 3, 1862, Vol. 1(6); *OR, Series 1*, Vol. 19, Part 1, 1057-1090.

142.   *Ibid.*, Lowry, 292-293; Telegraphic Dispatches to the Governor of Ohio, Series 145, Ohio Historical Society, Columbus, Ohio.

143.   *Ibid.*, Lowry, 302-303.

144.   *Pomeroy Telegraph, October 24, 1862, Vol. 5(22), 1;* Fogg Letters, October 15, 1862.

145.   *The Weekly Register*, October 16, 1862, Vol. 1(30), 1; "A Correction," *Gallipolis Journal, November 13, 1862, Vol.* 27(51), 2. "Card from Miss Dayton's Father," *Gallipolis Journal,* January 1, 1863, Vol. 28 (1), 2.

146.   *Ibid*; "A Correction," *Gallipolis Journal,* November 13, 1862. Vol. 27(52).

147.   *Ibid*; December 16, 1862.

148.   Lowry, *Battle of Charleston*, 315-329; Fogg Letters, October 24, 1862.

149.   *Ibid.*, Lowry, 335-355.

150.   *OR, Series 1*, Vol. 19, Part 2, 522-523; Lowry, *Battle of Charleston*, 303-15; 329, 335-355; *Pomeroy Weekly Telegraph* newspaper, November 21, 1862, Vol. 5(46), 2.

151.   *Ibid.*

152.   *Ibid.*, Fogg Letters, November 2, 1861; William V. Brown Letters, November 5, 1862.

153.   Shrewsbury Letters, November 8, 1862; Blake Letters, November 17, 1862.

154.   *Ibid.*, Shrewsbury, November 25, 1862.

155.   William S. Hall Letters, November 25, 1862.

156.   William V. Brown Letters, November 28, 1862.

157.   Lowry, *Battle of Charleston*, 366.

158.   De Bussey Letters, December 1, 1862; 4th WV Regimental Order Book, December 1, 1862.

159.   Farrar Memoirs, December 4, 1862.

160.   CSR, RG 94, Columbus Shrewsberry, M508, Roll 121, National Archives; William V. Brown Letters, December 5, 1862.

161.   *Ibid.*, Brown, December 14, 1862; 4th West Virginia Regimental Order Book, December 27, 1862.

162.   *OR, Series 1*, Vol. 21, Part 1, 940.

163.   Gilder-Leherman Collection, Civil War Manuscripts, No. GLCO2414.161, Letter to E.P. Scammon from officers of the 4th West Virginia, December 29, 1862. Institute of American History, New York.

164.   Farrar Memoirs, December 28, 1862.

Chapter 3

1.   Barton.

2.   Hewitt, Janet B., (Ed.). *Supplement to the Official Records of the Union and Confederate Armies.* Part 2, Record of Events, Vol. 74. (Wilmington, NC: Broadfoot Publishing, 1998) (hereafter Hewitt, *OR Supplement* Vol. 74); Lewis Love, Camp Fire.

3.   *OR, Series 1*, Vol. 21, 319, 940; Shrewsbury Letters, January 3, 1863.

4.   *Ibid.*, Shrewsbury; Hewitt, *OR Supplement*, Vol. 74; William V. Brown Letters, January 3, 1863; 4th West Virginia Consolidated Morning Report and Order Book.

5.   De Bussey Letters, January 5, 1863; Farrar Memoirs, January 5, 1863; Shrewsbury Letters, January 5, 1863; CSR, RG 94, Joseph Roush, M508, Roll 120, National Archives.

6.   *Ibid.*, De Bussey January 8-9, 1863; Brown January 11, 1863; 4th West Virginia Order Book.

7.   Shrewsbury Letters, January 13, 1863.

8.   *Ibid.*, January 17, 1863.

9.   *Ibid*; Farrar Letters, January 19, 1863.

10.   William V. Brown Letters, January 21,1863.

11.   Barton; Bearss, Edwin G. "The Fall of Vicksburg." *Civil War Times*, (July, 2006); Hatfield, Philip. "The 4th West Virginia Infantry at Vicksburg." *Civil War Historian*,

(July-August 2008), Vol. 4(4), 24-42 (hereafter Hatfield); OR, Series 1, Vol. 24, Part 1, 11.

12.   *Ibid.*, Bearss, Hatfield.

13.   Hewitt, *OR Series 1, Supplement*, Vol. 24; Lewis Love, *Camp Fire.*

14.   CSR, RG 94, George Ackley, M508, Roll 113, National Archives; William S. Hall Letters, January 29, 1863; WV AG 4th West Virginia, Folder 9; De Bussey Letters, January 29, 1862.

15.   WV AG, 4th West Virginia, Folder 26; CSR, RG 94, Arthur Forbes, M508, Roll 116, National Archives; Fogg Letters, January 31, 1863.

16.   Farrar Memoirs, February 1, 1863; *OR, Series 1*, Vol. 24, Part 1, 20-21.

17.   Shrewsbury Letters, February 12 1863; Lewis Love, Camp Fire.

18.   *Ibid.*, Shrewsbury, February 16, 1863.

19.   William V. Brown Letters, February 18, 1863. CSR, RG 95, George F. Waugh, M508, Roll 122, National Archives.

20.   *Ibid.*

21.   *Ibid,* Brown, March 1, 1863; Fogg Letters, March 1, 1863.

22.   *Ibid.*, Fogg, March 2 1863; Shrewsbury Letters March 2, 1863.

23.   William V. Brown Letters: Letter by Robert W. Davis to Brown's mother informing her of William's death March 8, 1963; CSR, RG 94, William V. Brown, M508, Roll 114, National Archives; CSR, RG 94, Robert W. Davis, M508, Roll 115, National Archives.

24.   CSR, RG 94, John Luther Vance, M508, Roll 122, National Archives; Fogg Letters, March 9, 1863.

25.   4th West Virginia Order Book; CSR, RG 94, George S. Woodhull, M508, Roll 122, National Archives; WV AG 4th West Virginia, Folder 6.

26.   *OR, Series 1*, Vol. 24, Part 1, 449-450.

27.   4th West Virginia Order Book.

28.   *OR Series 1*, Vol. 24, Part 1, 454, 459. Lightburn's Report March 29, 1863; William L. Safreed Diary, March 17, 1863 (hereafter Safreed Diary); Fogg Letters, March 17, 1863.

29.   *Ibid.*, *OR*; 4th West Virginia Order Book; 1860 U.S. Census; CSR, RG 94, William S. Hall, M508, Roll 117, National Archives.

30.   *Ibid., OR.*

31.   Safreed, William L. Civil War Diary, March 21, 1863; Fogg Letters, March 21, 1863; Pierpont Telegrams, WVU.

32.   *Ibid.*, Safreed; *OR, Series 1*, Vol. 24, Part 1, 438.

33.   *OR, Series 1*, Vol. 24, Part 1, 454. Lightburn's Report March 29, 1863.

34.   Safreed Diary, March 24, 1863.

35.   *OR Series 1*, Vol. 24, Part 1, 454.

36.   *Ibid.*

37.   Fogg Letters, March 27, 1863.

38.   Hall Letters, March 27, 1863.

39.   Barton.

40.   Hardesty, *History of Gallia County; History of Mason County;* Captain Frederick Ford Navy Pension File, Feb. 15, 1882. Claim No. 7945, Microfilm T288, Roll 157, National Archives. (hereafter Ford Pension file)

41.   Barton.

42.   Hall Letters, April 2, 1863.

43.   Safreed Diary, April 1863. (Entry written between 3rd and 5th, undated)

44.   *Ibid*; Shrewsbury Letters, April 8, 1863.

45.   *Ibid.*, Safreed, April 23, 24 & 26, 1863.

46.   *Ibid.*, Safreed, April 27, 1863; Grayum Letters, April 28, 1863.

47.   *Ibid.*, Safreed April 30, 1863; Fogg Letters, April 30, 1863.

48.   *Ibid.*, Fogg, May 3, 1863.

49.   WV AG, 4th West Virginia, AR 382, Misc. Records, Box 30, Folder 15, WV State Archives. Lightburn telegram to H.J. Samuels, May 9, 1863; CSR, RG 94, Joseph A.J. Lightburn, M508, Roll 118, National Archives.

50.   Fogg Letters, May 11, 1863.

51.   *Ibid*; CSR, RG 94, 52nd United States Colored Troops, M2000, Rolls 113-131 National Archives.

52.   Barton; CSR, RG 94, Charles Holstein, M508, Roll 117, National Archives.

53.   4th West Virginia Record Order Book; Saunier, Joseph A. *A History of the 47th Regiment O.V.V.I, 2nd Brigade, 2nd Division, 15th Army Corps, Army of the Tennessee.* (Hillsboro, OH: Lyle Printing Company, 1903), (hereafter Saunier); Barton; Hall Letters, May 14, 1863.

54.   Safreed Diary, May 16, 1863; Barton.

55.   *Ibid.*, Safreed, May 18, 1862.

56.   Saunier, 147, 144.

57.   *OR Series 1*, Vol. 24, Part 2, 281-283. Report of Brig. Gen. Hugh Ewing.

58.   Veteran Letters No. 10 & 31, 13th U.S. Regulars File, Vicksburg National Military Park Archives, Vicksburg, MS. Used with permission. (hereafter 13th U.S. Regulars File).

59.   *Ibid.*; Letter, Thomas T. Taylor to W.T. Rigby, March 19, 1903.

60.   *Ibid.*, James Kephart to W.W. Gardner, January 16 1902.

61.   Boswell, History of the 4th West Virginia; OR Series 1, Vol. 24, Part 1, 283. Ewing's Brigade Casualty Report for May 19, 1863.

62.   CSR, RG 93, M508, Roll 0119, National Archives

63.   Mallernee, J. L., *Athens Messenger*, August 20, 1863, Vol. 20; Smith, Eugene, *Athens Messenger*, May 15, 1963. Vol. 120.

64.   13th U.S. Regulars File, Letter No. 31.

65.   State of West Virginia. *Report of the Vicksburg Military Park Commission.* (Charleston, WV: Jarnett Print Co., State of West Virginia Government Printer 1923).(hereafter *Report of the Vicksburg Military Park Commission)*

66.   Barton.

67.   4th West Virginia Infantry File, Vicksburg National Military Park Archives. Benjamin D. Boswell Letter, 1901.

68.   Farrar Letters, May 20, 1863.

69.   Lewis Love, Camp Fire.

70.   Chamberlin/Vance.

71.   David Russel Widow's Pension File, Application No. 759981, March 31, 1902, CSR, RG 15, T289, Roll 3791, National Archives.

72.   CSR, RG 94, David Bartlett, M508, Roll 113, National Archives.

73.   Ancestory.com: Genealogy Report, Descendants of William Lowry; CSR, RG 94, William Lowry, M508, Roll 118, National Archives; CSR, RG 94, Joseph L. Cooper, M508, Roll 115; CSR, RG 94, Jacob Crossen, M508, Roll 115; CSR, RG 94, Robert W. Davis, M508, Roll 115, National Archives.

74.   Safreed Diary, May 22, 1863.

75.   Cantrell, Thelma Collection. Family History including Taylor, Sampson, et. al., Vol. 6, Manuscript Collection, Ms92-29, West Virginia State Archives; CSR, RG 94, Robert Henry Sampson, M508, Roll 121, National Archives.

76.   John Y. Jarrett Pension File, Application No. 227537, November 11, 1876, (Invalid), CSR, RG 15, T289, Roll 600, National Archives.

77.   CSR, RG 94, William S. Hall, M508, Roll 117, National Archives; Barton.

78.   Hardesty, H.H. *Presidents, Soldiers, Statesmen. Vol. 2, (New York*, H. H. Hardesty & Co., Publishers, 1898).

79.   Lightburn Collection, Ms94-2, Letter to "George," June 23, 1863. WV State Archives.

80.   CSR, RG 93, Henry Grayum, M508, Roll 117, National Archives; *Gallipolis Journal*, September 17, 1863, Vol. 28(43).

81.   *Gallipolis Journal, June 11, 1863*, Vol. 28(29); CSR, RG 94, Philemon B. Stanberry, M508, Roll 121, National Archives; Barton.

82.   Russell, Daniel A. Collection. Courtesy Eugene Smith, The Plains, OH. Terry Lowry Collection; Smith, Eugene. *Athens Messenger*, May 15, 1863 (Vol. 120); Barton; CSR, RG 94, *Wheeling intelligencer*, June 23, 1863. Vol. 11 (261).

83.   OR Series 1, Vol. 24, Part 2, 281-283. Report of Brig. Gen. Hugh Ewing.

84.   *Gallipolis Journal* 6/25/1863 Vol. 28(31); Barton.

85.   CSR, RG 94, Finley Davis Ong, M508, Roll 120, National Archive; Ong Family History. Courtesy Richard Sheppard, Boerne, TX.

86.   CSR, RG 94, James M. Hodge, M508, Roll 117, National Archives; Terry Lowry Personal Correspondence with James C. Cline, Beverly, OH, regarding John Perry Wolfe, 2000; Hartley, Charles A. "Cpl. Wolfe Delivered $5 Million In 1864 Calmly, as he Would His Weekend Laundry." Reprinted in *Pomeroy Tribune–Telegraph, · February 4. 1929; original article appeared in 1908.* Newspaper Reading Room, SN 87075197, Library of Congress; CSR, RG 94, Michael Richard, Jr., M508, Roll 120, National Archives.

87.   John Douglas Pension File, Application No. 312753, (Invalid), October 3, 1879, RG 15, T289, Roll 600, National Archives.

88. *Gallipolis Journal* June 11, 1863, Vol. 28(29); CSR, RG 94, James H. Ralston M508, Roll   120, National Archives. (hereafter CSR Ralston)

89. Barton.

90. 13th U.S. Regulars File, Letter No. 31, Vicksburg National Military Park Archives.

91. *Report of the Vicksburg Military Park Commission*; *OR, Series 1*, Vol. 24, Part 2, 163. Casualty Report of Ewing's Brigade, May 22, 1863; Barton.

92. Saunier, 146-147.

93. *Ibid.*, 147-148.

94. *OR, Series 1*, Vol. 24, Part 2, 282-283. Brig. Gen. Hugh Ewing's Report.

95. Saunier, 148.

96. 55th Illinois Infantry File, Accounts of the Forlorn Hope Assault, May 22, 1863, accounts of J. Larabee and H. Nouse. Vicksburg National Military Park Archives, Vicksburg, MS.

97. Charles E. Haley to Terry Lowry, February 19, 2001. Personal Correspondence with unidentified newsclipping of William H. Barringer's gravestone dedication and account of his role in the Forlorn Hope at Vicksburg, May 22, 1862. Terry Lowry Collection.

98. CSR, RG 94, Joseph Nicholson, M508, Roll 119, National Archives; Norma Frank to Terry Lowry, February 18, 2006 with Nicholson family history; *OR, Series 1*, Vol. 24, Part 2, 282-283; CSR Ralston.

99. Grayum Letters, June 5, 1863; CSR, RG 94, John L. Vance, M508, Roll 119, National Archives.

100. *Jackson Standard, September* 21, 1876, Vol. 32(38).

101. J. L. Vance Pension File, Statement of Sgt. Donald McDonald.

102. Grayum Letters, May 24, 1863.

103. Safreed Diary, May 22, 1863; Shrewsbury Letters, May 24, 1863.

104. Fernandes [Fernandis] Jeffrey Pension File, Application No. 310228, (Mother), November 5, 1888, CSR, RG 15, T289, Roll 600, National Archives. (Hereafter Fernandes Jeffrey Pension File)

105. Safreed Diary, May 24, 1863; Lewis Love, Camp Fire. Letter written to Clarkson Fogg's father about his death.

106.   Safreed Diary, May 25, 1863.

107.   Grayum Letters, June 6, 1863.

108.   CSR, RG 94, James Driver, M508, Roll 116, National Archives; Gallipolis Journal, June 11, 1863, Vol. 28(29).

109.   Fernandes Jeffrey Pension File.

110.   Hatfield; WV AG 4th West Virginia, Folder 9, Lightburn Letter to "George," June 17, 1863.

111.   Safreed Diary, June 20 & 25, 1863; CSR, RG 94, William Bell, M508, Roll 113, National Archives.

112.   CSR, RG 94, Calvin Sheppard, M508, Roll 121, National Archives; CSR Swinfield Hill; *Gallipolis Journal*, June 18, 1863, Vol. 28(30).

113.   Grayum Letters, June 30, 1863.

114.   *OR, Series 1*, Vol. 24, Part 2, 191-192, Report of Capt. William Kassak; Hall Letters, June 4, 1863.

115.   Grayum Letters, August 23, 1863.

116.   Fararr Letters, August 23, 1863; CSR, RG 94, Joseph B. Price, M508, Roll 120, National Archives.

117.   Saunier, 167.

118.   CSR, RG 94, Thomas Carol, M508, Roll 114, National Archives.

119.   Grayum Letters, September 27, 1863.

120.   CSR, James H. Ralston; CSR, RG 94, Homer C. Waterman, M508, Roll 122, National Archives.

121.   Caroline Taylor (McCabe) Pension File; CSR, RG 94, Caroline Taylor, Laundress, 67th U.S. Colored Troops, USCT 067, BX58, National Archives.

122.   *Ibid.*, Taylor Pension File: Peter F. Zeis Letter supporting Caroline Taylor application.

123.   CSR, Fernandes Jeffrey; Fernandes Jeffrey Penson File. Henry Dawson Letter to Milton Jeffrey.

124.   Grayum Letters, August 5, 1863.

125.   *Ibid.*, August 23, 1863; CSR, James H. Ralston.

126.   4th West Virginia Order Book; CSR, RG 94, Alpheus Beal, M508, Roll 113, National Archives.

127.   *Gallipolis Journal*, September 24, 1863, Vol. 28(44).

128.   4th West Virginia Order Book; Fararr Letters, October 3, 1863.

129.   Safreed Diary, September 27, 1863, October 1 & 3, 1863.

130.   *Ibid.*, October 6-7, 1863; 4th West Virginia Order Book.

131.   *Ibid.*, Order Book.

132.   *Ibid*, Safreed, October 16, 1863; CSR, William Grayum.

133.   *Ibid.*, CSR; Austin, Carol R. Some Descendants of Joseph Grayum of Connecticut. Unpublished manuscript, Garden Grove, CA. (2001). Family History Library, Salt Lake City, UT.

134.   Safreed Diary, October 17 & 18, 1863; 4th West Virginia Order Book.

135.   *Ibid.*, Safreed, October 20, 23, & 25, 1863; Grayum Letters, October 25, 1863.

136.   4th West Virginia Order Book; *OR, Series 1*, Vol. 31, Part 1, 763-764. Maj. Gen. Frank P. Blair's report.

137.   *Ibid.*, OR; Grayum Letters, October 28, 1863.

138.   Safreed Diary, October 30 & 31, 1863.

139.   *Ibid.*, November 1-3, 1863.

140.   *Ibid.*, November 4-7, 1863.

141.   *Ibid.*, November 8-10, 1863.

142.   *Ibid.*, November 11-14, 1863.

143.   *Ibid.*, November 15-18, 1863.

144.   *Ibid.*, November 19-21, 1863.

145.   *Ibid.*, November 23, 1863; *OR, Series 1*, Vol. 31, Part 2, 629-630; Gilliland, *Camp Fire.*

146.   Powell, David. *Battle above the Clouds: Lifting the Siege of Chattanooga and the Battle of Lookout Mountain: October 16-November 24, 1861.* (El Dorado Hills, CA: Savas Beatie Books, 2017) 2-15.

147.   Gilliland, Campfire, *OR Series 1,* Vol. 31, Part 2, 629-630. Brig. Gen. Joseph A.J. Lightburn's report.

148.   Safreed Diary, November 27, 1863.

149.   *OR, Series 1*, Vol. 31, Part 2, 629-630.

150.   Gilliland, Campfire.

151.   Safreed Diary, November 28, 1863; James C. Cline to Terry Lowry, Personal Correspondence regarding John Perry Wolfe, 2000. Terry Lowry Collection.

152.   *Ibid.*, Safreed.

153.   Gilliand, *Camp Fire*; *OR Series 1*, Vol. 31, Part 2, 629-630; Grayum Letters, November 28, 1863; CSR, RG 94, John Greer, M508, Roll 117, National Archives; CSR, RG 94, Josiah W. Vance, M508, Roll 122, National Archives.

154.   *OR, Series 1*, Vol. 31, Part 2, 629-630. Brig. Gen. Joseph A.J. Lightburn's report. Note that the service records of Josiah Ryan, Peter Hoffman, and Leander Harris and Wallace McCully do not mention their being wounded.

155.   *Ibid., OR.*

156.   *Ibid.*

157.   4th West Virginia Order Book; Safreed Diary, December 1-3, 1863.

158.   *Ibid.*, 4th West Virginia Order Book; Gilliland, Campfire; OR, Series 1, Vol. 31, Part 2, 571-579.

159.   *Ibid.*, Safreed, December 8, 1863.

160.   *Ibid.*, December 13-15, 1863; 4th West Virginia Order Book.

161.   *Ibid.*, December 16-17, 1863.

162.   4th West Virginia Order Book.

163.   *Ibid.*, Order Book; CSR, RG 94, William M. Hovey, 4th & 13th West Virginia Infantry, M508, Rolls 117 & 206, National Archives.

164.   Safreed Diary, December 25, 1863.

165.   *Ibid.*, December 29-30, 1863; 4th West Virginia Order Book.

166.   *Ibid.*, Order Book; Barton.

Chapter 4

1. Boswell; Barton.

2. 4th West Virginia Order Book.

3. *Ibid.*

4. *Ibid.*, 4th West Virginia Order Book.

5. Ibid., Order Book; *Gallipolis Journal,* Feb. 4, 1864. Ibid., Order Book; *Gallipolis Journal,* Feb. 4, 1864.

6. Barton; Lieutenant William Sisson, *Gallipolis Journal,* February 25, 1864.

7. 4th West Virginia Order Book.

8. *Ibid.*

9. *Ibid.*

10. 4th West Virginia Order Book.

11. *Ibid.*

12. *Ibid.; Gallipolis Journal, March 17, 1864.*

13. *Ibid.*, Order Book.

14. *Ibid.*

15. Farrar Memoirs, March 22-27, 1864; Mellott & Snell, 7th West Virginia History, 164.

16. 4th West Virginia Order Book.

17. *OR, Series 1,* Vol. 33, 813, 832, 986.

18. Farrar Memoirs, May 4, 1864.

19. *Gallipolis Journal,* May 5 1864.

20. *OR, Series 1,* Vol. 37, Part 1, 396-398; 4th West Virginia Order Book.

21. *Ibid.*, Order Book.

22. *Ibid.*

23. Gilliland, Camp Fire.

24. *Ibid.*

25.   Grayum Letters, May 16, 1864.

26.   Pierpont Telegrams, May 17, 19 & 20,m 1864. WVU.

27.   *Ibid.*, May 21, 1864.

28.   Warner, Ezra. *Generals in Blue*, 243; Eicher, John H. and Eicher, David J. *Civil War High Commands*. (Stanford, CA: Standord University Press, 2001), 310; 4th West Virginia Order Book.

29.   Gilliland, Camp Fire.

30.   CSR, RG 94, George W. Gandee, M508, Roll 116, National Archives; CSR, RG 94, John C. Dawson, M508, Roll 115, National Archives.

31.   4th West Virginia Order Book.

32.   *OR, Series* 1, Vol. 37, Part 1, 94-95. Report of Maj. Gen. David Hunter; Patchan, Scott C. *Worthy of a Higher Rank*, 39-41; Patchan, Scott C. *The Battle of Piedmont and Hunter's Raid on Staunton*, 52-77; 79-99. (hereafter Patchan, *Battle of Piedmont*)

33.   *Ibid., Battle of Piedmont.*

34.   *OR, Series 1*, Vol. 37, Part 1, 94-100, 104, 119, 128. Reports of Maj. Gen. David Hunter, Brig. Gen. George Crook, Col. Issac Duvall; 4th West Virginia Order Book; CSR, RG 94, William Shannon, M508, Roll 121, National Archives.

35.   *Ibid., OR*; Report of Maj. Gen. David Hunter; Samuel Sampson Pension Application No. 648527, April 2, 1888, (Invalid), RG 15, T289, Roll 600, National Archives.

36.   Vance Pension File.

37.   Stone, James F. *Company F, 4th West Virginia Volunteer Infantry.*

38.   Grayum Letters, July 3, 1864.

39.   William S. Hall Pension Application No. 417466, March 14, 1881, (Invalid), RG 15, T281, Roll 600, National Archives. (hereafter W.S. Hall Pension File)

40.   Gilliand, *Camp Fire.*

41.   *Ibid.;* Personal Correspondence, Terry Lowry with Bill Schenk, July 6, 2010.

42.   *Report of the Vicksburg Military Park Commission.*

43.   Barton; Personal Correspondence, Terry Lowry with Bill Schenk.

44.   *OR, Series 1*, Vol. 37, Part 2, 90; 4th West Virginia Order Book; Vale.

45.   Patchan, *Worthy of a Higher Rank*, 61.

46. *OR, Series 1*, Vol. 37, Part 1, 287, 290.

47. *Gallipolis Journal* August 8, 1864.

48. *Ibid.*

49. Stone, *Company F, 4th West Virginia Infantry*; CSR, RG 94, M508, Finley D. Chalfant (Roll 114), David Hamilton (Roll 117), Daniel F. McNeer, (Roll 119), George A. Scott (Roll 121), George F. Stone (Roll 121), National Archives.

50. *Gallipolis Journal* August 4, 1864; CSR, RG 94, M508, William S. Hall (Roll 117), Michael Christopher (Roll 114), Calvin A. Sheppard (Roll 121), Joseph A. Walsh, (Roll 122), National Archives.

51. *Ibid., Gallipolis Journal.*

52. *Ibid.;* J.L. Vance Pension File.

53. Hewitt, William, *History of the Twelfth West Virginia Infantry.*

54. Farrar Memoirs, July 20, 1864.

55. *Ibid.*

56. *Ibid.*

57. OR, Series 1, Vol. 37, Part 1, 288, 292-293, 301-302. Reports of Col. Joseph Thoburn and Col. William Ely.

58. Farrar Memoirs, August 12, 1864.

59. *Ibid.*

60. *OR, Series 1*, Vol. 37, Part 1, 287, 290, 547; Patchan, *Worthy of a Higher Rank*, 78-80.

61. CSR, RG 94, M508, George S. Woodhull, Roll 122, National Archives (hereafter CSR, Woodhull); Fararr Memoirs, August 6, 1864.

62. *Ibid.*, Farrar.

63. 4th West Virginia Order Book; Daniel A. Russell Collection, Co. E, 4th West Virginia Infantry.

64. *OR, Series 1*, Vol. 43, Part 1, 360; Stone, *Company F, 4th West Virginia Infantry.*

65. Farrar Memoirs, August 16, 1864; CSR, Woodhull.

66. 4th West Virginia Order Book; *Report of the Vicksburg Military Park Commission)*

67. *Ibid.*, Order Book; Boswell, History of the 4th West Virginia; *OR, Series 1*, Vol. 43, Part 1, 709.

68.   *Ibid., OR*, 360-361; Grayum Letters, September 3, 1863.

69.   Newspaper clippings (undated, news organ unidentified) in Terry Lowry's private Collection.

70.   4th West Virginia Order Book.

71.   *OR, Series 1*, Vol. 43, Part 1, 116, 361-362.

72.   Farrar Memoirs, September 20, 1864. Note that Farrar refers to the Third Battle of Winchester as "Battle of Bunker Hill" likely due to the proximity of that West Virginia town.

73.   Patchan, *Worthy of a Higher Rank*, 96.

74.   William S. Hall letters, September 26, 1864.

75.   4th West Virginia Order Book.

76.   *Ibid.*

77.   *Ibid.*; WV AG Papers, Union Regiments, AR 383, 12th West Virginia Infantry,

Box 19, Field & Staff, Colonel William. B. Curtis, Special Order No. 2, Folder 18, WV State Archives.

78.   Farrar Memoirs, October 15, 1864.

79.   4th West Virginia Order Book.

80.   *OR, Series 1*, Vol. 43, Part 1, 365-366.

81.   1860 U.S. Census; Boswell Family History; CSR, RG 94, M508, Benjamin D. Boswell, Roll 114, National Archives. Boswell previously served as Acting Adjutant General on Colonel Joseph A.J. Lightburn's staff in 1862, and was promoted to 1st Lieutenant on December 8, 1862, and to Captain of Company H on January 5, 1863. He was wounded in the side at Vicksburg on May 19, 1863. See also Ancestry. com.

82.   Farrar Memoirs October 20, 1864; Hartley, C.A., *Pomeroy Tribune–Telegraph, February 4. 1929.*

83.   William S. Hall Pension File.

84.   Grayum Letters, October 27, 1864.

85.   Matthew S. Glover Pension Application No. 74282, December 2, 1864, (Mother), RG 15, T289, Roll 600, National Archives; 4th West Virginia Order Book.

86.   *Ibid.*, Order Book; CSR, RG 94, M508, James H. Dayton, Roll 115, National Archives.

87. *Ibid.*, Order Book; Grayum Letters, December 1, 1864.

88. *Ibid.*, Order Book.

89. *Ibid.*

90. WV AG Papers, Union Regiments, AR 382, 2nd West Virginia Veteran Infantry, Box 26, Folder 3, WV State Archives (hereafter WV AG Papers, 2nd West Virginia Veteran); Stone, *Company F, 4th West Virginia Infantry.*

91. *Ibid.*, WV AG Papers, 2nd West Virginia Veteran, Folder 3; Grayum Letters, December 26, 1864.

92. *Ibid.*, WV AG Papers, Folder 1, Jacob Weddle's History of the 2nd West Virginia Veteran Infantry. (hereafter Weddle's History)

93. *Gallipolis Journal,* September 21, 1865; CSR RG 94, M508, William P. Mowery, Roll 119, National Archives.

94. WV AG Papers, 2nd West Virginia Veteran, Folder 2; CSR RG 94, M508, George Nagle, Roll 119, National Archives.

95. 4th West Virginia Order Book.

96. *Wheeling Daily Intelligencer,* February 22 & 23, 1865, *Vol. 13(54);* Wright, Simeon Miller. "The McNeill Rangers: A Study in Confederate Guerilla Warfare." *West Virginia History,* Vol. 12(4), (July 1951), 338-387. At least one correspondent claimed that McNeill's Rangers fired upon the Union pickets before capturing them, but other accounts omitted that claim.

97. Stone, *Company F, 4th West Virginia Infantry.*

98. Weddle's History, March 1865.

99. *Company F, 4th West Virginia Infantry;* Grayum Letters, April 22, 1865.

100. *Ibid.,* Grayum, June 2, 1865; Weddle's History.

101. *Ibid.,* Weddle.

102. *Ibid.*

103. *The Weekly Register,* July 27, 1865, Vol. 3(68); *Gallipolis Journal,* July 27, 1865, Vol. 30(36).

104. Dyer, Frederick H. A Compendium of the War of the Rebellion: Compiled and arranged from Official Records of the Federal and Confederate Armies, Reports of the Adjutant Generals of the several States, the Army Registers, and other reliable documents and sources. (Des Moines, IA: Dyer Publishing Co., 1908), 289-307.

105.   Boswell, History of the 4th West Virginia.

Chapter 5

1.   *Gallipolis Journal*, September 21, 1865.

2.   "Historic Drum in Parade", *The West Virginia Daily News*, Lewisburg, WV, October 3, 1908.

3.   A Confederate Yankee." *Nashville Banner*, December 23, 1927, Vol. 148(68), 4, Newspapers.com; CSR, RG 94, M508, Roll 119, National Archives.

4.   *"Belated Respect."* Steelhammer, Rick. *Charleston Gazette-Mail*, November 1, 2019, Newspapers on Microfilm, Misc. Reels M-17, WV State Archives.

5.   William H. H. Russell Obituary, *Sacramento Evening Bee*, 1898, Newspaper Reading Room, SN 84025962, Library of Congress; CSR, RG 94, M508, Roll 121, National Archives.

6.   Benjamin D. Boswell Military Records (MSS Boswell), Oregon State University Special Collections and Archives Research Center, Corvallis, Oregon; CSR, RG 94, M508, Roll 114, National Archives.

7.   Waterman, David. Letter, February 9, 2004. Personal correspondence. Terry Lowry Collection; CSR, RG 94, M508, Roll 121, National Archives; Annual Report of the Adjutant General of the state of West Virginia, December 31, 1864, 94. This information was found in the Record of Captain William Grayum's Company "G," 4th Regiment West Va. Infantry Volunteers, (three years' service), showing the changes in said company from the date of organization to the date of muster-out on the 24th day of August, 1864, by Henry C. Peck, 1st Lieut., 14th U.S. Infantry. Compiled from the muster out rolls. The editor, a Mr. Armstrong of the St. Louis, Missouri newspaper, *The Rustic*, claims to have obtained the information on Saunders from an unidentified Parkersburg, WV, newspaper dated July 4, 1877, while a modern correspondent with Terry Lowry indicated he found the information in an unspecified edition of the Cincinnati Commercial newspaper. Neither news organ was found containing the account.

8.   Schenkman, *David E. Civil War Sutler Tokens and Cardboard Scrip*. (Hampton, VA: Multi-Print, Inc., 1983).

Bibliography

Books & Monographs

Barton, Thomas H. *Autobiography of Dr. Thomas H. Barton including a History of the 4th Regt. West Va. Vol. In'fy.* (Charleston, WV: West Virginia Printing Company, 1890).

Bishop, William H. *History of Roane County, West Virginia: From the Time of Its Exploration to A.D. 1927.* (Spring Valley, NY: Apple Manor Press, 2007; Original published by W.H. Bishop, 1972).

Chamberlin, W.H. (Ed.). *Sketches of War History 1861-1865: Papers Prepared for the Ohio Commandery of the Military Order of the Loyal Legion of the United States 1890-1986*, Vol. 4. "The Retreat of Union Forces from the Kanawha Valley in 1862." by John L. Vance, 4th West Virginia Infantry. (Cincinnati, OH: Robert Clark Co., 1896).

Cole, Scott C. *34th Virginia Cavalry.* (Lynchburg, VA: H.E. Howard, 1993).

Cox, Jacob Dolson. *Military Reminisces of the Civil War*, Vol.1. (Whitefish, MT: Kessinger Publishing, 2004 Reprint, Original 1900).

Cressman, Frances Lightburn. *Joseph Andrew Jackson Lightburn, Union Brigadier General and a Baptist Pastor, or "Here by a Quarter of an Inch."* (Jane Lew, WV: Unpublished monograph by Frances Lightburn Cressman, 2001).

_____ *Kanawha Valley Campaign of 1862.* (Jane Lew, WV: Unpublished monograph, 2001).

Dyer, Frederick H. *A Compendium of the War of the Rebellion: Compiled and arranged from Official Records of the Federal and Confederate Armies, Reports of the Adjutant Generals of the several States, the Army Registers, and other reliable documents and sources.* (Des Moines, IA: Dyer Publishing Co., 1908).

Eicher, John H. and Eicher, David J. *Civil War High Commands.* (Stanford, CA: Stanford University Press, 2001).

Egan, Michael. *The Flying Grey Haired Yank, or the Adventures of a Volunteer.* (Leesburg, Virginia: Gauley Mount Press, 1992 Reprint).

Ervin, Edgar. *The Pioneer History of Meigs County, Ohio to 1949 including Masonic history of the same period.* (Pomeroy, OH: Meigs County Pioneer & Historical Society, January 1949).

Evans, Nelson W. *A History of Scioto County, Ohio Together With A Pioneer Record of Southern Ohio.* (Portsmouth, OH: Nelson W. Evans, 1903).

Gibbs, Mildred Chapman. *Mason City: W. Va.: The History of the Town. (Middleport, OH:* Quality Printing Shop, 1978).

Graham, Michael B. *The Coal River Valley in the Civil War.* (United Kingdom: History Press, 2014).

Hardesty, H. H. *History of Gallia County, Ohio.* (Chicago, IL: H. H. Hardesty & Co., Publishers, 1882).

_____ & Cochran, Wes, (Ed.). *Mason County, West Virginia: Hardesty's Bibliographic Atlas, Vol. 2. (Parkersburg, WV: W. Hardesty, 1892, Reprinted 1946).*

_____*Presidents, Soldiers, Statesmen. Vol. 2, (New York,* H. H. Hardesty & Co., Publishers, 1898).

Harper, Robert S. *Gallipolis: 1861 – 1865.* (Columbus, OH: The Ohio State Museum, 1961).

Hess, Earl J. *Storming Vicksburg: Grant, Pemberton, and the Battles of May 19-22, 1863. (Chapel Hill, NC: Un*iversity of North Carolina Press, 2020).

Hewitt, William, Miller James M. (Ed.). *History of the Twelfth West Virginia Volunteer Infantry: The Part It Took in the War of the Rebellion 1861–1865. (Charleston, WV: 35th Star Publishing, 2010, Original published by the Twelfth West Virginia Infantry Association, 1892).*

Hill, Jeffrey A. *The 26th Ohio Veteran Volunteer Infantry: The Groundhog Regiment.* (Bloomington, IN: Author House Publishing, 2010).

Kempfer, Lester L. *The Salem Light Guard: Company G, 36th Ohio Volunteer Infantry. (Chicago, IL:* Adams Press, 1973).

Lang, Theodore F. *Loyal West Virginia 1861–1865.* (Baltimore, MD: Deutsch Publishing Co., 1895).

Larkin, Stillman C. *The Pioneer History of Meigs County.* (Columbus, OH: The Berlin Printing Company, 1908).

Lowry, Terry. *The Battle of Charleston and the 1862 Kanawha Valley Campaign.* (Charleston, WV: 35th Star Publishing, 2016).

Maxwell, H. & Swisher, H.L. *The History of Hampshire County.* (Parsons, WV: McClain Publishing. 1897).

McDougal, Henry Clay. *Recollections 1844–1909. (Kansas City, MO:* Franklin Hudson Publishing Co., 1910). (Contains detailed post-war account of Reuben A. Vance of the 4th West Virginia Infantry).

Mellott, David W., and Mark A. Snell. *The Seventh West Virginia Infantry: An Embattled Union Regiment from the Civil War's Most Divided State." (Lawrence, KS:* University Press of Kansas, 2019).

Moore, Frank. *The Rebellion Record: A Diary of American Events.* (New York, NY: G.P. Putnam, 1862).

Ohio Roster Commission. *Official Roster of the Soldiers of the State of Ohio in the War of the Rebellion 1861 – 1865.* (Akron, OH: The Werner Company, 1893).

Patchan, Scott C. *The Battle of Piedmont and Hunter's Raid on Staunton.* (Charleston, SC: History Press, 2011).

_____ *Worthy of A Higher Rank: The 1864 Shenandoah Valley Campaign Journal of Colonel Joseph Thoburn, Commander, 1st Infantry Division, Army of West Virginia. (Charleston, WV:* 35th Star Publishing, 2021).

Powell, David. *Battle above the Clouds: Lifting the Siege of Chattanooga and the Battle of Lookout Mountain: October 16-November 24, 1861.* (El Dorado Hills, CA: Savas Beatie Books, 2017),

Robinson, James I., Jr. (Ed.). *Soldier of Southwestern Virginia: The Civil War Letters of Captain John Preston Sheffy.* (Baton Rouge, LA: Louisiana State Press, 2004).

Rollins Family History: Unpublished Manuscript. Typescript of original in Terry Lowry Collection. Courtesy Barney Rollins.

Saunier, Joseph A. *A History of the 47th Regiment O.V.V.I, 2nd Brigade, 2nd Division, 15th Army Corps, Army of the Tennessee.* (Hillsboro, OH: Lyle Printing Company, 1903).

Schenkman, *David E. Civil War Sutler Tokens and Cardboard Scrip.* (Hampton, VA: Multi-Print, Inc., 1983).

Smith, Timothy B. *The Union Assaults at Vicksburg: Grant Attacks Pemberton, May 17-22, 1863. (Lawrence, KS:* University Press of Kansas, 2020).

Stillman, Larkin C. *Pioneer History of Meigs County, Ohio.* (Columbus, OH: The Berlin Printing Co., 1908).

Stone, James F. *Company F, 4th West Virginia Volunteer Infantry.* (Ravenswood, WV: J.F. Stone Newsprint, 1914).

Stutler, Boyd B. *West Virginia in the Civil War.* (Charleston, WV: Education Foundation, Inc.,   1966).

Sutton, Joseph J. *History of the 2nd Regiment, West Virginia Cavalry Volunteers.* (Huntington, West Virginia: Blue Acorn Press, Reprinted 1992; Original publication 1892).

Taylor County Historical and Genealogical Society. *A History of Taylor County, West Virginia.* (Parsons, WV: McClain Printing Company, 1986).

Taylor, James. *With Sheridan – Up the Shenandoah Valley 1864 – Leaves from a Special Artists Sketch Book and Diary.* (Dayton, OH: Morningside Books, 1989).

The Camp Fire: Letters written by former soldiers about their experiences in the Civil or any other War. (Pomeroy, OH: Meigs County Historical Society, 1999, Vols. 1 & 2).

Vance, John L., Late Lieutenant Colonel 4th Virginia Regiment. *Sketches of War History 1861-1865: Papers Read Before the Ohio Commandery of the Military Order of the Loyal Legion of the United States*, Vol. 4, "The Retreat of the Union Forces from the Kanawha Valley in 1862." (Cincinnati, OH: R. Clarke & Company, 1896).

Walker, Charles M. *History of Athens County, Ohio.* (Cincinnati, OH: Robert Clark & Co., 1869).

Wallace, Lee A. *A Guide to Virginia Military Organizations 1861-1865.* (Lynchburg, VA: H.E. Howard, Revised 2nd Ed., 1986).

Warner, Ezra. *Generals in Blue.* (Baton Rouge, LA: University of Louisiana Press, 2006).

Whitney, Carrie W. Kansas City, Missouri: its history and its people. Vol. 2. (Chicago, IL: S.J. Clarke Publishing, 1908).

Williams, Frederick D. (Ed.). *The Wild Life in the Army: Civil War Letters of James A. Garfield. (Lansing, MI:* Michigan State University Press, 1964).

Winschel, Terrence, J. *Triumph and Defeat: The Vicksburg Campaign.* (New York, NY: Savas Beatie, 2004).

Wintz, William D. *Civil War Memoirs of two Rebel sisters.* (Pictorial Histories Publishing, Charleston WV, 1989).

Woodhull, Mary G. Francis B. *Woodhull Genealogy: The Woodhull Family in England and America. (*Philadelphia, PA: Henry Coates & Co., 1904).

Manuscripts

Austin, Carol R.   *Some Descendants of Joseph Grayum of Connecticut.* Unpublished manuscript, Garden Grove, CA. (2001). Family History Library Salt Lake City, UT.

Blake, Cincinnatus B.   Letters. Company H, 4th West Virginia Infantry. Wayne Farley Collection. Used with Permission.

Blundon & Matthews Family Papers, Edgar Blundon Civil War Diary and letters, typescript, 1861-1920, West Virginia Civil War Manuscripts Collection, Ms 89-94, Folders 1 & 2, West Virginia State Archives, Charleston, WV.

Brown Family Collection, 1843-1866. MSS018, William V. Brown Letters, Company D, 4th West Virginia Infantry. Ohio University, Alden Library, Athens, OH.

Cantrell, Thelma Collection. Family History including Taylor, Sampson, et. al., Vol. 6, Manuscript Collection, Ms92-29, WV State Archives.

Civil War Regimental Papers. 4th West Virginia Volunteer Infantry. Record Group 94. National Archives, Washington, D.C.

Civil War Regimental Papers. 2nd West Virginia Veteran Volunteer Infantry. Record Group 94. National Archives, Washington, D.C.

Cook, Theodore, "The Diary of Theodore Cook." 1st and 2nd West Virginia Veteran Infantry, MS 79-18, No. 70, WV State Archives.

Cline, James C. Beverly, OH, to Terry Lowry regarding John Perry Wolfe, 2000. Terry Lowry Collection.

Craig Family Scrapbooks, 1861-1865. Civil War Manuscripts, Sc86–201. WV State Archives. WV.

De Bussey, Adolphus. Company F, 4th West Virginia Infantry, Civil War Letters, Collection number A&M 3296, West Virginia Regional History Collection, WVU Library, Morgantown, WV.

Farley, Wayne (Private Collection). Arthur Watts, Pomeroy, Ohio. Charleston battle map; Cincinnatus B. Blake letter August 30, 1861. Used with permission.

Farrar, John G. Company E, 4th West Virginia Infantry. *Personal Account of the Civil War. February 14,* 1895. Typescript of original held in Vicksburg National Military Park Archives, Courtesy Diane Farrar. Used with permission.

_____ Personal Account of the Civil War; WV AG Papers, AR 452, Box 12, 4th West Virginia, Folder 1. WV State Archives.

Fifty-fifth Illinois Infantry File, Larrabee, J. & Nousse, H. Accounts of the Forlorn Hope assault, May 22, 1863. Vicksburg National Military Park Archives, Vicksburg, Mississippi. Used with permission.

Fogg, Clarkson. Corporal, Company E, 4th West Virginia Infantry. Original letters held in the Private Collection of Alan Sessarego, Gettysburg, PA. Used with permission.

Fogg, Clarkson. Corporal, Company E, 4th West Virginia Infantry. Transcribed copies of Civil War Letters 1861-1865, Civil War Artificial Collection, MS 79-18, Series 1, No. 74, West Virginia State Archives, Charleston, WV. Courtesy Brian Kesterson, Vienna, WV.

Fogg, Clarkson. *A Soldier's Life and Death at Vicksburg.* Monograph, (Unknown publisher, 2005). Acquired at the bookstore, Old Fort Jackson, Savannah, Georgia 2005.

Forbes, Arthur. Letter from Camp Piatt, Red House, Virginia, May 3, 1862. Original in private collection of Mae Persinger, Nitro, WV. Used with permission.

Ford, Frederick. Navy Pension File, Feb. 15, 1882. Claim No. 7945, Microfilm T288, Roll 157, National Archives.

Fourth West Virginia Infantry File, Vicksburg National Military Park Archives, Vicksburg, Mississippi. Used with permission.

Gilder-Leherman Collection, Civil War Manuscripts, E.P. Scammon Letters, No. GLCO2414.161, Institute of American History, New York, New York.

Grayum, William. Company G, 4th West Virginia Infantry. Letters 1862 – 1865. 4th West Virginia Infantry File, Vicksburg National Battlefield Park Archives, Vicksburg, Mississippi. Used with permission.

Hall, John T. Papers. Transcriptions of original copies of letters by Major John T. Hall, 4th West Virginia Infantry, held in Heidi Klein Collection. Original letters held in William Matthews Collection, Huntington, WV. Terry Lowry Collection. Used with permission of Heidi Klein and William Matthews.

_____ Student File, Virginia Military Institute, Archives and Records, Preston Library, Lexington, Virginia.

Hall, William S. Civil War Letters. Civil War Collection, (Artificial), MS79-18, No. 64, WV State Archives.

Hatfield, Philip. "4th Regiment West Virginia Volunteer Infantry: A Brief History As Told By The Veterans." Unpublished manuscript. (Wilmington, NC: December 2007).

Hill, Dallas to Terry Lowry regarding Swinfield/Winfield Hill,2005. Personal Correspondence. Terry Lowry Collection.

Kooken, Tom. "Formation of Company K, 4th West Virginia Infantry." Online: http//:www.rootsweb.com.

Lightburn, General Joseph A. J. Collection. 1865-1904. Civil War Manuscripts, Ms94-2, WV State Archives.

Lightburn, Joseph A.J. Wartime Misc. Correspondence 1861-1865. West Virginia Adjutant General Papers, 4th West Virginia Infantry, AR 452, Box 12, Folders 1 & 9. WV State Archives.

Love, Lewis. "Company A, 4th West Virginia Infantry." (1899) Monograph, *Camp Fire*, (Pomeroy, OH: The Meigs County Pioneer and Historical Society, 1995, Vol. 1,(25).

Maggio, David and Geiger, Joe with Terry Lowry. Personal Correspondence, January 18, 2007. Terry Lowry Collection.

Ong Family History. Unpublished manuscript, undated, Courtesy Richard Shepherd, Boerne, TX.

Pierpont, Francis H. Civil War Telegrams. West Virginia Regional History Center, West Virginia University, Morgantown, WV. Online: https://civilwarwv.lib.wvu.edu.

_____, Governor. Executive Papers, 1861-1865. Accession 36928, Box 6, Folder 3, H. Halleck to Pierpont Telegram, May 5, 1863. Library of Virginia, Richmond, VA.

Pomeroy, Arthur Watts. Company E, 4th West Virginia Infantry. Letter and Map. Lewis Leigh Collection. U.S. Army Military History Institute, Carlisle Barracks, PA.

Records of the Adjutant General's Office. Record Group 94. Book Records of Volunteer Union Organizations. 4th West Virginia Infantry. Regimental Consolidated Morning Report & Order Books. National Archives, Washington, D.C.

Records of the Colonial Militia through World War I. Manuscript Collection, Ca. 1936, MS80-22, 50-53. WV State Archives.

Rollins Family History: Unpublished Manuscript. Typescript of original in Terry Lowry Collection. Courtesy Barney Rollins.

Russell, Daniel A. Collection. Company E, 4th West Virginia Infantry. Courtesy Eugene Smith, The Plains, OH. Terry Lowry Collection.

Safreet, William L. Civil War Diary. *Jackson County Historical Society Newsletter*, Ripley, WV. (May 1983).

Shrewsbury, Columbus. Letters. Company A, 4th West Virginia Infantry. A&M 3216. Roy Bird Cook Collection, West Virginia Regional History Center, West Virginia University Library, Morgantown, WV.

Taylor, Caroline. (McCabe) Laundress, 67th United States Colored Troops. U.S. Pension Records. Application No. 1153797, October 9, 1893. United States General Index to Pension Files, 1861-1934", *FamilySearch* (https://www.familysearch.org/ark:/61903. 20 February 2021), Entry for Caroline Taylor Formerly McCabe, 1893.

Teays, Victoria Hansford. Civil War Diary. Boyd Stutler Collection, MS78-1, Series 1, No. 8, July 1861, WV State Archives.

Thirteenth United States Regulars File. Vicksburg National Military Park Archives, Vicksburg, Mississippi. Used with permission.

Vale, James B. C. Journal. 1891. Company D, 4th West Virginia Infantry. Civil War Manuscripts, A&M 3593, West Virginia Regional History Center, West Virginia University Library, Morgantown, West Virginia.

Waterman, David. Letter, February 9, 2004. Personal correspondence. Terry Lowry Collection.

West Virginia Adjutant General's Papers, 1861-1865. AR 382, Folder 10, Field History of the Thirteenth West Virginia Volunteer Infantry, Parts A and B, WV State Archives.

_____, AR 382, Field History of the Fourth West Virginia Volunteer Infantry by Benjamin D. Boswell, WV State Archives.

_____, AR 382, Union Militia Records, WV State Archives.

_____, AR 373, Misc. Records & Court Martials, WV State Archives.

_____, AR 452, 4th West Virginia Infantry Regimental Correspondence, Muster Rolls, WV State Archives.

_____, AR 1722, Pierpont – Samuels Papers, (includes wartime telegrams), WV State Archives.

_____, West Virginia State Service Commission, 1901, Ar402-403, Logan County, Gordon and Patterson Riffe, WV State Archives.

John V. Young Letters and Young Family Record of Births, Deaths & Marriages. Roy Bird Cook Collection, Call No. A&M 0895, West Virginia Regional History Collection, West Virginia University Library, Morgantown WV.

Young, Sarah Francis. Civil War Diary 1861-1862. Typescript. Roy Bird Cook Collection, Call No. AM 1651, West Virginia Regional History Collection, West Virginia University Library, Morgantown WV.

Government Publications

Annual Report of the Adjutant General of State of West Virginia for the year ending December 31, 1864. (Wheeling, WV: John F. Dermont, Publisher, 1865).

Civil War Widow's Pensions, Record Groups 15 & 94, National Archives.

Compiled Service Records, Record Groups 94 and 109, Microfilm 109 and 508, National Archives.

Grand Army of the Republic, Department of Ohio Records, Vol. 1, Call No. MSS-715, Ohio State Archives & Library, Columbus, Ohio.

Hewitt, Janet B., (Ed.). *Supplement to the Official Records of the Union and Confederate Armies.* Vols. 52 & 74, Part 2. (Wilmington, NC: Broadfoot Publishing, 1998).

Journal of the Congress of the Confederate States of America, 1861-1865, Vol. 5. (Washington DC: Government Printing Office, 1905). Original copy at Library of Congress, Washington, DC.

Lightburn, Joseph A. J. *U.S. Army Generals' Reports of Civil War Service 1864-1887.* Microfilm Publications M1098, 1980. National Archives, Washington, DC.

State of West Virginia. *Report of the Vicksburg Military Park Commission.* (Charleston, WV: Jarnett Printing Co., State of West Virginia Government Printer 1923).

Telegraphic Dispatches to the Governor of Ohio, Series 145, Ohio Historical Society, Columbus, Ohio.

The Seventh United States Census: 1850: Records of the Bureau of the Census, Record Group 29; National Archives, Washington, D.C.

The Eighth United States Census: 1860: National Archives Records of the Bureau of the Census, Record Group 29, National Archives, Washington, D.C.

U.S. Pension Files Index, 1861-1865, 4th West Virginia Infantry, RG 15, T289, Roll 600, National Archives.

U.S. Statutes at Large of the United States of America, from December 1899 to March 1901, and Recent Treaties, Conventions and Executive Proclamations, and the Concurrent Resolutions of the Two Houses of Congress. Vols. 31 & 32, (1900-1901), 56th & 57th Congress. (Washington DC: U.S. Government Printing Office, 1901-1902). Library of Congress.

United States War Department. *War of the Rebellion: Official Records of the Union and Confederate Armies.* (Washington, D.C., Government Printing Office, 1901).

West Virginia State Service Commission, West Virginia Adjutant General Papers, AR 202-403, West Virginia State Archives, Charleston, WV.

Magazines, Journals & Periodicals

Bears, Edwin C. (2006). "The Fall of Vicksburg." Civil War Times, (July 2006), Vol. 45(5).

Cook, Roy Bird. "Joseph Andrew Jackson Lightburn." *West Virginia History*. Vol. 15, (October 1953).

_____ "The Civil War Comes to Charleston." *West Virginia History*, Vol. 23(2), (January 1962).

_____ "Joseph Andrew Jackson Lightburn." *West Virginia History*. Vol. 15 (October 1953).

Farnsworth, Ronald. "Joseph Andrew Jackson Lightburn: Gallant Soldier and Christian Minister." *West Virginia Review*, (May 1938).

Ford, Frederick. "Riddled With Bullets." *National Tribune*. June 3, 1886, Vol. 5(43).

Hatfield, Philip. "The 4th West Virginia Infantry at Vicksburg." *Civil War Historian*, Vol. 4(4), (July-August 2008).

Miller, Edward A. "VMI Men Who Wore Yankee Blue." *Virginia Military Institute Review*, Spring 1996.

Safreed, William Lewis. 1863 Diary, Company B, 4th West Virginia Infantry. *Jackson County Historical Society Journal*." Vol. 31, (1989).

Newspapers

Athens Messenger
Cincinnati Daily Commercial
Cincinnati Daily Times
Cleveland Morning Leader
Gallipolis Daily Tribune
Gallipolis Dispatch
Jackson Standard
Sacramento Evening Bee
The Capital
The Hancock Jeffersonian
The Pomeroy Weekly Telegraph

The Pomeroy Tribune-Telegraph
Republican and Herald
The Fairmont West Virginian
The Guerilla
The Wheeling Intelligencer
The Weekly Register
The West Virginia Daily News

Digital – Online Sources

Ancestory.com.

Biography of William V. Brown, Sons of Union Veterans of the Civil War. https://suvcw.org/past/cwrbrown.htm.

Findagrave.com.

Spared & Shared. https://sparedshared22.wordpress.com/category/4th-west-virginia-infantry/. Spared and Shared No. 22. Word Press: Category Archives: 4th West Virginia Infantry.

Name Index

Ackley, George Knight 42, 55, 66, 80, 116, 151, 155
Ackley, Jeremiah B. 71
Anderson, Jack 96
Armstrong, William L. 142
Bailey, William C. 11, 13, 78
Baggs, John (Snake Hunters) 95
Barlow, Charles Augustus (Augustus C.) 42, 67
Barringer, Martin 222
Barringer, William 191, 193
Bartlett, Gamaliel 174, 176
Barton, Thomas H. 23, 24, 27, 51, 55, 66, 70, 75, 90, 112, 119, 125, 132, 145, 150, 161, 162, 165, 166, 173, 178, 179, 183, 221, 222, 235
Beal, Alpheus 19, 65, 205
Bearss, Edwin G. 151
Beckley, Wallace 18
Bell, Elias B. 63, 64
Bell, Samuel 175
Bell, William 175, 199
Benedict, Samuel 136
Bing, Francis Marion 79
Birch, Charles 223
Blake, Cincinnatus Benjamin "Nat" 31, 32, 46, 79, 83, 95, 98, 101, 104, 109, 119, 128, 140
Blackburn, Joe 130, 132, 133
Blair, Francis "Frank" P. 173, 175, 204, 207
Bly, Douglas 193
Boley, John W. 194, 243
Boone, Sanford "Doc" 52
Booram, John B. 31, 38, 68

Booth, John Wilkes (Boothe) 256
Boreman, Arthur I. 224, 225, 227, 243, 252
Boswell, Benjamin Dempsey 1, 7, 90, 173, 174, 223, 245, 248, 249, 251, 252, 253, 258, 261
Boyle, J.T. 147
Bradshaw, John W. 18
Bragg, Braxton 211, 216
Bratton Sr., Adam 16, 17, 87
Bratton, Purley (Pearley) 18, 69, 86, 96
Brown, Edgar C. 242
Brown, William Robert 21, 23, 59, 66, 90, 119
Brown, Willian Van 17, 18, 34, 49, 71, 74, 75, 78, 79, 81, 87, 89, 91, 96, 101, 110, 111, 115, 116, 124, 125, 127, 128, 130, 132, 140, 141, 142, 143, 147, 148, 149, 153, 154, 155
Brunker, Patrick H. 38, 63, 99, 141
Buck, George 163
Buckley, John C. 191, 244
Bumgarner, William 191
Burdett, William H. 178
Burk, William B. 85
Burnside, Ambrose 113, 115, 164, 216
Butcher, Gibson Jackson 37
Cantwell, James 58
Carroll, Thomas 202
Carson, Ephraim C. 21, 23, 78
Carter, John 161
Chapman, Augustus A. 222
Chapman, Henry Daniel 55
Chalfant, Finley D. 237
Christopher, Michael 239

Clark, William 191, 256

Clarkson, John 67

Clendenin, Francis M. 179, 193

Coates, John D. 86

Cobert (Covert), John 92

Cochran, Zachquill "Zack" 35

Conner, Milton 34

Conrad, C.B. 8

Cook, Britton 24, 132

Coon, Jacob S. 175, 178

Cooper, Joseph L. 177

Cox, Jacob Dolson 1, 3, 17, 34, 38, 39, 49, 56, 77, 78, 83, 84, 88, 89, 96, 97, 98, 113, 114, 115, 125, 138, 139, 143

Cox, William T. 267

Crane, Charlie 11, 19

Crawford, Samuel 33

Craig, Clark 85

Cressman, Francis Lightburn

Crossen, Jacob 177

Crook, George 70, 88, 97, 235, 242, 244, 245, 246, 247, 248, 249, 250, 251, 253, 255

Cunningham, John S. 136

Curtis, Samuel 202

Curtis, William Barlow 247, 248, 251

Dale, James W. 59, 179, 180, 249, 251, 259

Davis, George W. 250

Davis, Jeff 91, 104

Davis, John W. 11, 116

Davis, Robert W. 154, 155, 177, 199

Davis, William H. 95

Dawson, John C. 229

Dayton, James Hart 8, 9, 19, 35, 37, 39, 45, 46, 49, 58, 65, 66, 67, 71, 78, 92, 99, 103, 104, 113, 115, 137, 153, 157, 159, 164, 165, 167, 179, 183, 194, 202, 203, 205, 218, 224, 231, 236, 250, 266

Dayton, Rebecca 137

Dawson Henry 204

Dean, John N. 249, 251

De Bussey, Adolphus 29, 34, 39, 45, 53, 55, 67, 68, 78, 80, 91, 98, 99, 100, 101, 103, 147, 148, 149, 152, 154

De Grasse, Francis 174

Dejernatt, John 58

DeLille, John 31, 63

Donnally, Henderson F. 38, 39

Douglas, John 181

Driver, James 197

Duval, Isaac 244, 246

Dyer, Frederick 258

Dyke, Robert 203

Early, Captain 34

Early, Jubal 240, 248

Edwards, (Edmonds) George W. 107, 112

Elliott, Philip H. 267

Ely, William G. 236, 241, 242, 244

Emmon, Silas H. 121

Evans, James 69

Everett, Louis 13, 194

Ewing, Hugh B. 142, 143, 147, 159, 163, 169, 171, 173, 174, 179, 181, 189, 191, 193, 201, 222

Facemyer, John 85

Farrar, John G. 24, 33, 51, 73, 80, 81, 85, 120, 127, 141, 143, 147, 149,

152, 174, 175, 202, 205, 224, 225, 240, 241, 242, 246, 249
Fitch, William G. 236
Floyd, John B. 57
Fogg, Clarkson 27, 68, 69, 71, 72, 81, 83, 84, 85, 86, 89, 93, 95, 96, 97, 98, 111, 117, 119, 132, 136, 137, 138, 139, 140, 152, 154, 155, 157, 159, 160, 164, 165, 174, 175, 176
Forbes, Arthur 90, 91, 152
Ford, Frederick 7
Foreman (Forman), William 32
Friedline, Abraham 247
Fremont, John C. 86, 88, 89
Frost, Daniel 237
Fugate, Robert 95
Gandee, George W. 229
Gardner, Perrin 232
Garfield, James A. 78, 79, 84, 88
Gatchell, David 233
Gibson, S. 52
Gilbert, Samuel 135
Gilliland, George W. 15,16, 32, 51, 70, 80, 105, 107, 109, 112, 210, 211, 213, 215, 217, 227, 228, 229, 235
Gilmore, Quincy Adams, 136
Glover, Matthew S. 250
Goodspeed, Arza Mathias 16, 17, 87, 89, 92, 116, 142, 164, 166, 171, 173, 206, 267
Grant, Ulysses S. 3, 142, 145, 149, 152, 156, 160, 167, 179, 189, 193, 211, 244
Grayum, Henry 31, 32, 46, 63, 67, 69, 79, 80, 98, 104, 178, 206, 215, 249, 259

Grayum, William 80, 113, 163, 194, 197, 200, 201, 202, 204, 205, 206, 207, 208, 215, 222, 228, 232, 249, 250, 251, 255, 256, 259
Greer, John 215
Gregg, Andrew W. 109
Griffin, Charles 132
Groce, John H. 189
Guthrie, James V. 47, 49
Gwinn, William M. 157, 160, 161
Hall, James R. 41, 73, 104
Hall, John, Sr. 41, 42, 103
Hall, John Taylor 41, 42, 59, 73, 85, 90, 91, 100, 101, 103, 104, 105, 107, 109, 110, 111, 112, 115, 117, 119, 267
Hall, William S. 29, 93, 140, 151, 157, 161, 162, 165, 178, 201, 233, 239, 246, 249
Halleck, Henry 92, 225
Hamilton, David 239
Hamilton, William 191
Hankinson (Hankinsson), George W. 17, 78, 103, 142
Harman, Elias V. 99
Harris, Leander 215
Harris, Thomas M. 250
Harrison, James 191
Heth, Henry 97
Hill, Ambrose Powell 115
Hill, J.R. 160, 161
Hill, Swinfield 74, 200
Hodge, James M. 181, 249, 251
Hoffman, Peter 215
Holmes, Robert A. 162
Holstein, Charles 115, 117, 125, 165
Hornbrook, Mr. 243

Hovey, William M. 55, 57, 218
Hunter, David 229, 231, 232, 236
Hutchins, William 119
Jackson, Henry J. 256, 257
Jackson, Joseph Blackwell 8
Jackson, Lydia 257
Jackson, Thomas Jonathan "Stonewall" 37
Jarrett, John Y. 178
Jeffrey, Fernandes 195, 199, 204
Jeffrey, Milton 204
Jenkins, Albert G. 79, 90, 120, 121, 161
Johnson, Lewis 174
Johnston, Joseph 201, 202, 227, 233
Jones, Salathiel 181
Jones, Theodore 213
Jones, William E. "Grumble" 231
Kassak, William 201
Kelley, Benjamin F. 35, 39, 65, 67, 69, 225, 228, 250, 252, 253, 255
Kelloussouski, W.A. 70
Kershaw, Joseph B. 244
Kilpatrick, Judson 227
Kincade, Robert 175, 176
Kincaid, David 176
Kinnard, Dorel C. 260
Lamb, Thomas 197
Lambert, Philip 99
Lang, Theodore F. xi
Lee, Robert E. 123, 156
Lee, Stephen D. 208
Lewberry (Lineberry), Jacob C. 107
Lightburn, Calvin Luther 178
Lightburn, Joseph Andrew Jackson 3, 8, 18, 19, 37, 38, 39, 41, 45, 55, 57, 59, 61, 63, 66, 68, 69, 71, 74, 75, 78, 79, 80, 81, 83, 84, 87, 90, 91, 92, 93, 95, 98, 101, 104, 116, 117, 119, 121, 123, 124, 131, 133, 138, 139, 141, 150, 155, 157, 159, 164, 165, 171, 178, 181, 199, 202, 204, 207, 210, 215, 216, 223, 224, 251, 259
Lightburn, Martin Van Buren 178, 223
Lincoln, Abraham 5, 71, 115, 229, 255
Logan, John A. 200, 221, 224
Longstreet, James 216, 217
Loring, William W. 78, 120, 121, 123, 124, 129, 136, 137, 139
Love, Lewis 11, 25, 33, 52, 129, 146, 151, 153, 175, 176, 195, 223
Lovell, Richard Channing Moore 25, 29, 31, 59
Low, William R. 162
Lowe, John W. 34
Lowry (Lowery), Samuel Russ 86, 177
Lyons, James Perry 162
Lyons, Marshall 162, 163
Mahaley, Thomas M. 251
Mallernee, John Lacey 16, 74, 78, 99, 141, 148, 171, 213, 260
Malone, Charles B. 249
Malone, William R. 251
Malony, E.H. 175
Mansell, James J. 19, 65, 153
Marshall, Humphrey 96, 101
Martin, S. 52
Matthews, Philip 123
Maulsby, Thomas 227
McCabe, Carolyn (Caroline) 203
McCausland, John 129, 242

McClaskey, Ephraim 56, 57
McClellan, George B. 27, 113
McCown, Albert F. 11
McCully (McCullah), Wallace 215
McCurdy, John 99
McDonald, Donald 194
McDonald, John, 249
McGinness, Thomas 66
McGonegal, James 191
McKee, John 175, 191
McMaster, William L. 52, 109, 110,
    111, 117, 250, 251
McNeer, Daniel Forney 237
McNeill, John H. 253, 254
McPherson, James C. 227
Means, Charles E. 64, 66
Mellon (Melon), Samuel 253
Miller, John (Forked John) 92
Milroy, Robert H. 137
Miner, Robert 162
Moore, (Moor) Augustus 231
Morford, John R. 141
Morgan, Ephraim P. 267
Morrow, (Bob) Robert E. 96
Mosby, John S. 250
Mower (Mowry), William P. 190,
    253
Naret, Edward 120, 121
Nagle, George 253
Neal, James C. 179
Newton, W.I. 79
Nicholson, Joseph 193
North, Jasper N. 191
Northcott, R.S. 246
Nowlen, James W. 47
Nutter, Thomas 104
Oakes, James 9, 15, 65

O'Neal, George E. 189, 190, 191
Ong, Finley Davis 29, 153, 179, 180
Ours, Jehu 175
Ours, John 175
Palmer, George W. 64, 66
Palmer, John 53, 55
Parry, Augustus 160, 167
Parsons, Joel 191, 222
Patten, Joseph 73, 263
Paxton, John C. 121
Paxton, Lyle 52
Pell, William 51
Pemberton, John C. 149, 166, 167
Phelps, Lorenzo A. 137, 138
Phelps, Matthew 90, 91
Philson, John Rush 69, 71, 137, 155,
    160, 203, 204
Piatt, Abram 58
Pierpont, Francis H. 39, 61, 63, 69,
    92, 103, 115, 117, 119, 155, 159
Porter, David D. 156
Powell, Walter Angelo 98
Price, Joseph B. 202
Pritchett, Duckett T. 161
Purnell, John H. 197
Ralston, James Hoffersett 123, 131,
    153, 159, 183, 193, 202, 204, 259
Randolph, George W. 137
Reeves, William Henry 222
Reno, Jesse 113
Richard Jr., Michael 181
Rife (Riffe), Gordon (Grandville)
    112
Rife (Riffe), Patterson 112
Riffle, James 191
Rigby, William T. 169
Rockhill, Tilton B. 9, 11, 65

Rogers, Washington (Wash) 175

Rollins, Barney J. 15

Rook, Samuel C. 47

Rosecrans, William Starke 27, 39, 45, 57, 61, 63, 67, 70, 71, 84, 88

Rowley, Henry C. 267

Ruggles, George 101

Russell, Daniel Albert 175, 176, 179

Russell, David A. 119, 173, 216, 243, 259

Russell, Florence 176

Russell, William Henry Harrison 27, 29, 41, 45, 56, 57, 61, 80, 91, 96, 98, 99, 124, 127, 128, 148, 151, 152, 261

Ryan, Josiah 215

Safreed, William Lewis 157, 159, 160, 162, 163, 166, 177, 195, 199, 201, 206, 210, 213, 214

Sampson Jr., Robert Henry 177

Sampson, John 177

Sampson, Samuel 177, 232

Samuels, Henry J. 56, 66, 68, 71, 78, 79, 87, 164

Saunders, Jesse C. 262

Saunier, Joseph 167, 190, 191, 202

Savage, Squire 83

Scammon, Eliakim P. 142, 197

Scott, George A. 237

Shannon, William M. 231, 232

Schenck, William C. 164

Sheppard, Calvin Alexander 59, 98, 119, 200, 225, 239

Sheridan, Phil 244, 249, 250

Sherman, William T. 3, 145, 149, 150, 156, 159, 163, 164, 189, 190, 201, 202, 205, 207, 216, 217, 222, 224, 227, 233

Shrewsbury, Columbus 57, 81, 97, 140, 142, 147, 148, 154, 163, 195

Siber, Edward 104, 116

Siber, William 124

Sigel, Franz 225, 228, 229, 243

Sisson, William 222

Smith, Benjamin F. 42

Smith, Dioclesian "Dan" A. 11, 45

Smith, Giles A. 209, 224

Smith, Jim 79

Smith, J.P.R.R. 116

Smith, Morgan Lewis 221, 222

Smith, Thomas Jefferson 15, 24, 45

Spencer, Ogden 103

Spooner, B.J. 213

Stanberry, Philemon Beecher 21, 23, 42, 65, 93, 179

Starr, William C. 78, 103

Stevens, Jesse Vinton 15, 42, 55, 79, 84, 85, 86

Stewart, Milton (M.S.) 85, 96, 103, 107, 109, 119

Stinchcomb, James 25

Stone, James F. 24, 25, 31, 53, 70, 74, 232, 243, 252, 255

Stone, George F. 237

Storey, (Story) George W. 90, 91

Stratton, William 107, 112, 113

Strong, William Kerley 85

Stuart, David 159

Sullivan, Jeremiah C. 225, 229, 231, 237, 240

Summers (Somers), James C. 191, 260, 266

Taylor, Alfred 203

Teays, Victoria Hansford 124

Thoburn, Joseph 225, 231, 236, 237, 241, 242, 244, 245, 246, 247

Thrall, Henry 74

Tidd, A.C. 25

Tod, David 79

Toland, John T. 63, 137, 141

Trickle, Edward H. 244

Trogden, Private (first name unknown) 189

Tulleys, Lysander 131

Turnbull, John 132

Ullom, John 191

Vale, James B.C. 17, 18, 33, 34, 49, 55, 57, 58, 64, 73, 74, 89, 90, 93, 97, 99, 124, 127, 236

Vance, Alexander 59, 90, 95, 164, 259

Vance, John Luther 11, 13, 15, 34, 59, 93, 103, 120, 127, 129, 142, 155, 159, 164, 175, 176, 194, 200, 205, 209, 225, 228, 232, 236, 237, 239, 240, 242, 243, 244, 245, 247, 259

Vance, Josiah W. 215

Vance, Reuben 59

Voges, T. 223

Von Blessing, Louis 213

Walker, John E. 80, 81

Wallar, James L. 78

Walsh, Joseph A. 237, 239

Ward, James 58

Wartenburg, Alexander 98

Washburn, James 239

Waterman, Homer C. 155, 202

Waugh, George F. 153

Weaver, George 199

Weddle, Jacob 251

Weldon, Private (unknown first name) 52

Weldon, J.J.C. 175

Wells, George 237

Wells, Milton 237

Welton, Henry Samuel 9, 24, 25, 27, 46, 65

Wheat, James S. 8, 39, 41, 45, 46, 57

Wheeler, Joseph T. 47

White, Lyman S. 53, 242

Wilkinson, Nathan 225, 227

Willard, George W. 174

Williams, Caleb 33

Williams, Thomas 149

Wise, Henry A. 25, 34, 42

Witcher, Vincent Addison "Clawhammer" 105, 107, 109, 112, 267

Wolfe, John Perry 181, 214

Woodhull, George Spofford 43, 85, 155, 161, 205, 242, 243

Woomer, William 222

Young, John Valley 103, 121

Zeis, Peter F. 203

About the Authors

Philip Hatfield, Ph.D., is a member of the Company of Military Historians, and holds a doctorate in psychology from Fielding University; a master's degree in psychology from Marshall University; and a bachelor's degree in psychology and history from the University of Charleston. Dr. Hatfield is a veteran of the U.S. Air Force and served during Operation Iraqi Freedom. He is the author of seven books and numerous scholarly articles related to the Civil War.

Born in Charleston, West Virginia, Terry Lowry attended South Charleston High School and graduated from West Virginia State College (now a university) with a B.A. in History. He has written seven books on the Civil War in West Virginia and one on World War II. In addition, he has written numerous articles on the Civil War for newspapers, magazines, journals, and online articles, as well as given many lectures throughout the country. Terry worked for three years at the historic Craik-Patton House Museum and from 2001-2017 he was historian for the West Virginia State Archives. His history background has also included participation in living history groups, Civil War roundtables and historic archeology. Although a major loss of vision occurred after a heart attack in 2022, he continues to share his love and knowledge of history online. Terry has also been a professional musician for sixty years and continues to perform in concert.

Other Books by Philip Hatfield, Ph.D.

Other Books by Terry Lowry

The Battle of Scary Creek:
Military Operations in the Kanawha Valley, April – July 1861
(Charleston, WV: Quarrier Press, 1985)

22nd Virginia Infantry
(H.E. Howard Virginia Regimental Series, 1988)

26th (Edgar's) Battalion Virginia Infantry
(H.E. Howard Virginia Regimental Series, 1991)

Last Sleep: The Battle of Droop Mountain, November 6, 1863
(Pictorial Histories Publishing, 1996)

Images of the Civil War in West Virginia
(co-authored with Stan Cohen, Quarrier Press, 2000)

September Blood: The Battle of Carnifex Ferry
(Quarrier Press, 1985, Revised 2011)

The Battle of Charleston and the 1862 Kanawha Valley Campaign
(35th Star Publishing, 2016)

www.ingramcontent.com/pod-product-compliance
Lightning Source LLC
Chambersburg PA
CBHW060850120626
46553CB00001B/30